THE LAST BOHEMIAN

Irish Studies
Kathleen Costello-Sullivan, *Series Editor*

Select Titles in Irish Studies

Avant-Garde Nationalism at the Dublin Gate Theatre, 1928–1940
    Ruud van den Beuken

Broken Irelands: Literary Form in Post-Crash Irish Fiction
    Mary M. McGlynn

Modernity, Community, and Place in Brian Friel's Drama, Second Edition
    Richard Rankin Russell

Poetry, Politics, and the Law in Modern Ireland
    Adam Hanna

Politics, Culture, and the Irish American Press: 1784–1963
    Debra Reddin van Tuyll, Mark O'Brien, and Marcel Broersma, eds.

The Rogue Narrative and Irish Fiction, 1660–1790
    Joe Lines

Stepping through Origins: Nature, Home, and Landscape in Irish Literature
    Jefferson Holdridge

Unaccompanied Traveler: The Writings of Kathleen M. Murphy
    Patrick Bixby, ed.

For a full list of title in this series, visit
https://press.syr.edu/supressbook-series
/irish-studies.

THE LAST BOHEMIAN

BRIAN DESMOND HURST,
Irish Film, British Cinema

LANCE PETTITT

Foreword by Mark Cousins

Syracuse University Press

Copyright © 2023 Syracuse University Press

Syracuse, New York 13244-5290

All Rights Reserved

First Edition 2023

23 24 25 26 27 28   6 5 4 3 2 1

∞ The paper used in this publication meets the minimum requirements of the American National Standard for Information Sciences—Permanence of Paper for Printed Library Materials, ANSI Z39.48-1992.

For a listing of books published and distributed by Syracuse University Press, visit https://press.syr.edu.

ISBN: 978-0-8156-3743-1 (hardcover)
      978-0-8156-3729-5 (paperback)
      978-0-8156-5530-5 (e-book)

Library of Congress Cataloging-in-Publication Data

Names: Pettitt, Lance, author. | Cousins, Mark, 1965– writer of foreword.
Title: The last Bohemian : Brian Desmond Hurst, Irish film, British cinema / Lance Pettitt ; foreword by Mark Cousins.
Description: Syracuse, New York : Syracuse University Press, [2023] | Series: Irish studies | Includes bibliographical references and index.
Identifiers: LCCN 2022054093 (print) | LCCN 2022054094 (ebook) | ISBN 9780815637431 (hardcover) | ISBN 9780815637295 (paperback) | ISBN 9780815655305 (ebook)
Subjects: LCSH: Hurst, Brian Desmond. | Motion picture producers and directors—Northern Ireland—Belfast—Biography. | Motion pictures—Great Britain—History—20th century.
Classification: LCC PN1998.3.H85 P482 2023 (print) | LCC PN1998.3.H85 (ebook) | DDC 791.4302/33092 [B]—dc23/eng/20230103
LC record available at https://lccn.loc.gov/2022054093
LC ebook record available at https://lccn.loc.gov/2022054094

Manufactured in the United States of America

Contents

List of Illustrations *vii*

Foreword, BY MARK COUSINS *xi*

Acknowledgments *xiii*

Photo-portrait of Hurst, ca. 1946 *xvii*

Chronology *xix*

Abbreviations *xxiii*

Prologue: *Titanic Studios, Belfast* *xxv*

Introduction
Fugitive: Becoming Bohemian in a "Cinema Astray" 1

1. Formation
Belfast, Gallipoli, and the 1920s 20

2. Filmmaker
From Avant-Garde to Elstree, Films 1934–39 49

3. Fame
Cinema, Wartime, and Film Work in the 1940s 104

4. Finale
Adaptation, Revival, and Remnants of Empire 165

5. Forgotten
Hurst and the Wake of Fame 218

Conclusion
Found: Critical Redemption? 239

Appendix A. *Irish and Irish-Related Films Released in IFS and UK during the 1930s* 253

Appendix B. *Hurst's Filmography* 257

Notes 263

Bibliography 297

List of Films Referenced 317

Index 319

Illustrations

Photo-portrait of Hurst, ca. 1946   *xvii*

1.1. Ontario College of Art, Grange Park building, 1922   *33*
1.2. Group of Seven exhibition catalog, 1922   *35*
1.3. Hurst standing with Norman Dean, Arts Ball, Ontario College of Art, 1923.   *36*
1.4. "A Masquerade par Excellence," *Toronto Daily Star*, 1923   *37*
1.5. *L'Oeil de Paris*, program cover, Paul Colin, ca. 1926   *42*
1.6. Hurst as extra: *Hangman's House*, 1928   *43*
2.1. *The Night Nurse*, J. J. Abrahams, 1935: literary source for *Irish Hearts*   *65*
2.2. *Irish Hearts* on location: Trinity College, Dublin, 1935   *66*
2.3. Prefilmic sketch, *Riders to the Sea*, 1935   *69*
2.4. Bridie Laffan on location, *Riders to the Sea*, 1935   *70*
2.5. Crew shot, *Riders to the Sea*, 1935   *72*
2.6. *Ourselves Alone*, 1936: dramatic three-way profile   *78*
2.7.1 Maugham's play "retold" as prose fiction with visualization from *The Tenth Man*, Heinemann "Pocket Editions" series, 1936   *88*
2.7.2 Hurst on-screen cameo: *The Tenth Man*, 1936   *89*
2.8. London's speed and mobility: *Sensation*, 1936   *91*
2.9. Suburban Englishness: *Sensation*, 1936   *92*
2.10. *Glamorous Night*, 1937   *94*
2.11. *Prison without Bars*, 1938   *97*
2.12. *On the Night of the Fire*, 1939: prewar British film noir   *99*
3.1. "Brian's Barn," Wardrobes Lodge, Buckinghamshire, 1945   *106*
3.2. *The Lion Has Wings*, 1939   *109*
3.3.1 *Miss Grant Goes to the Door*, title credits, 1940   *111*
3.3.2 *Miss Grant Goes to the Door*, 1940   *112*
3.4. "Thumbs Up Patriotism": *A Call for Arms!* 1940   *114*
3.5. *A Letter from Ulster*, 1943: a moment of fraternal tenderness   *116*

Illustrations

3.6.1. *Letter*: tableau of GIs listening to "The Rose of Tralee" 117
3.6.2. *Letter*: impromptu barracks performance of "Ragtime Joe" 117
3.7. *Letter*: police and military border confusion 119
3.8. Warsaw devastation: *Dangerous Moonlight*, 1941 122
3.9.1. Heterosexual seduction: *Dangerous Moonlight* 123
3.9.2. *Dangerous Moonlight*: queer homosociality 125
3.10.1. Tableau of grief: *Dangerous Moonlight* 127
3.10.2. Stefan's tear shot: *Dangerous Moonlight* 127
3.11. Hurst and Sally Gray at Hurst's home, June 1947 128
3.12. Gambling with the middle-class family: *The Hundred Pound Window*, 1943 130
3.13. Continental crime and corruption: *Alibi*, 1942 131
3.14. *Alibi*'s theatrical release poster 132
3.15. Location shooting in Arnhem: *Theirs Is the Glory*, 1946 134
3.16. *Theirs Is the Glory*: reconstructive realism 135
3.17.1. *Theirs Is the Glory*: sculptures in light 137
3.17.2. *Theirs Is the Glory*: quasi-religious masculinity 137
3.17.3. *Theirs Is the Glory*: "poetic realism" 138
3.18. The Two Cities Dinner, London, 1948 143
3.19. Hurst's celebrity photo-portrait, ca. 1946 144
3.20. Irish land rebellion: *Hungry Hill*, 1947 149
3.21. Ballroom dance scene: *Hungry Hill* 154
3.22.1. "Look . . . with all that quality": *Hungry Hill* 155
3.22.2. The excluded mob: *Hungry Hill* 156
3.22.3. A moment of class "intermingling": *Hungry Hill* 157
3.23. *Mark of Cain*, 1948 159
3.24. *Trottie True*, 1949 161
3.25. Hurst in the top rank of British cinema: Hurst, Walter Sistrom, and J. Arthur Rank, 1947 163
4.1. Adolescent male camaraderie: *Tom Brown's School Days*, 1951 174
4.2. "In nature's garb": *Tom Brown* 175
4.3. Alistair Sim as Scrooge, *Scrooge*, 1951 177
4.4.1. *A Christmas Carol*, illustration, John Leech, 1843 178
4.4.2. *Scrooge*, 1951: "Ignorance and Want" 179
4.5. "Serial Picturisation," *Daily Graphic*, December 10, 1951 180
4.6. *Scrooge*, 1951: "The air filled with phantoms" 182
4.7. *Malta Story*, 1953: theatrical release poster, press book 184

4.8.1. *Malta Story*: solemn arrival   *186*
4.8.2. *Malta Story*: Maltese endurance   *187*
4.8.3. *Malta Story*: Alec Guinness's quiet heroics   *187*
4.9. *Simba*: Mau Mau conflict in 1950s Kenya, 1955   *189*
4.10. *Simba*: British detention camp in Kenya   *190*
4.11. *Simba*: "Is he East Africa's only hope?"   *192*
4.12. *Black Tent*, 1956: Daoud chooses Arabic heritage   *193*
4.13. *Dangerous Exile*, 1957   *195*
4.14. *Dangerous Exile*: theatrical poster   *196*
4.15. Doctor's dilemma: *Behind the Mask*, 1958   *201*
4.16.1. *Behind the Mask*: modern televised surgery   *203*
4.16.2. *Behind the Mask*: male domain, the doctors' common room   *203*
4.17. *His and Hers*: poster, 1960   *205*
4.18. Hurst directs his last film, *Playboy*, July 1961   *208*
4.19. Hurst directs Siobhan McKenna and Gary Raymond in *Playboy*   *210*
4.20. *The Playboy*, 1962: US press card   *212*
5.1. "London Exile": Hurst in Belgravia, September 1969   *221*
5.2. Hurst and George Cukor, 1975   *222*
5.3.1. Hurst's ninetieth birthday party, BAFTA, London. *Screen International* feature, 1985   *224*
5.3.2. Hurst and Astrid Frank, BAFTA, London, 1985   *225*
5.4.1. Hurst's civic, local, and national recognition: Directors Guild of Great Britain plaque, 2011   *234*
5.4.2. "Brian Desmond Hurst," Ulster History Circle plaque, Strand Arts Cinema, 2022   *234*
5.5. The Hurst and MacQuitty Sound Stages, Titanic Studios, Belfast   *236*
5.6. "Hurst Stage" plaque, Titanic Studios, Belfast   *237*

A quizzical subject: Hurst photo portrait, Angus McBean, ca. 1946   *238*

Foreword

MARK COUSINS

The year 1946, a British black-and-white war movie. Nighttime, in the dormitory of paratroopers who are about to risk their lives to secure a bridge over the Rhine River in Arnhem in Holland. The camera tracks left, past young men who are about to fall asleep. As it does so we hear their names and where they come from: Ballymena, Staffordshire, London.

But this is no ordinary tracking shot. The film is *Theirs Is the Glory*, and the men aren't actors; they're soldiers re-reacting, for the camera, things they did in the attempt to take the Arnhem bridge a year earlier. The beautiful tracking shot is a statement, a rhetorical visual attack on several things—films with movie stars, inauthentic portrayals of war.

That it's a reenactment in a documentary is striking in itself, but it's also hard not to notice the beauty of the men and the complexity of the lighting. The burnished image celebrates the contours of their faces, like Greta Garbo's cinematographers celebrated hers. Call it fated beauty, if you like, or think of the reifying elegance of the tracking shots in the films of Terence Davies, such as *Distant Voices, Still Lives*.

The tracking shot was directed by a filmmaker who, like Davies, was working class, queer, and from a northern industrial city. He was born in the year that cinema was born, 1895, so he was about fifty when he made this image, an image repeated near the end of the film, when four out of five of the men had been killed. Ten thousand soldiers attempted to open up that bridge across the Rhine, but only two thousand survived. The second time we see the tracking shot, the tone is different. Just as loving, just as morally serious, but this time even more somber. Most of the beds are empty; most of the men are dead.

Theirs Is the Glory was perhaps the director's personal favorite of his films. His *Riders to the Sea*, made more than a decade earlier, had a similar sense of resignation, of doomed youth, and, again, there was a camera expressing what William Blake called "the lineaments of gratified desire."

As Lance Pettitt's rewarding new book shows, this filmmaker was a human being, a soldier, a painter, an art director, a mendicant, and a bohemian who knew a thing or two about the lineaments of gratified desire. Over the years I'd seen some of his films, not always realizing that he came from where I come from—Belfast—and its working classes at that. I'd noticed his close-ups, his tracking, and the shadows in his movies, their moments of intensity or revelation, but, overall, his work hadn't come into focus for me. They seemed to be hiding behind conventions, subjects, stories. Private passions leaked from films such as *Dangerous Moonlight*, in which Anton Walbrook plays a Polish pianist and composer who's haunted by war, and the tracking shot in *Theirs Is the Glory* is repeated in other of this director's films, such as the *Trottie True* and *A Letter from Ulster*, but when I was young I wanted angry cinema or euphoric cinema, and this filmmaker didn't seem to do enough of either. The amplitude of his feeling seemed too small.

But then I read the book you have before you, and I better understood that amplitude, and those tracking shots. *Theirs Is the Glory* has a lot of detail and realism, and an interest in tactics, process, faces, geography, and what actually happened at Arnhem. Pettitt's book gives us a great context for these things.

What actually happened in the life of this man who saw battle, Paris's movable feast, Hollywood in silent times, and London's queer La Ronde? Pettitt has many answers. As he mentions, Northern Ireland and Ireland in the last generation have become more interested in transformation, the fluidity of identity, and in-betweenness. No surprise, then, that this penumbral figure, this exile, this Irish-Britisher, this foot soldier–deserter, this bisexual, conservative bohemian, classical avant-gardist is now catching our imaginations again. His in-betweenness was a product of his class, of his sexuality, and of empire. As I read this book, I saw my own in-betweenness.

At its close I wanted to drink fine wine with, and argue with, Brian Desmond Hurst.

Acknowledgments

I have been researching, writing, and talking about Hurst and his films for more than a decade. *The Last Bohemian* represents a bringing together and condensation of these activities between the covers of one book. I would like to thank the following people, publications, and institutions for allowing me to develop my ideas into this fuller study: Laura Izarra at the University of São Paulo for inviting me to write on Hurst's memoir in 2010, Ruth Barton and Neil Sammells at *Irish Studies Review* for its special issue in 2011, and John Hill and the editors at *ODNB* for asking me to write the Hurst entry in 2014. Some of this material has been reworked in the introduction and parts of chapter 4 and 5.

A number of scholarly associations, conferences, and film festivals have provided a platform from which to talk about Hurst and his films, notably: ABEI in Brazil, the Belfast Film Festival, the "Trinity Hub" Trinity College (Dublin), and IASIL, Toronto; in London: the Irish Literary Society, Clare Wills at the Irish Seminar within the School of Advanced Studies, Ian Christie and London Film, and Birkbeck's postgraduate seminar and the NFT "archive projects" series. I would like to thank Francis Campbell and Jeremy Sullivan for making it possible for me to give my inaugural professorial lecture at Europe House, London, in 2014. Such occasions for public speaking with the feedback that is generates have helped me to focus my thinking greatly.

Aside from these acknowledgments I would like to record my sincere thanks to several individuals and institutions who have enabled my research, through funds or facilities, or who have commented on my work in earlier forms or draft chapters of this thesis: Nigel Arthur; Simon Audley; Charles Barr; Ruth Barton; BBC Written Archives; Belfast Film Festival; Birkbeck Library staff; Stephen Bourne; all the librarians at the BFI/Reuben Research Library, London, but in particular Johnny Davies in

Special Collections; the British Library and its staff, particularly in Special Collections and the News Library; Joanne Carroll at the National Library, Dublin; Ian Christie at Birkbeck; my Belfast friend Stephen Douds; Martin Doyle at the *Irish Times*; Jeff Dudgeon on matters PRONI; Liz Duffy; Roddy Flynn; Dan Ford for kind permission to use materials and quote from his grandfather's correspondence; Roy Foster for advice and leads on the 1930s; the late Philip French for his support and encouragement; Maud Hamill; James Harte at the manuscripts department of the National Library, Dublin; John Hill at Royal Holloway; Sean Hutton; Fiona Kelly at the IWM; Michael Kennedy at the RIA; the Kennelly Archive, Beatriz Kopschitz Bastos in Sao Paulo; Sebastian Lassandro; Johanna Leech; the Linen Hall Library, Belfast; the Margaret Herrick Library, Los Angeles; Patrick Maume; Brian McIlroy; Sarah McElroy Mitchell at the Lilly Library, Indiana University; Danny Meegan; Massimo Moretti; Redmond Morris for kind permission to use materials from the Killanin Archive, Dublin; Laura Mulvey; Tony Murray; the National Archives, Kew; Damien O'Byrne; Sunniva O'Flynn at the Irish Film Archive; Alison Oram; Ruairí Ó Scanaill; Paddy O'Sullivan; Daniel Payne at Ontario College of Art and Design; Michelle Paull, Julian Petley, and Peter Power-Hynes for sharing historical research; Mark Riordan; Alyson Rodgers, the Ronald Grant Archive at the Cinema Museum, London; Ann Saddlemyer; Paul Sharkey; *Screen Daily*, Anthony Slide; Claire Smith; Jonathan Smith, librarian at Rugby School; John Stape for help with shipping and Canadian archival research; Dale Stinchcomb at the Houghton Library, Harvard; StudioCanal, Talking Pictures, Angela Waters; and Stephen Wyatt.

In terms of the book's commissioning and production, I would like to thank Deborah Manion sincerely for taking on the project and Syracuse's editorial, legal, and production teams, in particular Johanna Bermudez, and the two Syracuse readers whose reports contained several acute points and helped to polish the book's argument. Any errors lurking in the text remain my responsibility. It's fitting for a book on Hurst that my final thanks in this regard are to another Belfast filmmaker, writer, and cinephile, Mark Cousins. I appreciate the care he has taken in the strangest of periods and at the busiest of times to write such an elegant and perceptive foreword to frame my work.

Every effort has been made to trace the copyright owners of illustrations and to acknowledge them appropriately.

It only remains for me to thank my partner and soul mate of over thirty years, Matthew Daines, for sharing his love and life with me and his unerring support. Finally, I dedicate this book to four remarkable women in my family: Kate Pettitt (née Robbins, 1891–1951); Gladys Templeton-Gray (1914–2002); to her daughter and my mother, Sally Pettitt (1939–); and my sister, Gina Pettitt (1965–).

Brian Desmond Hurst, 1895–1986

Angus McBean photo-portrait of Hurst, ca. 1946. © Harvard Theatre Collection, MS Thr 581, Houghton Library, Harvard University.

Chronology
Hans (Brian Desmond) Hurst, 1895–1986

ORIGINS AND EARLY LIFE

1895   Born in Belfast, Ireland. Father a blacksmith in Belfast shipyard. Presbyterian upbringing.

1899   Mother dies.

1900S: CHILDHOOD, EARLY MANHOOD, AND WORLD WAR I

1901   Father remarries wife's cousin. Older sister, Patricia, goes to Glasgow.

1909–12   Leaves school, works as linen-mill worker, signs Ulster Covenant (1912).

1912   Father dies.

1914   Enlists in Royal Irish Rifles, adopts name "Brian" instead of "Hans."

1914–19   Serves in and survives Gallipoli but suffers bayonet injury and contracts malaria; recovers in Cairo; deserts, reenlists in RASC; service in Middle East, Salonika, and Balkans.

1920S: STUDENT LIFE AND WORK IN CANADA, PARIS,
NEW YORK, AND LOS ANGELES

1919–20   Returns to Belfast, the partition of Ireland, and the "Troubles." Immigrates to Canada on government grant. Manual work on a golf course.

1921–23   Enrolls Ontario College of Art; falls in love with fellow student Norman Dean. Fails to graduate. Adds "Desmond" as a second name.

1923–27   Living in Paris with Dean; informally studying at Beaux Arts.

1925	Period of study at Artists Union, New York, and commercial work as interior designer/painter.
1928	Appears as extra in John Ford's *Hangman's House* in sequences shot in Ireland and in United States, alongside Marion Morrison (later John Wayne).
1928–31	Hollywood. Living in Laurel Canyon, working as assistant and then art director for Ford in Hollywood studios.

1930S: LONDON, DIRECTORIAL DEBUT, AND ESTABLISHING A PROFILE

1931	Holidays in Hawaii with the Fords. Tightening immigration law forces Hurst to leave the United States. Moves with Dean to London where sister Patricia now lives.
1934	First films as director: *The Tell-Tale Heart* and *Irish Hearts* with location shooting in Ireland. Independently produced and funded by Harry Clifton.
1936	"Rescue director" for *Ourselves Alone*, BIP: box-office and critical success. Contracted to Alexander Korda at Denham studios. Publishes film essay in *Kinematograph Weekly*. Meets Lord Killanin and Terence Young in Cambridge. Contract to direct film about "Lawrence of Arabia."
1938	Owns property in Buckinghamshire and apartment in Belgravia, London.
1939	*On the Night of the Fire* and codirects *The Lion Has Wings*.

1940S: ENDURES LONDON BLITZ, ENJOYS SOCIETY LIFE, AND FINDS PROFESSIONAL REPUTE

1940–45	MOI work includes *A Letter from Ulster* (1943)
1941	*Dangerous Moonlight*: box-office and critical success.
1946	*Theirs Is the Glory*. Twin premiere in London and Ottawa.
1947	Formally converts to Roman Catholicism.

1947–50   Under contract to J. Arthur Rank; *Hungry Hill* (1947); portrait photograph by Angus McBean; profiled in *British Film Yearbook, 1949–50* with Lean, Asquith, Powell, and others.

1950S: CAREER PEAKS AND SUSTAINS, ENJOYS TRAVEL,
AND ACQUIRES HOME IN MOROCCO

1950   Publishes essay on British cinema in *Sight and Sound*

1951   *Scrooge*. Biggest box-office hit.

1953   *Malta Story* (Rank)

1955   *Simba*

1957   Visits Russia as film-jury judge. Publishes "director" essay for *Films & Filming*. Board member of "Four Provinces Films" with Ford, Killanin. *Dangerous Exile* (Rank)

1958   *Behind the Mask*

1960S: LAST FILM, BELFAST RECONNECTION,
STRUGGLES TO ADAPT TO NEW CINEMA

1962   Synge's *Playboy*—shot on location in Inch, Kerry. Irish Cultural Relations Committee fails to support *Playboy* as official entry for film festivals. Several other film projects fail to find funding.

1969–70   *Punch* magazine interview; *Guardian* article: "The Films"; BBC radio film pundit.

1970S TO THE 1990S: MEMOIR, TWILIGHT,
AND CRITICAL WILDERNESS

1975–76   Tape-recorded conversations with Christopher Robbins with editorial assistance from Stephen Wyatt, become "Travelling the Road" memoir typescript.

1970s   NFT occasional screenings of his films

1985   Ninetieth birthday party event at BAFTA, Piccadilly, London.

1986	Dies intestate in a London care home. Cremation and ashes to Dundonald Cemetery, Belfast. In London, Astrid Frank deposits typescript copy of "Travelling the Road" at BFI with public access. Obituary essay by Brian McIlroy published in *Éire-Ireland* (1989).

2000S: REDISCOVERY, RECOGNITION, AND CRITICAL AFTERLIFE

2004	Robbins's *The Empress of Ireland* memoir published. Cork Film Festival screens Hurst retrospective curated by Mick Hannigan. Ruth Barton's *Irish National Cinema* includes Hurst and IFTV Research entry online, Trinity College Dublin.
2009	Probate legally establishes the Hurst Estate. "Travelling the Road" at BFI removed from public/research access by estate.
2010	Brian Desmond Hurst website created as "Official Legacy Website."
2012	New "Titanic Studios" facilities Belfast named after Hurst and Bill MacQuitty. Directors Guild blue plaque unveiled at Queen's Film Theatre, Belfast.
2013–14	Hurst entries appear in *Dictionary of Irish Biography* (Maume), *Oxford Dictionary of National Biography* (Pettitt), and *Ulster Dictionary of Biography* (Kennedy).

Abbreviations

BAFTA	British Academy of Film and Television Arts
BBCWAC	BBC, Written Archives, Caversham
BBFC	British Board of Film Censors
BCL	Belfast, Central Library
BFI	British Film Institute, London
BFISC	BFI, Special Collections, London
BL	British Library, London
BNA	British Newspaper Archive, British Library, London
COED	*Concise Oxford English Dictionary*
DIB	*Dictionary of Irish Biography*
DUB	*Dictionary of Ulster Biography*
DUP	Democratic Unionist Party
HJFRTV	*Historical Journal of Film, Radio and Television*
IFI	Irish Film Institute, Dublin
ISR	*Irish Studies Review*
JFLL	John Ford Papers, Lilly Library, Indiana University
KAIFA	Killanin Archive, Irish Film Archive, Dublin
LOLNL	Liam O'Leary Papers, National Library, Dublin
MLA	Member of Legislative Assembly
MOI	Ministry of Information
NAK	National Archives (UK), Kew, London
NFT	National Film Theatre, South Bank, London
NL	National Library, Dublin
OCAD	Ontario College of Art and Design, Toronto
OCIH	*The Oxford Companion to Irish History*
ODNB	*Oxford Dictionary of National Biography*
ODOS	*Oxford Dictionary of Surnames*
PRONI	Public Record Office, Belfast, Northern Ireland

Prologue
Titanic Studios, Belfast

On a gray, sullen morning in Belfast in October 2012, a desultory crowd had gathered around the massive frontage of a new building on the site of a former shipyard works area now redeveloped and known as the "Titanic Quarter." Amid the corporate executives in suits, photographers, and journalists from the city's press, a TV presenter and camera rehearsed its prerecorded package. Among those persons lining up to speak and be photographed were a mother and her suited middle-aged son who talked with the two VIPs who were honoring the occasion. The VIPs were none other than the late Martin McGuinness, Irish republican, Sinn Fein, MLA, Deputy First Minister of NI Assembly, and First Minister Rt. Hon. Peter Robinson, MLA, First Minister of the NI Assembly, and leader of the DUP. They made small talk, and two characters in costume from the HBO series *Game of Thrones* stood mock-menacing on the edge of the photo lineup looking slightly incongruous.

What was the reason for the gathering, the photo op? What was the news that would go out on BBC Ulster that day? The film and television industry in Northern Ireland was booming; it needed these two new soundstage studios to cope with the work highlighted by the presence of HBO in Northern Ireland and the phenomenal success of *Game of Thrones*. The Titanic Studios project was an £8.3 million investment in the future, but it was drawing on the cinematic kudos of the past. Part of the speech ceremony involved unveiling plaques to commemorate the two figures after whom each studio was named. Who were they? Both were "sons" of Belfast though from completely different backgrounds. One was William (Bill) MacQuitty (1905–2004), former banker, film producer, photographer, and writer, best known for *A Night to Remember* (1958) about the ill-fated *Titanic*. The other was Brian Desmond Hurst (1895–1986), linen-mill worker, soldier, artist, film director, and producer, best known for his Dickens adaptation *Scrooge* (1951) but responsible for nearly thirty films in his career. The two had become acquainted after MacQuitty had made a film about silage production and Hurst had returned to make a propaganda film for the British war effort. In fact, they made two films together: *A Letter from Ulster* (1942) and a World War II desert epic called *The Black Tent* (1956). But who, apart from the cluster of the family relatives present enjoying the moment of civic and business limelight, actually knew much at all about either man or could recall their other films?

This book sets out to reevaluate for the first time the entire range of Hurst's film work and to understand better the way that he made films over three decades. It also tries to explain why Hurst in particular was being honored in this way and why the memory of his cinematic achievements was being mobilized at this particular point in time.

To begin to do so, we have to go back over a century to Hurst's birth in 1895, an inaugural date in cinema's history. This is the beginning of understanding the journey of his life, his involvement in cinema, and the transformation that film direction would bring to that life. How did this son of a Belfast shipyard blacksmith become "the last bohemian"?

THE LAST BOHEMIAN

Introduction
Fugitive: Becoming Bohemian in a "Cinema Astray"

> The Irish eyes twinkle wickedly out of the big Ulster face, expressing a cheerful pragmatism towards the fact of his own exile.
> —Wilfred De'ath, "Exiles in London"

The Last Bohemian examines the biography, films, and critical reputation of the Belfast-born filmmaker known as Brian Desmond Hurst (1895–1986). Until relatively recently, Hurst's name appeared mainly in the footnotes and film-directory entries of British and Irish cinema history as a "B"-movie bohemian figure, part of what Tom Gunning has suggestively called a "cinema astray."[1] Hurst learned about filmmaking in the "silent" 1920s under John Ford and was still making movies in the Cinemascope sixties. Surviving into his nineties, he outlived most of his British, Irish, and European director contemporaries, save Michael Powell. Hurst stands out as lacking sustained critical attention as a filmmaker. The work and reputations of a host of major and lesser figures—think Ford, think Hitchcock; think Renoir, Pabst, or Clair; think Rex Ingram, Raoul Walsh; think Emmet Dalton, Lance Comfort, or Anthony Asquith—all have been the subjects of book-length studies. Hurst marks the end of a bohemian cinematic generation, yet his films have been the last to receive their critical due.

This study argues that the most productive way to think through his body of films is as the works of an exilic director, a "creative migrant" from Ireland working principally in the British film industry and domiciled in London from the middle part of the last century.[2] The particular nature of his exilic status is defined in this introduction, elaborated upon in chapter 1, and traced as a thread through his film work in the following chapters. As is outlined, the specific coordinates of his exile produced a shifting set of conditions in which nationality, class, and sexuality became key vectors in the films that he found himself directing. The way these three vectors intersect is key to understanding Britain's society and cinema culture during the period that he worked in the industry. Hurst's Ulster exilic perspective as a professional creative in London combined in fascinating ways with people from other parts of Ireland, displaced continental Europeans, émigrés and artistic figures, and others who saw themselves, on the surface at least, as unproblematically "English." In an important sense, however, "exilic" is not a quality that inheres to an individual person or indeed to particular films; it is produced by the historical and cultural conditions of each time and place that forces exile to be performed and represented.

To get an initial sense of Hurst's measure and significance, consider that his corpus of films spans a critical period of cinema history, from the 1930s to the early 1960s. It ranges in subject and genre from *Irish Hearts* (1934) to his adaptation of J. M. Synge's *The Playboy of the Western World* (1962), and from popular wartime movies like *Dangerous Moonlight* (1942) and *Theirs Is the Glory* (1946) to adaptations like *Hungry Hill* (1947) and *Scrooge* (1951). Reflecting on his full filmography, the volume and the range of Hurst's work alone demand a critical assessment of his significance as a film director and the kind of critique that is responsive to the contexts within which he operated. A consideration of Hurst's work suggests how he might feature in a wider history of Irish exilic filmmakers who were active during the middle years of the twentieth century in the United States and Britain.[3] Hurst, I argue, was definitively shaped by his Ulster Protestant birth and upbringing, modified by his early transatlantic journeys, and then remolded again in the specific nexus of entanglements that obtained between Ireland and England during his domicile and professional work in London. These connections resulted from a particular subset of wider Irish–British Empire relations and post–World War I exilic experience whose impacts were articulated through British cinema in the same period.

BELFAST, BRITISH, BOHEMIAN, . . . AND IRISH?

These four words help to frame the material discussed, so some initial explanation might help to introduce the main themes, the scope, and the approach that I have adopted. At this point, reference might also be made to the "chronology" provided above. At the time of Hurst's birth, Belfast was the most modern, developed, and populous city in Ireland, well integrated by political union, industrial links, and imperial connection within the "United Kingdom of Great Britain and Ireland" formalized since 1800. Yet Ireland's "Britishness" and connection were contingent: they were seriously but incompletely decoupled within a generation by political events that came to a crisis point between 1912 and 1922.

Hurst's identification with Ireland and the particular form of his Irishness happened because he left home, traveled, and lived elsewhere during this crucial period of national redefinition. Leaving Belfast when he did was both personally and publicly significant. With Hurst, the adoptive transformation from "British" to "Irish" mattered because he grew up as a working-class Ulster Protestant confronting what fellow Belfast man Louis MacNeice called "this division of allegiance!"[4] As a nineteen-year-old, Hurst volunteered for the Royal Irish Rifles, a regiment in the British army, to fight for King George V against Germany, the Austro-Hungarians, and the Ottoman Empire in World War I. But a significant part of Ireland engaged in what became a five-year guerrilla war (1916–21) and a fiercely contested political argument for Irish national independence. This conflict resulted in the geopolitical division of the island of Ireland with a border in 1920, the creation of a partially independent Irish Free State (Saorstat Éireann) in 1922 with dominion status, and a smaller state, "Northern Ireland," in 1921 that retained an uneasy union within the United Kingdom.

Taking part in an international conflict overseas transformed Hurst's sense of British Irishness, and in time he fashioned what I term an "Ulster exilic sensibility." The detail of this matter is discussed in the course of this introduction and developed further in chapter 1, and it informs the analysis of his films in later chapters. By 1919–20 Belfast was riven by sectarian conflict along the lines of national affiliation badged by religion. To Hurst, arriving back to his home city with the recent carnage of war haunting him, Belfast held few prospects or welcome. The city's predominately Ulster Presbyterian character offered little possibility for Hurst to explore his creativity and make his life anew. Apart from anything else, Hurst had deserted in 1917, and his service medals remained uncollected.[5]

Staying in his home city was increasingly perilous; being elsewhere, going into exile, was a necessary move.

Thus, if bohemianism is defined as life "lived experimentally,"[6] then Hurst's early adult life was definitively shaped by two sea journeys, maritime experiments into the unknown. The first in the summer of 1915 was in a troop ship from Liverpool to the Mediterranean island of Lemnos and thence to Gallipoli. That brutal battlefield confronted Hurst with life at its violent extremes: mortal combat, mutilation, and the deadly diseases that resulted from an ill-conceived military campaign. The second decisive journey, just five years later in December 1920, was the transatlantic crossing to Canada that allowed him to invent himself as a bohemian Irish painter at an art school in Ontario. And that led to further journeys back and forth to Paris, London, New York, and Los Angeles throughout the 1920s. How this phase of fugitive exile provided successive temporary locations for Hurst's bohemianism to develop is discussed in chapter 1.

Suffice it to note here, following Jerrold Seigel, Hurst's was a generation for whom the idea of "bohemia" pointed to a central "dilemma about the nature of modern individuality." The artistic bohemianism that Hurst acquired in his midtwenties meant that he shared "a marginal existence based on the refusal or inability to take on a stable and limited social identity. All [bohemians] lived simultaneously within ordinary society and outside it."[7] In the next section, we examine in more detail some of the key biographical coordinates of Hurst's exile and develop an understanding of how that term serves best to explain Hurst and his filmmaking. Hurst's sense of his Irishness was, as we will see, shaped not only by the fact of being born in Ulster pre-1920 but also by the fact that almost all of his professional work took place beyond Ireland.

THE BIOGRAPHICAL COORDINATES OF EXILE

How can we understand Hurst's films given the situation that he was an Irish-born filmmaker working in the British cinema industry? It helps to journey back to think of his birth date, the location of his birth, and his given names. We know he was born in 1895 and that his full given name was "Hans Moore Hawthorn Hurst." The family names of his parents were combined with a Germanic first name that may have been a less odd choice than it now seems.[8] He was brought up in Protestant east Belfast "between the mountain and the gantries / To the hooting of lost sirens and the clang of trams," in a working-class family recorded in the 1911 Census as "Presbyterian."[9]

It was a large, bustling, extended—what we now call "blended"—family of nine that lived on Tamar Street, Belfast, most of whom were in school or employed locally. Hurst's mother had died in 1899; his father (Robert) who worked as a shipyard blacksmith had remarried, so Hans grew up with a stepmother (Margaret) and step- and half siblings, and his oldest sister, Patricia, was by 1911 away working in Scotland. Hurst had already left school to work, and in his midteens he was employed in a local linen mill. In quick succession, he experienced the death of his father, signed the Ulster Covenant in 1912 at age seventeen, and in 1914 enlisted in the British army, survived campaigns in Gallipoli and the Balkans (1915), sustained combat injuries, and contracted malaria but recovered in Egypt. The National Archives at Kew in west London records that Hurst deserted his regiment in July 1917, possibly during a period of convalescence, but bizarrely reenlisted under a false name in a different regiment.[10] Under military regulations at the time, desertion was a capital offense, but under an assumed name Hurst seemingly demobilized back in Belfast in 1919 and secured employment at the British Legion, a social club network for former soldiers and their families. His memoir recalls how sectarian violence became outright political conflict in his home city in the lead-up to partition (1920).

Given his criminal status, disillusionment, and poor future prospects in Belfast, Hurst took the opportunity to avail himself of a British government grant to immigrate to Canada, doing manual labor, and then shortly after enrolling to study art in Toronto (1922–24). There is some evidence that he may have visited Antwerp in 1923 on a study tour before spending some time in Paris during the mid-1920s.[11] He may also have had a spell in New York at its International League Art School in 1925 before crossing the Atlantic again, to find work in commercial mural painting and then art direction in Hollywood from 1926, initially for the Fox Corporation. He became close to the influential but maverick film director John Ford and worked as his assistant before the Wall Street crash in 1929. The collapse of Fox, the Depression, and tightening immigration laws prompted him to move to London in 1931.[12] It was the third instance of physical exile in his life, in this case the threat of expulsion by the US authorities representing a rejection by the state.

Yet by the mid-1930s, he had gained employment in the British film industry's major studios. With the success of an Irish War of Independence film, *Ourselves Alone* (1936), Hurst became established as a contract director at Elstree Studios, was able to retain residences in London and Buckinghamshire for the duration of World War II, and later also owned a residence in Tangiers until the 1970s. As a film director he produced a wide-ranging body of work, after which he enjoyed retirement in a Knightsbridge mews living on his royalties and reputation until his intestate death in a nursing home in northwest London in September 1986. This summary risks the biographer's curse of conferring undue coherence on their subject but with the merit of giving it meaningful shape. It also pinpoints the issue of Hurst's successive personal experience of exile and the ways he dealt with the encounter of "diasporic space." Avtar Brah's influential concept describes the overlapping real and imagined space inhabited by exiles interacting from different places and their encounters with the people, culture, and symbols of those who define themselves as "native" to a place, be it a city or country. For Brah, then, space is "inhabited not only by those who have migrated and their descendants, but equally by those who are constructed and represented as indigenous."[13] The displaced nature of these overlapping exilic networks of Hurst's adoptive culture in England, created in and by the conjunction of historic and more recent migrations, is key to understanding his working environment, his social life, and his lived culture.

In *The Last Bohemian* the "exilic" is presented as a productive critical optic for considering Hurst's life and film work as a director. My emphasis on the Ulster exilic is to modify the term "exile" (*deoíreacht* in Irish), perhaps one of the most persistent tropes of Irish social experience, political history, and cultural expression. In a deep, historical sense, Hurst was born in a place that developed its modern character as a result of much of its population having been "planted" there in the sixteenth and seventeenth centuries for political or religious persecution or for economic reasons. In this sense, then, Hurst grew up in a culture that was already exilic before he had physically departed his home country. The Ulster Protestant internalization of exile, banishment, and exodus with its biblical resonances of "diaspora" became part of the self-narrative of the community in which he was nurtured. At a cultural and a familial level, exile imbued the lives of Hurst's contemporaries.

In accounts of writers from the northern counties of Ireland whose creative expression was stifled by a close-knit, theocratic culture, their sense of feeling "inner exiles" is discussed by Seamus Heaney.[14] With Hurst and other young men like him in 1914, going off to fight in a war was an adventurous, exciting form of escape, caught up in conflict in strange places, not knowing when or if they would return home. His circumstances in 1920 were different again. Immigration to Canada was a different prospect: the transatlantic journey was a greater distance, Hurst as a deserter was more of a fugitive, and he was undertaking a trip from which he probably did not plan to return. In fact, the 1920s saw Hurst adopt a more fluid, transient, and mutable exilic existence, perhaps developing what might be called a transatlantic subjectivity. He retained the name "Brian" that he had adopted ad hoc in the army at the suggestion of his sister to avoid anti-German sentiment and added "Desmond" as a "painter's" name and also routinely stressed his Irishness as well as his ability to speak some French and a little Arabic. This notion of artist in exile tapped into tradition of a socially mobile, self-consciously bohemian lifestyle in major urban populations (Toronto, New York, Paris, Los Angeles), cities of strangers where creatives enjoyed a cosmopolitan milieu. For such people, the notion of "home" or a return to an originary place is endlessly deferred. Hurst adopted an Irish identity in the United States that he used within the movie business in which enterprising immigrant individuals featured strongly.

By the early 1930s, Hurst seemed positioned so that he could have become Irish American. But as a "resident alien" lacking proper papers, the tightening immigration laws post-1924, the crash, maybe tax registration issues, and possibly a vindictive rival in Hollywood meant that he was advised to leave the United States. Exiled again, his ship sailed for London, not Belfast. Clearly, Hurst and his male partner, Norman Dean, who traveled with him, would not return home to Belfast and could live more easily together though still illegally in London. Economically, there were more opportunities for work in the cinema industry in London, where he could to try his luck at becoming a director.

But becoming exilic Irish in England marked another shift: the proximity of Ireland to Britain put him in another position, enmeshed in the complex constitutional, political, and economic relations between Ireland and the United Kingdom. Of course, the relatively short distances between Ireland and Britain meant that some migration east–west had always been seasonal, short-term, and built into the economies of rural and urban Ireland. Hurst's own father may have been absent for periods of work in the Govan shipyards of Glasgow, for instance. Perhaps between 1800 and 1922, this human traffic might be seen as a form of internal labor migration, not exile as such. But many who arrived in Britain did not return and raised families, making a new home. "Out"-migration from Ireland continued between the two world wars, increasing slowly from the Irish Free State and again heavily in the 1940s and 1950s. This migration mirrored a similar pattern of population movement from rural England, Wales, and Scotland to major English cities. In becoming part of what might be termed the "near diaspora," Hurst had come closer to home, but home itself had changed since he had left. The pre-1920 province of Ulster with nine counties had become the smaller six-county state of "Northern Ireland" in 1921. As Stuart Hall has noted, in a profound sense, for all exiles, "migration is a one-way trip, there is no home to go back to. There never was."[15]

Given the contexts just outlined, it is important then to counter both critical and popular accounts of Hurst that have a tendency to characterize him as an *exceptional* Irish migrant figure, "as untypical and fantasticated an Irishman as it would be possible to find," as Adrian Frazier has put it.[16] Instead, in many ways, as an emigrant statistic he was typical of his era both in his exit to Canada and in his "reentry" to Britain as part of the "second wave."[17] That said, in terms of being a working-class Protestant, his career arc and social mobility do stand out but in ways that need to be carefully contextualized. His presence in London bears comparison with

George Bernard Shaw, a lower-middle-class Irish Protestant (1856–1950) from Dublin who made himself into a professional Irishman of letters in London, declaring: "Every Irishman who felt his business in life was on the higher plans of the cultural professions . . . felt that he must have a metropolitan domicile and an international culture: that is, he felt that his first business was to get out of Ireland."[18]

Such sentiments might also be shared by a clutch of Belfast-bred writers with Ulster Protestant backgrounds with whom Hurst might be compared, including Nesca Robb (1905–76), Louis MacNeice (1907–63), John Hewitt (1907–87), or Robert Greacen (1920–2008), all of whom, though of differing class, denominational, and educational upbringing, moved back and forth between Belfast, Oxford, London, and Coventry—and lived with the consequences. MacNeice's autobiography, *The Strings Are False*, begins memorably on board a boat from Canada to wartime Britain, and he writes, despite having been schooled there as a boy, of returning to "England the unknown."[19] Heaney writes about MacNeice's "bilocated extraterritorial fidelities" in ways that are echoed in Hurst's exilic formation. For MacNeice, according to Heaney: "His ancestry in Mayo gave him a native dream-place in the south which complemented his actual birthplace in the north, while his dwelling in England gave him that critical perspective on the peculiar Britishness of that first northern environment."[20]

Certainly, Hurst's adoptive names of "Brian" and "Desmond," his affinity for aristocratic Ireland, and Ulster's significance in premodern Ireland suggest a similar "dream-place" function in his self-fashioned family past. A former linen-mill worker, Hurst seems to have developed a fascinated predilection for landed, titled Irish and English aristocratic types and international royals: he became a close friend and business partner with Michael Morris, Third Baron Killanin, whom he met in Cambridge in the mid-1930s, a journalist and executive administrator who worked on film production over three decades. Despite the differences, these figures shared a complex adjustment to life in England and a deracinated relationship with Irishness and Ireland. This point is memorably captured in a line from MacNeice to his friend Eric Dodds: "I wish I could either *live* in Ireland or *feel* oneself in England."[21] Much of Hurst's domicile and creative work in London seems characterized by this tension.

Stressing Hurst's Ulster exilic status contributes to the academic field of Irish diaspora studies in that it addresses the seriously underexamined Protestant Irish in Britain and builds on the work of R. F. Foster (1993), J. W. Foster (1987, 2001), Sloan (2000), Patten (2011), and most recently by Reid (2016), who characterized this social group (after Shaw) as "Citizens of Nowhere."[22] The "exilic" optic has a second dimension in that it connects Hurst precisely into the European émigré constellation of film people who were so influential in the 1930s and 1940s within British cinema. Typically, the Irish in exile look backward, but, as Hamid Naficy shows, connecting "horizontally" with others also from elsewhere is part of a diasporic formation.

As we have seen, Hurst had lived on three continents before he was thirty, but as he started out a film director he found himself in proximate exile, in the familiar but estranged culture of England. To some middle-class Ulster Protestants, many of whom had been educated in England, those individuals in business or the professions, the move to England seemed a natural relocation, a kind of coming home, so strongly did British values impose themselves on those growing up in Northern Ireland. John Wilson Foster suggests that "it is the relationship with Britain (principally England) that has for obscure reasons damaged the Ulster Protestant as well as aided him," creating an "injurious feeling of inferiority beside England . . . a feeling I believe widespread but masked by patriotism, and not one explained by mere provincial pique."[23] In Hurst's time, 1930s Britain was a place that was itself undergoing epochal change in the economy, socially, and culturally. I argue that for this part of the twentieth century, being an Irish creative professional at the London hub of the British cinema business was to occupy an uneasy sociocultural space. To come to live and work there from elsewhere was to experience, as Naficy puts it, a "slipzone of anxiety and imperfection, where life hovers between heights of ecstasy and confidence and the depths of despondency and doubt."[24] Naficy's elaboration of the exilic in the context of the cinema industry stresses that such filmmakers "operate within and astride the cracks and fissures of the [studio] system . . . [and that they] . . . are not so much marginal or subaltern as they are *interstitial, partial and multiple*."[25]

It is in highlighting these qualities and applied with qualified specificity to Hurst that, I argue, the exilic helps us understand Hurst's films and is essential to a proper evaluation of his work in the British studio system.[26]

HURST'S PROFILE AS A FILM DIRECTOR

The Last Bohemian tracks how Hurst has been critically evaluated as a film director. But while it recognizes the history and indeed resurgence of debates about notions of authorship and film, this book does not present itself as a conventional auteur study of Hurst.[27] Toward the end of the 1950s and early 1960s, as auteur criticism came to be defined and named as such, some critical assessments of Hurst's work pointed out the absence of the qualities of coherence and recurring personal, "signature" motifs that marked the recognizable individual, artistic sensibility associated with the term "auteur." Indeed, the generic range and uneven quality of his films is generally seen as a weakness, indicating a director lacking talent and individuality, or as one profile, published in the late 1950s, put it: "Such versatility makes it difficult to pin down any one aspect of a shifting talent."[28] In contrast, this study recognizes his directorial versatility as one of the material necessities that conditioned his situation and others like him. Indeed, in my reading, the exile's social and cultural adaptability becomes a positive attribute.

Historically, the critical evaluation of Hurst has three broad phases: The first can be seen as he emerged and became established in the 1930s and 1940s. The press review and commentary material associated with this phase is assessed in the context of the individual films within each period of his directorial activity across chapters 2–4. The most damning critic of the early period was Graham Greene, who, in his 1939 review of *On the Night of the Fire*, wrote witheringly of Hurst's "second rate cinema mind."[29] There is some suggestion from remarks by Greene and other industry insiders explored in chapter 2 that his fairly well-known sexual proclivities may have hindered his advancement, but his record of achievement with box-office hits, the recognition that he produced some quality "art," and his solid "war work" record discussed in chapter 3 give ample evidence for his deservedly high status by 1950. Not long after Greene's remarks, a profile in *Screen* in 1942 could assert with more evidence of "his right to be regarded as a front-rank director," and Hurst had certainly attained that status by the end of the 1940s.[30] The second phase, with naturally a greater degree of retrospection, after Hurst had gained seniority, began toward the late 1950s and lasted until his obituaries in the mid-1980s. The third phase of critical evaluation is the current generation of scholarship, reference work, and popular writing from the late 1980s to the present juncture. Three examples of a popular memoir mode estimation will suffice here: first, that Hurst was "a routine director but [an] exuberant and amiable person"; second, that he was "an amiable but wicked old queen . . . who had an acid tongue and a hedonistic approach to life and work [and] a long and not undistinguished career"; and, finally, the even more bitchy, unfair summation that he was "a famously lazy director who got by for years by employing brilliant technicians. He was a gregarious, outrageously roguish old reprobate."[31] Other academic and scholarly portraits of Hurst are discussed in chapter 5.

For the moment, we can note that the two main themes that stand out in this contemporary phase are the oscillating tensions between Hurst's Irish and British affiliations and, second, the interest generated by his biographical profile versus the film material itself.[32] Early work by Slide (1988) and McIlroy (1989) established him within an "Irish" framework as an act of assertive recovery, but even Slide refers to him as a "major British director."[33] A later, second, essay by Brian McIlroy (1994), Jeffery Richards's comment that Hurst was "British cinema's equivalent of [John] Ford,"[34] and Ruth Barton (2004) do much to realign attention to Hurst's work in the British studio system, with John Hill (2006) providing a Northern Ireland grounding for Hurst's films. The present study revises the notion of Hurst's "indeterminate," hybrid, hyphenated "Northern-Irish"[35] identity, offering the concept of Ulster exilic identity, formed in the intersection of British and Irish national politics and culture. Hurst's case, then, is productively problematic, uneven, and awkward: he doesn't quite fit within existing borders of either British or Irish cinema history. But maybe that is the point: as a figure, he remains perpetually out of place, in between, and that condition is expressed in and through his films.

It is important to the broader argument about seeing Hurst as in some senses *un*exceptional by comparing him to other Irish-born directors. Rex Ingram (1893–1950) and Herbert Brenon (1880–1958) and film producer and Ardmore Studio cofounder Emmet Dalton (1898–1978) provide precursor or parallel examples, though distinguished from Hurst by class, denomination, and being Dublin born.[36] Interestingly, all three have been the subject of recent biographical, critical studies, ranging from the scholarly to the independently researched and published. Chapter 1 shows how Hurst's formative years of artistic development were spent in Canada and the United States, where the role of Jewish, Italian, and Irish immigrants and their offspring in the New York and California film industries is well documented, where Raoul Walsh (1887–1980), Sidney Olcott (1872–1949), Robert Flaherty (1884–1951), and John Ford (1895–1973) are the influential figures.[37] The specifics of Ford's stylistic influences have been noted by critics, and Hurst's professional collaboration with Ford on the Four Provinces Films enterprise in the 1950s is examined in chapter 4.

In a similar comparative vein, three director/producers should be mentioned as part of a constellation of Hurst's contemporaries in London of the 1930s. These are Herbert Wilcox (1890–1977), based in London with Cork origins; Alfred Hitchcock (1899–1980); and Montgomery Tully (1904–88), the latter two of whom had Dublin connections through one or both parents. Wilcox was a well-established, highly successful producer and director in the British industry who had assimilated culturally and reflected publicly on his Irishness only in late retrospection. Hitchcock had an international reputation against which up and coming directors like Hurst, Reed, Asquith, Powell, and others were measured. Less is known or made of the second-generation aspects of Hitchcock's Irish Catholic upbringing in London. Charles Barr has reasoned that "Hitch" actively suppressed his Irishness because of racism and political antipathy toward Irish republicanism in the 1920s as he tried to secure work. Tully is perhaps the least known director whose work has barely been considered. He started out as a screenwriter who broke through as a director in the late 1940s and turned to directing crime and horror movies and then television. Interestingly, Tully cultivated a professional biographical profile that constructed his Irish origins, fabricating his birth in Dublin and possibly an "earlier career" as a novelist to enhance his status.[38]

The process of positioning particular directors, connecting them, and highlighting certain films for critical study will always remain a contingent, selective process. Reflecting on a generation of British film studies, John Hill notes that invoking the terms "lost" and "unknown" as a methodological rationale is in "danger of becoming an exhausted critical manoeuvre with very little actual purchase on what might legitimately be held to be 'unknown' or 'undervalued.'"[39] Given my topic is Hurst's body of work, it's pertinent to reflect on the methods I devised to do the research.

RESEARCHING HURST AND HIS FILMS

The Last Bohemian examines a group of films made by one film director over a career that spanned thirty years. Hurst also had a hand in writing scenarios, wrote and cowrote some screenplays, and was an independent producer on several films. My primary emphasis at the outset was to critically analyze these films by paying close attention to their cinematographic qualities. Doing so involved as a secondary focus the methods required to better understand the contexts and conditions that produced Hurst and the circumstances in which his films were made and critically received at different phases of his career.

Over a period of about six years, I set about viewing Hurst's films in London and Dublin mainly. I had read Hurst's unpublished memoir, "Travelling the Road," then available at the British Film Institute (BFI) in London, and made archival visits to Dublin and Canada, the BBC in Reading, the Public Record Office of Northern Ireland (PRONI), and other locations in Northern Ireland. I made a set of notes of what was a systematic program of close visual analysis of all films credited to Hurst. This program was undertaken across different viewing formats and quite an extensive period of time.[40] Getting to know and understand the production and reception of his films involved extensive use of archival collections and library research, mainly in London and Dublin. Over a period of time, it has also involved recording some audio and note-taken interviews with individuals, such as the late Lord Beaulieu, Gerald O'Hara, and Dudley Sutton, who knew him from the 1940s onward, socially and professionally. These interviews are documented in the notes and bibliography. Another dimension of this secondary research has included reading Hurst's interviews in print or transcripts and consulting popular memoirs by Hurst's contemporaries to compile a sense of how he was viewed by actors, producers, writers, and other directors in the film business. The key source here is of course Christopher Robbins's memoir-biography *The Empress of Ireland*, but also of interest is its relationship to "Travelling the Road" and the work published under the auspices of the Hurst Estate. This work is critically discussed in detail in chapter 5 with the idea that contemporaneous views and voices of the period provided the best context for thinking about the films during the period in which they were made and shown. In this regard, my research has of course made much use of the critical appraisal of press reviews of Hurst's films across his career using British, Irish, and North American sources. Finally, I have located and critically analyzed discussions about Hurst in academic film studies, reference works, biographical studies, and the few documentary sources that exist. So, overall, the films themselves are considered within a framework of interlocking contexts that are severally historical/critical, visual/oral, personal/professional, and academic/popular.

A FUGITIVE SUBJECT

There is a sense, though, that, despite all this assiduous, carefully organized research, Hurst and his films remain a fugitive subject. My final chapter and conclusion show how Hurst and his films were forgotten and why over the past decade or so he and they have been "found." From the perspective of the early twentieth century, the focus in this last chapter is to explore how and why he has been reclaimed. Enigmatically, Hurst remains a figure on the move, avoiding scrutiny, even as he enjoys a greater profile, and my aim certainly is to cast a critical eye on the nature of that profile. His films survive and rightly, I argue, deserve the critical redemption that they are undergoing. But we still do not have a record of his art-direction work in his Hollywood apprentice years and need a fuller account of the tantalizing, unmade films from the 1960s. These and other topics for future research are discussed in the conclusion.

The Last Bohemian is organized into five chapters that follow a chronological approach to Hurst's filmmaking career to locate him between the history of the British cinema industry and Irish filmmaking. I argue that this positioning was determined by his interstitial status as an Ulster exile in London. In this regard, in social and cultural terms, Hurst may be seen as part of a new generation on the move, who came to be known pejoratively as "middlebrow," a term that we will discover in chapter 2 has been critically revised.[41]

Often characterized dismissively in standard cinema reference works as a "jobbing" director working across differing genres, his exilic sensibility predisposed him be adaptable and eclectic and to develop effective filmmaking attributes. These qualities were recognized by his peers: he achieved considerable professional status and financial success by the late 1940s. To luminaries like fellow director Michael Powell, there was no doubt: Hurst was "the brilliant Irish director, a follower of Renoir with a gift for poetic realism."[42]

Considered at different historical conjunctures, his films register the social and cultural anxieties of Britain from the 1930s to the early 1960s, with a particular concern over issues of national belonging, social-class distinction, and sexual expression that were part of a national cinematic imaginary. Film critics like Brian McIlroy, sympathetic to Hurst's wide-ranging output, do point out the difficulties that his oeuvre presents but try to rationalize its variety thus: "While Hurst's full filmography is, indeed, mixed, we can find '*progressive*' or '*countercurrent*' themes being explored."[43] These elements are present, but this study also allows for the fact that Hurst's films also project the conventional conservative and regressive strands of the culture in which he worked.

Taken together, his British *and* Irish films also offer an exile's view of Britain's particular relationship with Ireland and the Irish, the wider world, and the creative migrants who had arrived in Britain, many with whom Hurst worked. *The Last Bohemian* also tracks Hurst's changing relationship to the place he left (Belfast), his adopted place of domicile

(London and England), and how he strove to reinvent a new set of connections with "Ireland" at three different moments by trying to develop filmmaking in Ireland, none of which were welcomed or successful. Chapter 5 brings us up to date to see how Belfast has been encouraged to acknowledge and embrace an idiosyncratic creative figure whose lifestyle, values, and outlook were alien to its own civic image in his lifetime.

Chapter 1, "Formation," offers a contextual synthesis developing the significance of his origins and formative experiences in Belfast as the coordinates of his upbringing, culture, and domestic pressures that created the predisposition for departure. Moving from "inner" to "fugitive" exile, the chapter then examines a phase of transnational subjectivity for Hurst as exilic Irish based in Toronto, Paris, and Los Angeles during the 1920s. Chapters 2 and 3, and 4, "Filmmaker," "Fame," and "Finale"—forming the bulk of the material discussed in the book—deal with Hurst in three successive phases of his career within British cinema from the 1930s to the 1960s. The analysis seeks to isolate how—through the Ulster exilic that became more sharply defined from his arrival in London—the material conditions of national affiliation, social class, and sexuality shaped the productions that were embodied in the themes and visual matter of films discussed.

By the end of the interwar period, Hurst was forced to come up with a workable sense of "national" connection, as determined by the shifting definitions of Irish and British nationality. In class terms, Hurst became part of a generation in transition between the traditional classes and occupations of a modernizing Britain. The former mill worker turned fine artist rapidly rose to become a Bentley-owning member of London's creative "haut bohemia" and cinema "dreamland."[44] Socially and sexually, Hurst crossed class divides, "queered" the conventions of straight culture, and lived out his criminalized sexuality with some bravura. His films illustrate Andy Medhurst's point that "those on the margins of a culture know more about its centre than the centre can ever know about the margins." He is talking here specifically about the "codes, mechanisms and ideologies of heterosexuality itself" as they are reproduced in cinema and the wider culture.[45] Indeed, chapter 1 explores the bohemian nature of Hurst's heterodox thinking on matters social, sexual, and spiritual and the formation that in middle age became an unconventional conservatism. Chapter 5 brings us full circle but also updates Hurst and observes how he has been "found" and "reinvented" for a new era. Patrick Maume sums it up succinctly in his biographical appraisal: "In a twenty-first century Ireland, north and south, where fluid identities were regarded more favourably than in previous decades and where increasing attention was given to audio-visual culture, Hurst has attracted increasing attention."[46]

The periodization adopted in *The Last Bohemian* is suggested by particular kinds of filmmaking activity: Chapter 2 begins with the context of his directorial debut in 1934, moving from "artistic films" to crime-film "quota quickies," leading into the outbreak of World War II; chapter 3 focuses on his war-films work, comparing treatments of public information, documentary, and melodramatic film output; and chapter 4 deals with Hurst's postwar engagement with English literary culture, Britain's imperial legacy, and societal change as portrayed in popular cinema. It also analyzes Hurst's final film and considers some of his unmade film projects for which there is evidence. Chapter 5, "Forgotten," details how Hurst and his work were marginalized or disappeared from historical accounts of British and Irish cinema and reflects on the ways that since 2004 Hurst has been rediscovered through academic and popular writing, the establishment of the Hurst Estate, the selective rerelease of films on DVD, archival screenings, and other such "legacy" events marking his public significance.

As the prologue indicates, one such event occurred in October 2012. It was perhaps significant that the new Titanic Film studios in Belfast, a key facility for the HBO TV production *Game of Thrones*, supported by state and commercial redevelopment funds, was heralded with a ceremony jointly presided over by the late Martin McGuinness (Sinn Fein, MLA) and Peter Robinson (DUP, MLA). In a rare gesture of political ecumenism, the province's two leading politicians were there with Hurst's extended family relations and business chief executive offers to attend the formal opening and naming event that recalled two figures from Northern Ireland's cinema history: William (Bill) MacQuitty and Brian Desmond Hurst. A century after the doomed ship was built and completed there in 1911–12, the studios were constructed in what was the newly dubbed "Titanic Quarter." Indeed, it is this location and that moment in Belfast's history that created the conditions for Hurst's departure from his home city in the tumultuous years that led up to World War I that are explored in the next chapter.

1 Formation
Belfast, Gallipoli, and the 1920s

On September 28, 1912, a seventeen-year-old Hans Hurst walked into City Hall in Belfast and signed a petition, known as the Ulster Covenant. He joined nearly a half-million others to protest against nationalist "Home Rule" legislation being considered by Herbert Asquith's government in London and to protect their "heritage of British citizenship." The covenant provided a popular political rallying point for Irish Unionism, and its orchestrated signing in churches and halls across the province, in Scotland, and as far away as Canada was "conducted in an atmosphere of near religious fervour" on a carefully stage-managed, much-photographed "Ulster Day."[1] For the young linen-factory worker, this signature act was the first expression of a young adult public identity that can be traced.

This declarative act of putting his name to a document, announcing the self, forms the starting point in a chapter that charts a set of transformative points that track Hurst's itinerant movements and the early formation of an exilic identity. This chapter discusses five interrelated themes from the formative years of Hurst's life that include nationality, conflict trauma, spirituality, sexuality, and social mobility. These topics inform the outline of the rest of his personal life and his professional work as a film director. As for many young European men of his generation, the central event of Hurst's early adulthood was the period that he spent in the British army fighting in World War I campaigns in the eastern Mediterranean—notably surviving the slaughter of Gallipoli (1915), North Africa, and the Balkans. In the post-1918 era covered in this chapter, we consider three highly influential locations and their impacts on Hurst: art school in Toronto, the cosmopolitan collisions of the avant-garde in Paris, and the commercial film studio practice of Los Angeles, notably at

Fox Corporation and under John Ford. This chapter shows how Hurst's Edwardian working-class outlook was transformed in just over a decade of peripatetic migration between locations that shaped a generation and brought him to London in the early 1930s. The particular matrix he experienced formed the practical social skills and techniques of working with moving images. Combining them allowed him to actively participate within the milieu he came to inhabit in the interwar period as he began to make films, as discussed in chapter 2.

The bulk of the material discussed in this chapter is contextual, based on available print and still-image archival and secondary sources that range across sociopolitical and art history and cultural theory. This synthesis allows us to critically analyze the key theme of Hurst's various easterly and westerly migrations and to see how the formation of transnational subjectivities such as Hurst's were constitutive of the British Empire, its cultural forms and lived experience. By focusing on Hurst, we can examine closely how specific modes of Irishness-within-Britishness were woven into the routes of cultural traffic, exchange, and identity.[2] It shows how particular kinds of Irishness could inhabit successive diasporic realms and that these realms were forged in material as well as symbolic ways in combination and that overlapped with other migrant creatives. The aim is to illustrate Brah's insight about the nature of the "diasporic space" discussed in the introduction and to place Hurst as an Ulster Protestant in London alongside the list of "micks on the make" discussed by Roy Foster.[3]

Through his social life and professional creativity, Hurst participated in and drew character from those elements of hegemonic Englishness and British culture that were themselves under the flux and pressures of imperial modernity.[4] From this experience came the development of a cosmopolitan, bohemian outlook with which Hurst came to identify. These latent predispositions were made manifest by the historical conditions of his generation. Identity here is "formed at the unstable point where the 'unspeakable' stories of subjectivity meet the narratives of history, a culture."[5] It shows how he became professionally positioned at the interstices of particular social and aesthetic formations that Raymond Williams characterizes as "fractional" elements of an international cultural formation in the interwar period.[6]

IRELAND, BELFAST, AND EDWARDIAN EMPIRE

Growing up in the first decades of the twentieth century, Hurst experienced Belfast as a bustling industrial, mercantile, provincial Irish city, yet one that was also an imperial city that was globally connected.[7] To move, as many of its inhabitants had done, from the rural countryside to the rapidly expanding city districts was to shift into a new urban modernity. It linked to Glasgow, Liverpool, and London and from there to the trading, military, and political coordinates of the empire in ways that were ingrained into the life, work, and pastimes of Belfast's population. It was a significant part of a mind-set that was defined by an interaction of "here" and "elsewhere," and it is to this aspect of the character of Edwardian Belfast that we briefly now turn.

In the year prior to Hurst's signing the Ulster Covenant, the 1911 National Census returns indicate the socioeconomic conditions for a family in east Belfast. The nine members of the Hurst family on Tamar Street occupied an overcrowded domestic space headed by the stepmother, her children, some of Hurst's own siblings, and his younger half siblings.[8] Hurst's mother had died in 1899; his shipyard worker father, Robert, had remarried his cousin. Hurst's devoted older sister, Patricia, had immigrated to Glasgow, and it's likely at the time of Census he was working away. They were all physically or spiritually somewhere else, and Robert Hurst died a year later. These telling psychological absences made their mark on Hurst, but the material pressures for space, the need to earn money, and the struggle to define himself in a large, fractured family stayed with him. The city of Hurst's birth had expanded enormously from the mid-nineteenth century, as a generation of rural workers migrated to the jobs available in shipbuilding, engineering, rope making, linen weaving, and other manufacturing.[9] With this industrialization came modernity: urbanization, trains, trams, gas and electricity, and the novel pleasures offered by the variety hall and picture house as the region's first purpose-built cinemas emerged. But the Belfast in which Hurst grew up had a particular religiosity born of its ferment of different established, independent, and evangelical Protestant churches in parallel tension with Catholic institutions and demotic culture. In its civic character and cultural expression, Belfast's daily life had a Presbyterian stamp. If by his own account Hurst's was not a devout upbringing, the Census formally records that all those at Tamar Street were Presbyterian, and elements of its Ulster strain stayed with him despite his midlife spiritual conversion to Catholicism in the 1940s.

Economically, Belfast was Ireland's major industrial city. Politically, culturally, and spiritually, the Hurst household and majority of the neighborhood identified with the British monarchy, the empire, and its dominions and adhered to the continued political union of Great Britain and Ireland. However, the status quo of this constitutional connection was under threat from the political thrust of "Home Rule" politicians in Ireland, with British Liberal Party support in Westminster. The gathering momentum of labor politics in pre-1914 Ireland and Great Britain also threatened to undermine the honeymoon decade of the new Edwardian century. Part of east Belfast's manual laboring class, at the hub of resistance to Home Rule, Hurst and his brothers were behaving entirely consistently with what George Boyce has termed "Ulster political Protestantism," publicly affirming their loyalty to the Crown, being fiercely protective of religious rights, and taking for granted their status as part of a civic, political, and cultural majority within Belfast.[10] Within two years, people in the North of Ireland saw the formation of a Protestant paramilitary force (UVF in 1912) the passing of the Home Rule Bill (1914), the arming of Irish republican (Sinn Féin) and socialist paramilitary groups across Ireland, and the outbreak of war between the major European powers. A popular patriotism within Ulster's Protestant population, his own cramped domestic life, and a sense of youthful adventure that was common enough in teenage years led Hurst and a friend to respond to General Kitchener's recruitment campaign and enlist in the Royal Irish Rifles in the summer of 1914.

Signing the Ulster Covenant and joining the Royal Irish Rifles were the clearest articulations in Hurst's early manhood of an Ulster Protestant identity, its particular kind of Irishness-in-Britishness at that moment in history.[11] His military service in the British army during the horrors of the Gallipoli Campaign of 1915 and subsequent tours of duty with the Royal Army Service Corps in the Balkans, the Middle East, and North Africa were life-changing experiences, in profound and more trivial-seeming ways. One of the latter was that he informally dropped his given name, "Hans," to avoid barrack-room anti-German sentiment and adopted "Brian." More profoundly, what he participated in and witnessed forced him to question some of the core values instilled in the formative years of his Belfast upbringing and ultimately led him into lifelong exile from his home city.

WORLD WAR I AND ITS AFTERMATH

What is striking about Hurst's life is the range of fundamental transformations that he experienced during the course of his life arc, notably those issues concerning his name, faith, social class, geography, nationality, sexuality, and aesthetic principles. We have already mentioned that the catalyst for Hurst's reinvention of himself was essentially the outcome of two decisive long-distance journeys and the life-changing experiences that he encountered as a consequence of them. Now, the nature and mode of the exilic migrations were not untypical for his generation, nor were his practical, psychological, and creative responses. But I think we can identify five interrelated, overlapping themes that offer us the coordinates for discussing the particularity of his Ulster exilic identity:

- Ireland, Ulster, and British/Irish nationality
- Ulster Presbyterianism, Roman Catholicism, and spiritual (non)conformity
- World War I and the Blitz: trauma, comradeship, and homosociality
- sexuality and morality
- class, social mobility, and conservatism

Taking these themes in order, we can begin simply by observing that Hurst was born in an era when Ireland was linked to the United Kingdom under the Act of Union (1800). For reasons of birth, geography, class, and religion, he grew up with a dual sense of nationality as being British and Irish, but in quite complex ways this notion was already in flux in the late-Victorian and Edwardian era. To take one example, most Protestants in Ulster that had valued their British connection since the Union were

"Irish," though Unionists. Most Irish unionists became *Ulster* unionists between 1886 and 1912 and stressed their Protestant identity and loyalty to the Union as against Home Rule, Irish nationalism, and Roman Catholicism.[12] As the introduction has already indicated, in early manhood he clearly most strongly affiliated with the politics of Ulster Unionism and Britishness. But in the Royal Irish Rifles away from Belfast, he mixed with Irish Catholics and other British nationals, including English infantry and officer classes, some with Anglo-Irish backgrounds. The meandering exile of wartime postings allowed Hurst to begin a process of name-changing, shape-shifting, and a kind of impersonation.[13] In the ranks his given name made him a target for increasingly anti-German prejudice, which his older sister advised him to deflect by informally adopting the name "Brian," although his official military enlistment was as "Hans" and he retained his birth name with family and friends from home. "Brian" seems innocuous and non-German, but in an Irish context it carries particular heroic and aristocratic connotations, associated with Brian Boru (ca. 941–1014), the wily, ruthless, but charismatic king of pre-Norman Ireland who died fighting Viking Brodir at the Battle of Clontarf. The name that Hurst adopted and used thereafter, the example of the Republican rebellion of Easter 1916, and the sense that the English and other people he encountered abroad responded to him as "Irish" all contributed to the attractiveness of it as an identity that he could embrace.

John Wilson Foster has argued that "many Northern Ireland Protestants feel estranged from both Britain and Ireland,"[14] and Hurst is surely one of a long line of Protestants from Ulster that have had to negotiate this estrangement. For Hurst to go absent-without-leave and desert the army in 1917 also suggests a fundamental rejection of the military as an institution, to Britishness as a national allegiance, and to the imperial politics of war. His alleged reenlistment under a false name, "Brian Henry Hurst," for the remainder of the war and then his departure from Belfast as the Government of Ireland Act (1920) divided Ireland says much about his resourcefulness, desire for comradeship, and adventure, as well as his disillusionment with Britishness, the politics of Ulster Unionism, and the fact that "Northern Ireland" was not a state in which he could feel at home. We do not have a record of Hurst's identity papers or later what national passport he traveled under, but ships' passenger lists for the 1920s and 1930s show Hurst's movements recorded with his nationality given as Irish, British, and even Canadian on different journeys. He was not able to take out US citizenship and chose London as his long-term domicile, living under the travel and nationality protocols that evolved as Ireland and the United Kingdom managed a drawn-out process of close, diplomatic coexistence during Hurst's lifetime.

So much then for becoming an Irish national in exile, but what about Hurst's sense of spiritual affiliation? Here too we find a particular kind of heterodox thinking. Hurst was formally raised in the Presbyterian Church, the majority institutional faith at the turn of the nineteenth century for Belfast's working classes. By his account, it was not a strictly adhered to upbringing, but there were the staple observances. There were both Bible reading at home and Sunday school instruction, as well as an imbibed, everyday proverbial wisdom filtered down into his life. Hurst was of course aware of Catholicism growing up, but only as a mysterious, forbidden realm; or, in the street vernacular, Catholics were "papish" or "taigs." Yet as Robert Wilson Lynd has commented, "The Ulsterman's religion has been at once his making and his undoing. It has sent him about the world with a flame in his head."[15] Like a latter-day "mad" Sweeney astray—"away in the head" and wandering abroad—Hurst's first encounters with Catholicism beyond the sectarian geography of Belfast came via his regimental training in the Royal Irish Rifles in Hampshire: it recruited both Catholics and Protestants. This continued in the 1920s in Canada and Paris through sexual encounters with women and the Catholic history and milieu of Paris. Hurst formally entered the Roman Catholic Church in midlife—perhaps around 1947—but during the interwar period had developed his own idiosyncratic devotional practice that led to particular interest in the French martyr Saint Thérèse.

Hurst was also interested in the aesthetics of religious belief, studying sacred art formally and informally, and developed his artistic practice sufficiently competently to produce religious panels and his own favored portrait of Saint Therese. Hurst's spiritual profile puts him among a generation of Catholicism converts, but he retained a strong culture of nonconformity associated with aspects of his Ulster Presbyterian origins. There is a further demotic dimension to Hurst's belief system that again had its roots in his Ulster upbringing in pre-1914 Belfast.

In *The Empress of Ireland*, Robbins records how Hurst recalled memorable incidents, family lore, and alternative non-Christian beliefs in fairy folk, magic, spirits, and ghosts. Hurst's encounters with ghosts of his mother and a German servant stand out. Roy Foster, explaining Yeats's connections to theosophical circles in London, has brought out a "supernatural dimension of the Irish Protestant subculture."[16] Selina Guinness likewise has explored how Irish Protestantism of the late nineteenth century—across denominations—turned toward more charismatic practice. But it was also associated with various strands of theosophy and spiritualism in response to the rationality of scientific ideas, utilitarianism of modern life, and the conventions of orthodox religious thought.[17] While we do not have any evidence to substantiate Hurst's claim to have met W. B. Yeats in London, we do know that Hurst was interested in spiritualism, attended meetings of the Marylebone Spiritualist Association in the 1950s, and was featured in one of its publications.[18]

Hurst's upbringing, religious conversion, and practice all suggest a man with highly individual, eclectic, unorthodox ideas about faith and spirituality that fed into his artistic expression in the visual arts, as themes or outsider characters in his films, and a generally open-minded attitude to other people's spiritual beliefs. If, for some of his generation, the experience of the Great War shattered any sense of God, the scale and utter horror of modern warfare epitomized by trenches, shelling, machine guns, and gas led others like Hurst to turn toward some transcendent order for solace and meaning.

Hurst was a soldier living with the memory of direct firsthand combat experience in Gallipoli and the Balkans and then as a civilian "Blitzed" Londoner during 1940–45. Recognizing these troubling memories does help us understand Hurst's attitudes and his film work across a range of themes, and it is significant that a number of his films deal with state violence, conflict, and guerrilla war. There is little doubt that Hurst sustained considerable trauma as a result of his Gallipoli and subsequent experience. Hurst recuperated from bayonet injury and malaria in Cairo and then saw further active service in Serbia and Macedonia before succumbing to malaria again at the Strauma River. He returned to England, stopping off in Greece, and then to recuperate in Neath, Wales. His recall of his military service is key to understanding the nature of what he experienced and the violence that he witnessed, including hand-to-hand combat and the rape of a female Turkish sniper. *The Empress of Ireland*, with Robbins as Hurst's interlocutor, somberly addresses Hurst's anguished reflection of a deeply buried memory: "Brian sat for a moment, lost in thought. 'How could that man in hand-to-hand combat with a bayonet have been me? The capture of the sniper remains vivid today . . . too vivid.'"[19] It is a regrettable fact that sexual violence has been associated with men in conflict, often with civilian populations but also with prisoners of war and sometimes as here with combatants, including torture, mutilation and rape, and unlawful killing.[20] These are the extremes of human degradation and behaviors that Hurst understood, as well as his memory of killing and disease, and of being a noncombatant victim of the air-raid terror of the Blitz in the 1940s.

Processing these kinds of experiences, Hurst brought a particular sensitivity to bear when portraying men on film dealing with the privations of war and the pressures of armed conflict that is explored further in chapters 3 and 4. In this instance, the conflation of sexual acts and killing "sanctioned" by war is perhaps at the extreme end of the misogyny that some view as inherently "between men" in the male homosocial institutions, networks, and practices defined by late Victorian and Edwardian masculinity within which Hurst was socialized.[21] He held male comradeship in high regard and retained strong affiliation for "ordinary" soldiers, their bravery and fortitude and vulnerabilities in the face of killing others like them. There is a heightened awareness of homosociality in Hurst's films—not unlike his mentor, John Ford, in his westerns and war films—that has led some critics to "spot" gay characters or claim in Ford's case that he was a closet homosexual.[22] As many have noted about Hurst, he did not observe the niceties or necessities of "closeted" homosexuality in an era of criminalization, medicalization, and moral taboo.

Indeed, Hurst's attitudes to sexuality and morality derive from a modern bohemian revolt from bourgeois social norms that was rapidly apace by the 1920s, particularly in the cosmopolitan, urban situations where Hurst found himself. Yet prior to his departure from Belfast, Hurst testified to

Robbins as to his sexual experimentation in teenage years with both sexes. Hurst's memoir leaves us a frank record of his libidinous life. It is a first-person retrospective account of the conditions within which male bisexuality could be experienced in particular social situations. The diversity of Hurst's relationships with both sexes over his lifetime is remarkable. It ranged from a long-term relationships with Canadian Norman Dean whom he met at art school—which was an "open," nonmonogamous one—to one-night stands or chance encounters, including male-female-male ménage à trois, short-lived marriage engagements, a "live-in" male "personal assistant and secretary," paid-for sex with (usually) younger military men, and visits for sexual tourism in Morocco in the 1960s and 1970s.

He lived through a period in which for most of Anglo-American society, homo- and bisexuality were illegal and publicly taboo. But both were nevertheless actively present in cosmopolitan cities, occurred within and between classes, and were experienced in the situational circumstances of all-male institutions (school, armed services, youth and sports clubs, church, and universities). Finally, of course, it was also associated with and indeed sought out by those persons in the creative arts and world of professional entertainment. It is possible to read between the lines of his memoir and see in it an aversion to the overt politicization of male sexuality that began in Britain in the aftermath of 1945 and is perhaps most popularly associated in the 1950s with what became known as the Wildeblood sex scandal.[23]

Like his friend Lord Montagu whom he met in the late 1940s, Hurst articulated a complicated set of attitudes toward sexuality that were at once both nonconformist *and* conservative. Their shared bisexuality traversed class boundaries in ways that irked authoritarian strands within the political establishment and ran against its social convention but were quietly accepted by its liberal wing. While high-profile peers like Montagu and Michael Pitt-Rivers and figures like journalist Peter Wildeblood, actor Ivor Novello, photographer Angus McBean, and actor John Gielgud were all prosecuted by laws that criminalized male-on-male sex, Hurst's importuning of young men, casual sex, and sexual "tourism" seems not to have attracted the interest of the Metropolitan Police in an era of entrapment, blackmail, and "witch hunts" that prevailed into the mid-1970s and beyond. Hurst was bisexual in practice for much of his life rather than homosexual and certainly not "gay" in the contemporary sense of the word. Robbins cites a conversation between Hurst and a gay-activist agit-prop director that makes this point.[24]

Hurst's own brand of sexual politics would not endear him to social reformers such as Edward Carpenter (1844–1929) and later postwar liberal law-reform campaigners like Wildeblood.[25] The disruptive "queerness" of closet homosexuals and bisexuality will be discussed at various points in the analysis of the films in chapters 2, 3, and 4, and some do lend themselves to queer interpretation.[26] But it is equally interesting to reflect on how Hurst and other exilic queers—some like Anton Walbrook escaping Nazi persecution—were somewhat bizarrely central in representing the changing patterns of heterosexual desire, love, and relationships as part of a British cinematic imaginary.[27] It is the flip side of the "it takes one to know one" idea about a closet homosexual inadvertently revealing themselves. Those individuals who habitually hide their desires and dreams because they are vilified, marginalized, and traduced develop perceptive antennae about what defines the sexual norms of mainstream society.

One final theme to isolate for consideration to close this section is Hurst's social class, his mobility, and the social networks that he traversed professionally and privately. In popular accounts, it is the "rags to riches" story, from the Belfast poor working-class boy to the Bentley-owning bachelor of Belgravia narrative. First, this description takes us only so far and does not account for the specificity of class positioning for different kinds of Irish migrants to Britain or their offspring. It disguises Hurst's nonidentification with the Irish working-class culture active in Britain, whether rural or city born. Such fellow Ulster men with whom he was friendly, like Bill MacQuitty, were middle class. This class disavowal is in stark contrast to his active socialization with Anglo-Irish habitués, various exiled international aristocrats domiciled in London, and exiled creatives from Europe. Second, from this position, it is his exilic take on the class structure and social habitus of English society at different conjunctures—interwar, wartime, and postwar—that is of interest to this study.

The analysis explores how Hurst wrote screenplays and produced and directed films about the place that he made his permanent place of residence and its wider imperial connections. But this analysis is fundamentally linked to the ways that he looked back at an Ireland he had left, rarely returned to, and inhabited in his cinematic imagination. That imagination was stimulated by a keen interest in art, history, and literature as well as practical skills in drawing, portraiture, stage design, and graphic design. Working in film production, he developed the practical knowledge of story structure from adapting novels, plays, and writing scenarios as well as preparing shooting scripts.

Although Hurst failed to complete either his primary education or his tertiary training, he was a keen autodidact who learned French and some Arabic and read eclectically throughout his life, as is evidenced by what we know of his art and book collection. At the height of his career, Hurst had acquired considerable social and economic capital and affected a cultured manner, displayed his learning, and spoke with an accent that masked his working-class Belfast origins.[28]

As a self-styled bohemian of the 1920s and 1930s, he held bourgeois mores in contempt and was a spendthrift and sexual libertine. Yet for more than thirty years, he worked as a contract or independent film director within a demanding industry, having ditched his youthful avant-garde shape for a growing cultural conservatism that combined with a raucous, unconventional personal life. As a younger man, that irresistible urge to experience something else grew out of the poverty, disillusion, political violence, and lack of expressive opportunity in Belfast in 1920. Taking up a British government-sponsored immigration grant to Canada became a catalyst for what would become a period of bohemianism in exile, a decade of transatlantic travel, artistic training, and creative exploration in North America and Europe.

ONTARIO COLLEGE OF ART AND CANADIAN CULTURAL NATIONALISM

Disillusioned and eager to escape a city sundered by heightened sectarianism and "fierce riots"[29] from 1920–21, Hurst took up a government grant of £100 and in December 1920 set sail from Belfast to Montreal, a key port for many thousands of Ulster emigrants who had left for Canada before him. The British government had engineered a controversial compromise between Irish nationalists and unionists that resulted in the formal establishment of two new polities known as "Northern Ireland" and the "Irish Free State," the latter having the status of a "dominion," not unlike Canada. It was in Canada that Hurst transformed himself from a factory-linen worker to a fine-art painter. From a series of temporary manual jobs he saved up enough money to enroll for a four-year diploma course in fine art at Ontario College of Art (OCA, now the Ontario College of Art & Design University) in Toronto with fees of $100 a year.[30] In existence since 1912, the college received extra state funding that enabled it to expand, and it had just taken up residence in brand-new buildings at Grange Park in 1920, adjacent to the Art Gallery of Ontario. As a city Toronto was distinct from Francophile Montreal, and as an institution OCA became an innovative hub of creativity and social daring that challenged the aesthetic and social establishment. The OCA became synonymous with a rising tide of Canadian cultural nationalism through the movement known as the Group of Seven.

The OCA's prospectus stated that its purpose was "the training of students in the fine arts . . . and in all branches of the applied arts in the more artistic trades and manufacture,"[31] but its teachers, activities, and legacy questioned British/European models of artistic merit and by implication the assumed imperial rights of the political control of the "dominion."

Hurst found himself living in another city where the limits of empire were being challenged, albeit here through aesthetics rather than armaments. The comparison between Belfast and his adopted city would have been difficult for Hurst not to have made. Toronto was in part an imperfect copy, a hybrid whose character was defined in significant part by successive migrants from Ulster, Scotland, and northern England, giving the city a palpable character that would have been all too familiar to Hurst. However, although Toronto had a significant "Orange" and Presbyterian presence as a result of migration, Hurst's interactions during this period were with the artistic, culturally radical, and socially bohemian exilic fringe culture of the city.

While commentators often note that Hurst became a "painterly" director with a highly developed sense of visual composition, no one to

1.1. Ontario College of Art, Grange Park building (*right*), 1922. City of Toronto Archives, Fonds 1231, Item 135.

date has explored the *kind* of painter that he was trained to be, the influences that eddied about him, and how they were subsequently applied in the interactions between art and film practice in the interwar period.

Formal records show that Hurst was a diligent freshman student in 1921–22, successfully completed his first year, and got an honorable mention for design in 1922. The teaching faculty at the OCA comprised three of the most influential educators in Canadian art of this period: Arthur Lismer, F. Horsman Varley, and J. E. H. MacDonald. All were in fact English émigré artists from Sheffield and Durham, though with some experience of studying or working in Europe prior to immigrating to Canada. Lismer (1885–1969) trained as a commercial designer, immigrated in 1911, and eventually became vice principal at the OCA in 1919. He is credited for developing schools programs in art education and wrote on this subject too. Varley (1881–1969) had left England in 1912 and specialized in landscapes and portraiture. After his time at the OCA, he took a post in British Columbia. The last, MacDonald (1873–1932), is credited as the founder of the Group of Seven, which came together in 1920. A Presbyterian by upbringing, he worked at the OCA, was a member of the Arts and

Letters Club in Toronto, was interested in theosophy, and was one of the group's "thinkers." He was a noted muralist and clearly influenced Hurst's skills in this form of painting that stood him in good stead.[32] The group took influences from Scandinavian and northern European impressionism, blending it with the poetry and philosophy of Emerson, Thoreau, and Whitman and typically focused on the wilderness of the Canadian landscape. Lismer, as vice principal of the OCA, writing in the *Canadian Theosophist*, declared: "The imminent generation of the youth of Canada will come to produce fine art and fine craftsmanship because gradually they will become aesthetically aware of their environment."[33]

At the time that Hurst arrived to study, the Group of Seven had just held their first exhibition and were seen as experimental and challenging to the orthodoxy of the Canadian art establishment. Hurst would have undoubtedly visited this exhibition, and in class Lismer set out to impress on his male students that "to be a man, one has to be a non-conformist."[34] Within an otherwise conservative city at the far edge of the British Empire and close to the United States, it was a fascinating place for an Ulster Protestant to find himself. It also offers an episode of exposure to aesthetic and political issues at a remove that prefigures later cinematic engagements with conflict, trauma, and colonialism that are explored in the subsequent chapters of this book. MacDonald had sounded a fresh postwar departure for Canadian art in an essay in *New Statesman* (published in London in 1919): "Opening a new world the Canadian artists respond with a spirit that is very good. This world has not the picture-dealers' tone nor the connoisseur atmosphere . . . not often so softly beautiful as ruggedly strong, large, homely, free, and frankly simple in colour."[35]

In the first book-length appraisal of the "movement"—a term conferred upon it by critics and commentators, not themselves—Housser defined "tradition" as a "handing on" and said that "modernism is a movement of life and is not restricted to schools of art nor methods of painting."[36] Seen in longer historical perspective, however, its recent revisionist literature shows that the contemporary impact and historical legacy of the Group of Seven is complex and contradictory and must have offered a challenging set of circumstances for a young Irish artist to encounter.[37]

1.2. Group of Seven exhibition catalog, 1922. Art Gallery of Ontario.

Contemporary politics of art movements and their historical significance aside, the social milieu in which Hurst moved in these years provided the context for a wider range of masculinities and sexual expression to be explored. The archive of OCA press cuttings for the period indicate that the annual Arts Ball of the college attracted headlines with mildly scandalized headlines such as "Youthful Spirits with French Ideas People Toronto's Bohemia" (*Telegram*, April 1924) and "Art Students at Bohemian Dance" (*Telegram*, February 1925). There were also predictable complaints about nude posing before mixed-sex art classes. Hurst became more socially active and connected in his second year of study and made friends with

1.3. Arts Ball, Ontario College of Art, 1923. Hurst standing extreme left with Norman Dean to his left. Unknown photographer. Image courtesy Dorothy H. Hoover Library, Ontario College of Art & Design, 2009.

several influential people beyond the world of art, including Merrill Dennison and the Hart House theatrical group. "Christmas Frolics" reported that he was vice president of the Students' Club and acted in a biblical spoof in which he played Noah's first son.[38] He also took part in the end-of-year Arts Ball, dressing in costume for that year's Oriental theme.

These connections add to the "painterly" dimension to Hurst's artistic training in this period—encompassing the importance of theater, designing for stage, and composition for human figures, poetry, and theosophy. Dennison (1893–1975) was a playwright and polemic who was part of the Canadian "Little Theatre" movement and wrote for periodicals such as the *Canadian Bookman*. Like the Group of Seven, Dennison supported a

1.4. "A Masquerade par Excellence," *Toronto Daily Star*, 1923. Unknown photographer. British Library, Newspaper Archive.

new, culturally distinctive independence movement that sought to avoid "transplanted British mediocrity and anti-Americanism."[39] He was the son of Flora MacDonald Dennison, a suffragette and theosophist, a millennial religious movement originating in the 1890s that was an esoteric form of Westernized Buddhism. Its popularity in Western imperial countries whose cosmopolitan capitals Hurst visited or lived in is not coincidental and has particular resonances and strains within Irish contexts, notably within Anglo-Irish and middle-class Protestant social class circles, but also strains within Ulster evangelicalism, popular folk faiths, and other esoteric belief systems.[40] Hurst's family lore, alluded to in the introduction, and his personal conversion from Ulster Presbyterianism to Roman Catholicism came to the fore with the Canadian theosophists and his encounter with Parisian Catholic culture during this decade.

With Flora Dennison as host, the Bon Echo Inn had become a well-known retreat, a "gathering place for artists, thinkers and writers, all under the northern lights beside the great cliffs of the Bon Echo Rock."[41] At one point during their second year of study, Hurst, Dean, and two other students set off on a study tour to Antwerp. Such was Hurst's ability for self-publicity that the occasion of their departure was marked with a lunch at the Heliconian Club hosted by the college principal and reported in the *Toronto Globe* (April 30, 1923).

There is good evidence of collaborations between the art school and the Hart House Theatre, facilitated by Bertram Forsyth, who was the theater's artistic director (1921–25), an Oxford-educated practitioner with experience from theater in England.[42] Hurst appeared in the children's play *Castles in the Air*, and in 1924 they staged a production of J. M. Synge's *Riders to the Sea* (1904), with the "interior of the Irish cottage designed by Muriel Hedde and done by students of the OCA."[43] It is highly likely that Hurst not only assisted in the set painting but may also have suggested the play itself. Needless to say, being involved in this stage production meant that Hurst was practically very familiar with the Synge text that he would film in Ireland a decade later in the early flurry of work that is discussed in detail in chapter 2.

It is unclear exactly when or why Hurst left Toronto. He does not appear as a third-year student on the 1923–24 class lists, but he may have stayed for part of the college year just for the social scene in which he was very active. In April 1924, for instance, he was photographed at the end of term "Merrie Pageant" Ball, winning "best pair" in the fancy dress competition with his sister ("Miss Hurst") as a "Red Cardinal" with a "Carmelite Sister" as a "Stained Glass Window."[44]

For whatever reason, Hurst felt he needed to experience Paris and learn more about portraiture. He may also have become bored with Toronto and hankered to be at the center of what had become *the* international city in Europe for where its avant-garde collected. Hurst and his circle may have been influenced by Ernest Hemingway's series of articles written from Paris that were published in the *Toronto Star* throughout 1922–23. Ranging from the practical ("Living on a $1,000 a Year in Paris") to the political and opinionated, Hemingway's travel-writing essays were part of a North American wave of interest in the cultural exchange at the heart of the still war-bruised European capital. Paris became a focus for the avant-garde, a "recurrent reflex of revolt or renewal," best conceptualized as a network consisting of "transnational relationships and journeys."[45] Such multiple nodes of creative energy across the arts, architecture, design, art theory, and politics arose from the arrival and commingling of exiles from Spain, Italy, Romania, Ireland, and Russia, among others.[46] Hemingway's trenchant warning to would-be travelers that "Paris is the Mecca of the bluffers and fakers in every line of endeavour"[47] may have positively attracted Hurst, who in Toronto had added "Desmond" to his "Brian," achieved some formal education at a reputable college, and rehearsed the role of a promising young Irish artist in a small-scale bohemian setting, all within the space of about three years. It was perhaps time to extend this role in the capital of 1920s bohemian creativity. In the next section, we explore the impact of Paris on Hurst before tracking him back across the Atlantic to Los Angeles and Hurst's first professional work in cinema.

PARIS AND THE "COCKTAIL EPOCH"

> The unprecedented influx of foreigners since the War has helped to throw the classes together in a higgledy-piggledly vulgarity and has converted Paris into a vast bazaar of pleasure. A cocktail epoch!
> —Sisley Huddleston, *Bohemian Literary and Social Life in Paris*

Hurst may have intended to enroll at the École des Beaux Arts in Paris in the autumn of 1924, but no record of a formal registration during this period exists. It may be that he chose to "audit" courses—to pay to attend certain classes on an ad hoc basis but not be examined and take no diploma.[48] In later life, Hurst found it useful to stretch the truth to impress people, but he clearly did learn a lot from his improvised absorption in Parisian artistic life and how to speak French. Within Paris at the time, the École des Beaux Arts was seen to be a rather academic and conservative establishment,[49] but it offered a series of courses in very basic premises for life drawing in which celebrated artists, Beaux Arts, and nonenrolled students sketched together for a small fee. Hurst's engagement with art and the aesthetics of the period appears to be relatively conservative and developed along culturally traditional lines, even if his social life was more experimental and bohemian. Despite the disruptions of World War I that broke up the "French schools" that had established their artistic preeminence before 1914, Paris remained a vibrant cosmopolitan city for artistic innovation, training, and several notable "revolutions" in painting, sculpture, architecture, design, and couture fashion. In the mid-1920s the so-called School of Paris referred to foreign artists who had flocked to the Montparnasse district and its opportunities.[50] The factual details of this episode in Hurst's life are difficult to verify, as are some of the claims made in his own unreliable account "Travelling the Road,"[51] discussed more fully in chapter 5.

It is useful perhaps to briefly indicate the kind of domestic arrangements, the varied social connections, and the cultural networks that he explored in what was a three- or four-year sojourn in Paris. Hurst went to Paris with Norman Dean, but they enjoyed an open bisexual relationship and Hurst had female lovers and many random sexual encounters with both male and females (and sometimes couples) across a wide range of social classes—from servants to military, diplomats, and titled people from Europe's aristocracy either in déclassé exile themselves or enjoying Paris as a place to experiment in relative toleration. Like Toronto, the Beaux Arts held an annual ball, and Hurst ensured that he was on its organizing committee. By his own account he was thoroughly involved in the drinking, nakedness, and debauchery associated with the event on rue Bonaparte, Montparnasse. Program designs with graphic illustration from the period indicate the kind of sexual license permitted, and other firsthand witnesses such as Nina Hamnet corroborate the scene.[52]

More sustained acquaintances became friends with whom he would reconnect when he subsequently lived in London in the 1930s. Such figures included Patrick Guthrie and his lover Lady Duff Twysden, Irish writers James Stephens and Liam O'Flaherty, and artist Nina Hamnet.[53] Living with Norman from hand-to-mouth in cheap shared accommodation, occasionally selling paintings to wealthy widows, and getting dinners and hotel rooms paid for with sexual favors, Hurst was able to get by. He improved his sketching and painting technique and formed a number of connections to others in the overlapping social, literary, and artistic circles that formed the cultural life of Paris *à rive gauche* in the mid-1920s.[54]

Paris was a city that teemed with artistic talent, produced manifestos, and published journals like *L'Esprit Nouveau* (1920–25), and in the spring of 1925 the city had hosted a huge exposition of "high-end" modern decorative and industrial arts open to the public. Meanwhile, Le Corbusier was offering modern housing designs and urban living in the "Pavillion de L'Esprit Nouveau" as a counter. In terms of his direct tuition, Hurst claims to have been taught by a number of figures associated with impressionism, cubism, and the futurists, such as painters Juan Gris and Georges Braque, Romanian abstract sculptor Constantin Brancusi, and Fernand Léger.[55] The latter is interesting in that with Dudley Murphy, a young Irish American artist living in Paris, he produced and directed an experimental film, *Ballet mécanique* (1924), with music by George Antheil, which it appears Hurst may have seen while in Paris. He also refers to a student revue at "l'Oeil de Paris" (the Eye of Paris), renowned for theater and other kinds of performances on Montparnasse.

The show may have been in the style of a ballet, a collaboration between Léonide Massine, with set design by Picasso, Satie's music, and Cocteau's staging, including "the use of typewriters called for in the score."[56] Hurst recalled visiting a small cinema near his atelier that showed what he termed "art films" and said that his friends "considered ourselves very avant garde."[57] He recalled viewing Jean Cocteau's *Sang d'un poète* (*The Blood of the Poet* [1930]). Although the film was made during 1929–30—with its formal premiere delayed until 1932—even in its earliest form, Hurst had left Paris for North America in 1927–28 and couldn't have seen it when and where he said he did. Perhaps he was retrospectively projecting himself in memory to enhance his avant-garde credentials, or perhaps it is a case of the imagined past being more flattering than the actuality of events. Similarly, one figure from whom Hurst claimed to have directly received instruction in painting is Auguste Rodin, but the leading impressionist of the early twentieth century had in fact died in 1917!

Whatever his autobiographical fabrications, Hurst's first practical involvement in filmmaking was as an extra in John Ford's *Hangman's House* (1928), some scenes of which were filmed on location in Ireland during March and April 1927. It seems likely that Hurst met Ford first in Paris, since the director had been filming for Fox in Germany, touring in

1.5. *L'Oeil de Paris*, program cover, Paul Colin, ca. 1926. © ADAGP, Paris and DACS, London 2021.

1.6. Hurst as extra (*in hat, left*): *Hangman's House*, 1928. Screengrab.

France, and had also visited his ancestral homeland.[58] Ford astutely took the opportunity while in Ireland to film some horse-racing scenes, and Hurst found employment as a bystander (alongside Marion Morrison, later known as John Wayne). Whether Ford suggested that he return to the United States or not, passenger records show that after filming, Hurst set off on a ship called *France* and arrived in New York in early July 1927.

NEW YORK, LOS ANGELES, AND FORD

Once back in Manhattan, Hurst reconnected with various artist friends perhaps associated with his stay at the Art Student's League, and in 1928 he decided to follow up a connection with Hugo Ballin (1879–1956), who had promised him commercial interior decoration work in California. Although by training an artist, Ballin was by this time a producer and director in Hollywood. He had studied at the Art Student's League, then in Europe, before returning in 1921 to work for Samuel Goldwyn as a scenarist and art director. He went into independent film production, specializing in adaptations of English literary classics. He was also a muralist with corporate and public commissions, including the synagogue on Wilshire Boulevard in Los Angeles, a project on which Hurst assisted.[59] Although John Ford has been routinely recorded as Hurst's movie mentor, Ballin was equally important as a role model to Hurst in his early thirties. Decorating the domestic interiors of wealthy clients, Hurst was able to make a reasonable living such that he rented a bungalow in Laurel Canyon.

At this time it was a pleasant suburb of the city of Los Angeles, only formally part of the city since 1923. It was wooded and relatively secluded and had become a desirable residence for Hollywood's movie celebrities, producers, and associated trades. Hurst and Ford socialized here; Ford gave him work to appear in more scenes in *Hangman's House*, but he also made him serve an apprenticeship as a scene designer and art director in both Fox and MGM studio productions.

It is not possible to document the productions on which Hurst worked owing to the absence of comprehensive credits at this time, but he claims to have worked on *Arrowsmith* (1931)—a "sound movie" with Ford—and been on set to watch Von Sternberg directing Marlene Dietrich in *Shanghai Express* (1932). Hurst consciously developed his understanding of film design, camera setups, and lighting by observing Ford and many other directors at work in the specialized studio conditions of the Hollywood system. He was also able to access the best of the current European art cinema in specialist film theaters like the one on Vine Street where Hurst recalled seeing Dreyer's *The Passion of Joan of Arc* (1928) with Ford. The Hollywood system was going through a transition that was the result of new technological and economic conditions. Synchronous film sound changed the writing, acting, directing, and creative collaborations at the heart of Hollywood process, and it coincided with the fiscal shock waves that the Wall Street crash had brought to the financial models of the major studios. The latter prefigured events in the British industry in the mid-1930s that are explored in the next chapter. But Hollywood partially drew on and absorbed the aesthetics provided by the international circulation of art cinema outlets and was influenced by the traffic of actors, screenwriters, art designers, and directors who adapted their practice to the highly demarcated studio system.

Amid this backdrop in Los Angeles, as the twenties ended and the economic downturn of the 1930s set in, Hurst rode his luck and worked his connections. He distinguished himself as a French-speaking, Parisian-trained Irish artist who could draw to technical specifications as well as paint murals and sets and generally presented well as a cultured "old European." Socially, he moved in mobile networks of creative exiles who had migrated to the studios and their associated professions. Before he left the United States, Hurst traveled as a guest with Ford and his wife for a holiday in Honolulu, Hawaii, during October–November 1931. Here he socialized with the island's royals, Princess "Cappi" and her son, David, and an Anglo-American international set, including Noël Coward and the eccentric speedboat racer Betty "Joe" Carstairs (1890–1993), the daughter of an American heiress to the Standard Oil fortune and one of an international group of lesbians with Ruth Baldwin and "Mabs" Jenkins.[60]

It is also probable that he crossed paths with Ivor Novello, the writer/composer and actor who had been in Los Angeles earlier that summer, and indeed six years later in London they collaborated on the screen adaptation of Novello's highly successful stage musical *Glamorous Night* (1937). It was also during his time in Los Angeles that Hurst had the fortune to become good friends with a visiting Englishman named Harry Clifton, who it transpired was the heir to a considerable property and fortune in Lancashire.[61] They stayed in touch, and when Hurst moved to London he reconnected with Clifton, as we see in chapter 2.

As well as his art design work for Fox and then as an assistant to Ford, he remained active within theatrical circles and internationally renowned visiting productions. One notable such event was to work as costume and set designer to the Japanese dancer Michio Ito, whose shows at the "Playhouse" in January and March 1931 were reported in the *San Diego Union* (January 22) and *Hollywood News* (February 20).[62] In addition, Hurst also directed his own translation of the French mystery cycle Grand Guignol Plays, in Ralph Herman's *The Play Shop* production at its studio theater and tea rooms on Gower Street. Hurst understood the bourgeois and popular interest in and the market for imported film and theater culture, a "reciprocal movement of European and Russians traversing the Atlantic in order to work . . . in the sub-orbits between America's filmmaking metropolises" of New York and Los Angeles.⁶³

For Hurst, this interest in the macabre would find expression in his first project as an independent film director three years later. He showed how back across the Atlantic in a London studio the American short-story classic "The Tell-Tale Heart" could be transferred to film and take its place within a US and European tradition of silent and early sound-screen gothic.⁶⁴

AN IRISH ARTIST "RETURNS" TO FIND ENGLAND

This chapter has detailed a series of migrations back and forth across the Atlantic in order to show how an exilic Irish identity could be formed for a Belfast-born male in the early decades of the twentieth century. The nature of Hurst's "Irishness" was, first, inflected with class, religious, gendered, and national specificities that were particular to his era. But it was also, to develop the argument set out earlier in the chapter, a protean identity carrying the traces of travel routes and the imperfect imprint of short-stay destinations. The formation of this exilic identity was determined by social and cultural transformations that were taking place in three key locations: Toronto, Paris, and Los Angeles. Each of these geographical locales in the 1920s provided Hurst with an emerging political and cultural zeitgeist—be it Canadian cultural nationalism, Parisian avant-garde, or capitalist consumption epitomized by Hollywood's cinema industry—that was defined at a deeper level by the concussions of the war between the world's major powers. In each location, Hurst was himself a marginal figure, an ingenue outsider within circles of influence and patronage. The zeitgeist in each location had its contradictions: the Group of Seven's philosophy was partial, claiming to kick against "dominion," empire, and old Europe but denying Canada's indigenous culture and new diasporic heterogeneity. How did this paradox seem to an Ulster man, a British army deserter escaping from the "Troubles"?

Hurst stated in a later interview to have been drawn to film because of its capacity for the manipulation of light and shadow within the space of the canvas/screen frame.⁶⁵ Based on the few extant examples of his painting, portraiture, and other artwork that we can view in photographs or on-screen, what we can venture to say about Hurst is that his style was heavily influenced by French impressionism. This style mutated under the pressure of popular tastes for interior design in his commercial work post-OCA in the 1920s. He also developed a penchant for religious art, and Patrick Maume has noted Modigliani, Aubrey Beardsley, Wilde, and the decadent movement as influences.[66] Tableaux groupings associated in classical art with strong lines and perspectives, or the high contrasts of figurative art, also seem to have appealed to Hurst's eye. Aspects of the elementalism that marked Canadian landscape painting that emerged in the early century seem to have influenced his visualization of Synge's West of Ireland in *Riders to the Sea* as well as obvious comparisons with Jack B. Yeats's earlier work. In terms of film, Hurst was drawn to European émigrés working in Hollywood in the 1920s and 1930s: Hurst claims to have observed Von Sternberg at work on set, for instance. He was alert to the French surrealists and German expressionist techniques as absorbed by his mentor, Ford, as well as Scandinavian directors such as Carl Dreyer. Such art films that Hurst saw were screened in specialist theaters in Hollywood and then in Paris when he lived there mid-decade.

From even this short summary, Hurst's eclecticism and ability to absorb the essential elements from different aesthetic styles stood him in good stead as an art director on a film set and later as a film director in his own right, serving a script by organizing the visual look of a film. What it does indicate is that he perhaps failed to develop a singular artistic vision and that this lack was accentuated by the conditions of his film practice in the 1930s onward. Aesthetically, Hurst acquired an impressionist eye for natural landscape that he later transferred to his treatment of filmed locations, but he retained a classical style of portraiture that recurs in his screen composition of actors. The avant-garde attitudes and expressionist preoccupations of the 1920s—even as they were imported into Hollywood and exemplified in some of Ford's key films—are carried forward into Hurst's early "artistic films" within the British industry.

Hurst acquired this aesthetic from the exilic identity and cultural predilections developed in the diasporic spaces that he occupied temporarily during this period. He drew on these eclectic sources, oscillating back and forth over a decade, led as much by circumstance and opportunism as a worked-out scheme or a methodically planned set of career moves. His lack of fixed position, reluctance to assume doctrinaire ideas, adaptability, and sociability were necessary attributes and strengths for a creative migrant seeking to survive in volatile times. This predicament finds no better illustration than his requirement to leave the United States because of tightening legislation (1921, 1925, and 1929) designed to restrict immigration from Europe, Russia, and Asia.[67] Hurst "returned" reinvented as an Irish artist to England and its cosmopolitan capital. He and Norman Dean, his "traveling companion"—as the shipping company register recorded their relationship—hoped to use what contacts they had in London. He thought he had a better chance of making the transition from art design to directing his own films in a revived, partly subsidized British cinema industry. How he fared in these new circumstances is discussed in the next chapter.

2 Filmmaker
From Avant-Garde to Elstree, Films 1934–39

From his directorial debut in 1934, Hurst worked intensively over a five-year period, notching up no fewer than ten film credits, and landed a contract with Alexander Korda, then Britain's leading movie mogul at Elstree Studios. This chapter charts how Hurst transitioned from art direction, working for Ford in Hollywood's studio system, to become a filmmaker in his own right within the contexts that defined the British cinema in the mid- to late 1930s. He had embarked on a career during a period of mass unemployment and widespread austerity but in a London-focused industry where the numbers of "new studios mushroomed." Remarkably, Hurst achieved prominence even as the industry business sustained a financial "crash" in 1936–37.[1] Hurst developed a set of connections within a cosmopolitan network of Irish and other European exiles that was increasingly socially mobile yet positioned in Naficy's "slipzone of unfitting" as the end of the decade moved toward a widely anticipated world crisis.[2]

This chapter argues that Hurst's exilic trajectory enabled him to establish a social and professional status that drew upon particular notions of national, class, and aesthetic affiliations accessible at the time. They are consciously and unconsciously etched into the films on which he worked and into the discursive web of commentary about them and him, and in the critical tensions of wider cultural debates that marked the decade. My analysis draws on Jamie Sexton's work on "alternative film cultures" in the interwar period as distinct from what in a continental European context might be termed "avant-garde." It also situates Hurst's output in this phase in relation to Lawrence Napper's critical rereading of British "middlebrow" culture in the interwar period. Woolf disparaged this emergent culture's social and cultural mixing because it lacked singular vision and was vulgar: "In pursuit of no single object, neither art itself nor life itself, but both mixed indistinguishably, and rather nastily, with money, fame, power, or prestige."[3] Napper counters the negative characterization of "middlebrow," pointing out how it actively engaged with change, in attitudes to modernity and nationality, and in debates as to what constituted "culture." The adaptability required for class mobility and cultural blurring spoke to the social aspiration and cultural anxieties of middlebrow tastes and represented elite class fears.[4] On the level of national concerns and affiliations, I situate Hurst's profile in relation to the prevailing, still fraught cultural politics of Anglo-Irish coexistence in the 1920s and 1930s that have been the subject of analysis by Mo Moulton.[5] She elaborates on the idea that "Irishness" operates as an exemplary intersectional element within Anglo-British culture that connects with other major shifts, namely, those of social class and suburbia, the cultural consequences of impacts by migration from Europe, and a loosening of old-order imperial power coupled with the tensions associated with the formation of new transatlantic connections.

Putting these ideas in terms of the films that Hurst worked on, it is clear that in this phase he enjoyed partial autonomy, moving between independently sponsored films and studio contract work. It is also interesting to explore the extent to which his particular training and experience in painting, illustration, and graphic art, and his professional experience with art direction, staging, and camera work in silent movies under Ford, became adapted to new conditions and different materials in the 1930s. Indeed, citing Hurst's art school origins, Sandford Sternlicht characterizes his abilities as a director thus: "He saw film as a series of carefully composed stills on the storyboard. There was always something distant and detached in his film work. He was taken by 'composition' like a formalist stage director. In particular, he liked the portrait-posed two or three shot, 'staged' with the front-open triangulation. . . . [His] creativity is in the prevision rather than the lens eye-inspired shot."[6] This assessment will be tested in the film analysis sections a little later in this chapter. In terms of subject matter, Hurst showed an interest in Irish topics in some of his early work, namely, *Irish Hearts* (1934), *Riders to the Sea* (1935), and *Ourselves Alone* (1936). But this chapter analyzes quickly made crime dramas like

The Tenth Man (1936), *Sensation* (1936), and *On the Night of the Fire* (1939) as well as films with romantic themes or social comment such as *Glamorous Night* (1937) and *Prison without Bars* (1938) that were based on film adaptations typical of the British studio system of the period.⁷ Within a comparatively short period, his initial "avant-garde" credentials attributed to and perhaps encouraged by him with *The Tell-Tale Heart* (1934) were absorbed by the routines and scale of studio practice at Elstree, where he became a contract director in 1936.

Yet as later chapters will show, he continued to operate with an independent spirit, negotiating a career path at the margins of an "inner" circle within the studio system. Insofar as he joined creative exiles from other parts of Europe, Hurst was typical of an era and particularly for London in this period. Although he had spent important years in Hollywood and Paris, his being originally from Belfast accented his exilic status based as it was on an Ulster Protestant sense of displaced familiarity with England that we explored in chapter 1. This chapter shows how he joined others in London with Irish connections already established in literature, the arts, and creative networks.

Finally, this chapter offers a reading of two films about revolutions, one in Ireland and the other set in the Middle East, viewed in the contexts of empire diplomacy from Hurst's exilic position in London. *Ourselves Alone* (1936) has attracted considerable exegesis, whereas Hurst's unproduced *Lawrence of Arabia* (1936–38) has had, understandably, much less in this particular context.⁸ The topics that began to dominate the high politics of Anglo-Irish debates in the 1930s after Eamon de Valera returned to political power in 1932. His diplomatic thrust focused on Irish independence from its dominion status within the British Empire, notably an economic tariff war with the United Kingdom, and Éire's passing of the 1936 (External Relations) Act and the 1937 Constitution. With the climate for defining Irish separateness politically and culturally, Hurst's success with *Ourselves Alone* (1936) carried over into press releases about plans for setting up an Irish film production studio by the end of decade that were associated with Hurst, but these ideas came to nothing.⁹ However, our focus is on the work that Hurst made within the British film industry where circumstances had led him to base himself. It makes sense then to consider some of the pertinent prevailing conditions within the city of Hurst's domicile early in the 1930s.

IRELAND AND ENGLAND: LONDON CONNECTIONS

During the interwar period, Ireland's relations with Britain, the subject of "Irishness," and the Irish community in Britain suffered from an ambivalent recoil. This reaction came in the context of a series of crises that were part of a wider destabilizing of the British Empire in the aftermath of World War I. But Mo Moulton argues, "The connection between England and Ireland remained objectively important in the interwar decades: as a source of political, military, and economic instability. . . . The Irish are important both as reality and as metaphor, a dual position they have often occupied in English history."[10]

The cumulative outcome of events between 1916 and 1923: the Easter Rising, the Anglo-Irish War, the partition of Ireland, and the establishment of separate political entities within the island of Ireland—the "Irish Free State" (Saorstát Éireann) and "Northern Ireland"—and the Irish Civil War were a legacy of awkward connections with Britain that "created both bitterness and tolerances of unusual refinement."[11] The implications of this unresolved, unsettling ambivalence that Moulton characterizes as "uncanny" can be traced through British cultural production and are explored briefly here in film and popular culture.[12] As Moulton details, concerning matters Irish—through political, diplomatic relations and familial connections, in journalism, advertising, and fiction—the presence of Irish people in British society and Irishness in cultural expression were occasions for intrigue, bafflement, and hostility, but also deep affection, admiration, and good humor. This disposition she evidences in newspaper and magazine articles and advertising copy, but also in private correspondence, diaries, and memoirs, often reflecting the thoughts of those individuals with family connections, military ties, professional links, and less direct responses achieved through going to plays, reading novels, or seeing films with Irish themes.[13]

Most of her sources tend therefore to reflect the variegated mind-set of the middle, professional, or upper classes enmeshed in some way in the Irish-British connection. In his own way part of such a connection, Hurst therefore can be seen to occupy the terrain of this kind of social and cultural "space" living in London but with his particular Belfast origins. Through his work in the film industry, he lived, appraised, and helped to represent different kinds of an emerging modern "Britishness": urban space on-screen, particular locations within London, and the homes and ordinary lives at its newly growing suburban fringes. But his film work also showed audiences extraordinary lives in imagined and actual rural or urban locations in England, Ireland, and foreign exotic places, both contemporary and historically set. As an outsider who worked to achieve an insider status socially and culturally, he joined a number of creative exiles who helped constitute the cosmopolitan character of diasporic 1930s London.

For most Londoners in this decade, their material existence was shaped by poverty, unemployment, and the meanness of living through an economic depression that rippled out from the Wall Street crash of 1929 to the world's other financial cities and didn't begin to lift until 1934.[14] Yet even in the Depression of the interwar period, London—like Paris and other European capitals—remained a draw to other creative and artistic exiles trying to eke out a living through writing, journalism, design and fashion, and film. Thus, Hurst's arrival and adjustment to his new circumstances in London in 1932 were far from uncommon, though not that well documented. Arrival in London must have been a considerable climatic jolt for Hurst, used by then to mild and sunny California. We know also from autobiographical sources and archives of passenger lists that Hurst had holidayed in Honolulu with the Fords in October–November 1931.[15] Yet the locale of his new residence, the social circles within which he moved, and the cultural milieu of the time to which he aspired can be pieced together. These contexts form the basis for evaluating his initial impact and early trajectory in British cinema from 1934 to 1939 and help us to understand the films with which he was creatively engaged.

That Hurst was able to take up residence with little known savings or regular income in a flat in Lancaster Gate, north of Hyde Park, is probably owing to the support of his well-connected elder sister Patricia and through being able to initially use Harry Clifton's Mayfair apartment off

St. James's Street. Hurst indicates that he may have lived, at least for part of this early period, in a steady but nonmonogamous relationship with Norman Dean. Over the course of the next few years, Hurst established himself in Belgravia, south of Hyde Park—first at Grosvenor Park Mews and then in a studio flat on Kinnerton Street that he kept for the duration of World War II. By his autobiographical account, Hurst tried to use powerful connections from the California industry—such as Irving Thalberg and Jack Warner—to gain employment in art direction within the burgeoning studios around London, but to no avail.[16]

Hurst deepened his friendship with Ford and his wife and claims to have brokered the sale of the film rights of Liam O'Flaherty's novel *The Informer* (1928) to Ford. Released in 1935, Ford's film garnered much critical acclaim and set the critical expectations for the reception of Hurst's own early work.[17] Hurst may have lacked economic capital, but precisely because he lived in London, he was well positioned to activate his social capital. He reconnected with Parisian friends, including novelist Liam O'Flaherty, who had returned from there to live on Ebury Street in Belgravia. O'Flaherty, an ex-Irish Guards veteran of World War I turned socialist, was a shrewd critic of Ireland in the interwar years who not only wrote fiction, but in this period also crafted screenplays and an autobiography, notably *Shame the Devil* (1934).[18] Another London-based Irish outcast with whom Hurst was acquainted was novelist Francis Stuart. His novels from this period included *Pigeon Irish* and *The Coloured Dome* (both 1932); an early memoir (at age thirty-two), *Things to Live For* (1934); and a satire on the film industry called *In Search of Love* (1935).[19] Always an outsider, Stuart lived and worked in Germany during World War II. Closer to Hurst's artistic and theatrical interests were painter Nina Hamnet with whom he had become acquainted in Paris, sculptor Patrick Kirwan, and painter John Flanagan, the latter being a friend of Gracie Fields, the hugely popular singer and film star who was at the height of her fame in the 1930s. Different again was the playwright Denis Johnston, a Dublin-born barrister who had studied law in London, but became a playwright and artistic director of Dublin's Gate Theatre (1931–36) and also worked for the BBC.[20] So if Hurst lacked cash, he certainly cultivated connections, particularly on the axis between London and Ireland, inhabiting a post-Bloomsbury social scene overlapping the tattered margins of the bohemian area of Fitzrovia, north of Soho and Oxford Street, and the more upmarket, uppercrust Belgravia, to the south and west of Hyde Park.

This social network included another important personal connection at this time that came via a friendship with Lord Michael Killanin. Newly graduated from Magdalene College, Cambridge, the young earl was from a landed Anglo-Irish family in Galway, educated at Eton and the Sorbonne, and was also president of the Footlights, Cambridge's drama club. Indeed, it was through a visit there in May Week of 1936 that Hurst first met Terence Young performing in a show, who went on to serve as a captain in World War II and later became mentored in screenwriting and direction by Hurst. Of independent income, Killanin nevertheless worked as a journalist in London and China during the 1930s and collaborated with Hurst on film production and shared his ambition to establish a film studio in Ireland.[21] Although Hurst's ambitions to direct for cinema were shaped very much from a view of film as an art form, he understood the business of financing film but lacked Killanin's broader organizational acumen. From this set of personal connections, Hurst reestablished contact with his wealthy acquaintance from his California days Harry Clifton, and, using his friendship with John Flanagan to reach Fields, Hurst was able to raise sufficient money for two of his early films. The question then arises: What was the nature of the industry into which Hurst sought entry in the mid-1930s?

INTERWAR BRITISH CINEMA

The British cinema industry underwent a number of transformations in the interwar period, characterized positively by Sarah Street as "consolidation and expansion," framed by state interventions in the form of two decisive pieces of legislation, the Cinematograph Films Acts of 1927 and 1938.[22] These acts, responding to internal and external forces, shaped the economic reorganization of studios, increased production, and helped studios respond to technological innovation, notably sound. But cinema was also itself part of social and cultural change, and it involved filmmakers confronting new creative, formal, and aesthetic challenges. From the debris of the Great War in the early 1920s to the onset of the Second World War in 1939, the British cinema industry remained defined by the powerful economic and cultural presence of the Hollywood product in its midst. But cultural models of filmmaking in European and other world cinemas also shaped the industry, not just by the screening of particular films but also by the presence of creative, technical, and entrepreneurial people employed by British studios. Jamie Sexton has detailed how some British filmmakers (Adrian Brunel, Anthony Asquith) and artists interested in film as an expressive medium (Len Lye) in its own right engaged practically with making and screening experimental work. They also programmed screenings of films from France, Germany, and Soviet Russia and generated theoretical and cultural debate through journals and film societies. The network that was created was an alternative to the commercially available cinema that became integrated into larger studio combines.[23]

The increase in production to the midperiod of the 1930s provided valuable opportunities for young men and some women to gain experience in documentary work and commercial studios. An influx of European cine-émigrés—many fleeing Germany and Austria under the Nazis—meant that some of the techniques and styles of working developed in international studios worked their way into British film studios. According to one film historian, German, French, Hungarian, and Austrian émigrés were "engaged in all capacities in the production of British films, they trained the future generation of native-born film technicians," and they influenced a generation of directors too. What emerged over the decade was a mainstream production structure. For the most part commercially funded, it turned out feature films and "quota quickies" but with an emerging state-supported documentary output too. This structure came to be defined entrepreneurially and creatively by a "particular combination of imagination and technical skill which the Europeans brought to the cinema."[24] Coexisting and emerging from these conditions developed what Sexton identifies as an alternative film network: artistic films created within the commercial industry aimed at a more middle-class or "intellectual" viewership.[25] They provided the basis for a strand of filmic alternatives to British versions of entertainment for the "mass-mind" tastes that emerged in the sound era as popular comedies/musicals, crime films, and historical dramas.[26]

Given the above discussion, it is pertinent to ask, is there any evidence of Hurst's engagement with these debates in terms of the films that he worked on and the critical commentary about them? The single most significant engagement in a critical forum was Hurst's essay "The World's Only New Art Form," published in the trade journal *Kinematograph Weekly* in 1936.[27] One of the key titles at the time, it provided distributors, cinema managers, booking agents, and so on with production information about latest films and offered commentary and reviews in its columns. Hurst's op-ed piece from this crossroads point of his early career appeared on the back of his considerable success with *Ourselves Alone*, which had opened earlier that summer. It was clearly intended to increase Hurst's profile, to suggest the young director's critical acumen and rising cultural capital. In the essay Hurst initially aligns himself by declaring the "kinematograph camera" and "film as a new art form" and sets it alongside the other arts of drama, literature, and painting. Hurst observes: "The new interest the cultured classes are taking in the kinema is significant and there can be little doubt that it is now being recognised as an Art as well as an Industry."

This observation is somewhat after the fact, given the small but significant network of film-appreciation societies, alternative screening circuits, and growing periodical literature, which had been in existence since the late 1920s, especially in London. Hurst refers to his own early art school training yet signals a turn away from "highbrow" film, urging instead a focus on the "business of making good pictures." In particular, his statement that he is "a great believer in keeping the camera close on the heels of the story," that the action follows a linear form, and his comment that "we must get back to straight story telling" are suggestive of a director fashioning a rationale for his studio practice based on the experience of efficiently turning around projects on time, on budget, and pitched at a mid-market audience. It is certainly borne out in his output between 1936 and 1939, discussed later in this chapter. In the article, Hurst moves on to question what he terms "weird camera angles and lighting effects," characteristics of "artistic" films praised by critics and "picture patrons," and seeks to explain the dangers of overusing "cross-cutting" within a scene and argues for very careful use of the "close up," which can be "a blessing and a curse" as a "method for emphasis" for the director.

Again, these particular points can be explored in examples of Hurst's filmmaking during this period, as we shall see in due course. In discussing use of space and movement within the cinematic frame, Hurst compares it to what he was taught about using the full scope of the canvas at art school. Yet he moves quickly to deflect the idea that he is somehow espousing "highbrowism" in film because he is claiming it an art form and recognizes the need for cinema to operate in a commercial realm.

It seems, through this article, Hurst is articulating the middlebrow tastes of English cinema-going classes, lower and upper middle classes, and aspirant, mobile working-class audience groups. Hurst's views were noticed and echoed in other cultural spheres, as is evidenced by a *Country Life* film reviewer who appreciatively cited Hurst's views in his column some six weeks later.[28] This example shows how Hurst was developing a sense of dual address, creating a set of class, cultural, and national affiliations with and through which he could find identification. For the moment, having outlined the main contours of the interwar context and influences on Hurst, we can now examine the detail of how he got started as a director in his own right with more modest productions.

GETTING STARTED: INDEPENDENT AND "ARTISTIC" FILMS

Hurst made his first forays into the writing and direction of film with *The Tell-Tale Heart* (1934) and *Irish Hearts* (1934, released in the United States as *Nora O'Neale*). These films were followed up quickly the following year by his first Synge adaptation for the screen, *Riders to the Sea* (1935). Although each film is distinctive, they share a number of production features as well as aesthetic strategies and attracted a pattern of critical responses that justify their consideration together. All three are extant and viewable, except that *Irish Hearts* is clearly missing a central section of its narrative and the only copy available offers the viewer an abrupt, unsatisfactory final scene.[29] All three films are based on preexisting though different kinds of literary sources: an Edgar Allan Poe short story of macabre horror, a popular romantic novel set in middle-class Dublin, and a one-act stage tragedy set in the west of Ireland. All also bear the visual imprint of Hurst's training in fine art, and, in the case of *Tell-Tale*, Hurst's art school illustration training was deployed in the gothic-themed artwork for the film's press book, and his own paintings from Toronto–California make an appearance as "props" in one scene.

In production terms, this cluster of films was all funded privately through the largesse of a landowner heir, Harry Clifton, and, in the case of *Riders*, through Hurst receiving money from Lancashire music-hall singer and film star Gracie Fields. Typical of experimental, independently produced films, the core of the creative and technical crew for these films involved Hurst's close friends and associates in writing and as performers. They involved Hurst multitasking production roles and employing continentally trained art design and cameramen. Ambitiously, two of the films combined location filming in Ireland and England; they provide for some striking rural landscape sequences but with a mixed quality of studio-based scenes. While it is possible to claim Hurst as the first director to film Synge's drama, in choosing the Poe short story as a source text, Hurst publicity alludes dismissively to previous film versions: "One or two abortive attempts were made in the United States during the silent days to translate Poe for the screen."[30]

His own version of *The Tell-Tale Heart* borrows elements from German expressionist conventions of lighting, design, and camera style.[31] It opens in an asylum where a young artist is being treated for catalepsy following his confession of the brutal murder of an old man who was his landlord. It is possible that the sensitive artist represents the febrile psyche of a young war-damaged interwar generation, and to this extent it looks forward to the impact of sustained conflict on the creative sensibility of the Polish pianist airman Stefan in *Dangerous Moonlight* (see chapter 3). Here, though, instead of music being the key sense, Hurst self-consciously explores the optical field with the eye as its chief instrument, first as a diseased or surreptitious all-seeing "Evil Eye" of Poe's source story or in his adaptation making the young man a painter with a feverish artistic vision, as evidenced in his paintings displayed in his rooms at several points in the film.[32] The paintings are conventional female nude studies sitting alongside the strikingly bold, more abstract painting of Saint Theresa displayed on an easel.[33] At one point, the young man himself is framed, if not nude then as a shirtless torso like a model alongside the other finished paintings.

The other scopic field explored in the film is of course the apparatus of the camera itself, of film and the voyeuristic drive of cinema to look without being seen. The old man is seen secretly following and spying on the young man and the girl on their visit to the river and woods, and the viewer is sutured into this point of view. The young man feeling spied upon by the grotesque eye sneaks into the old man's room at night to look at him asleep, fascinated by his ocular deformity. Told in an extended flashback, the film effectively establishes its disturbed, manic state through its askew camera angles, recurring pattern of close-ups of eyes and slow dissolves to abstract spirals or circular shapes, and chiaroscuro lighting of the interiors of his lodgings. As Ian Conrich has commented, "It is a striking production, not just for the photography but also for its visual design."[34]

The central narrative of violent paranoia and subsequent guilt that lead to the mental breakdown of the young man is conveyed less by the conventions of spoken dialogue, which was so minimal that some would be forgiven for thinking that Hurst was making a silent film. While the dialogue is very spare, the film uses an insistent "heartbeat" sound effect—"the hellish tattoo of the heart increased,"[35] as Poe put it—to signify the young man's gnawing guilt that draws the viewer into the aural contours of his mindscape. It is significant that in opening out the source story that has no locatable setting, *Tell-Tale* provides some rural location sequences in a lyrical "romantic" interlude between the young man and his girlfriend as they take an excursion together. To the strains of Debussy, the couple, shot in low angle, walk through fields, row a boat on a lake, walk through a wood, and are framed in an apparently arboreal idyll. These sequences were shot in Burnham Beeches, some twenty miles west of London, but rather than affording a naturalistic location, they visualize the young man's psyche.[36] One shot shows a scene of blissful completeness, yet the trees are surreal, grotesquely exaggerated, and the knotty whorls resemble the old man's diseased eye in his imagination.

These images are perhaps instances of Andrew Moor's notion of the "magical spaces" in the films of Powell and Pressburger where it is linked, as he argues, to the switch from a topographical real location, eschewing naturalistic veracity, that gives way to poetic and cultural and in some cases psychological terrains on nonrealistic locations. This propensity offers "a cinema of transition, alternatives, journeys, borders and flights of fancy, constructing a multiplicity of spaces, an alien or exilic sensibility."[37] In this regard, Hurst's discussion of *The Tell-Tale Heart* is illuminating for its exilic contexts. According to the press release/trade publicity notice, up until this film:

> Poe, as far as the Grand Moguls of Filmdom were concerned, was uncommercial and untranslatable. Hollywood shook its head. Europe shook its head. Elstree was far too busy with Ruritania. . . . So an Irishman did the job for them, with a light in his eye and fire in his heart, Desmond Brian Hurst [*sic*] did the job so thoroughly that the privileged few who have seen the finished film declare him to be Great Britain's first director to rank with the Pabsts, the Claires and the Eisensteins. . . . [T]he film was made in Great Britain, with British capital, technicians, players and locale.[38]

Allowing for the inaccuracies of the self-promotional public relations "puff," this statement is interesting because Hurst's Irishness is emphasized within the context of a Britishness that includes "Great Britain" but not "Northern Ireland."

In another piece in the press, a reviewer discusses how the film "shows a most unusual sense of pictorial beauty, especially in its exteriors," filmed "within twenty miles" of "lovely London," mentioning "clouds over Wimbledon Common" and the "woods of Burnham Beeches." Not only is Hurst introduced in this piece as "an Irishman" who has worked in Hollywood, but he talks of "returning to England," skates over his Belfast birthplace and home country, and appropriates the English countryside: "Since I returned to England, he said, I have been struck by the amazing beauty of *our* countryside. It reeks with scenic possibilities. I have the feeling that I never want to go into a studio again. England has the most marvellous scenic possibilities."³⁹ This quotation shows Hurst professionally aligning himself with the British industry in which he sought future employment (and he soon would be working in a studio). But in another way, it enacts a deeper disavowal of the Ulster exilic, "the injurious feeling of inferiority beside England" identified by J. W. Foster that we discussed in chapter 1.⁴⁰ The other side of the projection of self in a new place is the rejection of the actual connections to the old place. The production of Hurst's exilic form of Irishness is one that simplifies origins, occludes some affiliations, and invents new ones. In postcolonial terms, the Ulster Protestant Hurst would exemplify the inferiority complex of a colonist who is ashamed to accept provincial status within a backwater of the United Kingdom and an exaggerated patriotism characterized by a heightened "exultation-resentment."⁴¹ He has a love of the "mother country" that is so misplaced that he can talk in terms of returning to a place where he is not "from." In terms of exile theory at a personal level, Hurst is engaged here in reconciling himself to being in England and cleaving toward it. He is simultaneously actively forging a version of his Irishness that maintains a connection to "Ireland," but not the actual basis of his birth city: Belfast and his urban working-class Presbyterian roots. It is, as we shall see, something that Hurst had to negotiate endlessly over the course of his life and career and through his films. Exilic theory works at a cultural level, which is to say that these omissions, misplacements, invented connections, and senses of affiliation operate collectively. Most important, it is reciprocated by "Englishness," an "Anglo" host culture at the core of an imperial mind-set, that outwardly considers its nationality as an unproblematic constituent of Britishness. It feels "at home" in England; it is from "here" and not "foreign" or even from one of the "Celtic fringe," what are known as the "home countries" of the Union.

The Tell-Tale Heart achieved reasonable coverage in the trade press and made critical impact on release, despite the scale of its production and budget.⁴² At thirty-five minutes in duration, it was a support film, and evidence suggests that it was distributed widely in the United Kingdom outside of London, where it received its initial run. It found its home in specialized cinemas, as "an amazing thriller," and in regional centers like the Prince of Wales Cinema, "Liverpool's home of artistic film." In some cities *Tell-Tale* achieved notoriety for being banned by some local authorities, even though it was less graphic than the original story, and Hurst was compared to Hitchcock and Capra.[43] Perhaps more important, it was picked up and distributed in the United States by the Fox Corporation. Previewed in the trade journal *Variety* with its "British-made" title, the first line is deceptively unpromising: "This is one that can be carded quickly and easily enough as an artistic flop."[44] However, somewhat contradictorily, the review goes on to praise the film's qualities as having "sufficient importance from a technical standpoint to command attention." Referring to "Desmund [sic] Hurst, an adventurous and young Englishman [sic]," the reviewer judged that Poe's mystery and gruesomeness were delivered "in an overdose" but that "half the time the audience won't know what's going on."

Hurst's cinematography and pared-back dialogue are the key features of praise: "Photographically it is a gem, some of the shots reminiscent of Harry Lachman and Rouben Mamoulian at their best." It continued: "The shadow photography is especially apt and successful . . . using pantomime and silent screen technique to manage [the minimal dialogue]," and that it was "on the whole, artistically successful." The review closed by urging the industry "to watch for Hurst's future work. If this is a sample of his first effort he conceivably can become one of the cinematographic magicians." The *New York Times* was no less impressed, praising it as a "fascinating motion picture," noting its judicious adaptation and additions to the story, and admiring its pace ("no slackening in interest"). It lauded the accuracy of the period atmosphere reproduced in the film and said "the light effects are particularly impressive. The very sparseness of the dialogue adds to the illusion."[45] The film performed sufficiently well at the box office to return a small profit on the investment as well as garnering a significant critical profile. As ever, the issue was the next film and how to fund it.

Set in middle-class south-side Dublin, *Irish Hearts* was a medical melodrama that was adapted from a slight 128-page cheaply priced volume, a "Newnes Ninepenny Novel." Titled *The Night Nurse*, the original emphasized a romantic plotline, favored the point of view of twenty-three-year-old nurse Norah Townsend, and was aimed at a lower-middle-class reader.[46] The film follows the book in its plot obstacles to Norah's eventual final-page scene union—suggested by the book's cover illustration—in the arms of Dermot Fitzgerald, the young, impoverished trainee surgeon. He finds it difficult to overcome his emotional reticence ("so coldly correct"), and there are a "love triangle" in the form of a more sexually forward Nurse Otway with whom he is temporarily engaged, the testing of his vocation in the form of a typhus epidemic, and his own illness. The film struggles cinematically to convey Norah's inner turmoil, and Dermot's fever-induced delirium in the novel doesn't make it from the page to the screen.

But the attempt to focus on the interior world of emotional states and subjective angst does align it with the concerns of "artistic film" debates in the early 1930s. In Britain these debates circulated in the films, essays, and talks associated with the Film Society, the journal *Close-Up*, and then the formation of the BFI. We have no evidence of Hurst's active participation in the Film Society at this time or connections with its membership, but his essay in *Kinematograph Weekly* suggests he was aware of these debates. In Ireland a fledgling alternative group of intellectuals and practitioners eventually formed the Irish Film Society in Dublin in 1936. As the National Library's archives show, a young Liam O'Leary photographed Hurst's crew on location for the Trinity College scenes. O'Leary was gay and knew Hurst, and the older man may have been a guest speaker at early IFS meetings.[47]

Hurst shot most of the film in London at Twickenham Studios (run by Julius Hagen) under "quota quickie" conditions, but he achieved some fine-looking urban location photography of central Dublin (Trinity College and its sports park), student rowers (probably shot on the Thames, not the Liffey), and a well-shot rural interlude sequence. Full appreciation of the film is rendered difficult by the absence of a complete version of a film print.[48] Rarely if ever screened since and with no extant screenplay, it is hard to evaluate. One interesting pivotal character in the novel, La Touche, a bohemian artist friend of Dermot's, appears to have been dropped from the scenario, although he may have featured in the missing reel of the original.[49] The film was effusively reviewed in Dublin's *Evening Herald* on its screening in March 1934, comparing it in the same bracket as and a kind of "corrective" to *Man of Aran*:

2.1. *The Night Nurse*, J. J. Abrahams, 1935: literary source for *Irish Hearts*. Book cover. British Library, Rare Books Collection.

2.2. *Irish Hearts* on location: Trinity College, Dublin, 1935. © Liam O'Leary Collection. Courtesy of the National Library of Ireland, MS 50.000/326/16, Dublin.

> As well as being the most ambitious, [*Irish Hearts* is] also the most daring film made within the four shores of Ireland. Hitherto . . . Irish-made films, with eyes trained on the foreign market, especially the United States, have depicted, almost to the exclusion of everything else, the simplicities of life in our whitewashed cottages and misty valleys. Although *Irish Hearts* does not neglect to give us such sequences, they do not constitute the whole film. . . . In our first Irish made feature-length talkie [*sic*] a leaf is taken out of Hollywood's much-thumbed book of romances. The story opens in modern Dublin, and about half-way through the love story is temporarily suspended while we view native song and dance in a seaside village. This latter sequence, beautifully set and photographed, is one which *Man of Aran* urgently needed . . . for many people thought that Flaherty's film only gave a one-sided view of life on the island.[50]

The film's presentation of the city as a modern, middle-class milieu with its emotional dilemmas and social status concerns is perhaps its most distinctive feature.[51] In the Irish Free State, whose Catholic social teaching and statutory legal requirements—soon to be passed as part of a new, conservative Constitution (1937)—women in teaching and other civil service jobs would have to give up their posts on marriage. To such audiences the film would have seemed "modern." When asked by Dermot about her choice of nursing career, Nora offers the socially progressive view: "because I believe in women having complete freedom and a career." A generation of Irish working- and lower-middle-class women immigrated to Britain in increasing numbers in the interwar period because of narrowing opportunities and found work as nurses, secretaries, retail assistants, and office administration. To them the film might have seemed an endorsement of their decision. However, *Irish Hearts*' narrative dilemma and its resolution (marriage) are anodyne compared to that of Michael Farrell's *Some Say Chance*. This silent feature—sadly also incomplete and made but not released in 1934—has a story line that deals with a middle-class mother estranged from her husband but paying her daughter's public school fees by money earned from her prostitution.[52]

However, in Ireland and in England, the qualities of *Irish Hearts* were recognized in newspaper reviews as well as trade and critical circles and favorably compared to Flaherty's film, and the *Monthly Film Bulletin* declared it "beautifully shot." Hurst had also managed to secure members of the Abbey Players to appear in it, including sisters Sara Allgood and Maire O'Neill, significant to his future plans. Hurst sought better and higher-profile source material, a darker-themed scenario, and more independent finance. These goals were realized over the coming months, as he teamed up with artist John Flanagan to set up Flanagan-Hurst Productions. They began to raise financing and audaciously set out to create a screen first from the theatrical canon of J. M. Synge by adapting *Riders to the Sea* (1907).

Synge's tragic one-act play is set in Connemara in the west of Ireland and focuses on a mother's loss to the dangers of the sea of her fisherman husband and all her sons during the course of the action. It ends with Maurya's fatalistic acceptance: "They're all gone now, and there isn't anything more the sea can do to me. . . . No man at all can be living forever, and we must be satisfied."⁵³ From a scenario cowritten by Hurst and Wolfgang Wilhelm, young novelist Francis Stuart and Patrick Kirwan produced a shooting script from Synge's stage text. Synge had created a new stage language for the Irish cultural revival and its Abbey Theatre company. Written in a hybrid Hiberno-English, supple, poetic, and raw, it was rooted in his acquired mastery of Irish speech rhythms and presented with a spare realism in staging. Delivered well, the result was shocking to early audiences in Ireland, but *Riders'* tragic symbolism evoked by the best theatrical productions retained the power to move audiences worldwide.

The collaboration between Parisian-influenced artists Flanagan and Hurst, the stamp of German theater aesthetics and film technique, plus Hurst's admiration for the stark cinematography and spiritual angst of Carl Dreyer's films combined to define the visual style of *Riders*.⁵⁴ Abstract framing (of objects and humans), chiaroscuro lighting, and strong stylized blocking of actors in midshot lines or tightly framed in close-up predominate. Using "old school" silent-movie methods, natural outdoor light and shade were used for some of the interior scenes that were shot on location using, according to Hurst, a cottage film set: roofless, built with three walls to enable camera shots through the windows, with sea views in the distance.⁵⁵ On the whole, the natural landscape—sky, shoreline, rocks, and hills—is well used, at times echoing the work of Jack B. Yeats, where the clouds occupy important, evocative elemental screen space and the diminutive situation of humans figures here and against geometric objects and man-made structures appears abstract.

The *Irish Times* reproduced a sketch drawing of Bridie that appears as a shot in the finished film (2:28 minutes). It could be Flanagan or Hurst's work, but given what we know from Hurst's account of frame sketching for *Ourselves* a year later (see later in this chapter), it might be an example of Hurst's prefilming technique.⁵⁶

Whatever the quality of its cinematography, the acting performances were decidedly uneven. Hurst's cast mixed accomplished Abbey professionals (Sara Allgood, Ria Mooney, Sheila Richards), amateurs (writers Denis Johnston playing Michael and Patrick Kirwan as a priest), Kevin Guthrie (playing Bartley), and nonactors such as Bridie Laffan and local

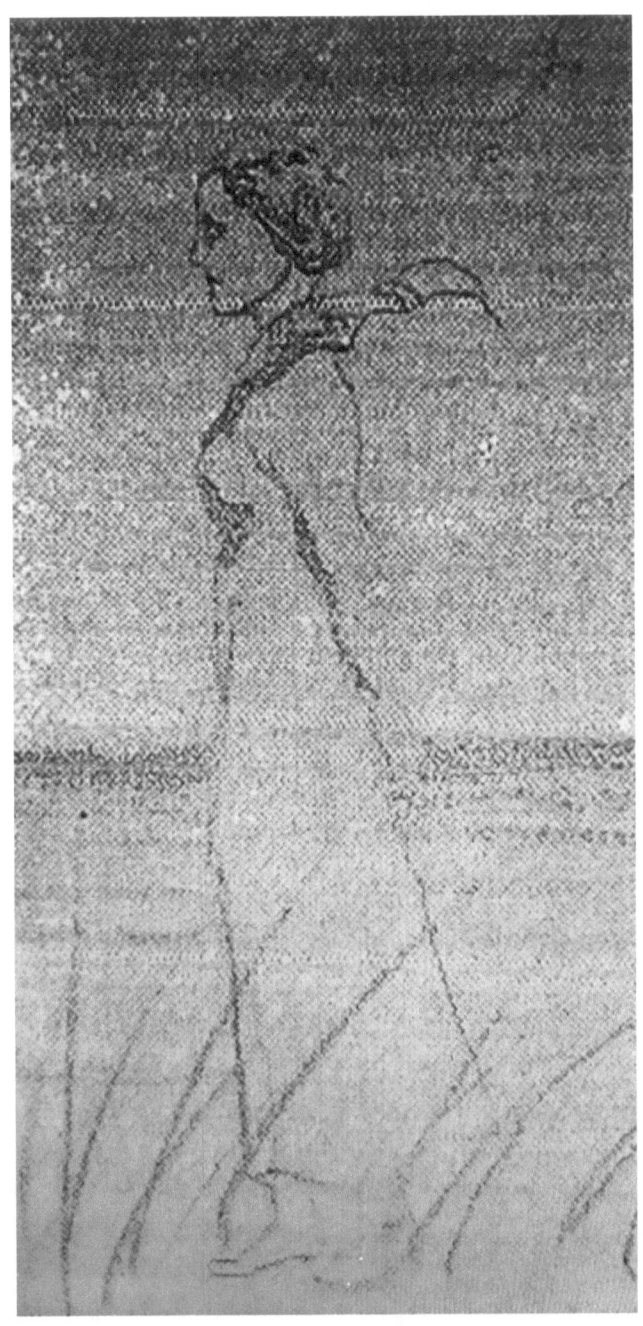

2.3. Prefilmic sketch. *Riders to the Sea*, 1935. Unknown artist. *Irish Times*.

2.4. Bridie Laffan on location, *Riders to the Sea*, 1935. Unknown photographer. *Irish Times*.

women keeners were brought in to enact age-old funeral rituals. Unsurprisingly, Allgood's handling of Synge's text was assured, effective, and moving, drawing on her experience of the original production. On being given a recovered stick, identifying a drowned body as her own son Michael, her words maybe spoke to a grieving generation of mothers and fathers mourning sons lost in 1914–18: "In the big world the old people do be leaving things after them for their sons and children, but in this place it is the young men do be leaving things behind for them that do be old."[57] In contrast, Guthrie's Anglo-educated accent is awful: his diction and the delivery of his lines are excruciatingly stilted, not stylized. His supposed love for the girl (Bridie Laffan) is wholly unconvincing, whereas hers is a simple and unaffected performance.

The keening sequence is striking and well directed for maximum effect, but some directorial decisions and editing are more questionable. For most of the film Hurst resists the temptation to visualize theater action that in the script takes place off-stage to be reported by characters. But Maurya's vision of her spectral son Michael riding on the gray pony alongside Bartley on the red mare is shown on-screen, thereby diminishing the effect of the actress's words to her daughter.[58] There is also a "frequent and flagrant breach of the 180° rule" (for example, at 23:47–49) that one critic has defended as an attempt to break continuity in a deliberately defamiliarizing effect, but this assessment is not consistent with the film's overall treatment.[59]

Progress on early filming was reported by the *Irish Times* at the end of May 1935.[60] Production base headquarters were at Renvyle House Hotel, Galway. Although the article misnames Hurst as "Mr John [sic] Desmond Hurst" and overcredits him as the director of five films, it does name-check John Ford as his mentor and the Abbey actresses' link to the original stage production of Synge's work. The journalist presents Hurst as one "who has so thoroughly studied the question of film production in Ireland" and reports: "Mr Hurst considers that there is a wealth of material for films in this country, and sees no reason why the screen should not extend over a wider area [sic] the thoughts and lives of our people as the Abbey Players have expressed them on the stage."

2.5. Crew shot, *Riders to the Sea*, 1935. Unknown photographer. *Irish Times*/Sebastian Lassandro.

Hurst's ideas to establish a film studio in Ireland would be reported in the Irish press over the 1935–38 period, most notably in a collaboration with Lord Killanin. They were in competition with the Hungarian émigré producer Gabriel Pascal, who had similar ideas to produce the works of Shaw for the screen.[61] *Riders* proceeded in production through the summer of 1935, with the *Irish Times* following its progress. In July it discussed the difficulties of logistics and, inevitably, the inclement weather's effect on schedules.[62]

Gracie Fields's backing of *Riders to the Sea* attracted attention in the London, Dublin, and provincial press in England who reported on a press screening in London in the autumn of 1935.[63] Having witnessed some of the studio work in London, Ernest Betts predicted that "it will make a superb film."[64] The *Evening Standard* noted that as a film it was "not everyday. It is one of the most moving and sincere pictures this country has produced."[65] In the piece Hurst is referred to as "an Irish painter," and it is noted that the film used Abbey Theatre actors, their cachet derived from London stage productions, and that its exteriors were shot in the west of Ireland and a makeshift studio in Marylebone, where apparently Hurst "made no concessions to film making traditions." Much is made of the local people from Connemara who were persuaded to "do their parts before the camera without conscious acting. . . . They performed with natural dignity and effect."[66]

The film opened in Ireland in December to a warm critical reception, being dubbed "An Irish Gem," and Hurst was commended: "As director [he] displays artistic subtlety and force and it would be well if this little photographic gem could be seen more widely in the public programmes."[67] The review went on to expatiate that "if literary masterpieces are to be made into films at all, it should be done with economy, almost with parsimony and with the fewest possible additions or embroideries." The film had its "distractions," "intervals of action," and what the reviewer called "scenes of purely visual interest," and it even claimed that Synge's words were "treated with respect and admirably spoken; the acting throughout is sincere and affecting." Reviewers in Ireland and Britain seemed mostly to want to claim the film for its authenticity, based on its location and use of nonacting "natives of the locality in which the scenes are set," who "acted with natural dignity and affect," "outstanding too is Brigit Lafferty, a local girl who has never seen a film." The *Limerick Leader* concluded that "the cumulative result is an unforgettable masterpiece of screen realism."[68] Other trade responses in London reminded its readers that this film was based on a theater play and that its genre might exceed mere mimetic realism.[69] The critic of the BFI's house journal praised elements of the technical and acting achievement but questioned the conception for the material: "[The film] unfolds in a slow, funeral tempo, and the direction and handling of the actors is patently sincere. The development is in the main by means of 'realistic photography' and straightforward cutting. It is doubtful whether a play of this kind which depends on poetic imagery, can be filmed successfully by naturalistic methods."[70]

The print of the film perhaps prepared for British and US release had pretitles that framed the film for its viewers, its wording stressing literary and linguistic heritage and its value as a kind of film anthropology of

Irish spirituality: "In this story of Western Ireland, the most famous surely of Ireland's greatest dramatists John Millington Synge is brought to the screen. It tells of a deeply religious people who speak English with all the poetry and strange turn of phrase of their Irish mother-tongue."[71]

In its assessment, the *Era* reviewer, recalling *Man of Aran* and its "certain noisy success" and Hurst's own *The Tell-Tale Heart*, claimed *Riders* "moves with the inevitability of a Hardy theme, and had a high compositional value worthy of Millet or Whistler."[72] Much less impressed was the acerbic reviewer of the *Spectator*, who declared archly, with a hint of coded insinuation: "There is something altogether too private about this Synge film, a touch of mutual admiration about the continual close-ups of the individual players, a self-conscious simplicity. The camera is always delayed for Synge's words, when in true film the words are less important than the camera."[73]

Greene felt that people who admired Synge would not enjoy what the film had done to the play and picked up on some technical faults, its pace, and shortcomings in the concept of the adaptation itself: "Something has gone badly wrong with the continuity; the loss of act divisions [sic] has upset the sense of time. Though the movements of the actors, between the set speeches which are nearly always delivered in close-up, are intolerably slow, so that most of the film seems to have been getting from door to fire and back again, and the events outside the fishing village follow quite another order of time, without interval or preparation."[74]

It is significant that *Riders* got a notice in *Life and Letters Today*, a quarterly arts and intellectual journal that featured new fiction, essays, and reviews and took a keen interest in international film. Contributors were eclectic: C. L. R. James, Edith Sitwell, Sergei Eisenstein, and so on. But the review concurred with the crux of Greene's criticism: "It must then be admitted that the film is as was expected. Quite real-looking, very reverent (almost refined). But the problem of giving screen-form to a one-act play has not been solved."[75] Overall, it concluded pointedly: "The impression [is] that the film is a revival not a re-creation." Years later, Hurst ruefully recalled of *Riders* that although it screened for "trade shows," it was shown once at the National Film Theatre in April 1977, some forty years after the film was made, and was never released in England.[76] Indeed, although the film was reviewed in the *Monthly Film Bulletin* in 1937, described as "a one-act photoplay," and listed among a group of "films for release" that April, no evidence can be found that it was actually released.

The uneven circumstances of Hurst's first three films were partly owing to the fact that they were all substantially reliant on privately sourced funding. Despite this situation, however, some of them were seen by significant metropolitan and regional audiences in the United Kingdom and Ireland and enjoyed some exposure in the United States, and *Tell-Tale* made its money back plus some. Almost as important, critical notices in the transatlantic trade press and press reviews recognized the promise shown by the newcomer director. Indeed, viewing *Riders* had prompted Walter Mycroft, head of production at British International Pictures at Elstree Studios, to contact Hurst. As it would happen, 1936 would prove to be the moment at which Hurst became a contracted director with one of the major film studios of the period, being paid £40 a week, or about ten times the average weekly wage. He was able to apply the skills acquired in this trio of independently produced films to altogether much more substantial studio projects.[77]

Ourselves Alone (1936) and the unproduced *Lawrence of Arabia* (1938) make for a fascinating comparison, as we explore in a moment. With the former, there is a considerable trail of production documents, contemporary reviews, and later secondary critical appraisals of the film. As recently as 2015, *Ourselves* has been remastered, released on DVD, and screened as part of an archival project at the National Film Theatre London, giving it a renewed currency and moment for fresh appraisal. By contrast, *Lawrence of Arabia* from T. E. Lawrence's *Revolt in the Desert* (to give the 1938 scenario's full title) remains an early episode in the long genesis of the better-known *Lawrence of Arabia* (1962, directed by David Lean). Although Hurst's co-written film received some academic attention following the publication of its script in a scholarly edition in 1997, we can make further interpretative use of extant script material, setting it within a wider set of political contexts in an effort to suggest new perspectives on Hurst's film work.[78] In order to do so, we need to consider the historical moment of 1936.

STUDIO FILMS I: 1936, CRISIS, AND CONFLICT

In the interwar period, at home and abroad, the British Empire was embroiled in several long-running crises, ructions with allies (principally the French in the Middle East), and new nationalist uprisings.[79] It was forced into committing its troops and resources to expend its diplomatic capital in negotiating favorable terms of agreement and trying to realign itself as the axes of world power shifted. But despite the partition of Ireland in 1920, the signing of the Anglo-Irish Treaty in 1921 to end military engagement, and the establishment of the Irish Free State with a government in Dublin, Ireland remained a persistent concern to the British government throughout the 1930s.[80] British senior military figures made explicit the similarity between the nature of the underlying political conflict in Ireland during its War of Independence (1916–21) and the contemporary armed unrest in Egypt, Palestine, and Transjordan of the mid-1930s, however crudely put: "The problem of Palestine [was] the same as the problem with Ireland, namely two peoples living in a small country hating each other like hell."[81] This section briefly considers two films that were conceived in the mid-1930s: one, *Ourselves Alone* (1936) was successfully brought to the screen; the other, *Lawrence of Arabia* (1935–38), was shelved and remained unproduced; both were troublesome projects that Hurst inherited.

First, Hurst was asked to take over from director Walter Summers who was struggling on *Ourselves Alone*, one of a clutch of films in the mid- to late decade that featured the Anglo-Irish War (1918–21) and more broadly "empire" films.[82] Post-1922, the "Irish question" meant the challenges presented by the Irish Free State to tax, strategic and symbolic obligations to Britain and its status equivalence of "dominion" within the empire, and Westminster's new axis of relations with the Ulster Unionist majority in parliament in Stormont. These issues continued to reverberate through British politics and society in the 1930s, particularly after Eamon de Valera returned to power in 1932. In these contexts, the recent military conflict of the 1916–21 period remained a topic of interest in drama, film, and literature.[83] *Ourselves Alone* was based on a stage play called *The Trouble* by Dudley Sturrock and a Noel Scott short story titled "River of Unrest."[84]

Ourselves Alone generated considerable critical hype on its release in London's West End and English provincial cinemas, and it was subject to censorship and banning north of the Irish border.[85] Hurst's own account in retrospect sets out clearly how he came to the project under Walter Mycroft, chief of production at British International Pictures, taking over the direction duties from Walter Summers, who continued as the film's producer/production manager. The script is credited to trio of writers (Marjorie Deans, Lesley Dudley, and Philip MacDonald) with Denis Johnston brought in by Hurst to work on "additional dialogue" to add some Irish authenticity to it. Hurst effectively wrote a shooting script and story-boarded it himself and insisted that Walter Summers's existing footage was discarded and refilmed from the start with (another Walter) W. J. Harvey on "photography."[86]

Ourselves Alone is set at the height of the guerrilla war that defined the War of Independence, much of which was fought in the rural counties of the south and west of Ireland against the existing civilian police force, the RIC (Royal Irish Constabulary), and its much-feared Auxiliary Division, the British army itself, and its infamous "auxiliary forces," otherwise known as the "Black and Tans" because of their uniforms, recruited from former World War I service men. The film opens with the escape from RIC captivity of notorious Irish Republican Army man "Mick O'Dea" (Niall MacGinnis), whose identity remains a mystery to the viewer until toward the end. The film opens with an impressive IRA flying column ambush-rescue sequence of O'Dea that for a modest budget achieves an authentic feel with moments of wry humor (Private Parsley played by Jerry Verno). *Ourselves Alone* sustains its melodramatic tension, showing the state (army, auxiliary, and its police) trying to suppress armed insurgents amid a civilian population, some of whom are loyal, others who are not. Conventionally, the film places a love triangle at its center. English Captain Wiltshire (John Loder), serving his country as an intelligence officer in Ireland to quell "the Troubles," falls in love with Maureen Elliott (Antoinette Cellier), a well-to-do daughter on an Anglo-Irish estate but is already in a relationship with the local county inspector of the RIC, John Hannay (John Lodge).

2.6. *Ourselves Alone*, 1936: dramatic three-way profile. Courtesy of Studiocanal Films. Still supplied courtesy of the Ronald Grant Archive.

While both men are united in their search to recapture O'Dea, neither realize that he is in fact Terry Elliott, Maureen's wayward brother, whom she suspects is up to no good (smuggling contraband) but not that he is in the IRA. Wiltshire hears from his informer Hennessy that O'Dea has called a meeting of other IRA activists, Connolly, Maloney, and Hennessy, at Ballyfinnon Tower on the Elliott estate where they in fact turn on the informer among them. The IRA court-martial is interrupted by the RIC and army, and in the confusion Terry is shot dead, we think by Wiltshire. News gets back to Maureen that her brother has been shot by her new admirer, who is then captured by a revengeful IRA for execution, and Hannay gives chase in an armored car. Hannay saves Wilshire from the IRA and takes the blame for the shooting of Terry. He realizes that Maureen loves Wiltshire and not him, magnanimously allowing them some future happiness.

The critical reception of *Ourselves Alone* is illuminating in the context of this study. In Ireland the *Irish Times* (August 17, 1936) reported on its record five-week run at the Grafton cinema in Dublin and double run in London and also confidently predicted it as "picture of the year." The *Irish Press* declared that it was "the sweetest piece of exciting unhistoric history that has come our way," but noted that the film was hugely popular with audiences. John Hill, summarizing the English press coverage of *Ourselves*, shows how their reviews followed the two main lines of preferred reading suggested by the publicity package put out by British International Pictures. The goal was to stress the accuracy and veracity of the events portrayed yet to play up the romantic "love interest" and melodrama.[87] Hill shows that it is an "unusual film" because "while is it possible to argue that the film probably privileges a 'British' perspective, there are nonetheless sufficient subordinate strands within the film to subject this dominant discourse to strain."[88]

But press discussion of the film also mobilized it as a cultural product in a competitive cinematic market, principally demonstrating the quality and talent of the British industry in a bigger trade war. So a *Sunday Mercury* headline declared "Another British Film Success . . . Hitchcock, Capra . . . Desmond-Hurst" and the *Daily Mail* offered: "Hollywood made a picture like this . . . But . . . Elstree does it better" and predicted it might be judged the "best picture in either London or Hollywood during 1936."[89] The *Evening Standard*'s headline claimed, "Elstree made a star of a Man Hollywood neglected." This quote refers to the actor John Lodge, but interestingly the review also contains a particular reference to Hurst: "A new director has broken into British films. He is Brian Desmond Hurst, a solid framed, ruddy-faced Northern Irishman [sic]."[90] As we have seen from the review of press coverage earlier in this chapter, Hurst in this period is presented sometimes as a "British director," sometimes as "from Belfast," occasionally labeled as "English," but mostly tagged as a young "Irishmen" or "Irish artist" and on this occasion a "Northern Irishman." This pattern represents the process by which his public profile was being shaped and coming into some kind of resolution, but at this stage it was somewhat mutable.

Ourselves Alone was certainly a box-office success, and it elevated Hurst into the spotlight of interest in Britain and Ireland. Most commentators from Brian McIlroy and John Hill, to Ruth Barton and others, have approached the film with regard to its politics of representation of conflict in Ireland. Such critics make use of textual readings of the film and cite published remarks made by Hurst at the time, official statements that condemned the film's political leanings (as "Sinn Fein propaganda" or as too "pro-British"), and the many press reviews that the film generated. What is chiefly of interest for the present study is how Hurst is positioned in terms of national affiliation, the boost that the film gave to his career, and how his activities within the film culture of Britain and Ireland assume considerable public profile. A further dimension is the film's profile in the United States and the terms in which Hurst is discussed that have received less analysis by commentators.

In the US trade press, the film is well praised, with the focus of the conflict seen to be an "internal" struggle between Irish combatants, and reported as historically accurate and the setting "authentic." One review picks up on how British censorship has been avoided: "A Sinn Fein story of brutal ruthlessness, showing with meticulous detail the unceasing feud between the RIC and the IRA. Splendidly directed and produced with detail that would be difficult to challenge, minor types impossible to improve upon."[91]

The *New York Times* contextualized *Ourselves*, now "playing in the 55th Street Playhouse," noting cinematic comparisons between Irish and Russian history: "The Irish rebellion, which has become as recurrent as a motion picture theme as the Russian revolution, has set off another melodrama," with its "fascinating but if by now familiar background." Without naming other "Troubles" films, the reviewer argues that *Ourselves* "manages to sensibly preserve an objective point of view": "Possibly because they truly understand the situation better than the Hollywood historians, the English producers [sic] have not seen fit to glorify the Irish patriots."[92] Rather mutedly, "it emerges under Desmond Hurst's direction and the competent acting performances of its cast, as one of the better things of its kind."[93] When the film was on release, in some theaters titled as *River of Unrest*, *Variety* gave a second notice to the film, remarking that "[the] Technical end is A-1. Acting is well, if not brilliantly handled, with bit players especially effective." As regards its handling of history, it was more critical: "It is probably a very good film from an accuracy standpoint, and it has a good deal of artistic merit. But the story matter is not readily exciting." It too contextualized the film's release: "There have been two or three Sinn Fein pictures produced in Hollywood. None of them may have equalled this Britisher from the standpoint of historical truth, but they had a better story background." The reviewer refers to the political tensions of the Anglo-Irish conflict topic, but "in an attempt to assuage feelings dramatic value was lost sight of." Nothing comes across in the coverage mentioning Hurst's "Irishness," how that might have accented his direction of the material, and the film is deemed to be presenting a "neutral" "Britisher" view of a studio picture. The review does show a familiarity with Hurst's reputational rise in the business and provides some solid professional advice as to his future direction: "[Hurst] has been making rapid strides in England the past couple of years. He started as an indie producer but is now considered near the tops. This is understandable more from a directing standpoint than a producing standpoint.... This picture shows that he has the makings of directorial importance. But he is still obsessed too much by arty valuations and not sufficiently with story design."[94]

So, on both sides of the Atlantic during the autumn of 1936, Hurst's "directorial stock" was high and to rise higher over the coming months.

With *Ourselves* screening nationwide and awaiting its opening in the United States, he went to Dublin to explore the feasibility of setting up a production base in Ireland. The *Sligo Champion* confidently reported:

> Next April [1937] will see a permanent Irish film company at work on the first of a series of pictures which, it is hoped, will lead to the establishment of a large Irish film industry. Mr Hurst, who is in Dublin at the moment with Lord Killanin, who is also interested in the project, explained that it his ambition to produce films which, technically can rank with the best work of Hollywood or Elstree and can take full advantage of working in Ireland by employing Irish players and using Irish scenes . . . that Irish people would as far as possible be used exclusively.[95]

Hurst as a director and producer-entrepreneur and his business partner, Killanin, were seeking to strike while Flaherty's *Man of Aran* (1934) and Ford's *The Informer* (1935) as well as his own work defined a moment of attention toward Irish-themed films. It was in 1936 that Hurst was approached by Alexander Korda and with a view to direct a film about Lawrence of Arabia, because of his Eastern experience and smattering of Arabic. It was, as Hurst recalled, "the plum job of the year."[96]

He was contracted to direct but is credited with coscripting a film about perhaps the most well-known, controversial English popular hero of the interwar period who had died dramatically a year earlier. Cinematically, such a film would allow Hurst to extend his range, ambition, and project scale.

Finding a narrative for a figure such as Lawrence would allow Hurst to revisit his own soldiering experience in North Africa, the Middle East, and the Balkans and to explore the disguised Irishness of an "English" war hero.[97] Although it is not referred to directly in his own memoir, some have speculated that Hurst met and fought with Lawrence after he had reenlisted to the RASC motorized transport ("armoured cars and a repair unit") in 1916–17 where he was posted to "Egypt and the Middle East," including a desert advance against the Turks across the Sinai from Alexandria to Jaffa.[98] Coincidentally too, of course, Hurst was embarking on a film about the troubled history of empire that, although more distant geographically, had discomforting contemporary parallels with Anglo-Irish affairs, Middle Eastern history, and Britain's continuing contemporary difficulties as it attempted to quell Arab nationalist movements. As we will see in chapter 4, Hurst would return to the issue of Britain's colonial conflicts in the African setting for *Simba* (1955), illustrating that there is a thread running through Hurst's work that offers a countervailing impulse to those films that represent Britishness in the "patriotic" mode explored in chapter 3.

Lawrence of Arabia is a problematic film in a different sense to *Ourselves Alone* in that it exists only on the page and in the imaginations of those several people who tried to realize it on-screen. Although unmade, it does deserve some attention in this study partly because of what it signals about Hurst's reputation in mid-decade but also because it has assumed a critical significance as a case study in censorship and as a ghost precursor to Lean's finally realized *Lawrence of Arabia*. What I also want to conjecture is that a fuller consideration of the Irish dimensions and parallels of the *Revolt* project suggest that if it had been made, rather than merely offending the Turkish authorities, it would have been as discomforting to audiences in Britain and Ireland. Its dissonance lies closer to home.

A scholarly edition of the script "Lawrence of Arabia: From *Revolt in the Desert*" published in 1997, noted in its introduction that "both artistic and financial problems beset the production [of *Revolt*] along the way, but its fate seems to have been determined ultimately by politically inspired censorship."[99] What the editors seem not to find significant or worthy of comment is the number of Irish film directors and scriptwriters associated with the project in its development stages. In the 1920s, no less a figure than Rex Ingram was in correspondence about directing *Seven Pillars of Wisdom*, and Ingram's lavish and exoticizing aesthetic getting to work on Lawrence offers a tantalizing prospect. At a later stage, Herbert Wilcox retrospectively claims to have turned down the project to adapt the book a year earlier, on grounds that the material was "sordid" and uncinematic. Under Korda's sponsorship, the project was revived in the mid-1930s, and he commissioned two scripts by James Lansdale Hodson and John Monk Saunders in 1935. Hodson's script carried within it a trenchant critique of British imperial policy in the Middle East.[100] Two attempts to produce the film (to be directed by first Lewis Milestone and then Zoltan Korda) during 1936–37 had fallen through because of censorship as well as diplomatic and financial difficulties.

During 1937 Hurst actually also wrote a 121-page "scenario" and then worked on a "screenplay" sharing a writer's credit with Miles Malleson and Duncan Guthrie that became the final version that Hurst was slated to direct.[101] Malleson was publicly associated with pacifism and conscientious objection in World War I, and, given the implicit critique of imperialism bound up in the film's presentation of its central troubled "hero" figure, it is interesting to speculate on Hurst's influence and the potential dissonance of "Irishness" running through the film at this conjuncture.

Although Lawrence was born in Wales, there is a part of his public profile as the quintessential English hero that had masked his illegitimacy until adult life and his Anglo-Irish ancestry. On his father's side, Lawrence's forbears in Killua, County Westmeath, were part of the "upper tier of Anglo-Irish landowning class" that carried aristocratic title, held expropriated land, and had a military pedigree.[102] His birth mother was the family's governess with whom his father had an illicit affair and then eloped, ending up in Oxford as "common-law" cohabitants under the assumed name of "Lawrence." It is possible to see the socially displaced, exilic Irishness of Lawrence as the root of his "awkwardness" and never quite fitting the assumed social position, culture, and rank that he attained and then rejected. The Oxford scholar and decorated soldier felt himself to be in but oddly not of the establishment, and he turned down a knighthood from King George V in 1918.

The Malleson-Hurst-Guthrie script repeatedly instances Lawrence's affinity with Arab culture, history, customs, and language, and his inability to think or conduct himself like a "proper" British soldier is ascribed to his being eccentric, odd, and unmanageable. The veridical Lawrence began to identify with his Irishness post-1919, building friendships with Bernard Shaw and his wife, and with other notable Irish public figures, including W. B. Yeats.[103] To Rex Ingram, the filmmaker already mentioned, when discussing a film of his life, Lawrence wrote: "The Arabs appealed to me because they had complete self-respect and no sense of being inferior to the English. That pleases me, for I'm Irish too, more or less."¹⁰⁴ Lawrence felt that his personal affiliation with Irishness connected him historically and politically with the Arab peoples with whom he had fought in 1916–17 against the Turkish Ottoman Empire, but for the larger British interest at the time.

According to Kevin Jackson, other evidence in Lawrence's correspondence indicates that he saw himself in a similar vein as Sir Roger Casement, "a broken archangel," hanged for treason for his part in the Easter Rising.¹⁰⁵ Lawrence supported Arab nationalism and felt that his efforts were thwarted by imperial diplomatic strategies, namely, the British-French Picot Treaty of 1919. Critics have claimed Lean's later film as a watershed moment in the cinematic portrayal of the declining British Empire but had *Lawrence of Arabia* been produced in 1938 it would have been ahead of its time.¹⁰⁶ In taking on the compelling narrative of Lawrence, British cinema was faced with risky ideas and reminders of the past. These reminders included that an "English" national hero had fought for an Arab cause that was unsatisfactorily settled and that British Empire policy was underpinned by racist thinking, prejudice, and laziness on the part of the ruling elite. At one point in the script, we get, in response to his colonel:

> LAWRENCE: (suddenly angry): There's nothing *inscrutable* about the Arabs . . . the word's an excuse for not troubling to know them. . . . It's just *laziness* to say they can't be understood, and *prejudice* to say they can't be trusted.¹⁰⁷

Lawrence of Arabia would have been a discomforting reminder to audiences that Britain's colonial politics remained patently unresolved in the mid-1930s. At points, the military language of the dialogue suggests parallels with the terms used to discuss the Anglo-Irish and Irish Civil Wars, with Arabs as "volunteers" compared to other troops, "Regulars and the Irregulars" (67). Furthermore, it is plausible to argue that "El Laurens" "going native" was partly conditioned by his own unresolved "Irish" filial connections. This is not to argue that Lawrence was "really" Irish, but simply to argue that his was an exilic Irishness within a publicly presented "Englishness." It was an unspoken reminder that Ireland's revolt was still working its way through the British body politic during the precise period of writing of the film (1935–38).[108]

Moreover, unlike the "wholesome" heterosexual narrative of *Ourselves Alone*, *Lawrence of Arabia* presents Lawrence's "otherness," his queered Englishness, as crucially linked to sexual deviance. The homosocial military for Lawrence incubated a personal asceticism, blended with a racialized homoeroticism and predilection for sadomasochism, that is explicitly brought out from *Seven Pillars* in the film's early script drafts as political and sexual violence are graphically conflated. Its opening scene—a graphic, savage whipping—features the sound of whiplash preceded aurally on the soundtrack before the visual comes up on-screen. The rest of the film originally featured hanging, torture, scenes of male nudity, and unlawful killing that duly attracted the official BBFC censor, but some remained, if toned down.[109] It is difficult ultimately to judge the checks and balances of external censorship, revision, and compromise within the internal dynamics of the screen-writing process at play here.

Compared to *Ourselves Alone*, *Lawrence of Arabia* would seem to contain more risky ideas and potentially subversive parallels, but we have to be open to the idea that Hurst was not necessarily the sole source of them, given Malleson's background. It might be argued that this idea is conjecture and circumstantial context based on a film that was not made and had no actual cinematic realization. But I hope to have shown how Hurst's involvement in the Lawrence project has a conjunctural significance at this point in his development. Even though the film was unmade, Hurst's envisioning of Lawrence expresses a tantalizing moment in the political and cultural history of British cinema that was ripe with contradiction and an underlying uneasiness, particularly in how Britain presented itself internationally. Although *Lawrence of Arabia* was not brought to the screen, Hurst's work ethic was vigorous at the time: "We really had to go at it then—making films was rather like scrubbing and washing at the tub."[110] He was involved in a flurry of films that addressed the equally urgent if domestic concern with crime in the films of this period, as we shall see in the next section.

STUDIO FILMS II: CRIME TO NOIR, 1936-1939

As a director on contract, Hurst's adeptness and effectiveness with a wide variety of miscellaneous material are demonstrated in the final clutch of films that he worked on over an intense three-year period, mostly revolving around the enduringly popular crime genre. All are adaptations from different kinds of sources including stage, screen, and fiction. The first, *Glamorous Night* (1937), was an Ivor Novello popular musical theater piece; the second, *Prison without Bars* (1938), was a refilming of a successful French film; and the last, *On the Night of the Fire* (1939), was an adaptation of an F. L. Green novel. Its contemporary, urban setting was adapted and cowritten by Hurst, Patrick Kirwan, and the young Terence Young, fresh out of Cambridge. As finished films, all three sustain different capacities for being interpreted as symptomatic of their times, from film production conventions to direct topical references to social or cultural concerns. Some of them included white-collar crime and its reporting, marital infidelity, and divorce, with indirect parallels to the political crises of the period, including King Edward VIII's abdication and the rise of fascism in Europe.

Hurst preceded this trio of films with *The Tenth Man* (1936), based on W. Somerset Maugham's 1910 stage play of the same title, adapted for the screen by a script team at Elstree (including, again, Marjorie Deans). An interesting hybrid "novelized" play was published to accompany the film, with theater action and dialogue put into prose by C. M. Martin and the novel illustrated with photo stills from the film.[111] The film itself struggles to register fully a generation of changes in its update, but visually the location of action in London's business and society districts (City and Mayfair) is contrasted to the provincial city of Middlepool, where "self-made" man businessman George Winter (John Lodge) is seeking to renew his parliamentary seat during a period of frenzied and unscrupulous dealing in the City and dodgy use of trust funds to finance investments in a gold mine in South America.

The opening montage sequences and scenes in the first twenty minutes suggest the pace, wealth, and modernity of the capital and the rugged, ruthless dynamism of Winter. The Elstree Studios interiors of Winter's

Persuasively Ford intervened. "George, we want you to be our member again. This wasn't my idea, but others have got to be satisfied. Won't you please ask Mrs. Winter to see us?"

The moment could no longer be postponed. George rang for the butler and sent word for Catherine.

In her lover's arms, Catherine's decision was taking shape. She knew now, beyond all doubt, the greatness of his love. For her, he would renounce all that he had achieved and might achieve.

"Robert," she said, "you do know I love you, don't you? But I don't think you quite realise how much!"

Catherine knew that he indeed loved her.

When the butler brought George's message, she went with Robert through the hall and saw him depart, knowing that it was a departure not only from her home, but from her life. For Catherine, too, could renounce.

George, awaiting her, experienced the tensest moment of his life. His wife had it in her power to extricate him from his difficulties, or to ruin him irretrievably.

"I warn you," he told the deputation, "that if my wife refuses to answer, I shan't say a word to persuade her."

She entered, wraith-like in her white dress.

"Sorry to trouble you, my dear," said George, almost pleadingly.

2.7.1. Maugham's play "retold" as prose fiction with visualization from *The Tenth Man*, Heinemann "Pocket Editions" series, 1936. Author's private collection.

2.7.2. Hurst on-screen cameo: *The Tenth Man*, 1936. Screengrab.

company offices, his and Lord/Lady Etchingham's town houses, the hotels, and cabaret parties are vast, stylish spaces that Hurst makes full use of to move his camera around in. These are offset with the less well-rendered Middlepool scenes, which are also the occasion of the film's comic scenes about political electioneering (farce and malpractice) that take place in the provinces. Like the use of his own paintings within the set of *Tell-Tale*, Hurst allowed himself to fleetingly appear, Hitchcock-like, in a cameo role within a "campaigning" sequence montage.[112] Apart from his early extra work with Ford, it is the only time the director appeared in front of the movie camera.

Modest though the film was, critics like C. A. Lejeune in her "Films of the Week" column noted the film and name-checked it with Hitchcock's *Sabotage* and the developing work of Carol Reed, urging "the British [film] industry to give newcomers" like Reed and Hurst "the best facilities that cast and studio can offer." Unimpressed by the acting skills ("mugging") of the cast and the general thinness of the plot, she did comment damagingly, "Mr Hurst is too good a craftsman ever to turn out a completely and inescapably bad picture but [*The Tenth Man*] is as near as makes no matter."[113]

A film that fared better was *Sensation* (1936), adapted from George Munro and Basil Dean's large-cast and complicatedly staged theater piece, *Murder Gang* (1935). It had been hugely successful in the West End and came with considerable reputation for controversy, with a review in the *Times* commenting that it was "a vivid and veracious and disgusting picture of crime reporting."[114] It set out to expose Fleet Street reporters' callous methods for securing the story behind a vicious murder of a young woman involved with a married commercial traveler in a quiet country town north of London. It thus picked up on the theme of sexual infidelity and marriage from the royals, society, and more humble social classes rife with news of King Edward VIII's affair with Mrs. Wallis Simpson.

The play's target for satire spread more widely into the legal profession and judicial system, but the focus in the film adaptation was the corruption of the press and incompetence of the police in solving crime ("I wonder what the police are doing?" "That's the greatest mystery of every murder story," comes the reply), with the eventual murder trial process truncated into a montage of newspaper headlines.[115] What's interesting here is how the seventeen different scenes, multilocation, and fluid action staging of the theater production may have lent itself well to being given a filmed treatment, albeit in a seventy-five-minute format. Lejeune in the *Observer* noted it was "a small picture with the big merit of pace" and stated that Hurst who "is at his best when he is dealing with the underdogs of life has handled the thing with increasing momentum; it begins fast and fairly pounds along to reach its climax."[116]

From the start of the film, using Dvorak's third movement from Symphony no. 9 as an urgent musical theme, Hurst's direction establishes two contrasting worlds. First, the modernity and frenetic upbeat pace of Fleet Street at the heart of London is captured by mobile camera on the street, and the mechanical production of "news" is suggested by spacious interiors full of activity and montage sequences where murder is routine. This action is starkly compared with the slower-paced, small country town epitomized by the King's Head Inn, which becomes a boozy base for the crime reporters attempting to dig the dirt and outwit the police in attempting to solve a murder, which is an exceptional event. These locales and the lives and actions of the main characters carry with them moral values and

2.8. London's speed and mobility: *Sensation*, 1936. Screengrab.

social comment as well as dramatic conflict. The "lone wolf" reporter, Pat Heaton (Lodge), is seen early in the film stringing along Claire (Margaret Vyner), his glamorously attired fiancée with a Mayfair address, unable to commit to her for the buzz of his work and the seedy male camaraderie of his competing reporters. The banter that cements this male world is neatly captured in the running gag between Heaton and Spikey (Jerry Verno), his sidekick photographer. Every time Spikey puts a cigarette to his mouth, Heaton contrives to snatch it from his hand or lips. More distastefully, Heaton is shown to be as unscrupulous as George Winter in *The Tenth Man*, stealing private letters of the dead girl who worked in the pub, tricking a young boy, and stealing family photographs to file his "scoop" story. He relents in the end at the plight of the murderer's wronged wife (Joan Marion) and withholds publishing her personal letters.

The direction and camera work lend greatest sympathy to the female characters in the action—the barmaid, the murdered girl, and the murderer's wife, left to bring up their young son. The lower middle-class

2.9. Suburban Englishness: *Sensation*, 1936. Screengrab.

ordinariness of 1930s suburban small-town life is presented as wholesome and desirable, and the domestic hub of married life is deftly captured in the scenes of Heaton's arrival at the unsuspecting wife's Tudor-fronted house and interior, where he wheedles information from, tricks, and steals from the mother and son. The sense of corruption and threat to this ideal is brought out from the hurt on Joan Marion's face as the wronged wife, or the barmaid (Diana Churchill) shown in massive close-up, perhaps providing a good illustration in practice of Hurst's views on this technique discussed earlier in his *Kinematograph Weekly* article.

Glamorous Night (1937) was hastily adapted from Ivor Novello's musical theater show set between London and the "Kingdom of Krasnia," a fictional country in Ruritania—a conventional stage setting standing in for any state in central Europe. The original Drury Lane production was, in the words of the Lord Chamberlain's Office report, "a romantic play with music . . . [and] there is nothing in the story itself to object to."[117] The staging itself was elaborate—cutaway sections of a row of London suburban terraced houses, a palace, forest scenes, cutaway four decks of a cruise liner—and with over twenty scenes, "many of which are of brief cinema-like spectacle," the script suggested its suitability for transfer to film.[118] This stage version framed its story of Ruritanian revolution and romance with the more prosaic setting of London suburban life, the lower-middle-class Allen family, and the frustrated ambitions of the son, Anthony, a young radio announcer-cum-inventor keen to promote the new technology of outside broadcast television. The play moved from different dramatic registers that oscillate between, in Novello's words, "pure pantomime" (act 1, scene 1) and contemporary naturalism, portraying the domestic life of the Allens in London with the fictional world of Krasnia.

It is this topsy-turvy world in which Anthony (Barry McKay) finds himself embroiled on the eve of revolution while visiting the country on a cruise. Krasnia has a benign King Stefan (Otto Kruger), who keeps an opera singer mistress, Militza Hajos (Mary Ellis), who is from Gypsy stock and connected to the rural heart of the country. But the capital's fickle urban mob is easily manipulated by a corrupt prime minister and the evil, authoritarian Count Leydyeff (Victor Jory), to effect a military coup. They force Stefan to abdicate to a new authoritarian regime, making his announcement on national radio. Militza survives an assignation attempt but is banished so joins Anthony back on his ship. They become infatuated, go back to her homeland, and raise a Gypsy counterrevolutionary force that returns to successfully depose the regime and reinstate Stefan as monarch.

He insists on marrying Militza, and Anthony returns to London to demonstrate his new invention of live outside television by telecasting Stefan/Militza's wedding live, during which ceremony she is shot and killed. The coda to this scene is Militza's voice filling the auditorium, singing the signature tune, "Glamorous Night," transporting Anthony, held in spotlight, as the stage directions suggest: "Spot on Antony. He is listening, but he is not here, he is somewhere far away with MILITZA. THE CURTAIN FALLS" (33). Novello's original frames its political romance narrative with a narrative of the arrival of television, yet it uses radio as a device to connect the staged action to the topical events of the mid-1930s.

2.10. *Glamorous Night*, 1937. Courtesy of Studiocanal Films. Still supplied courtesy of the Ronald Grant Archive.

In Mr. Allen's house the audience hears a news broadcaster's voice read out reports of Italian fascists led by Mussolini and then action in Paris and then in "Krasnia": "King Stefan this morning opened the new State Opera House. He was accompanied by Madame Militza Hajos, and met with mixed reception" (6). This mixing of real events with the fictional world of the play is also used to great effect in the film when Krasnian people at home and in factories listen to radio broadcasts of Stefan's abdication speech written by Leydyeff, clearly recalling for many film viewers their own recent experience of hearing King Edward VIII's abdication broadcast in December of the previous year.

In Hurst's version, there is much cod folk dancing, dubious costuming, musical sequences, and singing, and much of the stage spectacle has been transferred to the screen. However, the framing device of Allen and his television scheme is dropped, the film falling back on a more traditional "hand opening the pages of a book" device to open the action. Plotwise, Anthony becomes Angus, a hapless civil engineer working in Krasnia at the time of the coup. More topical events impinge on the plot in that Otto (the prime minister) and Leydyeff are motivated to annex the ancient Gypsy lands because of the valuable oil deposits that they have. Although the film's opening frame "Producer's Note" claims that "it has neither historical significance nor application," plots about territorial annexation, disputes over control of oil deposits, monarchical abdication scenes, and the rise of authoritarian dictators were obviously available to be read by audiences of the day into the domestic politics of Britain and the conditions in Europe and the Middle East that became the focus of a world war. The play's English hero who is working as an engineer in the country is embroiled in this plot, falls in love with the peasant-girl love interest, and sides with threatened folk in the countercoup fight against the would-be dictator.

In the film version, Melitza survives to marry King Stefan, and the generally "happier" and conservative resolution of the narrative might have suited the release date of the film two years after the stagey romp at Drury Lane. The film appears a hasty transfer of a moderately successful stage musical for quick financial return and popular cinematic pleasures.[119] But the setting, plot outline, and art design of the production do key into the political events of the period, allowing us to read the film's significance at the level of an allegorical working through of British anxieties about Germany's National Socialism, its politics, and its aggressive annexations, as diplomatic tensions increased toward the end of the decade.

Prison without Bars (1938) was a different type of project again in that as *Prison sans barreaux* it had been a well-regarded French production released earlier the same year, and Hurst's was to be its British copy.[120] In this period the audience for subtitled screenings was limited to film-appreciation societies, so Hurst's task was to remake the film in English using some of the original French cast under Elstree's production team. The film was aimed at a middlebrow audience whose interests might be attracted to a contemporary prison-reform melodrama. *Prison* carried with it the cultural capital of its French origin, a marked social issues agenda in the story line, and a strong cast. Hurst was employed as a replacement director for a BIP colleague whose treatment of the French work he dismissed.¹²¹ Hurst's efforts resulted in a screen remake that stands the test of time and critical reappraisal.

Produced by Alexander Korda, the art design was handled by his talented brother, Vincent, and the director of photography was Frenchman Georges Perinal, with Beral Browne. Korda adopted a stylized look that is suitably stark, stripped down in concept, and whose spatial layout served scenes of the regimented activities of the inmates. Visually, this conveys their entrapment—physical and spiritual—and the emotional toll on the warders, medics, and prison superintendent whose own personal lives and emotions were exposed as far from liberated or free from problems. Indeed, elements of the performance and framing suggest a nascent homosocial lesbianism, referred to as the film's "sordid element," but Hurst is praised here and elsewhere for confronting the topic.¹²² In this world the characters' moral dilemmas were suggested cinematographically, the film shot in crisp high-contrast lighting. In contrast to the British popular crime narratives of the 1930s discussed above and the rather crude confection of Novello's Mitteleuropa musical, *Prison* offers through the optic of the foreign a culturally liberal meditation on human rehabilitation versus authoritarian retribution in the justice system.

What turned out to be Hurst's last film before the outbreak of World War II, *On the Night of the Fire* (1939), had typically modest origins and billing as a "murder melodrama."¹²³ Hurst recalled it a "gloomy story about blackmail," but some early critics recognized its qualities.¹²⁴ The impressive opening montage of shots of *On the Night*, with the River Tyne's iconic iron bridge, establish the docklands location of Newcastle and retrospectively prefigures the theme of escape and exile that confronts the main character, Will Kobling (Ralph Richardson). But this visual expansiveness is very soon scaled down to the poorer districts of this northern provincial city, its streets, steps, alleyways, markets, small businesses, pubs, and modest working-class homes occupied by Kobling, his wife, Kit (Diane Wynyard), and their young family.

The respectable working class, their domestic lives, and their moral dilemmas form the heart of the dramatic action of a tense and emotionally draining narrative.¹²⁵ Will runs a barbershop, while Kit brings up

2.11. *Prison without Bars*, 1938. Still supplied courtesy of the Ronald Grant Archive.

their daughter, Lettie, but both are frustrated by their situation: "Being the same [as everyone else] won't get us no where," says Will at one point. The initial dilemma is caused by a moral lapse: Will's opportunistic theft of £100 through an open office window, a deed that Kit finds out about and colludes in covering up the evidence (an incriminating button off his jacket at the scene of the crime). Unbeknownst to Will, his wife has been running up a debt with the local drapery business run by Pilleger (Henry Oscar), who has been trying to exert pressure on her for sexual favors. When Will pays off a chunk of this debt, Pilleger suspects he is the thief, and as the local police and a fresh new detective (Wilson) snoop around, Pilleger tries to blackmail Will. On the evening of a huge blaze in the warehouse area of the local community, Will confronts Pilleger, they argue, and Will murders him.

The focus then falls on Kit, torn between loyalty to her husband but fearful of what will happen to their daughter. She goes to stay with her sister, who has married a local lad-made-good as a professional boxer. As with *Sensation*, the delineation between working- and middle-class residential life is clearly signaled in the domestic mise-en-scène. Will, on his own at the shop with no customers, left to fend for himself and the victim of gossip (a local char, played by Sara Allgood). He becomes isolated, watched by police, and hounded by angry locals in scenes reminiscent of Fritz Lang's classic exploration of the child killer, *M*. (1931). Assisted by a sailor named Jimsey (Romney Brent), Will plots to take a ship to escape and be reunited with Kit to start life afresh. Harking back to *Sensation*, Kit's situation becomes of intense interest to the local press, who hound her, and she is fatally injured in a car accident attempting to avoid journalists chasing her for a story. Reading of her death and facing the hangman's noose for a capital crime, Will's desire to escape turns into a fatalistic longing to be with Kit in a spiritual other world, and, cornered, he induces the police to shoot him, not unlike the ending of Johnny (James Mason) in *Odd Man Out*.[126] *On the Night of the Fire* was F. L. Green's fourth novel, and he went on to publish *Odd Man Out*, which was adapted and directed by Carol Reed in the 1947 film.

The cinematography and the situation of Will Kobling (with its suggestion of foreignness) may be seen as a precursor for Johnny (James Mason) as the "outsider," a reluctant IRA man hounded and tracked down in an urban landscape of a port (the setting is Belfast). The final scene where Will, cornered and desperate, provokes the circled police to put him out of his misery is very similar to the scenario of Reed's later film. Green was born in 1902 in Portsmouth of Irish extraction. In the 1930s he married an Irish woman and moved to live in Northern Ireland. This "return," perhaps an uneasy reconnection and of not quite fitting into a community is well conveyed in Patrick Kirwan and Terence Young's screenplay. The film was artfully designed and lit, Hurst working again with his painstaking Austrian cinematographer, Günter Krampf.

Although its production began early in 1939 before the outbreak of war that autumn, *On the Night* featured impressive scenes of firestorms and mass evacuation (complete with public address announcements) at the pivot point of a dark film that was screened in British cities whose own communities would soon be enduring the widespread bombing of

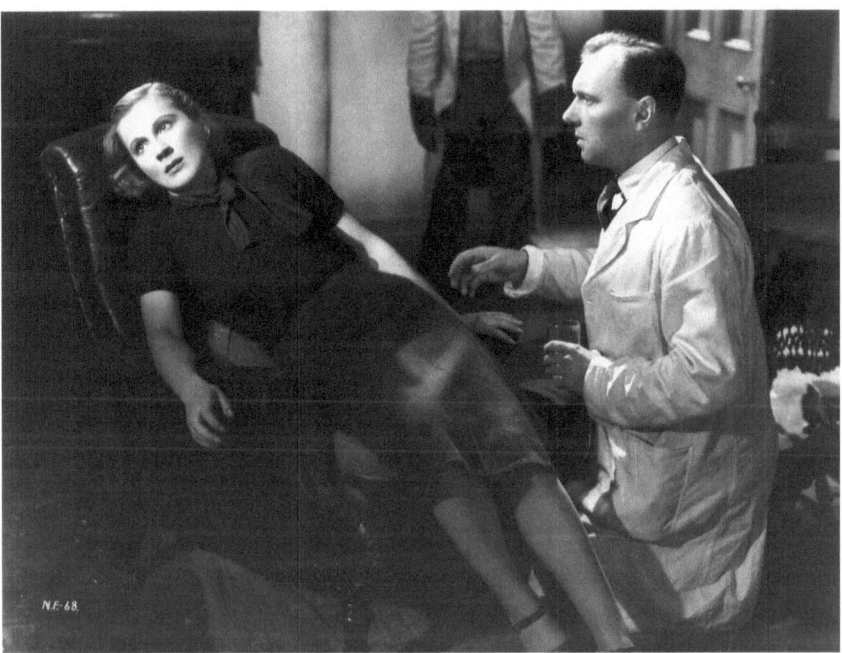

2.12. *On the Night of the Fire*, 1939: prewar British film noir. Still supplied courtesy of the Ronald Grant Archive.

the Blitz. In this way, it is eerily prescient. Indeed, Hurst recalls the press asked why such a "gloomy" film had been released with the onset of war, and it carried an "adult material" tag by distributors in the United States Attributing realism to the film does jar in that, despite its clear location in Newcastle in the northeast of England, the accents of most of its characters are a composite "working class," with some Irish. So while aspects of the working-class life portrayed are grounded in the observed particulars of screen naturalism, the film is stylized and heightened in its design, direction, lighting, and camera work that shifts its aesthetic into noir.[127]

In this respect, *On the Night's* genre conventions create a vision of English class and family that are far less cozy beneath appearances. Both Kit and Will harbor material and status aspirations for which they are punished: early on, with the stolen money, Will takes his wife past a passing Salvation Army band to spend thriftlessly at a teeming Sunday market. The ostentatious nouveau wealth of Kit's sister, Dora (Gertrude Musgrove), and Jim (Dave Crowley), her boxer husband, is seen to be causative of Kit's social envy that led her to excess, debt, blackmail, and Pilleger's sexual predation. The community is shown to be susceptible to gossip and mob violence, and it seeks its own rough justice for the uncharged Will, who evades traditional policing (epitomized by the inspector, played by Frederick Leister) and is driven to his end by the younger investigator Wilson's (Ivan Brandt) "modern" police tactics that border on harassment.

According to one review, the film—"a grim and drab story"—"is powerfully acted and skillfully directed . . . gripping and thought-provoking," but, it observed, "is not for those in search of light entertainment."[128] This review suggests that it may well have misfired with audiences otherwise distracted by new wartime realities. Critically, if it received a tepid but respectful reception by reviewers in London and the United States, it infuriated one in particular. Graham Greene noted sardonically that journalists at the press screening responded with "ribald laughter" at the accents and action. He went on to lay into the film's direction, tempering the praise poured on Hurst, accusing him of having a "second rate cinema mind," and complaining about the poor state of filmmaking in Britain:

> The director has taken most of the dreary story in medium shots, the camera firmly placed as it were in the front row of the [theater] stalls. Watching the dull distances, the ineffective angles and bad lighting, I found myself wondering—as I have before at Mr Brian Desmond Hurst's *Ourselves Alone* and *Riders to the Sea*—what constitutes promise in an English studio. Can it be the well-worn shot of a gramophone needle scraping to a close as a man dies out of sight? The second-rate cinema mind has always been attracted to symbolism—the apple blossom falling in the rain, the broken glass, all sham poetic ways of avoiding direct statement, which demands some insight into the way men really act.[129]

Having also seen the film at a London press screening (the same as Greene?), Aubrey Flanagan prefaced its US release by describing it as a "relentless study of human fear and inhuman cruelty, knitting in detail of meanness and treachery, suspicion and persecution."[130] Greene is unduly harsh on the cinematographic qualities of the film's direction, lighting, camera work, and design. In contemporary academic and popular discussions of British noir, *On the Night of the Fire* has been reappraised and rightly rescued from Greene's critical ire.[131] Nevertheless, it must have left Hurst feeling that he still had to prove himself as a director.

ESTABLISHING CREDENTIALS

This chapter has analyzed the five-year period of intense activity by Hurst in the febrile film industry that saw him work on ten films. In short, it's shown how the art designer became a filmmaker who established his cinematic credentials. He did so in the contexts of a British cinema industry whose contours and features I've outlined. They have included its political, economic, and cultural aspects but with a focus on the place of Ireland and Irishness. The 1930s has been characterized as a decade of considerable turbulence. Through this analysis we've gauged how Hurst's films were made, exhibited, received by cinema audiences, and judged by newspaper reviewers and by industry peers.

As well as some critical broadsides, it is also evident that there were occasional coded comments in print (Greene's "too personal . . . mutual admiration" phrase) and industry "gossip" circulating that implied something "unsavory" about Hurst's personal life and that perhaps questioned the core of his national allegiance during this defining period.[132] We have seen how the task of establishing oneself professionally in the British film industry involved a complex dynamic of positioning, self-presentation, and being positioned by others in social and cultural terms.

In part it was a consequence of choices to initiate or accept particular film projects, to develop that material, and to steer its production to completion within a set of circumstances that were constantly shifting and difficult to control. As an upcoming filmmaker, Hurst moved from the independent artisanal avant-garde margins to studio-produced genre mainstream within two years, with occasional prestige productions. As we have seen, as well as writing, directing, and some producing, Hurst also wrote about filmmaking and entertained the entrepreneurial development of cinema in Ireland. This activity shows that Hurst had a more serious, sustained engagement with film's wider infrastructure, culture, and debates than has been acknowledged before in critical estimations about him.

In the process of reporting on these activities, Hurst's nationality was variously tagged in interviews, articles, and reviews of his work that extended into early recognition in the United States. In a period of competitive definition of British cinema (as against "Hollywood"), his efforts to define himself personally as "Irish" were sometimes blurred or lost, or he was incorrectly referred to as "English." Did this matter? Yes, first because the cinema industry was wrestling with the issue of external US domination but also because—according to some views—"foreign" control was being unscrupulously exercised from *within* the British studio system, principally by a group of non-British-born producers, creatives, and technicians. Some thought that this trend was at the expense of jobs for homegrown talent and to the detriment of the "national character" presented on-screen.

Second, the issue of definition carried over into the context of the era's preoccupation with the politics of belonging, pressure on redrawing national territories and borders, as well as redefining racial and social class boundaries. As an Irish British subject domiciled in England, Hurst's was an already liminal identity, given particular accent by his pre-1920 Ulster birth, albeit transitionally rerouted via multiple international locations during the 1920s. The "Irishness" he invented for himself having left Ireland did require him to effectively disavow Belfast, his class roots, and most of his family connections, and at times in Paris in the 1920s he was mistaken and (in his phrase) "passed" as English.[133] He remained an expatriate of a state (Northern Ireland) that had not existed when he was born and with which he had little or no affinity. Yet being "Irish" in the 1930s did have the advantage of distinguishing him positively from continental "foreigners," dubious Russians, Jews, and troublesome "Arabs." However, in England the very Irishness he asserted was at certain times associated with a violent republicanism that brought bombs to London, Liverpool, Manchester, Coventry, and Birmingham in 1939 before the German Luftwaffe got properly going.[134]

On its part, Éire put its citizens living in Britain in an anomalous position as a consequence of differentiating and distancing diplomatic acts and legal moves between 1935 and 1939; the British state pragmatically fudged the issue of Irish people's "alien" status until after the Second World War, and Hurst had been born in a part of Ireland that remained within the British state after 1920. As war approached and *Prison without Bars* was released, the Press Service at Denham Studios pushed out a biography of its director. Containing his carefully crafted fabrications, it left no doubt about his class, culture, and war service: "Now only 38 years old, Desmond Hurst has a distinguished war career—he was a Gallipoli veteran at the age of fifteen, gaining the rank of Captain before the end of the last war. After leaving the army, he studied for the medical profession, but tiring of this he decided to become a painter and studied in Paris."[135]

The influential Alexander Korda and other directors like Michael Powell clearly believed in Hurst's directing talent, and his record of military service (albeit slightly doctored to omit desertion and promotion to the officer class) would have reassured Ministry of Information officials. He was given ample opportunity to display his skills and demonstrate that his own Ulster exilic brand of Irishness was perfectly compatible with British patriotism in his wartime film work, which is explored in the next chapter.

3 Fame

Cinema, Wartime, and Film Work in the 1940s

This chapter charts Hurst's most productive period and some of his most memorable films. It examines the range and dexterity of his work and the considerable success that he achieved across widely varying production contexts. He reached the height of his professional status within an industry that peaked in popularity for cinemagoers before it experienced a crisis at the end of the decade. Across his films of this period, Hurst's direction showed an uncanny ability to turn out films that articulated three related areas of human experience that connected to British wartime audiences and their postwar concerns. His films keyed into feelings of extreme emotions under pressure, and the sense of spatial and social dislocation felt by exiles and war's displaced persons. His better films connected affectively with popular patriotic sensibilities. This expressive ability came from his collaborations with creative and technically accomplished people across the disciplines of script writing, acting, production design, and cinematography. It also included, as viewing and cinemagoers' recollections of *Dangerous Moonlight* make clear, memorable music and musical performance, all of which we examine in the films of this period.

Hurst's working methods for studio and location work evolved in the uncertain conditions associated with "total war" but were also determined partly by a heightened social and aesthetic dexterity with the not quite "alien national" status of the Irish British population. He had developed this facility since his entry into the cultural and professional core of British cinema in the mid-1930s. His films, interviews, and an essay for *Sight and Sound* (1950) show the development of his creative skills and know-how and his view of film as a social medium. For Hurst, film was important because "it embodies all the other arts but at the same time is actually part of people's daily lives like washing up and preparing Sunday dinner."¹ His homely commitment to a British way of life and to "Britishness" was forged from his experience of the London Blitz.

However, although at the outbreak of war he had enthusiastically accepted an invitation to codirect *The Lion Has Wings* (1939), in the summer of 1940 he had written to John Ford, his old Hollywood mentor, complaining about the state of the industry in Britain, likening Wardour Street in London, where many film companies had offices, to the "Wailing Wall" pilgrimage and prayer site in Jerusalem. Hurst was looking for Ford's help to reenter the United States and even asked Ford to pretend that one of the studios was offering him a contract to satisfy immigration authorities.² Yet Hurst simultaneously pursued his efforts to connect personally and professionally with an "Ireland" and a notion of "Irishness" that did not exist, framed as it was by Éire's strategy of "external relations" with the United Kingdom and the neutral stance it took in relation to "the Emergency" of 1939–45. Indeed, Hurst's wartime films quietly claim recognition for the Irish contribution to the defeat of Nazi totalitarianism, and they explore historic Irish-British relations in an era of imperial uncertainty and crisis. In a film like *Hungry Hill* (1947), preceding the point at which Éire withdrew from empire in 1949, Hurst's address of Irish political source material is compromised. In another register, his films work through societal anxieties about changes that are connected to class and gender, and to the cultural mix thrown up by war damage, but arguably with increasingly conservative outcomes.

Domestically, Hurst maintained a pied-à-terre studio apartment in Belgravia where, according to one of his friends, "he lived in great splendour amidst wealth inherited from his Irish ancestors,"³ and he continued an active social life in town at clubs like the Bag of Nails[4] at the height of the Blitz and during the routine air raids thereafter. As another survivor of this experience put it, "For most of 1940 London by night was like one of those dimly-lit parties that their hosts hope are slightly wicked."⁵ Hurst's "wicked" neighbors included Hermione Gingold and Elizabeth Welch; Louis Mountbatten; various other international visitors, such as Hollywood director George Cukor, who stayed locally in Claridges and the Ritz; and his friend John Ford. Ford was working for the US Army coordinating

3.1. "Brian's Barn," Wardrobes Lodge. Buckinghamshire, 1945. Historic England Archive.

film photography crews operating in North Africa and attended a Hurst party at the Kinnerton Street mews flat in the summer of 1942.[6] Such was Hurst's disposable income that he had rented and then bought a house in the Buckinghamshire countryside that he co-owned with Terence Young, his protégé director whom he had met at a Cambridge Footlights revue performance in 1936.

The house, "Wardrobes Lodge"—dubbed affectionately "Brian's Barn" by his friend Hermione Gingold, became a place both to work and to entertain weekend guests with a live-in "man servant and secretary."[7] Its location was also convenient for work in Denham and the other studios dotted across outer West London.

Hurst enjoyed a personal and professional situation whose template had been set in place as war approached. He recalls how in London he had had a flat in Grosvenor Crescent in Belgravia, employed a Danish male cook called Fleming to help with his entertaining,[8] and lived, according to Rodney Ackland, "an Irish version of La Vie de Bohême."[9] Sexually promiscuous, open, and socially alternative to hetero norms, he continued to enjoy an upmarket bohemian excess that indulged fine wines, artworks, and a Bentley in an era of a "make do and mend" mentality. *Prison without Bars* was scripted and revised in Wardrobes Lodge during 1938. Hurst worked on *On the Night of the Fire* for G and S Films, independently produced by Josef Somlo, which was released with eerie prescience in the autumn of 1939, as discussed in chapter 2.

Film production in Britain continued throughout the war but obviously created a set of conditions that were challenging and restrictive in many respects but produced innovation from necessity.[10] Remaining in London and within the "home counties" for the duration meant that Hurst absorbed the unnerving terror of air raids, the demoralizing routine of rationing, and blackout restrictions. He, like others, mentally internalized the general disruptions to daily life and the underlying pressures of living through wartime. As an infantry veteran and Gallipoli survivor, Hurst, as we have seen, understood combat and conflict, which fed into his professional treatment of Second World War subjects in films that he made during and after the war. Hurst contributed to the collective war effort and morale by his work on government-sponsored information films, propaganda films, and entertainment movies. In this work he was publicly demonstrating an affiliation with Britain; its institutions, values, and history; and the people-nation of which these were symbols. He "did his bit" for Britain on its home front during 1939–45, as did many Irish-born and colonial subjects of the British Empire who died fighting in the British military services in its widespread theaters of conflict across the world.

So, Hurst is not unusual in his stance. But as we learned in chapter 2, Irish and British diplomatic relations became especially strained when de Valera declared Éire neutral at the outbreak of war in 1939 and there was an IRA bombing campaign in Britain at this time. To some, the Irish living in Britain during the war—aside from those men serving the historic "Irish" regiments of the British army—could be thought to harbor suspect loyalties.[11] If there were any doubts about Hurst, they would have been quickly quashed, as he readily took up the codirection (with David Lean and Adrian Brunel) of Korda's hastily assembled propaganda piece

The Lion Has Wings (1939). This film and three other shorter-form "public information" films are discussed next before moving on to examine more substantive, better-resourced feature films set in wartime and a succession of period-piece melodramas thereafter.

"THE FRONT LINE IS IN EVERY HOME": *THE LION HAS WINGS* AND PROPAGANDA FILMS

James Chapman's account of Britain's cinema industry during the war makes clear that as diplomatic solutions ran out and war seemed inevitable, the government in London had few concrete plans to organize film production, either as state-led documentary from the Crown Film Unit or the commercial cinema for entertainment.[12] Combining newly shot sequences and found footage, *The Lion Has Wings* (1939) was offered "gratis" by Korda to the war effort and gratefully accepted by the War Office but was viewed by one commentator, Tom Harrison, as "a powerful contribution towards Chamberlainish complacency."[13] Screened nationwide early in the war, it was essentially a film to convince the British viewing public that the Royal Air Force (RAF) was resourced, prepared, and ready to defend Britain against the Nazi Luftwaffe. Acidly, Graham Greene commented in his *Spectator* review: "As a statement of war aims, one feels, this leaves the world beyond the Roedean still expectant."[14] Later in the war, Hurst also enthusiastically directed other notable films at key junctures. His short *A Letter from Ulster* (1942) and feature-length *Theirs Is the Glory* (1946)—a docu-reconstruction of the ill-fated airborne invasion that centered on the Dutch town of Arnhem in 1945—both insisted upon Ulster's role in the war effort. *Letter*, a highly favorable picture of Northern Ireland welcoming US airmen to its bases, papers over the sectarian divisions of its host society, whereas the opening-prelude scenes of *Theirs Is the Glory* feature a tracking shot left past a row of British army barrack beds with a voice-over that names and places different kinds of Irishmen on the eve of the disastrous airdrop into Holland on which the film was based.[15] Providing a thread through Hurst's career, these films are significant for offering a contributory history of the Irish in the British military.

3.2. *The Lion Has Wings*, 1939. Still supplied courtesy of the Ronald Grant Archive.

The Lion Has Wings was extensively documented during its period of release nationwide,[16] as part of the activities of Mass-Observation and in subsequent academic work on wartime cinema.[17] Mass-Observation was set up in 1937 by an independent group of anthropologists, writers, and documentarists interested in measuring British social attitudes and behaviors. Its chief method was a system of observation, reporting, and analysis carried out by its "army" of volunteer "correspondents" across Britain. Anonymous individuals kept diaries, responded to surveys on specific topics, or listened, noted, and wrote up what they heard in public, at events or at home, and what they themselves were feeling on a regular basis. It was well suited to capture the habits of a cinema-going public and the impact of films during wartime. And while some press reviewers from 1940 praised *The Lion Has Wings* and understood its power to move minds, especially abroad,[18] many included critical elements. The *Sunday Dispatch* wrote that "it is in many ways a fine piece of work, but it is a hotch-potch of brilliant ideas and *dull, languid stuff* that should have been left on the cutting room floor."[19]

Hurst recounts that he directed the scenes with Ralph Richardson and Merle Oberon as well as the aircraft sequences.[20] The Richardson-Oberon scenes were in fact some of the most disliked aspects of *Lion*, though its aerial scenes were praised. However, the overall impact is summarized thus: "That the film will be a success can be determined not only from the fact that a West-End audience clapped and cheered, an incident rare enough itself to cause comment, but also from the fact that even a trailer evoked very considerable response."[21]

Flawed in ways, in British cinema history *The Lion Has Wings* is a significant example of an early war film, and as Robert Murphy summarized in his textbook overview of the topic, "its public schoolboy attitude to history is expressed with enthusiasm and conviction."[22] Perhaps significant too for this study is the impact that the circumstances of the war had on debates among practitioners at the time about documentary filmmaking practice and commercial "studio" film methods. Toward the end of the war, Anthony Asquith argued that "the commercial director has a lot to learn from the documentary approach" and that "the war has changed this situation [division between documentary and commercial] almost entirely. The chief reasons are, I think, that commercial directors have joined service or government units and have had, perforce, to deal with documentary subjects."[23]

This was exactly the case with Hurst, who, like others, oscillated between commercial and MOI projects for the duration. It is telling that with his personal favorite film, *Theirs Is the Glory*—made immediately after the war—he insisted with his producers upon a dramatized reconstruction mode, drawing on his MOI experience of working and embracing elements of a neorealist aesthetic most associated with postwar Italy and Europe's "ruined city films." This discussion will be picked up later, but his three short-form documentary war-service films will now be examined.

A more organized program of Ministry of Information–funded short films made during the 1940–41 period produced mixed reactions. Hurst was responsible for two, with other contributors, including Harry Watt,

Michael Powell, Adrian Brunel, and others. Hurst's *Miss Grant Goes to the Door* (1940) proved to be a seven-minute mini master class in suspenseful drama explaining what to do if a German paratrooper lands in your garden and how to be wary about spies! The screenplay was fashioned by Rodney Ackland (who is also given a codirector credit) from a story by Thorold Dickinson and Donald Bull.

It uses simple parallel action, is skillfully edited, and creates a chilling sense of the domestic space being violated in an imagined Nazi airborne invasion. Ackland claimed that it was "shot first as a horror film" but that the MOI thought it "too scary" and was "reshot as comedy,"[24] the wry humor of which comes through in the finished piece. The film was carried by the central performances of Mary Clare and Martita Hunt as the redoubtable Miss Grant and her resourceful sister, Carrie, "maiden aunts" against the deceitful Nazi spy (Manning Whiley, seriously sinister in his role), who pretends to be a lost British officer but is found out by the vigilant couple.

Miss Grant goes to get help, leaving Carrie with a revolver keeping guard over the dead paratrooper and the German spy. After the danger is

3.3.1. *Miss Grant Goes to the Door*, 1940. Title credits. Screengrab.

3.3.2. *Miss Grant Goes to the Door*, 1940. Screengrab.

averted and over a cup of tea, the ladies and Mr. Richards (Ivan Brandt), the Local Defence volunteer, reflect:

> MR RICHARDS: Well, if hadn't been for you, the Germans would have got away with it. We've rounded them all up before they had time to do any damage. The great thing is, ladies, is you kept your heads. The front line is in every home nowadays
> MISS GRANT: To think I wanted to stay in bed—I wouldn't have missed this for the world.
> CARRIE: If I hadn't noticed that mistake he made—Yarvis for Jarvis.
> MR RICHARDS: Now that's exactly what everyone should remember if they're not sure keep the man talking—if he's a German he'll give himself away soon enough.
> MISS GRANT: More tea?[25]

Hurst coaxed credible performances from his two leading female actors and worked effectively with the demands of the short-form drama, spiked as it was with necessary "public awareness" lines, which pointed to the future of how his strengths as a director might be deployed in his postwar work. Writing at the time, Tom Harrison offered the view that *Miss Grant* was the "best liked" of the MOI shorts and noted that "apart from terrifying some rural spinsters and widows, [it] was *incidental propaganda for a 'people's war.'*" He developed this point: "The whole solution of her problem depended on her getting a revolver (from the fortunately placed corpse). . . . The sight of this untrained hand wielding the weapon, however ineffectively, at once played on the secret wish to have some weapon of protection."[26]

Some later commentators have also suggested that this short film's premise inspired later feature-length productions that tapped into the disturbing prospect of an imagined occupation by an evil enemy. According to the BFI: "Some officials in the War Office considered the film too frightening, but its premise—the enemy in the heart of a docile English village—was later reused in the most famous 'invasion' film of the war, Ealing's *Went the Day Well?* (1944)."[27]

Hurst's second MOI film, *A Call for Arms!* (1940), is less sophisticated in its scenario or treatment: two revue dancers feel guilty at not serving the national need and swap profession to work in a munitions factory.[28] We have recollections of the writer, the film's director, and data from the Mass-Observation archive that show a more mixed response, particularly around class. Ackland offers insights into the production, stating baldly that "its object was to persuade shop girls, typists, manicurists . . . to become munitions workers," noting it was shot on location in Woolwich Arsenal and of "the effect of getting factory girls to 'act.'"[29] Hurst recalled the on-location preparatory work, planning shots, and his way of building up a rapport with the women workers who would appear in the film.[30]

Ackland claimed that the rough-cut screening for the MOI officials caused "much controversy" because it showed a girl fainting after a sixteen-hour shift but also noted: "All the documentary boys who were working for the MOI derided our munitions—propaganda effort as melodramatic and unreal, which, indeed it was. But the effect on the younger generation of female film-goers where it was shown . . . was exactly what Brian and I had intended."[31] The evidence for this statement is difficult to discern, but Tom Harrison questioned the film for its misguided, metropolitan address and distribution: "It is really amazing that any informed propaganda unit can have produced for *general* [sic] distribution a film like *Call to Arms* which was calculated to alienate many sorts of working-class or other feelings."[32] He goes on to accuse the Films Division of "being easily out of touch with the rather simpler reactions of industrial Lancashire or rural Somerset." Coleen Nolan was cast as a sympathetic supervisor character, continuing Hurst's habit of giving Irish-born actors roles in non-Irish-themed films, her accent contrasting with the voice of a working-class Londoner, the suffering Mrs. James (Kathleen Harrison). As Tom Harrison implies, the two leads' accents were more RADA (Royal Academy of Dramatic Art) than revue girl and more authentic, representative working-class representation in British film would take a generation to break through.[33]

Indeed, more recent research by Hollie Price, based on a Granada cinema manager's report of the audience at screenings actually in Woolwich and supplied to the MOI, indicates that the film did not go down well with locals: "This was received by our audience, consisting of a very

3.4. "Thumbs Up Patriotism": *A Call for Arms!* 1940. Screengrab.

large portion of Arsenal workers, with satirical laughter and a chorus of 'Oo's and 'Oh Yeah's."[34] Price indicates that not all of the MOI output was dismissed and, like Harrison, believes that some of its messages did alter behavior in viewers, working their way into the minds of audiences. But we will pick up the themes of class and women again later in this chapter when we examine a trio of Hurst films from the late 1940s.

Although the remainder of Hurst's war output was commercial feature-length material, he did accept one other short-form film project for the MOI as the United States entered the war in December 1941. *A Letter from Ulster* (1942) reflected the fact that troops armaments and the US Air Force soon became strategically stationed in the eastern counties of England's air bases and in Northern Ireland, taking Hurst back closer to home. The film's purpose, as recalled by Hurst, was "to show how splendidly [the soldiers were] getting along with the people of Ulster."[35] Its title echoes Michael Powell's deeply affecting five-minute short, *An Airman's Letter to His Mother* (1941), famously narrated by John Gielgud.[36] In preparation for the film, Hurst and Terence Young, who had written the scenario, visited Northern Ireland and met with troops, and the film developed into a script structured around a letter written home to their parents by two Minnesota-born "brothers" stationed there, played by serving soldiers Don Prill and Wally Newfield. Hurst's account of the film's genesis explains that he cast the two GIs, "one Catholic, one Protestant," but this isn't really borne out in the film, and, as John Hill has noted, it is unlikely that siblings would have different faiths. The film seems driven by Hurst's desire to promote a view of the interdenominational harmony *within* Northern Ireland, offering a quasi-travelogue structure of the shared Irish past of its sectarian traditions. Although the US troops are assisted in their billet by the "English guy," cockney-accented Private Staines, and are shown meeting a lot of local civilians, they do not seem to meet with any soldiers with accents from Northern Ireland.

The film skillfully manages to integrate the tonally contrasting sequences that show the GIs playing baseball with the kids, helping locals with the harvest, the brothers sightseeing, and then action sequences of physical training and tank maneuvers. These shifts are knitted together in the voice-over of brotherly banter that adds other emotional layers to

3.5. *A Letter from Ulster*, 1943: a moment of fraternal tenderness. Screengrab.

the film, those of comradeship, homesickness, and fraternity, which are visualized in a quietly tender manner.

The set-piece solo of Hurst's favorite Irish song, "The Rose of Tralee," performed by Denis Martin, sees the director adopting a tracking shot and assembly of male profiles similar to the ones we have seen used in *Riders to the Sea*, and it recurs in a setup for a scene in *Dangerous Moonlight* discussed shortly. The effect of these screen tableaux vivants is to create a hiatus, a moment of individual reflection that is possible when listening collectively to a musical performance and with which the film audience is invited to identify.

The communal singing of "Home on the Range" around a piano near the end of the film and the impromptu rendition of "Ragtime Cowboy Joe" by the GI guitarist in the billet conjoin with the popular Irish "standards" to offer an assimilative, nostalgic audio track that seeks to comfort and to deflect from the purpose of the US presence in Europe and the unspoken consequences for the young men.

3.6.1. *Letter*: tableau of GIs listening to "The Rose of Tralee." Screengrab.

3.6.2. *Letter*: impromptu barracks performance of "Ragtime Joe." Screengrab.

Of course, these directorial choices serve the chief propaganda purpose of the film: to address audiences back home in the United States, to assure them that the military presence in Northern Ireland was welcome, and to convince the local population that the US military was necessary for the war effort. There were Irish Republican objections to the presence of US troops in Ireland because under its Constitution (1937), "Ulster" was still part of the "national territory" of a neutral Éire and their presence challenged the terms of the Anglo-Irish Treaty (1921). Diplomatic differences aside, on location Hurst recalls that the disruptions of the troop movements, tanks on roads, and the noise of aircraft caused resentment and friction that led to a GI hotheadedly shooting a local bus driver in the arm. "That night the man's two brothers went into the American camp and shot an officer very deliberately in the arm" as a "punishment" and warning. As Hurst noted, Éire's neutrality was the source of ill feeling and rumor, that it was refueling German submarines and so on, ruefully joking that "it was in this atmosphere that I arrived to make a goodwill documentary."[37]

John Hill's analysis of the film points out that the overriding purpose of the film was to appeal particularly to an Irish American audience, with time given for the GIs to visit various places of historical interest with American connections.[38] This intended address necessitated an appeal to generalized "Irishness," rather than the specifics of an identity suggested by "Ulster" in the title. Indeed, as Hill concludes: "The film is unusual in attempting to offer a more inclusive 'imagining' of 'Ulster' than that found in earlier films [set in Ulster], as well as an element of 'balance' between the representation of Protestants and Catholics."[39]

The film plays with the idea that the GIs in their "Peep" (people-carrying Jeep) at one point get lost in their travels, unknowingly straying over the border into the "Free State," but are redirected by a friendly farmer. Checking with a bemused Royal Ulster Constabulary man on their return to Northern Ireland, Wally's comment that "there don't seem to be any boundaries around here" is met with the RUC man's: "Yes, it is a bit difficult. Sometimes I don't know where I am myself."

Gently poking fun at the "border" was a common comic trope in Irish and British films starring Will Hay and Jimmy O'Dea in the interwar

3.7. *Letter*: police and military border confusion. Screengrab.

years. But it is interesting to attribute the confusion; it is slipped in here in an official film funded by the Northern Irish state that is "dedicated to those members of the US Forces who are our guests *in these islands*" (emphasis added), an inclusive but nonetheless ambiguous formulation.

Although the film works hard to balance national and religious differences, there is a sequence in the film of a Catholic Mass that stands out: its setup, lighting, shot composition, and the one transition sequence of a tilt to a pan to a long, slow tracking shot with dissolves of the congregation's faces enrapt to the sounds of "Ave Maria" may be seen as a stylish homage to Hurst's mentor, John Ford.[40] As such, it carries more emotional weight for the viewer and pulls against the film's "official" function and its "preferred" meanings. William MacQuitty recalls that it was set up carefully "to be filmed in one take, a tilt down to the priest giving the Benediction and then a slow pan to the congregation and a track down the aisle." As the film's rookie assistant director, he had helped arrange the scene and had heard Hurst brief Chick Fowle on camera, but when he "whispered to Brian, kneeling in the front row [pew]," Hurst had replied: "'You direct,' he said, 'I'm praying,' and closed his eyes!" Even if it was a case of deus ex director, and the on-set crew "christened [the sequence] 'MacQuitty's wax-works,'"[41] the completed form of *Letter* was much heralded by Northern Ireland's prime minister, John M. Andrews, seeking to promote its contribution to the British war effort, and Hurst notes that he received a letter of commendation from US president Teddy Roosevelt.[42] In this double-coded manner, much like the analysis of *Ourselves Alone* and *Lawrence of Arabia* (discussed in chapter 2), *Letter* allowed Hurst to vicariously reconnect with the place of his birth, to reimagine "Ireland," and to forge a new working relationship with the assistant director of the film, one of Belfast's returned emigrants, William MacQuitty, with whom he would work again in the 1950s.[43]

On the basis of his prewar work, *The Lion Has Wings*, and his short-film experience, it was reported in the press that Hurst had been engaged to direct one of several forthcoming feature-length productions by British National Studios. Based on a story about the use of illegal radios by the German underground resistance, Hurst was set to direct *This German Freedom*, with "Diana Wynyard and Clive Brook playing together for the first time since *Cavalcade*." The report went on say the film's production under the direction of "Brian (Desmond) Hurst who had been largely responsible for *The Lion Has Wings*, is proving difficult because actors have to be found to play Hitler, Goering, Goebbels."[44] In fact, the film was taken over by Anthony Asquith and successfully released as *Freedom Radio* (1941). The reason for this change is that Hurst was also working on an RKO film about "a tramp steamer that was sinking a German submarine in the Indian Ocean," called *A Gift for the King*.[45] However, Hurst quickly recognized the potential in Terence Young's scenario about a Polish pilot fighting in the RAF, and RKO ditched *Gift* for the new idea that would become one of Britain's memorable wartime films: *Dangerous Moonlight*.

WARTIME MELODRAMA: *DANGEROUS MOONLIGHT* (1941)

Looking back at cinema trends in the previous year and the effects of the war on the film industry, Len England, reporting for Mass-Observation, noted the popularity of "glamorised accounts of our gallant airmen" as second only in popularity to the "Englishmen-chased-in-Germany" narrative.⁴⁶ Terence Young's script of *Dangerous Moonlight* clearly met this growing popularity for military-service-based narratives. In the hands of Hurst, an accomplished creative team, and leading actors in Anton Walbrook and Sally Gray, *Dangerous Moonlight* is one of this period's memorable films and gives support to Tom Harrison's idea that feature films might be more important in shaping attitudes than the purpose-made shorts and five-minute documentaries, even "if less direct" in their effects.⁴⁷

The film offers a melodramatic love story of a Polish pianist-turned-RAF pilot, Stefan (Walbrook), who meets and marries an American war correspondent, Carol (Gray). With the action of the film opening in a mental hospital, the viewer is asked to wonder what had brought Stefan to this demise, and it then enters into an extended flashback for the main body of the film to the moment of Poland's invasion by the German Wehrmacht forces that shattered Warsaw. In part, then, *Dangerous Moonlight* helped to cement the iconic status of the bravery of what Winston Churchill called "the few," the RAF outnumbered by the Luftwaffe, in what became known as the "Battle of Britain." Hurst and Rodney Ackland worked with Terence Young to complete the shooting script. The scenario was part of an upsurge of stories about pilots and fliers that were more popular than army and navy narratives.⁴⁸ The film's plot was especially important, since the love interest knitted British/Polish and American lives together onscreen, the intended audiences being in the United Kingdom—including US service personnel based there and their families in the United States, but also in this case the considerable numbers of Polish refugees and service personnel displaced when Poland suffered from blitzkrieg in 1939.⁴⁹

One of the film's most memorable scenes appears early on in devastated Warsaw during a bombing raid. Carol, the reporter, seeks refuge in an abandoned house from which she hears a piano being played. Inside she finds Stefan in a Polish air force uniform feeling out a tune on the keys of a grand piano as a way of cushioning himself from the bombardment outside. It is a stylish musical seduction scene in which the filmic elements of art design, lighting, script, and camera work combine with an evocative musical theme and on-screen acting performance.

3.8. Warsaw devastation: *Dangerous Moonlight*, 1941. © RKO Pictures. Still supplied courtesy of the Ronald Grant Archive.

The responses of actual viewers to *Dangerous Moonlight* rather than newspaper critics or trade reviews are, thanks to Mass-Observation, well documented.[50] For "No. 59," a female company secretary, aged forty-five from Warrington in northwest England, the film represented "an authentic wedding of two artists [sic]—music and film" (276). For "No. 39," a twenty-six-year-old public health official from Birmingham, it was remembered as "a very moving film in which the 'Warsaw Concerto' predominates, and acting of Anton Warlbrook [sic]" (233)" A male special constable, aged thirty-three, living and working in Doncaster, recalled that he "very much enjoyed: *Dangerous Moonlight*. Liked music, general atmosphere & acting" (232). But perhaps two responses to the film stand out as to their level of critical and emotional engagement. "No. 44," a male civil servant aged fifty-two from Morecombe, noted that he saw *Dangerous Moonlight* twice, commenting on a socio-artistic dilemma,

3.9.1. Heterosexual seduction: *Dangerous Moonlight*. Screengrab.

and showed an awareness of film form: "I liked this chiefly because it is not just a story, but deals with a very real and vital present-day problem—viz. what is the duty of the artist in wartime? Also, I enjoyed the music. Also, Anton Warlbrook's acting. When I first saw this film, too, the technique of starting at the end of the story was fairly new. It seemed to me then to be a clever and well-constructed film, and the impression remains although the novelty has gone" (271). "No. 42" from Portsmouth ranked *Dangerous Moonlight* as fourth on their personal list of memorable films, observing that it "is included not so much for the actual visual aspect but for its beautiful music. One scene from [the film] sticks in my mind: 'The Warsaw Concerto' was playing, to the accompaniment of bombs bursting: the scene had a *shivering montage effect*, and was very moving" (141). Interesting, here, for the viewer, the musical theme acts as an aural trigger for both a visual and an emotional memory.

In the year after the war, the *Daily Mail* instituted a National Film Award. In the inaugural awards, its scope was for the public to choose its most favorite films, stars, and so on between 1939 and 1945 with a half-million votes cast in a national popular vote. Anthony Asquith's *Way to the Stars* was voted "Outstanding Film." However, *Dangerous Moonlight* is tenth in the top twenty films after *Henry V*, *In Which We Serve*, *The Way Ahead*, and *This Happy Breed*, among others, but ahead of *Blimp* and *Millions Like Us*.[51] *Moonlight's* popularity contained a number of tensions about class, sexuality, and exilic nationality that spoke to audiences of the moment and remain significant from the perspective of a cultural historian.

For instance, critics then and since have pointed out how the film features a strong narrative exploration of exilic angst about belonging, personal love, and national duty.[52] This exploration was carried through the combination of its emotive musical motif, the so-called Warsaw Concerto, and its heightened visualizations in which Hurst excelled. Ruth Barton has pointed out how Hurst was adept at slipping in Irish roles and indeed actors into his films, showing how Stefan's friendship with another pilot, Carroll (Derrick du Marney), plays off of his Irishness, subtly showing how the RAF's resourcefulness and Britain's survival depended upon the courage of those displaced men being prepared to risk their lives.[53] An equally pertinent point about the film is the concern for gender and identity. In particular, it is telling how the homosociality of men in conflict and how sexuality and repressed emotion are represented visually and aurally.

Despite the screenplay's overt organization around a heterosexual, passionate romance involving a classical Hollywood competing triangle dynamic of two men and a woman, critics such as Stephen Bourne and Ruth Barton respectively have opened up the film to both queer and feminist readings that perhaps disrupt the film's obvious structure of feeling and offering instead a countervailing emotional key.[54] According to Bourne, Hurst's own bisexuality is adduced, as is the production's collective presence of homosexual men involved in the film, or showing textually how Stefan (Anton Walbrook) is visually feminized by Hurst's camera work, by the actor's mittel-European accent, and by the narrative fact that he is "musical." In interpreting these elements it is worth noting Richard Dyer's critical treatment of film authorship within a matrix of "material and semiotic circumstances."[55] In particular, his emphasis is that the

3.9.2. *Dangerous Moonlight*: queer homosociality. Screengrab.

director and his work occupy a "material social position in relation to discourses" (34) of sexual, ethnic, and cinematic codes and that "cultural production must be understood to take place within, and to be a struggle about" (36), these discursive limits. Thus, Hurst's exilic status is both conventional *and* subversive in this context. By his own account, Hurst had tried to direct Walbrook's performance away from being—in his terms— "sissy" or effeminate, yet Hurst's lens was looking otherwise.[56] Second, of course, Stefan and Mike are involved in a classic Hollywood love triangle that is explicitly referred to in the dialogue. In such an obvious—to use Bourne's term—"gay classic," it is odd that his interpretation does not even mention Mike! Barton does but fails to follow through a queer reading. Is it a coincidence that Mike's surname (Carroll) is the same as Stefan's lover/wife (Carol)? Or does it indicate that he is the homonymic supplement to Stefan's repressed "musical powers"—which are traumatically lost and transformed in conventional romantic heterosexual love?

According to the anonymous *Sunday Times* reviewer, the film's "banal and novelettish script" comes to a creaky conclusion. But the same critic nevertheless found the film scenario "moving and sincere," if only when it is dealing with "the business of flying, the casual heroism of airmen." The film's prepublicity describes Stefan's patriotic duty in terms of sensuous desire, "an irresistible urge"[57] that overcomes the social convention of marriage. He leaves his new wife in the United States to join the Polish squadron of the RAF where he enjoys intense male camaraderie with Mike in the officers' mess. The two men row over Carol, and it remains ambiguous if Mike actually has tried to give Stefan her letters.[58] After one such row, Mike dies in an air sortie—it is heavily hinted that he might have recklessly killed himself—and Stefan finds letters from Carol in Mike's papers. Was Mike withholding some of the letters? Although Stefan comes to realize that his wife does love him, does he weep more for the death of his "best friend"?

While most moviegoers and critics praise the surging orchestra of the theme music, a scene occurring the morning after Mike's death provides a minor musical motif of major thematic importance because of how its exilic significations are associated with this queer narrative subtext.[59] In the officers' mess, sitting at a piano, Stefan picks out the chords of a ballad that Mike has hummed, but nobody can remember and it becomes identified as a kind of musical obituary (the tune that none can name?). In one of Hurst's signature tableau scenes—straight diagonal lines of young uniformed men in profile—Stefan's fellow officers are drawn to the simplicity of the musical air, sharing its poignant tribute, but in this moment of musical mourning Stefan's intimate emotional vulnerability is intruded upon. It contrasts with the film's earlier, much more famous, scene in which Stefan plays the piano to seduce Carol during an air raid in Poland. Walbrook is—I venture—in this quieter scene actually playing the ballad "The Rose of Tralee" himself and gets it slightly wrong.[60] But as Barton astutely points out, using Noël Coward's idea of "the potency of cheap music," particularly in films, is such that ballads carry multiple valences.[61] Sung on film by John McCormack in *Song o' My Heart* (1930) and on record, this popular standard would be instantly recognized by Irish people in cinemas in Britain and in the United States, creating a musical exilic link emotionally evoking loss and separation. Here without the lyrics, the

3.10.1. Tableau of grief: *Dangerous Moonlight*. Screengrab.

3.10.2. Stefan's tear shot: *Dangerous Moonlight*. Screengrab.

transposition of this screen rendition masks the gender reversal to the original song-narrative. The lyrics (attributed to William Mulchineck and set to music by Charles Glover) tell of a male lover's grief over his *fe*male love's tragic death and their forbidden relationship that caused them to be apart. The tune had exilic resonances for Hurst—away from Ireland—and crucially it allows the possibility for homosexual desire to be screened and sonically signified via Stefan's playing and by Walbrook's performance. And in yet another layering, it was the case that off-screen, Walbrook's male lover had departed to Canada in 1940.[62]

3.11. Hurst and Sally Gray at Hurst's home, June 1947. Photographer: Francis Goodman. © National Portrait Gallery, London.

As a wartime film, its capacity to engage members of the audience separated from loved ones by British military service abroad or bereaved by bombs closer to home gave it a poignant popularity. Chapman has noted its powerful resonance and that it "suggests that realism and emotional restraint were not necessarily the only criteria of good propaganda" at this stage in the war.[63] *Dangerous Moonlight* can, however, as I have argued, best be understood as an exilic film and one in which the vector of queer sexuality, fashioned from the determining mesh of contexts, acknowledges the nature of Irishness and suppressed desire in Britain in the 1940s. Less expressive of Hurst's individual sense of self, the embodiment on-screen of Irishness through fictional characters and music ought to be understood as articulating collective identifications for those Irish people in the darkness of the auditoria in Britain and the United States. Crucially, however, the film also engages the feelings of wider audiences, other émigrés and displaced persons, lost ones, and loved ones, including those socially eclipsed because of their sexuality. The film also helped to boost Hurst's rising professional profile and his connection with Sally Gray, who became a baroness in 1951 when she married the Irish peer Dominick Browne, fourth Baron of Oranmore, in Mayo.

ALIBI (1942) AND *THE HUNDRED POUND WINDOW* (1943)

Following such considerable box-office and critical success on both sides of the Atlantic a year later, *Alibi* and *The Hundred Pound Window* make for interesting companion pieces to offset the high moral patriotism, self-sacrifice, and sensitive exploration of vulnerabilities that are presented in *Dangerous Moonlight*. In contrast, *Alibi* is set in an underworld of entertainment and turns on its exploration of how murder and criminal deception and detective subterfuge seem to be part of the environment of a louche Parisian cabaret culture of the late 1930s. *Hundred* presents an English lower-middle-class suburban family life whose respectability is compromised by addictive gambling of its father-family head and how he and his wife are drawn into a criminal racket. The lack of satisfaction and fulfillment offered by this "respectability"—with money, the thrill of consumption, and material gain seeming desirous—picks up the core moral

3.12. Gambling with the middle-class family: *The Hundred Pound Window*, 1943. Still supplied courtesy of the Ronald Grant Archive.

dilemma of *On the Night of the Fire*. But for the sake of brevity, I will focus for the rest of this section on *Alibi*.

In some respects, *Alibi* carries on from Hurst's sequence of crime films and communal melodramas that featured in the intense period of prewar work between 1936 and 1939 discussed in chapter 2. Like *Sensation*, *Alibi* exposes the entrapment tactics of police and, like *Prison without Bars*, was a remake of an already successful play and French film, in this case *L'Alibi* by Marcel Achard under the production arm of British Lion/Gainsborough Studios. The precredit title emphasizes that the story is taken from "the records of the Parisian Prefecture of Police from 1937." But for Britain's cinemagoers, the story and setting keyed into the demimonde reality of the wartime black market, organized crime, and illicit activities that ran alongside dutiful rationing and state-organized scarcity. Despite the distancing of period and geographical setting in Paris, the film presented audiences with an alluring view of a nightlife complete with a

3.13. Continental crime and corruption: *Alibi*, 1942. Still supplied courtesy of the Ronald Grant Archive.

Cuban orchestra, transatlantic star Elisabeth Welch singing in a cameo role, cocktail call girls, and a sinister cabaret mind-reader performer, "Professor Winkler," as the villain. With all of the principal characters (except Winkler) played by actors with English accents, the audience is asked to suspend its belief that the setting is Paris before the war, while clearly being asked to enjoy the pleasures of nefarious activities and recognize the "continental" accent of Raymond Lovell, a corpulent Canadian character actor as Winkler, and the "spiv" character/accent of Dodo (played by Philip Leaver).

The film was released in the United States, and a trade review cautioned about its "adult" nature. "British-made melodrama is fair program entertainment. Although the action lacks thrills, it holds one's interest to a fair degree, because of the story's developments. . . . The comedy relief is negligible, and the romantic interest is mildly pleasant. The Production values are good. . . . Adult entertainment."[64] Compared to meaner types

3.14. *Alibi*'s theatrical release poster. Supplied courtesy of the Ronald Grant Archive.

of production being made at the time in London's smaller studios like Welwyn, *Alibi*'s budget of £65,000 was lavish for wartime. Sets of the club, Helene's (Margaret Lockwood's) rooms, and street scenes display the skills of Alex Vetchinsky's set design and Hurst's penchant for French "authentic" decor, and a brief opening sequence of Parisian streets, lights, and glamour take us convincingly into this imagined world. Winkler is a theatrical, "high-class" con artist but worried that his fraudulent past will catch up with him and has John Gordon (Hartley Power), an associate from the United States in Paris, murdered by his sidekick, Fritz (Rodney Ackland: "Let *me* do it, Eric," he implores). To provide himself with an alibi, Winkler coercively bribes one of the call girls from the cabaret bar, Helene (Margaret Lockwood), who is in dire financial straits, to testify for him to the police investigating Gordon's death, led by Inspector Calas (Hugh Sinclair).

Unbeknownst to Helene, Calas uses a police officer, Andre Laurent (James Mason), as decoy to trap her into exposing her lie, but Mason and Helene end up falling in love, with her finally confessing her perjury. Winkler is protected by his trusty "servant, valet, confidante and part of his act," Fritz. Their interplay on screen suggests a covert homosexual relationship ("I'm sure he would do *anything* for me"). When the game is up, Fritz suggests an escape to Marseille to meet him later, but Winkler commits suicide by poisoning himself in his dressing room at the club. As we have seen from the analysis of *Dangerous Moonlight*, such on-screen queerness remains encoded in the performance and camera work at telling moments, but such presence is the marginalized counter to the film's main narrative. Its resolution sees the successful heterosexual union of Mason and Lockwood as they leave for Beauville by train to escape the immoral criminality of Paris.

"MAKING HEROISM ARTICULATE": *THEIRS IS THE GLORY* (1946)

Theirs Is the Glory is a dramatized reconstruction of an ill-fated Operation Market Garden airborne offensive in September 1944 by British and Allied forces (including Canadians, the United States, and the Polish army) that centered on Arnhem in occupied Holland. The German forces defeated

3.15. Location shooting in Arnhem: *Theirs Is the Glory*, 1946. © Liam O'Leary Collection. Courtesy of the National Library of Ireland, MS 50.000/326/21, Dublin.

the attack and inflicted heavy casualties, some eight thousand men killed or wounded out of a force of ten thousand, not to mention Dutch civilians and Resistance fighters. The 1st Airborne Division paratroopers took the brunt of what was an unmitigated military disaster. At the time, press and newsreels had to present events as a "magnificent losing fight that was as glorious as any victory when the sky rained men,"[65] and Hurst's film—made almost immediately after Victory in Europe (VE) was achieved in 1945—was a film tribute to the men who gave their lives, as is made clear by the prefilm "foreword" title. With its religious Lord's Prayer–echoing title, *Theirs Is the Glory* was Hurst's favorite film and the one with which he was most satisfied as a director. This satisfaction was first because it allowed him to honor the nation's debt to "just ordinary men" and second because of the sense of camaraderie with the soldiers that developed during the production. His recollections of the film's genesis and production stress the importance of using the actual survivors from the battle and

3.16. *Theirs Is the Glory*: reconstructive realism. © Rank Film. Still supplied courtesy of the Ronald Grant Archive.

shooting it on location, to re-create a "true documentary reconstruction of the event" and to achieve utmost verisimilitude.[66] From its premiere and through its general release, it made a strong public and critical impact. King George VI saw it at a special command performance at Balmoral, and it enjoyed joint premieres in Ottawa and at the Gaumont in Haymarket, London.[67]

Its immediate postwar afterlife was notable, too. Endorsing the idea of its accuracy and veracity, it was screened as part of their basic training for paratroopers during the 1950s.[68] It remains a remarkable cinematic reconstruction of an ill-fated episode on the way to Britain's defeat of Germany in Europe; it has been screened as part of a historical war-museum exhibition in the Netherlands and most recently been the central featured film of study of a battle of Arnhem book.[69]

To close this section, however, I want to critically examine claims made for its authenticity but also explore how Hurst creates the powerful emotional responses that the film engenders. To help with this endeavor, we also need to set it in context with earlier and later war films that emerged as a popular genre in the 1950s that are discussed in chapter 4. From the point of its instigation as a film, led by Castleton-Knight who was head of Pathé News, all through Hurst's account and most of the contemporary critical discussion of the film, its truth claims, accuracy, and fidelity to actual events are seen to be the guiding method to the treatment of the material. To my reading, the film adopts an odd, mixed mode of address to an audience who knew the outcome of the narrative. This mode is characterized by the tension between facts and fiction inherent in any dramatic reconstruction, but it is also specifically in this film between voice and image. Thus, instead of suspense or surprise, the film is tragically driven by a pathos of confirmation. It also requires the viewer to give of themselves, to open up to an emotional engagement, and for screen time to work in a noncognitive realm, that is, to feel with the men on-screen who are themselves, through the process of reenacting, remembering their experience.

The decisions to use nonactors who were the surviving soldiers from the battle, to have the war correspondent go back and revoice his reports, and not to mock-up using set and studio were significant. But to go back to shoot on location in the ruins of Arnhem itself does not, as Halpin has noted, necessarily confer an absolute form of representational "truth" on the film.[70] As Hurst admitted looking over the soldiers on exercises on Salisbury Plain at the casting stage, "I the selected men for the film very carefully and we had to pay the army three pounds a day for each paratrooper."[71] Although soldiers were "playing themselves," Hurst was choosing them for their accents and for what their photogenic looks might signify on-screen.

The film moves beyond retelling the story to find instead a way of expressing fear, male camaraderie, fortitude, suffering, and grief or, as one reviewer put it, "to articulate heroism."[72] In some of the most memorable sequences of *Theirs*, we are offered the male face as an object of beauty to contemplate in a quasi-religious state in moments of desolation and death.

3.17.1. *Theirs Is the Glory*: sculptures in light. Screengrab.

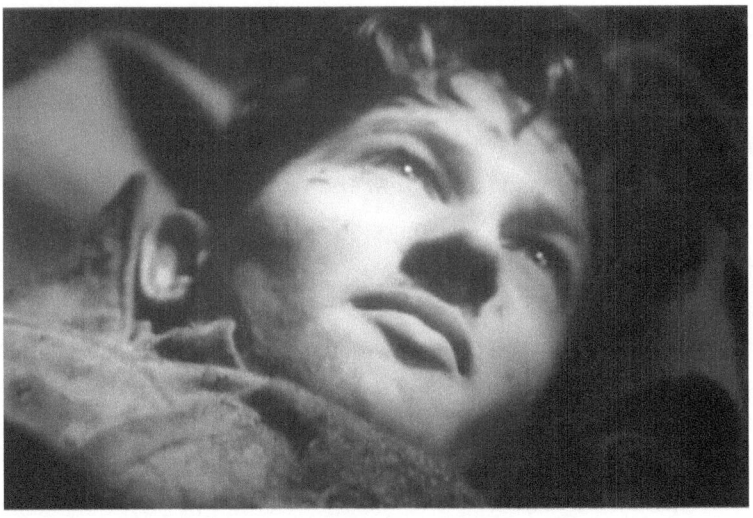

3.17.2. *Theirs Is the Glory*: quasi-religious masculinity. Screengrab.

3.17.3. *Theirs Is the Glory*: "poetic realism." Screengrab.

We can see from the analysis of Hurst's earlier films, like *Riders to the Sea* and *Letter from Ulster*, that Hurst drew on his knowledge of religious art and portraiture, his training with Ford, and his practice of sculpting with light within the frame of his camera. Hurst explained to Christopher Robbins how he worked with young nonactor soldiers: "I would lock the soldiers into a close-up so *they couldn't move* and say: 'Just think *what you felt at the time* when the RAF dropped the desperately needed supplies on the German lines [by mistake].' The results were superb."[73]

What Hurst describes is a technique of emoting, of drawing on a recent emotional memory, rather than acting as such, that is, pretending to be someone else or feeling something of the character you are playing. Hurst wants immobile figures, men composed in groups or a single face, held in an arrested moment shaped by angles, shadow, and light. "The effect of these sequences is to produce the qualities of poetic realism that Michael Powell praised in his memoir summation of Hurst that was cited earlier. Certainly, *Theirs is the Glory* did much to elevate Hurst into the pantheon of British post-war directors."

WAR DAMAGE AND IRELAND

Yet as Britain's postwar years moved toward the end of the decade, a short-lived euphoria soon gave way to war damage and a state of exhaustion. Personally, however, Hurst had indeed reached the height of his professional esteem, and, as his entry in *The British Film Yearbook, 1949–50* noted, he was "under contract to J. Arthur Rank."[74] This position had been sealed with Prime Minister Clement Attlee's presence at the screening of *Theirs Is the Glory* and its popular reception discussed in the previous section. In the material and mental aftermath, the foundations of Britain's bomb-damaged cities and social formation were shaken, its domestic interiors exposed—literally in some cases—to scrutiny. To some eyes, even, London's rubble-strewn devastation looked otherworldly, "like the moon's capital."[75] While for some, out of this leveling rubble the possibilities of a new era were glimpsed, for others the moment called for conservative retrenchment. These tensions were played out in the films of the era and experienced by avid cinemagoers whose weekly enjoyment reached the peak of its popularity in 1947–48. However, one critic sounded a note of caution about the state of the British industry: "As a result of the war, in spite of the fact that British films increased in standard and prestige, the number of films produced in our studios was considerably lessened."[76] Yet in the five years following the war, British cinema may in many ways be seen as a gilded period of quality productivity and filmic achievement.

Despite his residence in London, his clear attachment to England, and his professional success within the British industry, Hurst maintained contacts with Ireland, visiting Dublin in 1942 and working on location across Northern Ireland in 1943, as we have seen earlier with *Letter*. However, he sought in 1946–47 at this high point in his career to have an influence on the Irish Free State government's policy direction on cinema. This took the form of a meeting with Sean Lemass, the IFS's minister for industry and commerce, in Dublin.[77] would have been aware of Hurst from the press notices that his *Riders* (1935) and *Ourselves Alone* (1936) had received in Ireland. But as was noted in chapter 2, news reports at the time that Killanin and Hurst were planning to build a film studio had come to nothing. Back in April 1937, Lemass had come under clerical pressure in the person of a Jesuit, Father Devane, demanding that the government hold an inquiry into all aspects of cinema in Ireland. To head off clerical interference, Lemass finally set up the Inter-Departmental Commission on the Film Industry in 1938 to examine cinema production and the economic viability of an industry based in Ireland. The onset of the Second World War and internal departmental wrangles meant that the commission's findings were delayed, their report finally submitted in 1942.[78] It was not made public, so gloomy were its prospects.

But Lemass commissioned a further report that was published a year later that recommended the establishment of a National Film Institute with a small annual budget, whose focus would be educational and overseen by Father Devane. It was set up and got to work in 1944. The report did see merit in the state supporting the production and distribution of a newsreel service made by a modestly funded film studio, but a commercially viable Irish cinema industry was not envisaged. There was a growing public discourse on the cultural role of film, documentary, and cinema in modern Irish society in this, period characterized by a Catholic front of clerical intellectuals[79] and popular lay groups against a culturally expressive, more secular set of interests—filmmakers, artists, and writers—whose countervailing ideas found focus in cinephile activist Liam O'Leary and his book *Invitation to the Film* (1945). O'Leary and others contributed to the debate via the pages of the *Bell* and in proxy fashion via the London-based *Sight and Sound*.[80] O'Leary had summed up the position in his "Developments in Éire" article arguing for more than the piecemeal support for film in Ireland. Lemass and the state whose ministerial office he held found themselves in the vortex of clerical, commercial, and cultural forces swirling around cinema.

It is little known that at this juncture at some point during 1946–47, Hurst became a director of Mercury Films (Ireland) Ltd., a company financed and led by Dublin-born businessman Richard Bingham.[81] *Shadow of a Gunman*, scripted for screen by O'Casey, was reportedly planned for production "within the next few months," with an all-Irish cast. Moreover, Bingham was buying Gormanston Castle; architects' plans were drawn up to build a new facility on its grounds that would be the focus of Ireland's first film studio. To the press Bingham said: "Every country of importance in the world had its film industry and it's extraordinary that there was none here before now." Hurst and Lord Killanin managed to secure a meeting with Lemass and an aide to consider an offer from Hurst to forgo a lucrative Rank contract in London to set up the studios but were seeking the support of the Irish government. Rather undiplomatically, Hurst was talking to the newspapers prior to the meeting early in January with *Hungry Hill*'s release imminent: "Let them [the Irish government] just give me one and a quarter million pounds and that is all they would have to do. I would then erect a studio on the outskirts of Dublin and give them five first class films."[82] The actual meeting did not go well. Hurst recalled the minister's response:

> "Which part of Ireland do you come from, Mr Desmond-Hurst?" the Minister asked.
> "Northern Ireland."
> The Minister looked at the aide sitting beside him.
> "Mr Desmond-Hurst means, of course, the Six Counties."
> "No, Mr Lemass, I do not mean the Six Counties. I mean what is now and always has been the dominating province in Irish affairs—Ulster."[83]

The £1.25 million was not forthcoming, and Hurst took up the job offer at Rank back in London.

Perhaps this unwelcoming rebuke by Lemass contributed to Hurst's sense of estrangement from Éire's political and cultural establishment, despite the emotional attachment that he cultivated. Given the parlous condition of state finances, the capital development budget he pitched for was wildly optimistic. The National Institute's annual purchasing budget of a paltry £2,000 puts into further perspective. Even allowing for the point-scoring confrontation, this exchange crystallizes Hurst's response to his situation living away from Ireland. He had developed an imaginative affiliation shaped by a premodern ideal. He had little truck with Fíanna Fáil Irish nationalism that had dominated postindependence, yet he also knew from his brief location filming in Northern Ireland that it was incapable of providing a home for him or a place to earn a living. In later life, he ruefully commented of Belfast in an interview that "it's not just the lack of money and opportunity [there], it's the lack of appreciation that kills you in the end."[84] The economic, political, and moral substrata in either state within Ireland at the time simply could not sustain the kind of cinema system that Hurst knew and was thriving in his adopted London.[85] Moreover, culturally and practically, he was excluded from "Ireland," the place with which he identified and where he felt he belonged. But pragmatically, he had to remain in England.

POSTWAR CELEBRITY, SOCIETY CIRCLES, AND *SIGHT AND SOUND*

Indeed, back in England, secure under contract to Rank, Hurst's rising stock as a director and his social capital are exemplified by noting the circles he was moving in by the end of the decade. Two photographs help us to locate Hurst visually in this moment. The first records a lavish dinner at the Grosvenor House Hotel held in London in September 1947. Thirty-one producers and directors who had worked with Filippo Del Giudice, the Italian founder of Two Cities films, met in his honor. With Peter Ustinov as master of ceremonies, Laurence Olivier presented Del Giudice with a silver cigar case. Seated around the table were, among others, David Lean (*Great Expectations* [1946] and *Oliver Twist* [1948]), Carol Reed (*Odd Man Out* [1947], *The Fallen Idol* [1948], and *The Third Man* [1949]), Roy Boulting (*Fame Is the Spur* [1947]), Roy Ward Baker (*The October Man* [1947] and *The Weaker Sex* [1948]), Joseph Somlo (*Trottie True* [1948]), Anthony Asquith (*The Winslow Boy* [1948]), Anatole de Grunwald (screenwriter, *The Winslow Boy*), and, of course, Brian Desmond Hurst. The highlighted film credits for the period should also include Powell and Pressburger's *A Matter of Life and Death* (1946), *Black Narcissus* (1947), and *The Red Shoes* (1948) and Olivier's *Henry Fifth* (1946) and *Hamlet* (1948), but Hurst's place at the table of excellence at this point in his career was well deserved.

Hurst's social mobility and cultural capital at this particular point are also signified by the fact that he sat for theater and society photographer Angus McBean. Born in Wales, McBean had moved to London, worked as a window dresser, and learned photography as an assistant to Cecil

3.18. The Two Cities Dinner, London, 1948. BFI National Archive/Simon Hessel.

Beaton before establishing his own business on Belgravia Street and rapidly earning a reputation for photographing stage shows, publicity stills, and theater stars in the late 1930s, perhaps most famously capturing the looks of Ivor Novello in what became his signature classically romantic photo-portraiture style, whose "fabulously dark blacks, Velazquez-like in their density, and the dramatic chiaroscuro effects were McBean's hallmarks."[86] But in 1941 McBean had been arrested in Bath, where he had moved to avoid the bombing. He pleaded guilty to homosexual offenses with young men and served four years of prison with hard labor (1942–46). On release McBean relaunched his photography business in a new studio on Endell Street, his clientele picked up, and he quickly became internationally renowned for a new, whimsical photo collage style as well as the more conventional "McBean portrait style [that] had now [1948] reached its most burnished lushness."[87] His subjects included stage and screen stars, society figures, royalty, celebrities, and other notable international figures, including, among others, Ivor Novello, Audrey Hepburn,

3.19. Hurst's celebrity photo-portrait, ca. 1946. Photographer: Angus McBean. © Harvard Theatre Collection, MS Thr 581, Houghton Library, Harvard University.

James Agate, Beatrice Lillie, Vivien Leigh, Diana Churchill, Elizabeth Taylor, Mae West, Laurence Olivier, Maria Callas, and Elizabeth Bowen.[88]

Becoming part of the portfolio of such a feted photographer is a clear indicator of Hurst's public profile, putting him in the highest of social and celebrity echelons and associated queer networks that thrived in metropolitan London. Finally, in the *Times* of London's "Court and Social Circular," dated March 1, 1949, his dining circle is indicated by the following report: "Sir Campbell Mitchell-Cotts gave a dinner party last night at the Connaught Hotel, Carlos Place, W. to meet Mr Gabriel Pascal and Mr Brian Desmond Hurst."[89]

Gabriel Pascal, the eccentric Hungarian film director of *Caesar and Cleopatra* (1945)—whose production Hurst was involved in for a time—remained friends with Hurst throughout the 1940s and 1950s. Their host, Mitchell-Cotts, second Baronet of Coldharbour, Sussex, had read law at Cambridge; called to the Bar in 1928; inherited a fortune and title at age thirty; married a French princess in 1934 but got divorced after five years; and served in World War II in the Black Watch regiment. He was a journalist, publisher, sometime actor, and writer but generally enjoyed a bachelor life between Chelsea and a country estate until in 1964, as *Debrett's Peerage* might say, he "died without issue." Like Hurst, he was a convert to Catholicism, enjoyed fine wine and art, and possibly also shared Hurst's interests in guardsmen. Hurst's social life at exclusive hotel restaurants with peers and his links with an international set, reported in the press and his interviews within film magazines in the 1940s, project an astutely fashioned image of the "haute bohemian." Hurst appears a talented, cultured individual, comfortable within the circles of a postwar British social elite of Knightsbridge and Kensington.

Hurst continued to be productive as the decade worked to its conclusion but with a distinct shift. The three films that Hurst made in the late 1940s turn away from the docu-realism of *Theirs Is the Glory* and back toward literary-sourced, historical melodramas, all written by female authors. They might be seen to strike a chord with twin impulses of the period: one a tendency to look back to the past for reassurance, the other to look toward change and a more egalitarian future. They were screened in cinemas that, if viewed from certain perspectives and contexts, throw light on shifts within the industry, of technology and tastes that would exert their pressures on producers and filmmakers in the coming decade of the 1950s, discussed in chapter 4. By the start of that decade, the British studio duopoly of Rank and ABPC was forced to reorganize its funding models as the US industry itself restructured and increased its influence on European screens. As British studio contract directors, independent producers, and smaller studios came under pressure, Hurst was invited by Gavin Lambert, newly appointed as editor of *Sight and Sound*, the BFI's "terminally boring magazine . . . [to] bring it back to life,"[90] to contribute an article for the August issue of 1950 commenting on the situation.

Whimsically titled "The Lady Vanishes," Hurst begins the piece by likening the British film industry to an *Alice in Wonderland* scenario and explaining the absurdities of the financing and production of films in Britain.[91] To Hurst, the present circumstances produce a grim, abject attitude: "We are no longer astonished when we look in the [news] paper to see what's on at the local or enquire what companies are at present in the studios and find little that is British" (253).

By 1950 the wider British economy was struggling with its currency, "frozen sterling," and the funding infrastructure for British film production itself was outdated, flawed, a "mad hatter's tea party" in Hurst's words (253), especially for independent companies outside of the main studio setup. Since 1947 the UK and US economies and film in particular had been locked into a war of tariffs and takeovers with Rank and Britain losing out.[92] Hurst is in an opinionated, combative spirit, showing a keen working knowledge of the system that supports his livelihood, or not. Trying to organize a production as an independent, with a script but at the mercy of distributors and finance sources, risk-averse decision makers make it nigh impossible to complete a film. Hurst notes that only Anthony Asquith— one of the country's "important directors"—is working, while "our best director," Carol Reed, as well as Thorold Dickinson, David Lean, and himself, pointedly are not. He details how his own attempt to get *She Stoops to Conquer* produced fell by the wayside in this system. He summarizes without blame the "American bridgehead" of US dominance of the British industry and the attempts by two government working parties—one chaired by George Gater and another under the president of the Board of Trade, since 1947 Harold Wilson, MP.

Hurst analyzes the problem and applauds the efforts of Wilson as "a good friend" of the film industry. The NFFC had been set up in 1949 to support the development of film, and Hurst acknowledges its partial help for some films. Perhaps understandably, Hurst does favor greater support for independent producers, the presence on working groups of people with filmmaking experience, and praises efforts—backed largely by Rank—to launch a national film school "to lay the foundations of real film craftsmanship" (254–55), which would go on, after legislation passed in 1967, to become the National Film School in Beaconsfield (1971). The article is brought to a close with Hurst stressing again the importance of "establishing a sound and solid industry in which certain people would no longer be able to gamble with the livelihoods of their employees" (255).

But what is even more interesting is Hurst's call for a return to "our tradition of worthwhile pictures," a rejuvenation of the "national quality of selflessness," and the way that, in a patriotic gesture, he calls for "a flourishing industry which still expresses *our* way of life and way of thought. It is essential not only *to us* but to others who look to us as a bastion of our western civilisation" (255; emphasis added).

It seems to be an extraordinary statement underpinned by an assumed Britishness that Hurst is appropriating in this instance. For the exile to adopt such a position involves his taking on an advanced conservative stance that sits uneasily with other contra positions. Apart from this article in *Sight and Sound*, there is also some evidence that Hurst spoke on the active circuit of film societies in London in this period. One such occasion was to the Hammersmith Film Society in the autumn of 1949, where—sharing a platform with Jill Craigie—it was reported that "Mr Hurst believes in the partial nationalisation" of the film industry.[93]

Aside from these industry contexts, Hurst's film projects in this period do seem to indicate a creeping conservative tendency. This point is manifest in his working methods, the aesthetic that his films embody, and what we know of his wider sociocultural outlook that we can evidence from his public utterances. It might be that Hurst was responding, albeit unconsciously, to an ideological turning back to traditional moral and social certainties that began to reassert themselves in the postwar period. It is significant in this respect then to consider that the flurry of postwar films are period films based on contemporary popular literary sources authored by women and that one of the screenplays was cowritten by a woman. Du Maurier's epic family saga *Hungry Hill* appeared in 1943, *The Mark of Cain* film is based on a novel by Joseph Shearing (pseudonym of G. M. Vere Long [1885–1952]), *Airing in a Closed Carriage* (also published in 1943) is about a woman falsely accused of poisoning her husband, and finally *Trottie True*, by the Brahms and Simon writing duo, published in 1946.

MELODRAMA, CLASS, AND HISTORY: *HUNGRY HILL* (1947)

Daphne du Maurier had established a reputation as an author of note with *Jamaica Inn* (1936) and *Rebecca* (1938), both of which were adapted into successful films. Two Cities astutely optioned her 1943 novel, and Hurst was an obvious choice to handle the project. The lengthy three-hundred-page source novel with its five-book structure was transposed by Terence Young (following up from *Dangerous Moonlight*, with Francis Crowdy on additional dialogue) into a more manageable three-act screenplay structure. The plot is a family saga narrative that dramatizes how, over three generations, the economic and political power of the Anglo-Irish becomes attenuated owing to the rising interests of a rural Catholic tenant class over the course of the nineteenth century. This situation is typified into a family feud between the landowning Broderick dynasty that mines copper ore from the mountain known as Hungry Hill and the recalcitrant Donovans who down the generations attempt to frustrate their masters.

The film's setting is based on an actual location in County Cork, a real family known to Du Maurier, and, as John Oliver points out,[94] its production emphasis on its "meticulous historical research," *Hungry Hill* presented itself as a historical drama, not a "costume" piece like a Gainsborough film. But as a literary and film text, it elides history in a number of ways. The film replicates the cross-generational family-saga scope from

3.20. Irish land rebellion: *Hungry Hill*, 1947. Still supplied courtesy of the Ronald Grant Archive.

1820 to 1895, but significantly it ends at the end of "book 5" and omits Du Maurier's epilogue, "The Inheritance, 1920." Fanny Rosa's closing speech of conciliation between the two families offers the irrational prospect of a workable peace the terms of which cannot be reasonably anticipated: "Only the unexpected can hope to work in Ireland." This speech was not in the "Second Draft Script."[95] In these earlier drafts the reconciliation between Fanny Rosa (Margaret Lockwood) and the Donovans is off-screen, and we learn about it from a speech by "Young" Tim (Shamus Locke). But the shooting and postproduction scripts clearly indicate that Katherine (Eileen Herlie) has a part in gently nudging Fanny Rosa to reconsider. However, the final postproduction script shows that as Tim invokes the memory of John (Dennis Price), his voice is heard "in Fanny's head" as "Voice Over (sotto voce)," which Fanny Rosa repeats out loud as the film comes to its closing exterior shot of the mountains.

> KATHERINE [PICKING UP ON TIM'S SPEECH]: And he'd be right. I'm thinking what this will mean to the children there will be. Brodericks and Donovans.
> FANNY ROSA (TO KATHERINE): Katherine!
> TIMOTHY: It would be a hard thing for them to grow up with the Donovan curse on them.
> JOHN'S VOICE. OVER (SOTTO VOCE): I know it was an unexpected thing but only the unexpected can ever hope to work in this country.
> FANNY ROSA: Timothy! You may go and tell Mr Hennessy that I have changed my mind. I'm withdrawing the charge. You can tell him it's because only the unexpected can ever hope to work in Ireland. (14–15)

With the servant dispatched to save Sam Donovan (Michael Golden) from hanging and the other locals from penal servitude or riot, Fanny Rosa muses:

> (TO HERSELF): I hope that now after all the misery Hungry Hill will be at peace again. Once more green and beautiful and the Brodericks and the Donovans will live quietly together at last. (16)

The film's narrative resolution of the enmity set up in the opening scene remains unconvincing. Setting out to exploit the copper ore of Hungry Hill, Broderick's (Cecil Parker) bluff dismissal of the Morty Donovan's (Arthur Sinclair) family's prior ownership, that "these ancient quarrels are best forgotten," receives the following retort: "Yes, the land belongs to us be rights, aye and the copper in it too if we'd a mind to take it."[96] The mountain exerts its curse on both families across generations, killing off fathers and sons in fateful murder, explosions, and diphtheria that divided kin in the aftermath. Despite the title, "*Hungry* Hill," the period, and Munster setting, it is significant that both novel and film pass over An Gorta Mór/the Great Famine (1845–48) without mention. Hurst, Irish members of the crew, and indeed audiences of the film cannot have been unaware of the 1846–47 centenary of this historic starvation during its production in 1946–47 and the rancor of debates about its "natural," fatalistic, or political causes.

A second, perhaps more deliberate, excision of the political context of the novel is realized in the film version. As mentioned, Du Maurier's text includes an epilogue titled "The Inheritance, 1920" (327–44) that brings the action back to Cork during the "Troubles" of the Anglo-Irish conflict and at the moment of the partition of Ireland. In the novel John-Henry, the grandson, has grown up into a young man who is returning from Canada and contemplating his inheritance of the family estate at Clonmere House at Doonhaven on Mundy Bay. He visits his aunt Lizette, buys drinks for "Black and Tans," gets abducted by the IRA while they burn his inheritance down, and meets with Eugene Donovan, the cowhand grandson of Morty Donovan. The resignation of John-Henry at the end of the novel (342–43) is in contrast to the uplift of Mrs. Broderick's closing speech of forgiveness and reconciliation, "because only the unexpected can ever hope to work . . . in Ireland." Brian McIlroy summarizes what he sees as the incoherent politics of the film: "The key answer to the Irish question, it seems from this film, is in sharing of the land and in wiping the slate clean of personal grudges. This socialist theme periodically provokes a critique of class in English society, although it is suppressed in the adaptation as a whole."[97]

This comes in sharp contrast to the welfare socialism at work during the period of the making and screening of the film, and neither novel nor film offers a coherent critique of class in England or Ireland. Du Maurier's novel does detail the transformation of the Irish Protestant Ascendancy's slow succession of its power over the late nineteenth century to popular nationalist political claims, the IRA's separatist Republicanism, and the creation of the new state of "Northern Ireland" in the 1916–20 period. Terence Young's decision to cut "The Inheritance" section of the novel must have been discussed with Hurst and perhaps the film's producer, but we have no evidence of it nor of studio or BBFC intervention.

The effect is to close down and neuter the film's potential disruptiveness and keep it firmly in the historically distant past. It also for some viewers made it less than satisfying, Noël Coward noting in his diary, having seen it in November 1946, that it was "a dreary, long film with Margaret Lockwood as a suburban-Irish madcap who became a very old and very suburban lady. Oh dear."[98] For a slightly less bitchy overview, John

Oliver succinctly sums up its reception as a viewing experience: "The film itself, like Lockwood's performance, generated more good notices than indifferent ones, being compared favourably to contemporary Hollywood product."[99]

He cites directly the *Sunday Times* reviewer: "I find here as much skill and far more taste than in the comparable Hollywood cinema" and the *Kinematograph Weekly*'s view that it was "technically the equal of the best American film, its dimensions are indisputably box office." The *Manchester Guardian* alludes to the genre of the film and Hurst's capabilities working within it: "These family sagas have been the speciality of Hollywood: Mr Hurst has shown that a British studio can do the trick just as well." The competitiveness comparisons between Anglo-American industries are the dominant theme of the moment, but Hurst's specific Irishness is noted by the *Sunday Times* as a valuable attribute to his treatment of the material: "The director's sympathy with Irish characters and the Irish background helped warmth creep into what might have been a tedious record of marriage and violent death." In a review titled "Ireland in the Last Century," the *Times* noted that "some of the photography is charming and Mr Brian Desmond Hurst has accomplished the considerable feat of directing a long film about Ireland without mentioning either politics or religion."

During the autumn of 1946, as *Hungry Hill* was being adapted and filmed, Herbert Morrison, the new British Labour deputy prime minister, took a holiday in Ireland, informally meeting on separate occasions both Taoiseach Éamon de Valera and the Northern Ireland prime minister, Sir Basil Brooke. Since the Labour Party had come to power, Brooke and his Unionist Party had been seeking to secure the permanency of the Irish border that had been set up in terms of the Anglo-Irish Treaty of 1921. Northern Unionists were seeking political payback for their loyalty and sacrifice to the British Crown during the war. They feared that the Irish Free State would continue its dismantling of the terms of the Anglo-Irish Treaty (1921), signaled by the repeal of the 1936 External Relations Act, and use international diplomatic means to make good the (1937) constitutional claim to the six counties ("Northern Ireland") as part of the "national territory."[100]

Hurst's film should be seen among a clutch of other British studio titles released before and after *Hungry Hill* that feature Ireland as a setting, or key narrative, or with significant Irish characterization. These films included historical and contemporary scenarios addressing Éire's neutrality and IRA activity in Northern Ireland and Britain during wartime, as well as featuring "Irishness" within narratives across a range of popular genres. To list the following: *The Half Way House* (Dearden, 1944), *I See a Dark Stranger* (Launder/Gilliat, 1946), *Night Boat to Dublin* (Huntington, 1946), *Odd Man Out* (Reed, 1947), *Another Shore* (Crichton, 1948), *Daughter of Darkness* (Comfort, 1948), and *Old Mother Riley's New Venture* (Harlow, 1949) through to *The Gentle Gunman* (Dearden, 1952) is to appreciate a range from spy thrillers and noirish melodramas to more whimsical comedies and the gothic horror of Emmy in Lance Comfort's disturbing tale of a destructive Irish servant girl's sexuality. As such then, we can agree with Ruth Barton's summation that Hurst veered toward an uncontroversial British perspective in terms of *Hungry Hill*'s national cultural politics by "merely allowing himself to be blown along by the prevailing winds of popular British political thought."[101]

These matters of history are linked to the way that the film represents class, the gendered organization of social space, and sexuality. The world of *Hungry Hill* is obviously stratified by class—principally a Protestant—land-owning class but without obvious aristocratic title. The Brodericks are of a modern Victorian professional and entrepreneurial class (mining, the legal profession, and officer class connections). As a class they are seen as "interlopers" by the native Irish, Catholic tenant class (led by the Donovans) who work but don't own the land on which their families live and survive in relative poverty. The film visualizes this territorial and class division between locations of the village of Doona and the Castle Clonmere, its gardens, estate, and mine works, compared with domestic interiors of the Donovan house and the castle, notably in a ballroom dance scene. But we also get access to the servants' quarters of Clonmere and notably the exterior location of the lake and Hungry Hill itself. Finally, we have scenes of John's London residence/legal chambers near St. Paul's. In regard to the latter, although the Brodericks have City and legal connections in London, they remain Irish Protestants, not English.

3.21. Ballroom dance scene: *Hungry Hill*. Still supplied courtesy of the Ronald Grant Archive.

The film attracted review attention at the time and has subsequently been cited by more recent critics for the exuberance of the dance scene occurring twenty-nine to forty-four minutes into the film.[102] At this point, John and Fanny Rosa have been courting and attend the ball hosted at Clonmere where officers from the local garrison will meet possible suitors. The decorum of the evening is established with formal dancing to a small musical ensemble, including crane shots mixed with eye-level coverage of the dance as if within the ballroom. The proceedings reach an interval at which it is announced that the pianist will accompany Micky John, a "fiddler from the village," in a waltz. Around this moment, we are given two different perspectives of the interior space of Castle Clonmere. The first from within the ballroom is of the local villagers crammed in the French doors to the gardens, eager to view the proceedings. The second shift in perspective is from Old Tim's/Sarah's (played by F. J. McCormick and Eileen Crowe, respectively) servant quarters looking through the door into the ballroom scene, Sarah saying, "Look at Micky John in there with all that quality." Back in the hall, the pianist and fiddler awkwardly begin the waltz, and we see dancing pairs swirl around to the tempo of the music, intercutting between crane shots down on the dancers and medium shots of the two musicians. Micky John (Dock Mathieson) begins to speed up his playing, forcing the pianist to keep to his timing, because "the divil's in me fiddle and he wants to dance a jig." "The camera pans round with a gyrating pair of guests, as they pass the window. Through here we can see out on to the garden where the tenants, at last finding some music that they can understand, have begun a very gay little jig, the women all in their bare feet."[103]

The music builds up speed so that the waltz is overtaken by Irish jig, dancers drop their formal partner moves and break into "Irish dance" steps, and then they pour out of the French windows, the camera cutting to the outside space of the gardens where the local villagers, soldiers, and society ladies—taken in with crane-shot angles—all mix up in dancing with an

3.22.1. "Look . . . with all that quality": *Hungry Hill*. Screengrab.

3.22.2. The excluded mob: *Hungry Hill*. Screengrab.

abandon that reaches a climax: "60. EXT. LAWN. CLOMERE. NIGHT: L.S. THE DANCERS (SHOOTING PAST THE TREES TOWARDS THE HOUSE). More and more of the guests are coming out through the open French windows out of the stream of light into the softer illuminations of the open air. *It is by now impossible to tell who are the house guests, who are the tenants, for they are all dancing together hopelessly intermingled.*"[104]

John and Fanny collapse at the finish: "Oh it's wonderful and like wild things from the other side of the mountain." It is a virtuoso sequence of control, combining cinematic space and music to convey the interpersonal relationships of the lead characters. But as the script directions indicate, this moment is one of utopian feeling, where the screen space and musical infusion of native rhythm signify a momentary "intermingle" of class relations in the dance.

Beyond the diegesis of the film, the issue of class mobility and its gendered inflection were of course topics of popular interest and British

3.22.3. A moment of class "intermingling": *Hungry Hill*. Screengrab.

establishment concern in the period immediately following the Labour Party's general election victory in Britain. The class structure, its economic and legal underpinnings, and how woman's subordinate place within it are maintained are really at the heart of Hurst's two tonally very different films that he worked on at the end of the 1940s. Once again, film adaptations of contemporary popular novels set in the historic past might be seen to offer oblique commentary on the present. These Rank/Two Cities films form part of body of what Spicer has termed the "High Noir: 1946–51" period of British "noir."[105] If *Alibi* reflected a criminal underworld associated with wartime, then *Hungry Hill* and *Mark of Cain* operate within the gothic melodrama mode, as does *Scrooge*, discussed in chapter 4.

NOIR AND TECHNICOLOR MUSICAL: *THE MARK OF CAIN* AND *TROTTIE TRUE* (1948)

Made for Two Cities Films, *The Mark of Cain* is a period film beginning in 1898 in France but whose plot swiftly moves to Manchester. As its title suggests, it is a drama about the fortunes of a pair of brothers who co-own their cotton-milling business inherited from their father. Contrasting in character and temperament, Richard (Eric Portman) and John Howard (Patrick Holt) find themselves drawn into rivalry for the affections of Sarah Marguerite Bonheur (Sally Gray), a young English-French heiress. John wins her over, bettering his older sibling. However, once married to the younger, more industrious John, Sarah finds her life quickly becomes constrained and she is treated cruelly by her husband, preoccupied as he is by business and overcoming the class prejudice and xenophobia of his northern English society, but being frozen out of both French and English aristocratic circles. Sarah has children but also receives the attention of handsome nobleman Rochford (Edward Lexy) and Sir William Godfrey (Denis O'Dea), for whom she is seen to have some natural "titled" affinity. Richard becomes obsessively jealous and protective for his sister-in-law and hatches a plan to poison his brother, for which Sarah is accused and stands trial. A solid quarter of the film time deals with courtroom drama in which the increasingly histrionic Richard mounts an impassioned defense of Sarah, hoping vainly that it will win her over to love him instead.

W. P. Lipscomb's adaptation and Francis Crowdy's screenplay were sumptuously designed by Alex Vetchinsky and filmed by Erwin Hillier, the German-born cinematographer who had worked with Fritz Lang at UFA and then in England with Powell and Pressburger at the Archers film company. While undoubtedly visually stylish, the narrative of the wife and young mother as a victim-apex of a fraternal triangle base is oddly asymmetric, and the film does not live up to the scope suggested by its biblical title. The few reviews on its release were unimpressed: "This is a gloomy production, which induces little interest or belief. Once again the theme is murder, and it has not even the entertainment value of being an exciting one." The reviewer in *Today's Cinema* thought it a "ponderous story," with "implausible direction" whose "painstaking production qualities fail to redeem this picture from label of dismal entertainment," but gave a detailed, thorough analysis of its faults and missed opportunities: "For all its outmoded atmosphere, the piece might have amounted to something had it been put forward as a straightforward murder melodrama. [But instead] we have an arty pretentiousness which fumbles with fraternal egoism, a suggestion of domestic domination which has facility without feeling."[106]

The only element of praise was the performance of Eric Portman, who "brings intelligence and polish to a role whose extravagances he cannot be held responsible."[107] Indeed, Portman's performance of the eccentric, narcissistic Robert dominates the film as a suave, obsessive, and decidedly queer criminal driven by a perverse desire for his brother's wife.

Finally, under pressure from Rochford, Robert confesses his guilt, the widowed Sarah is reprieved and reunited with her daughter in a closing shot in France, and Robert is presumably hanged for his crime. The

3.23. *Mark of Cain*, 1948. Still supplied courtesy of the Ronald Grant Archive.

narrative resolution sees that misdirected, excessive (hetero-) sexual desire is punished, but the social class system presented—albeit in a pre-1914 past—is conservative, unforgiving, and rigidly demarcated between the provincial industrial class, a servant class, and Anglo-French land-owning aristocracy.

In contrast to the monochrome immobility of this world, *Trottie True*'s Technicolor brightness appears to offer a different tone and prospect. With an exterior shooting schedule over the sunny summer months of July and August 1948 in central London, its inner suburbs, and outer London countryside, *Trottie True* made full use of the decision to use the color stock, Hurst's first picture in this medium. C. Denis Freeman's screenplay, an adaptation of Caryl Brahms's novel, tells the story of how a lower-middle-class Gaiety girl singer (Jean Kent) becomes a duchess, having attracted the affections of Lord Digby Landon (James Donald). The story is told in flashback, with Trottie reflecting on the "many exciting moments" of her life, including her professional rise from the Camden music halls to "legitimate" theater as a performer, marriage, and Mayfair. At first she criticizes other girls: "You think more about marrying a lord than smiling at the gallery," but concedes, "I suppose I am bettering myself." She has suitors aplenty, from the honest working-class Sid Skinner, the balloonist (Andrew Crawford), to the aging industrialist northerner Arthur Briggs, both of whom she rejects. As a Gaiety star, she attracts the attentions of several titled gentlemen and as a commoner marries Lord Landon of Wellwater, only then to be subjected to aristocratic family scrutiny. She wins over the staff and icy mother-in-law (Mary Hinton), who declares "She'll do" at the end of a scene reminiscent of the *Hungry Hill* ball where again, for a moment, class differences dissolve.

With the scene set up and shot using similar techniques, at an annual party she melts the formality of the waltzing room first by singing one of her Bedford Hall favorites, with family, guests, and servants in a communal singsong ("Take my morning promenade") and then a moving ballad (possibly a Tom Moore lyric). When the marriage goes temporarily awry because of a misunderstanding, the elderly dowager advises her daughter-in-law on how to keep her man: "You are a born Duchess, consequently

3.24. *Trottie True*, 1949. Still supplied courtesy of the Ronald Grant Archive.

you are incapable of being vulgar.... I made sure my late husband gained the habit of preferring me to other women."

Husband and wife reconciled ("You'll be happy once again, never mind," as one song has it), Trottie can advise a new young bride on the eve of her wedding before joining her husband in a carriage ride through Hyde Park. It is difficult to accept McIlroy's assertion that *Trottie True* is a socially progressive text: "On the surface, the film is a light entertainment which, nonetheless, criticizes severely the institution of marriage as overly restrictive. It also *supports* (unlike *The Mark of Cain*) class mobility and the right of a lower class to bring its attitudes and values along with it."[108]

The script, with its screenwriter's final comment that the "wheels of the carriage—and the social machine go whirling on," suggests otherwise.[109] I argue that the film reinstitutes social conformity, and hegemony adjusts and reasserts its position of dominance in terms of gender and class. Although not a completely novel phenomenon, the business of social "left-hand marriage"; that is, titled aristocracy marrying "commoners," retained a popular fascination in Britain's popular class-defined society. As noted before in chapter 2, the interwar period saw an increasing emergence of "new money" peers, Anglo-American marriages, entrepreneurial American wealth dynasties and film stars, sportsmen, and famous people being treated "like royalty." Hurst's own social mobility was based on a disavowal of his class background, an invention of a family past, and an "Ulster planter" lineage, cultivating aristocratic friends and a set of cultural tastes, as well as developing a working practice and public persona that became increasingly conservative, as we will explore in chapter 4.

FASHIONING THE SHAPE OF BRITISH FILM: INTO THE 1950S

This chapter has charted Hurst's film career over a decade that spanned the upheavals, dislocation, and trauma of a global conflict. It has examined the cinematic contexts at play in Britain during this defining period and how Hurst negotiated the professional challenges thrown up by the necessities of state intervention, then international competition and the opportunities that arose as a result. Different kinds of evidence—peer

3.25. Hurst in the top rank of British cinema: Hurst, Walter Sistrom, and J. Arthur Rank, 1947. Photo by George Konig/Keystone Features/Hulton Archive/Getty Images.

recognition, popular memory, box office, and critical opinion—suggest that, overall, Hurst took his chances and prospered in the circumstances that presented themselves to him.

Indeed, by 1950, he was reckoned by one commentator to be one of a small group of seven filmmakers "who have largely fashioned the shape of British film as we know it. . . . [T]heir contribution as craftsmen has been the development of a recognizably British style."[110] Harry Wilson suggested that Hurst "is inclined to be over looked in any survey of British cinema, possibly because he has been denied the highest flights of fame by no more than sheer mischance," without explaining further. However, his conclusion makes some telling claims: "What makes Hurst's work stand out as being potentially of the first importance . . . is a certain clean-cut surface treatment, a very clever realism of the kind the documentary school developed, but without its somewhat arid conventions and lack of the warm touch of humanity, which needs only the impetus of the right ideas to achieve a real master-piece. He is obviously a director to watch closely, and one who is likely to play an increasingly important part in the development of British films."[111]

We have seen how Hurst, like others, learned from the demands of wartime production to combine techniques and different visual styles across documentary, drama, and mixed forms that culminated in *Theirs Is the Glory*. Hurst developed his direction of nonprofessional actors and location filming that would hold him in good stead for future projects. He engaged sporadically in writing about film practice and spoke publicly on the Film Society circuit, but he did not engage systematically in publishing his ideas, as Anthony Asquith and others did on documentary or neorealism.[112] We have also seen how music and scenes of musical performance have been some of the most memorable elements of the films in this period. Thematically, Hurst's output of films has been looked at as narratives with characters (and creative crew and performers themselves) who are out of country, exiled in conflict or socially marginalized, or straddle class boundaries. We have seen how some of Hurst's films—particularly the melodrama titles—are "double-coded" in terms of gender and sexuality, despite the fact, unsurprisingly, that male and female characters mostly conform to the prevailing roles of the era. But wartime films offer homosocial masculinity as the focal point for moral questions, intense emotional scrutiny, and physical beauty. The creative teams with whom Hurst worked produced films that created images of masculinity for pleasurable contemplation that contained heterosexual *and* homoerotic charges as well as instances of feminine disruptiveness, albeit fleeting. These charges gave a gendered and sexual inflection to the wider socioeconomic realignments that were forced upon Britain as it emerged into the postwar period of recovery. The cinematic possibilities during the 1950s, a period of austerity and critical decline, are the subject of the next chapter.

4 Finale
Adaptation, Revival, and Remnants of Empire

In 1951 Hurst entered a public debate about plans for the establishment of a National Film and Television Theatre, or "telecinema," sited on London's South Bank. In a letter published that August in the *Times*, Hurst argued that the "national telecinema should be retained and given a permanent place alongside the National Theatre and the Royal Festival Hall." The depleted postwar economy had delayed the redevelopment of London and many of Britain's other major cities: priority had gone to housing, roads, bridges, and vital infrastructure. But a cultural revival, a nationally coordinated series of events billed as the "Festival of Britain" showcasing British design, innovation, and culture was held during the course of 1951. Echoing the Great Exhibition of 1851, it was meant to signal a collective sense of renewal and the reassertion of British culture, its values and institutions, soon to be embodied in the coronation of the young Queen Elizabeth II in 1953. At this point in his career, Hurst was far from shy in sharing his opinions about the significance of film to national culture.

In the capital and elsewhere, new cultural venues were being commissioned, and the concrete modernity of London's "Rive Sud" was the site for the National Theatre, the Festival Hall for music concerts, and an art gallery. But the four-hundred-seat "telecinema" complex, capable of screening film and large-screen television, was envisaged as only a temporary structure. Hurst argued that "this opportunity for the State, as patron, to establish a living tribute to this art should not be missed." While Hurst's support for the project is perhaps unsurprising, the rhetoric of his high-flown patriotism is worth considering: "[Film is] an art that is capable of revealing to millions the English way of life, the English ways of thought and feeling, and, whether the balance of power is passing or not, England is the moral anchor of the world."[1]

Hurst's public exultation of Anglocentric notions of a British national culture whose international politics would be severely tested by the decade, notably Suez in 1956, is bizarre. It is significant nonetheless for what it indicates about a worldview that he promoted: his Ulster exilic view somehow reconciled his "Irishness" with a self-regarding English patriotism.

This chapter reassesses perhaps Hurst's most enduring film, *Scrooge* (1951), in light of his other literary adaptations of British and Irish canonical literature in the 1950s and 1960s, such as Hughes's *Tom Brown's School Days* (1951) and Synge's *The Playboy of the Western World* (1962). It also analyzes a selection of films exploring the Second World War, colonialism, and revolution. These films share concerns about questions of allegiance, mixed racial and cultural belonging, and the lingering memory of the war, the nature of Englishness, and monarchy. This examination is set within a wider context of Ireland's post-1949 relations with Britain and shifts within British society as reflected through its films.

In this period Hurst and Killanin tried—again unsuccessfully—to set up a film studio in Ireland. They lost out to Emmet Dalton's bid for creating an Irish state film studio in Ardmore, Bray, County Wicklow, in 1958 but were involved in an Irish film production company with John Ford. Hurst's essay on directing published in *Films and Filming* (1957) is analyzed, and his intriguing unmade film projects from this period are briefly considered. The aim is to exemplify Hurst's position asymmetrically straddling two industries: one, in Ireland, nascent, attempting to establish itself; the other, in Britain, desperately trying to restructure itself in the face of US competition, and changing domestic politics, demographics, technologies, and audience tastes.

The chapter also aims to explain Hurst's own increasingly dated cultural politics in relation to the British Empire, colonialism, and indeed notions of Irishness in relation to his long-term residence in England as a professional "Irishman." In this regard, the anomalous category of Irish British subjects (as distinct from Irish citizens resident in Britain) can be compared to the new commonwealth nationals who arrived from the West Indies, Africa, and India to work and build new lives to become part of British society. The working through of new national affiliations, more complex social class, and ethnoracial mixtures in a postcolonial era were some of the underlying currents that bubbled up in major studio and independently produced films for middlebrow and popular audiences in the 1950s. And Hurst's career, like those of Powell and Pressburger, David Lean, John and Betty Box, Lance Comfort, and others of their generation, was shaped by these new circumstances of uncertainty and redefinition.

POSTWAR GEOPOLITICAL CONTEXTS

The geopolitics of the world changed irrevocably in the years following the end of World War II, and Britain, as the world's foremost imperial power, was forced to adapt more than most. In the wake of the war, Britain's dominions and colonies exerted political, diplomatic, and physical force to claim their independence within a new world order under the United Nations and its charter (1948).[2] Other major powers stealthily moved to build new economic alliances; capture resource-rich territories in the coming continents of Africa, Asia, and South America; and establish new trading and ideological blocs that held sway for a generation from the 1950s until the end of the 1980s. These shifts played out in Britain in a multidimensional fashion: it began to absorb significant numbers of imperial subjects into its society as it rebuilt the country; it engaged in diplomatic war with India that resulted in a hasty partition to form East Pakistan and West Pakistan (1947–49); colonial Britain encountered political violence in northern Africa, the Far East, and the and Middle East, notably the issue of Egyptian nationalism and the Suez Crisis (1956), and colonial insurrections for independence in Kenya (1952–60) and against communist Malayan rebels (1948–60). Economically, Britain was crippled by the United States; Britain began to witness the rise of Japan and the emergence of a European trading bloc known as the European Economic Community (EEC) in 1957 without the United Kingdom as a member. As well as trying to reestablish the United Kingdom's standing in the world and modernize itself as an "equal partner" in the British Commonwealth through the newly crowned Queen Elizabeth II (1953), Britain had to recalibrate its relationship with its oldest neighbor, Ireland, which had pointedly exited the commonwealth in 1949 and began to engage with the consequences of de Valera's concept of "external association."[3]

Both states on the island of Ireland struggled economically during the 1950s with the consequence that emigration increased sharply, particularly from the Republic, and, as Clair Wills has explored, new Irish-born migrants joined Caribbean and later African colonials in Britain's cities.[4] As the immediate postwar phase stretched into the 1950s and 1960s, there were subtle shifts in relations at formal political and diplomatic levels. But these changes were anchored in and partly had to reflect the everyday practical business of accommodation, employment, as well as social and cultural adjustments that result from widespread immigration. This shift was felt by those individuals who defined themselves as "indigenous," new arrivals, and people who had partially assimilated or otherwise found a place as part of Britain's historic minorities, like the Irish or the Jewish.[5] Popular understanding of "immigration" (moving from necessity to novelty and then to "nuisance" and "problem") combined with developing ideas of the "postimperial" and "modernization." Working-class Irish men and woman became a significant part of an expanding nationalized workforce and infrastructure, notably in nursing, transport, and the commercial construction industries. There's little on record to show Hurst had any great interest in or connection with the Irish working classes, "an unconsidered people," as Catherine Dunne describes them, or even new Irish professional classes in London.[6] Middle-class Irish continued to occupy positions in the civil service, the professions, teaching, engineering, business, media, and cultural production. What did "external association" mean personally and professionally for people of Hurst's generation who had come to Britain in the interwar period, and how did they and he position themselves? The 1948 British Nationality Act provided Irish-born citizens with nonalien status and rights to live and work in Britain that were different from other commonwealth subjects. Yet for Bernard Shaw, "by birth a British subject" but also "a registered citizen of my native Ireland," it created a sense that he was "a Citizen of Nowhere" and that "in Britain I am still a foreigner and shall die one."[7] The ambivalent wariness of and warmth toward Ireland and the practicalities of the presence of Irish people in Britain were expressed in everything from travel permits to diplomatic status, and on cinema screens in films like *Daughter of Darkness* (Comfort, 1948) in which a troubled, nymphomaniac Irish girl arrives on a Yorkshire farm to wreak havoc on the locals.

HURST AND BRITISH POSTWAR CINEMA, 1948–1962

As was noted at the end of chapter 3, the British cinema industry in the postwar period was destabilized by an economic trade dispute with the United States that badly affected the supply of films to the market. The British studio duopoly (Rank and Associated British Picture Corporation) was restructured, and the state intervened to support film domestic production by means of a tax scheme, known at the Eady Levy. Introduced in 1950, it redistributed box-office receipts to qualifying British films depending on their take. Even in the best of times, filmmaking and cinema were enterprises with an unpredictable alchemy of capital and creativity: the period saw many realignments, changes in the cinema-going public, and a decrease in ticket sales.[8]

If it was tough for the major companies (Rank and ABPC) to respond to the US presence, the coming technology and new social medium of television, and changing audience demographics, it was a precarious decade for independent production companies.[9] According to Sue Harper and Vincent Porter, British cinema developed "a sort of cultural myopia" during the 1950s whose generic output "represented the rest of the world either as a site of exotic pleasures or as a source of regret." This tendency was accompanied by an inward turn, a focus on war films and comedies being the popular genres, but others like the historical and costume melodrama falling out of favor. For Harper and Porter, the films of the decade are characterized as "an anxious cinema, which worried away at the new social and sexual boundaries."[10]

Early in the decade, Hurst's active career peaked and was sustained as he navigated a course between major studio contracts and independent production projects. He directed a clutch of films mid-decade for Rank, whose strategy was to exploit overseas markets in the colonies and try to recapture British cinema success from the 1930s. It is instructive to explore Hurst's position as a director involved in popular colonial and costume dramas such as *Simba* (1955) and *Dangerous Exile* (1957), featuring as they do questions of allegiance, mixed racial and cultural belonging, and monarchy. His work on Second World War films such as *The Malta Story* (1953) and *The Black Tent* (1956) rehearse and comment on attitudes toward Anglo-British, national, and class character. As director/producer, Hurst worked in the struggling independent production sector, and his English literary classic adaptations exemplify the "anxious cinema" mentioned by Harper and Porter, preoccupied by belonging, the vulnerability of masculinity, and filial love (or its lack). Hurst's exilic situation, his work on location in overseas settings, and the dramatic narratives featuring exiled Irish or estranged "nationals" in "foreign lands" expose several interconnected, discursive tensions and limits.

ADAPTATION AS REVIVAL: *TOM BROWN'S SCHOOL DAYS* AND *SCROOGE*

British cinema in the post-1945 period witnessed a marked reversion to English literary source material with its high-culture values. In the wake of the threat to the "nation" and during a period of national renewal, it is perhaps unsurprising that this should be so. Olivier's production of *Henry V* (1945); David Lean's celebrated Dickens adaptations, *Oliver Twist* (1946) and *Great Expectations* (1948); and Alberto Cavalcanti's *The Life and Adventures of Nicholas Nickleby* (1947) offered Englishness and an assertion of its cultural values in a period when the experience of the majority of people was to question the basis of those values. Liberal, conservative, and new labor claims to British identity in the late 1940s highlight the contested nature of culture. As has been noted, the phenomenon of a liberal Victorian revival (1951 harking back to 1851) occurred in conjunction with a new "modern" monarch, a youthful Elizabeth II, and a nationally televised coronation, all signaling a new "Elizabethan" age.

In the middle of this period, Hurst found himself contracted by two independent companies, Talisman Films and Renown Films, juggling roles as a producer turned director of *Tom Brown's School Days* and *Scrooge* (both 1951). The first is a popular Victorian public school narrative that offered a reformist argument against bullying and a model for steadfast individualist heroism in an English middle-upper-class institution. The second, based on one of the most popular of Dickens's stories, *A Christmas Carol*, is a moral tale telling of the need for a generosity of spirit and the potential for personal transformation.[11] As works of literature, both titles had become canonized, retained a popular readership, and were ripe for screen versions. The Tom Brown story had been filmed in 1940 in a US production, and Hurst's *Scrooge* was the fifth screen version of Dickens's novel. Indeed, it might be argued that Dickens was as deeply absorbed in the popular visual culture as he was its literary fabric. Hurst gave valuable if partial accounts of the making of both films to Christopher Robbins in preparing his memoir, but it is useful to consider some of the broader political terrain at the time and to think how the films keyed into the topical debates in the minds of audiences.

The films were released in April and December 1951, respectively, as the first five-year term of Clement Attlee's postwar Labour government fell to Winston Churchill's Conservatives, demonstrating a political shift in Britain at the time. In the 1940s, Maynard Keynes and William Beveridge had propounded a state-led economic program to provide for a state secondary school system (known as the Butler Act, 1944), a program for the nationalization of key industries and services, a plan for the rebuilding of homes, and, crucially, the National Health Service, which came into operation under Attlee's government. To what extent do these films reconfigure Victorian reformist texts for the postwar agenda of rebuilding state Labourism? What attitudes toward class, privilege, poverty, and social exclusion do these films seem to display? As I have been arguing, as an exile himself, Hurst had sharpened his ability to articulate the emotional landscape of the social outsider or newcomer, to the stateless people who washed up in Britain during and after the war, and, more broadly, to connect with the plight of those individuals who found themselves excluded or socially marginalized. The films discussed in this chapter often feature child figures as victims, representing the vulnerability of the future generation, but the films discussed also extend sympathy toward an increasingly isolated older generation. The titular boy and pupils at the center of *Tom*

Brown and the elderly bachelor in *A Christmas Carol*, with its wretched orphans, father-son relations, and surrogate parentage, are themes that recur in *Dangerous Exile*, *Black Tent*, and *Simba*.

Tom Brown is set in mid-Victorian England and is a rite-of-passage story of the eponymous young teenage boy who goes off to Rugby School. The early scenes of the film portray Tom departing his family and encountering the strangeness of the school's building, its grounds, and Rugby's rituals, especially its strict hierarchy of authority, rules, and routine corporal punishment. Although Tom is befriended by the slightly older East, he is also soon subjected to the "fagging" system whereby the senior "boys" in the upper school treat younger ones as junior servants, subjecting them to initiation rituals and physical abuse that run alongside the team spirit of house games: rugby football, boxing, cricket, and cross-country running.

As in the original novel, the film features the villainous "Flashman," a raffish cad who picks on the impressionable Tom and mercilessly bullies him beyond the unspoken limits, at one point "roasting" him against an open fireplace. The source novel's author, Thomas Hughes, an "old boy" of Rugby himself under its most famous headmaster, Dr. Arnold, went on to become a barrister, writer, and Christian socialist, a movement associated with what is now known as "muscular Christianity." It espoused a set of values that was directed at providing a code of living for boys and young men to follow. Its character training stressed cleanliness, physical health, duty, service, courage, independence and loyalty, and "manliness" to produce in adulthood a morally anchored middle-class Christian gentleman. The open secret of bullying at England's public schools was only partly what drove Hughes to write the novel; the wider project was to improve the corrupted public school system for the Victorian middle classes and end some of the worst excesses of aristocratic privilege.[12]

Given this historical lineage, it is pertinent to ask how such a novel adaptation would work for its contemporary cinema audiences almost a century later, as Britain embarked on postwar broadening of educational opportunity and the construction of a modern meritocracy. From an overseas point of view, the *Variety* reviewer noted that a US version of the same story had been released in 1940 but responded to the press-book publicity praising the fact that this version was shot on location at Rugby School itself, such that the authenticity "of the background cannot be questioned," and used many of its own pupils as extras and in minor parts.[13] However, it continued: "It is acted with great sincerity by a name cast, but the script and direction go all out to emphasise the obvious emotional tear-jerker angles. Almost the entire script hinges on the popular angle of the new boy versus the bully."[14]

It wasn't just foreign eyes that saw the distortion of the novel that is at the heart of Noel Langley's adaptation. *Monthly Film Bulletin* noted, encouragingly to begin with: "The opening scenes of *Tom Brown* establish a pleasing atmosphere. Tom's arrival at the school and early scenes in Rugby (particularly a charmingly handled sing song) give rise to hope that the director might be able to pull off this almost impossible subject."[15] But it went on to pinpoint "the script fatally compromises," the scenes with the righteous headmaster (Robert Newton's performance was noted as "subdued"), the "awkwardly tacked-on sermonizing at the end," and the lack of a proper, "robust, *Boy's Own Paper* feeling of the opening." In fact, the film was faithful to the book's sermonizing sententiousness, but Tom is a much more mischievous, flawed character in Hughes's original. K. R.'s view was that "the film's main failure lies in John Howard Davies' lifeless playing of Tom. John Forest over plays Flashman atrociously, which might not have mattered had the film stuck consistently to its boisterous schoolboy intentions . . . while John Charlesworth and Glyn Dearman play naturally and well among a large cast of self-conscious boys."[16]

Howard Davies *is* rather insipid in performance, but Hurst's own account of the production catches at his own attraction to the project that was practical, cultural, and personal. His Rank contract had expired, and he was looking for work. Hurst seems drawn as an outsider in terms of class and nationality to the subject of an iconic English public school, a celebration of a quintessentially homosocial environment with its sexual undertow. The film's original director, Gordon Parry, left the project because, as its producer Hurst thought, "It was apparent the story wasn't getting through, and the director was paid off. I took over, and ended up directing 75% of the movie, although I refused to take off the director's original credit."[17] Apart from recalling how he displayed his superior knowledge of W. B. Yeats's poetry with an English master, Hurst recounted how he admired the physical looks of Ferguson, one of the school prefects, "an extremely handsome rugger player" whom he teased and flirted with in front of Beatrice Dawson, his friend and the costume designer.[18]

The film does well in conveying the adolescent camaraderie, competition, and physicality of an all-boys environment and the bitchy bachelordom of the masters' staff room. An early scene showing the boys singing the school song in the refectory is another example of how Hurst structures the organization of screen space for a communal, musical, or dance performance that we analyzed in *Letter from Ulster*, *Hungry Hill*, and *Trottie True* in chapter 3. Interestingly, in a quieter scene (fourteen minutes into the film), Hurst presents a sequence involving three youths at a piano singing the Irish ballad "Molly Malone" before the camera picks out another seated boy in the foreground who then moves to join three others toasting muffins at the fireplace.

Here in *Tom Brown*, Hurst's direction manages in such moments to catch something of the intensity of emotional attachments between boys and the vulnerabilities of masculinity in formation that underlies

4.1. Adolescent male camaraderie: *Tom Brown's School Days*, 1951. Screengrab.

Hughes's portrayal.[19] Bristow has noted how the novel and other examples of the genre disavow the underlying homosexual tension within a homosocial setup, and the same might be said of the 1950s film treatments of masculinity.[20] But in Hurst's version, there are two sequences of Tom, East, and the boys at the river swimming that presents the young actors in full rear nudity.

Following on from the previous chapter's exploration of *Alibi* and *Dangerous Moonlight*, we can show how *Tom Brown* offers a queer appropriation of the original text in two ways. First, the scenes of naked swimming boys in the Langley/Hurst adaptation in fact visualize what is *already there* in Hughes's archaic, euphemistic prose: "They spent a large portion of the day *in nature's garb* by the river side."[21] Second, these sequences also seem to draw on English, Continental, and US currents in nineteenth- and interwar twentieth-century art celebrating the homoerotic boy nude in nature such as Thomas Eakins's *The Swimming Hole*, Henry Scott Tuke's *Lovers of the Sun* and *August Blue*, and Frederick Walker's *The Bathers*.[22] The film shows then that Hurst shaped his historical source both by

4.2. "In nature's garb": *Tom Brown*. Screengrab.

drawing out from it and by imposing a distinct visualization on the film's mise-en-scène.

Hurst's second film of 1951, *Scrooge*, described by Jeffrey Richards as "a dark Gothic fable, which is a remorseless expose of heartless capitalism," is another instance of reworking Victorian literature for the new Elizabethan age.[23] It was the fifth British cinema version of Dickens's series, originally titled *Christmas Books* (1843) but known as *A Christmas Carol*, and was adapted for screen by Noel Langley and shot at Nettlefold Studios, Walton-on-Thames. *Scrooge* opened in November 1951 at the Odeon, Marble Arch, and went on to become an enduring seasonal film favorite. Claimed by some to be "the finest of all filmed adaptations of *A Christmas Carol*" (*Film Review*), it certainly provided George Minter, who owned Renown Pictures Corporation, if not Hurst, with his most successful box-office return, rivaling the popularity of his wartime romance, *Dangerous Moonlight*, and marked a high point in his career. By re-viewing the film and knowing something of its critical path, we can get a better perspective on the merits, flaws, and insights of Hurst's popular hit.

Scrooge is a well-crafted film, as would be expected from as experienced screenwriter as Noel Langley, who had worked in British cinema and for MGM in Hollywood on *The Wizard of Oz* (1939), no less. The script hugs the essentials of the story but adds new characters like Mr. Jorkins (Jack Warner) and emphasizes the isolated torment of Scrooge. Hurst as producer and director assembled an excellent cast (Hermione Baddley, Michael Horden, Mervyn Johns), and Scottish actor Alistair Sim produced a vivid, career-defining performance in the lead role that carries the film.

The London that Hurst offers shifts between a screen Victorianism established by Lean and Cavalcanti, lit and photographed by C. Pennington-Richards, but it is really Ralph Brinton's art design of the interiors of Scrooge's house and his mindscape that define the "Victorian noir" element of the film at its most disturbing. Oscillating between the ambivalent poles of Dickens's seasonal sentiment and darker angst, the finished film may feel uneven, as the creative treatment wrestles with the material. Although most obviously addressed by critics as a literary adaptation, Dickens's work carried a significant currency in popular visual culture,

4.3. Alistair Sim as Scrooge, *Scrooge*, 1951. © Renown Pictures. Still supplied courtesy of the Ronald Grant Archive.

4.4.1. *A Christmas Carol*. Illustration, John Leech, 1843. Public domain. Scanned image by Philip V. Allingham. Dan Calinescu/www.victorianweb.org.

including the legacy of the novel's original illustrations, stage versions, and the plethora of film and television versions.

A crucial moment in Hurst's film, the dramatic revelation of "Ignorance" and "Want" personified as two scrawny children, a boy and girl, in rags beneath the cloak of the Ghost of Christmas Present draws directly from John Leech's original illustration.[24] But Hurst's film itself generated a new "picture serialization" version of Dickens as part of a promotional deal struck by the film's enterprising producer with the *Daily Graphic*. The newspaper announced *Scrooge* would appear in its pages: "Today the *Daily Graphic* begins the picture serialisation of one of the best-loved stories in

4.4.2. *Scrooge*, 1951: "Ignorance and Want." Screengrab.

the English language," telling its readers that "the pictures are taken from the George Mintner film *Scrooge* now at the Odeon, Marble Arch."[25]

Extra-filmically, the press-book copy made much of Hurst's personal success and self-confidence at this point in his career. It outlines the director's professional profile with the now familiar Hurst inventions: "Born in Ireland 1900. Educated at Westminster and the Societe des Beaux Arts, Paris . . . associated for a long period in Hollywood with director John Ford."[26] This text takes five years off his age, gives him birth in "Ireland" (rather than Belfast), a completely fabricated education at Westminster School, stretches his informal attendance at Parisian art school, and stresses that he had been mentored by Ford. The profile continues by mentioning his wealth, homes in Belgravia and a country house in Denham, conveying the sense of "landed gentry," and ends with a final flourish ("he enjoys epicurean tastes"), suggesting pleasure in excess. *Scrooge*'s box-office success allowed Hurst to live a self-declared "epicurean" lifestyle as a celebrity, and he continued to work regularly during the rest of the decade.

But the record of its critical reception at the time shows that *Scrooge* was not universally applauded on its release. For Hollis Alpert, it had a

4.5. "Serial Picturisation," *Daily Graphic*, December 10, 1951. Newspaper Collection, British Library, London.

"magic allure," and he saw Alistair Sim's bravura performance as "the most wonderful and marvellous *Scrooge* of all." In the United States, distributed under the title *A Christmas Carol* to entice a family seasonal audience, the *New Yorker* was lukewarm: "There is enough good here to warrant the attendance of all save the hardest heart."[27] For "Brog" in *Variety*, the problems were greater—"too grim for children, too dull for adults"—and it continued that the film "will give tender-aged kiddies viewing it the screaming-meemies, and adults will find it long, dull and greatly overdone." Bosley Crowther in *New York Film Review* compared it to a previous version: "The last one [1938] was [a] ruddy and generally cheerful affair, this one is spooky and somber for the most part . . . full of heavy discords and harsh sounds of misery. And when the ghostly apparitions enter, it is a bit on the overpowering side.... In short, what we have in this rendition of Dickens' sometimes misunderstood [A Christmas] 'Carol,' is the accurate comprehension of a shabby soul." In short, it was an adult "art picture" that asked a lot of questions of the Dickens source material.[28] In London, *Monthly Film Bulletin* felt, somewhat begrudgingly, that "the film as a whole lacks style," and in its "recreation of the atmosphere of story in dramatic terms, it cannot be said that Brian Desmond Hurst has been altogether successful."[29]

More recent critics have taken to *Scrooge*, accepting the dissonance between its literary source and the fifties film. Anthony Quinn picked out a quality in film that he claimed worked against the original story: "Dickens was sentimental but in director Brian Desmond Hurst's adaptation it becomes a magnificent Gothic nightmare, steeped in shadows and a terrible remorse."[30] These more recent critical comments point up how, like Cavalcanti, it draws on gothic tropes in reworking English Victorian material for a post-1945 austerity. Hurst's own unorthodox spiritual beliefs—Ulster Presbyterian convert and local lore meets "bells and smells" Continental Roman Catholicism—resonate in the scenes of ghostly visitation, past hurts are revisited in the present; dispossession and commercial rapine; disputes over property/business ownership; Scrooge's enormous cavernous but empty house; the absence of the familial; and his own traumatic childhood. What might be termed an Ulster gothic sensibility was fused with Hurst's humanism to arrive at his own belief in personal spiritual redemption that he formally acknowledged in entering the Catholic faith in the late 1940s.

In contrast, Sir Christopher Frayling, in a DVD essay on the film, firmly locates the film less in spirituality and more in the social democratic moment of Clement Attlee's Labour government, beaten by a Tory electoral victory in 1951. Although Patrick Maume has inferred Hurst's Labour Party connection, and Robbins recalls firsthand mischievous quips about "voting Labour,"[31] there is little evidence that Hurst had a strong political bent for socioeconomic reform. But as we have seen in chapter 3, he did publicly acknowledge Harold Wilson's role as chair of the Board of Trade in its state support of British film. Frayling offers a concise, well-illustrated argument, drawing on a range of literary, visual, and cultural references to show how the adaptation adroitly commented on the key debates about social welfare that were at the heart of the election debates between Labour and Conservatives in 1951. It was a dark film for austere times and not, as we have seen, a family film, as its US distributors had wanted. For Frayling, Hurst is wrongly assessed as a "second-eleven type of filmmaker [or just] a very competent jobbing director without much personality," arguing instead that *Scrooge* is a "major film." To Frayling, what is striking about Hurst's film is not that it was actively advocating a "Dickens for our time" but providing a cinematic collision of expectations, "between dark Dickens and bright Dickens," showing how the novel's "after life" has got mixed up with earlier cinematic versions.[32] He rightly adverts to the ghostly, otherworldly aspects of *A Christmas Carol*, which, with the dark, expressively lit sets, oddly angled stairs, long shadows, distortions, special effects, sinister music, and grotesque characters offer a disturbing vision of London that ran at odds to the sentimental, "chocolate box" Dickens.[33]

4.6. *Scrooge*, 1951: "The air filled with phantoms." Screengrab.

Frayling draws attention to a brief screen moment when, through an open window, Marley's ghost shows Scrooge a portal to another dimension that also might be a visualization of Scrooge's tortured conscience. Frayling argues that the vision of the spirits of those who failed to do good in the world and have now lost the power ever to do so is like "one of the circles of hell" from Dante's *Divine Comedy*.[34] It is a filmic special effect but carries spiritual impetus explained by Hurst's Irish upbringing, a belief in the supernatural spirit world, and a saturation in religious art, particularly Catholic iconography. What it is not is a statement about Catholic social teaching or a socialist political program. But as an example of British postwar noir, *Scrooge* does make a cinematic statement about the moral dilemma of economic austerity and social deprivation. Britain's more recent past and the pressing contemporary position of Britain in a world context is something with which Hurst grappled in a group of films spanning the middle years of the decade.

WAR, COLONY, AND REVOLUTION:
MALTA STORY, *SIMBA*, AND *THE BLACK TENT*

In the 1950s, war films and colonial adventures dominated British cinema screens. Collectively, the nation was undertaking the process of working through the historical legacy of empire and imperialism through its public screens. This process was of course merely what was taking place at a political and diplomatic level in Parliament, the United Kingdom's relations with its territories in the commonwealth, and with the world's emergent powers. Riding on the success of *Scrooge*, Hurst secured a further Rank contract, and he contributed serviceable titles to these genres, working with some of British cinema's leading actors and up-and-coming talent, including David Niven, Alec Guinness, Dirk Bogarde, Flora Robson, Muriel Pavlow, and Virginia McKenna. He had to grapple with the challenges of shooting on location in Africa and the Mediterranean. In some senses, he can be seen to be building on the previous decade's "war work" in the affirmative, celebratory mode discussed in chapter 3. But what is particularly interesting for this study is to explore how Hurst's Ulster exilic status is accented post-1948 by his established position within the industry and with these particular topics to produce films that offer a more anxious, ambivalent, or reactionary set of values.

In the first of a trio of war films with overseas locations, *Malta Story* (1953), titled "A Bright Flame" in development, was originally to be directed by Thorold Dickinson. But Rank offered the project to Hurst, who initially turned it down but was then persuaded by John Ford to take it on.[35] Hurst was ably equipped to handle the material and the particular demands of the script with its producer, the South African–born Peter de Sarigny. Although based at Pinewood Studios, much of the film was shot on Malta and on monochrome stock, mixed with wartime archive footage, lending a historic, or at least documentary, feel to it. The film proved to be popular box office in Britain for the reasons rather gushingly listed by a trade promotion review: "Gripping sea and aerial war melodrama, finely acted and authentically staged. A worthy tribute to bomb-scarred Malta. . . . History and action-packed screen entertainment in one, the

4.7. *Malta Story*, 1953. Theatrical release poster. Press book. © Rank/Carleton. Supplied courtesy of the Ronald Grant Archive.

film never lets up and is bound to bring prestige and immense kudos to the universal box-office."³⁶

The plot centered on Flight Lieutenant Peter Ross (Alec Guinness), an archaeologist working as an RAF pilot in an aerial photography unit in transit to Cairo in 1942. On a refueling stopover mid-Mediterranean, he gets stranded on the British-occupied island of Malta, undergoing a prolonged aerial bombing siege from Axis forces. Far from comfortable in uniform, Ross is seconded by his commanding officer Frank (Jack Hawkins) to the Allied Command to use his photography skills to identify the sources of German air forces and help relieve Malta. Ross becomes romantically involved with Maria (Muriel Pavlow), one of the locals working at the air base, and they become engaged and try to plan a future amid the chaos. The script was based on an idea by Thorold Dickinson and worked up into a story by William Fairchild, who cowrote the screenplay with Nigel Balchin. Its exteriors were shot on location by Hurst, with Robert Krasker as his chief cinematographer, to produce the film's solid authenticity, assisted by the local civilian population, who reenacted air raids and other aspects of life under siege, much as Hurst had done in *Theirs Is the Glory*. Effective use is made of Valletta's Old Town, underground catacombs, the Neolithic site of Ħaġar Qim, and the harbor area. Hurst produced one of his trademark "tableaux" sequences of the arrival of the badly damaged SS *Ohio*, its injured crew, and the onlooking crowds of Maltese inhabitants at the quay and on the hillsides with reactive close-ups of lined, weary faces.

Indeed, the film was made to pay tribute to the fortitude of the Maltese people and to the brave sacrifice of the combined forces of the RAF and the British navy and army as well as the assistance of the US Navy a generation before. Connected by interest (archaeology) and sharing one of T. E. Lawrence's aliases, the central character of "Ross"—in Guinness's low-key performance—is quizzical, detached and donnish, and decidedly unheroic in performing his duty of spotting enemy supply trains.³⁷ Guinness, along with Dirk Bogarde, offered new postwar versions of masculinity for cinema audiences that were at variance to certainties offered in wartime portrayals, typified by the "meritocratic professional officer" played by Hawkins.³⁸

4.8.1. *Malta Story*: solemn arrival. Screengrab.

By contrast, at one point Ross asks Maria's mother (Flora Robson) if the Maltese might hate the British "for being here, bringing all this on you," which she denies. Her son, Giuseppe (Nigel Stock), we learn in a subplot, is a Maltese who is arrested for spying for the Italians and trying to disrupt the Allied relief convoy. He denies he is a traitor and confides to his mother: "The British are finished. They cannot win. Why should Malta go on being crucified when a few bold strokes would save us all?" "You chose your side," she blesses him, before she leaves him to be executed. Ross's disinterestedness and the brief moment of Giuseppe's dissidence give way to the overriding sentiment of the film, hammered home by the overinsistent film score. In the final sequence, Ross is detailed by the AOC to fly out solo at high risk to find an enemy convoy. Having done his job, inevitably he is shot down by enemy fighters, leaving Maria to contemplate a different future but justifying the film's honorable tribute: "We spent ourselves for the general good."

4.8.2. *Malta Story*: Maltese endurance. Screengrab.

4.8.3. *Malta Story*: Alec Guinness's quiet heroics. Screengrab.

While this type of film might still have worked with audiences in Britain, reviewers in the United States found the material and its treatment more questionable. "Clem" in *Variety* noted the star power of Guinness, likens it to *The Cruel Sea* (1953), but adds: "It is handled in a grimly realistic but over dramatic style. Camera work is excellent. . . . Supporting players are uniformly good while the direction is unerringly aimed to reveal the human and devastating side of war [and he] predicts 'universal appeal.'"[39]

But for another US reviewer, neither topic nor treatment connected with contemporary cinemagoers for whom Malta and the war were too distant and the cast overly stereotyped. Even though he praised Krasker's "lensing of rubbled Valletta": "This type of war story no longer packs the big punch. It's like watching a slightly aged film with its characters out of relation to the present time. . . . Not even this cast can make up for the date of the product." Of Guinness and Hurst's technique in directing him, the same reviewer noted shrewdly: "He isn't given much chance to emote and his performance is therefore slightly disappointing. In fact Hurst appeared to be satisfied with posing him mostly looking with a half-smile scanning various objects about him."[40]

The second of Hurst's fifties war trio was a Rank star vehicle with an African setting and a strong topical postcolonial conflict narrative, scripted by John Baines. *Simba* (1955) featured the strained relationship between Howard (Dirk Bogarde) and Mary (Virginia McKenna) as new, young settler farmers in Kenya during the unfolding anticolonial unrest in which Mau Mau guerrillas and political activists campaigned for independence from Britain between 1952 and 1960.

Wendy Webster has noted that the 1950s saw attempts by British studios to "modernise imperial identities" under the pressure of challenges to the idea of racialized boundaries, intermarriage, and the arrival of colonial migrants to Britain, the rebranding of "empire" to "commonwealth," and as a response to US global power. Images of rugged, adventurer British white men were softened by the introduction of white women to narratives, including heterosexual romance and marriage.[41] So in its national, racial, and gender politics, Hurst's film was thus highly topical.

But as Christine Geraghty shows, the film vainly attempts to articulate a reformist British position on Kenya that its narrative, mise-en-scène,

4.9. *Simba*: Mau Mau conflict in 1950s Kenya, 1955. © Rank/Carleton. Still supplied courtesy of the Ronald Grant Archive.

and central performances cannot reconcile "the attempt to accommodate the liberal discourse of the new Commonwealth within generic conventions that are strongly linked to the films of empire."[42] One can note the irony of Hurst's position, an ex-British soldier, an Ulsterman with broadly Irish nationalist sympathies, making a film during an anticolonial guerrilla war.[43] This paradox was something about which Hurst was acutely aware as he scouted locations and shot a lot of stock establishing footage and medium- to long-shot material.

Robbins writes that Hurst recalled challenging a Dubliner, a commissioned officer serving in the Kenyan police force, about the treatment of the Kikuyu population, comparing the Kenyan political situation to that of the Irish War of Independence and the British auxiliary forces known as "Black and Tans": "'When the people in the caged lorries were Irish Republicans.' The captain turned abruptly and marched away."[44]

4.10. *Simba*: British detention camp in Kenya. Screengrab.

As noted by Esler Smith, Hurst actually captured the barbed-wire compounds of the British detention camps on camera in one shot, and the film makes quite clear the terror and counterterrorist activities of the Mau Mau and the British.[45] Hurst's casting of the Belfast actor Joseph Tomelty in a minor but significant role as the film's moderate figure, Dr. Hughes, does allow us to see an Ulster exilic Irishness dimension imbued in this film that goes unremarked by Geraghty and is undeveloped by Esler Smith. As tension rises within the white settler-farmer community, Drummond (Donald Sinden), the police chief, holds a public meeting about how to deal with Mau Mau attacks, one of which had seen Alan's brother murdered. Making a significant intervention, Dr. Hughes berates the increasingly belligerent calls for counterinsurgency violence:

> I've got a family too; my stake in this place is every bit as big as any of yours—if not bigger. *I don't want my grandchildren to grow up in a country where they must wear a gun all day and sleep with it at night under the pillows.* That's what'll happen if you people carry on like a lot of hooligans.

...

[One settler shouts out: "you can't reason with the Kukes."] I know, I know, you can't reason with the Mau Mau, but you can with the Africans—and you must, otherwise you will force them over to the enemy. You must reason with them. You must make friends of these people, as otherwise you'll find yourself not fighting a few thousand fanatics, but five million angry people. You'll all be killed. Mau Mau must be stamped out, yes, but we've got to think of the future; we must use our heads—not lose them.... [He continues over rising disquiet] Give yourselves a chance; we're not the only people with a stake in this country. We must learn to live together side by side, black and white, and make a better world. There's no other way out.[46]

Hughes/Tomelty's lines about his children and "keeping guns under pillows at night" had a contemporary resonance and premonition closer to home in Northern Ireland as the IRA geared up for a low-level campaign of violence (1956–62) against the continued existence of the Irish border. A former Irish soldier in the British army, with colonial experience in the Middle East and Africa (1914–19), who left Belfast at the height of the Troubles in 1920, Hurst understood precisely the unsettling ambivalence of being Ulster exilic and being implicated in an empire's counterinsurgency measures.

The film received a broadly warm reception in press reviews. "Mr Hurst has directed soundly," and *Simba* was considered "a thought provoking and occasionally disturbing film," "a credit to Pinewood treating an important theme with dignity as well as excitement," an "outstanding British picture—although the red-hot political problem is handled with dignity it pulls no punches," and that its "direction was as sensitive as the script."[47] The *Daily Telegraph* noted the poignancy of the closing shot of the orphaned child: "The little Black boy toddling towards the camera—is *he* East Africa's only hope?"

The third of Hurst's overseas films from this busy period is based on a short-story and first-draft screenplay by Robin Maugham, *The Black Tent* (1956), which was filmed on location in Libya, London, and the English countryside.[48] The film opens and closes with contrasting images of

4.11. *Simba*: "Is he East Africa's only hope?" Screengrab.

"home": a colonel's English country house and gardens and a Bedouin tent in the desert. Charles Holland (Donald Sinden) travels to Libya to find out the truth of his army captain brother's disappearance during 1941 in North Africa. In the desert, he locates Sheik Salem (Andre Morell), whose family had sheltered the injured David Holland (Anthony Steel) from the Germans. However, Holland had fallen in love and married Mabrouka (Anna Marie Sandri), the sheik's beautiful daughter, and had a son, Daoud. In the final six minutes of the film, the teenage and very blond, blue-eyed Daoud is confronted by a moral dilemma. His choice is to "return" to England to claim his rightful inheritance, house, and considerable wealth or remain in the black tents of his grandfather's family, who puts this stark situation to him: "No man can serve two tribes, therefore you must choose between them."

Even if Geoffrey Unsworth's cinematography is admirable, the scenario, the dialogue, the casting, and the camera's exoticization of land, people, and culture carry all the hallmarks of a cinematic "orientalism" typical for the period. Written, produced, and directed by Maugham, William MacQuitty, and Hurst, respectively, this blend of Ulster Protestant and English aristocratic sensibilities explains how the film's increasingly dated worldview and production values combined in popular cinema during this decade. The casting of Donald Pleasance as Ali, the devious Arab guide for Charles, and the ridiculousness of Daoud's public school accent (interestingly, played by a child actor by the name of Terence Sharkey), ought to be understood as stress points in the film's representational limits that were symptomatic of a culture under pressure to reconcile itself to new political realities of Arabic resurgence and modern nation-state formation.[49] The film turns on Daoud's dilemma, which is either to disown his genetic and cultural "Arab" inheritance through his mother and grandfather or embrace his legal entitlement to the estate, land, and wealth of his "Anglo" father, the blond war hero, David.[50] The boy burns his father's will, thus choosing the culture of his upbringing rather than legal entitlement.

4.12. *Black Tent*, 1956: Daoud chooses Arabic heritage. © Rank/Carleton. Still supplied courtesy of the Ronald Grant Archive.

The script in its earlier versions provided a touching scene in flashback in the aftermath of the impressive desert tank battle. An injured Holland comes across a mortally wounded German who, knowing that he is dying, proffers his water flask, aware that he will not need it. The two soldiers find a moment's camaraderie, finding out each other's name and what they did before the war, and David stays to comfort the German as he passes away. Bryan Forbes, then a contract scriptwriter for Rank and an actor, had been flown over to help with rewrites to Robin Maugham's script, but was also cast in the role of the German, a scene that was filmed but did not make the final cut.[51] It hints at a subtly drawn scene about a moment of emotional connection and tenderness between men in extreme conflict. It would have added another texture to the film that, apart from its ready deployment of racial and national stereotypes, is not without value for some of its nuanced dilemmas that it struggles to portray, notably that of Daoud's mixed-race identity.

The agency indicated at the end of the film is subtly different from Maugham's original story, where it is Sheik Salem, not his mixed-race grandson, who destroys the paper-legal lineage in a fire, causing Charles to exclaim: "You've destroyed his chance of freedom."[52] The incidence of interracial marriages in England in the 1950s and 1960s and extramarital infidelities is indicated in deceptively casual exchanges between Charles and Baring (Anthony Bushell) early in the film, the latter a Foreign Office contact in Tripoli referred to as a "quinine queer" in the film's production notes.[53] The complex, unspoken questions of plural cultural identities arising from the diasporic exile are articulated in an indirect fashion by the script and the visual qualities of the mise-en-scène, with few London-set films of the fifties taking on racial narratives.[54]

In the final of Hurst's midfifties clutch of films to be discussed here, *Dangerous Exile* (1957), the exile in question is a boy-king, Louis XVII of France (Richard O'Sullivan). Despite the distancing layers of historical period, the scenario's flaky narrative does find resonance within the context of Britain's new "Elizabethan age" and its monarchic commonwealth. In the opening scenes of the film set in France, the Duke de Beauvais (Louis Jourdan) has sacrificed his own son's life as a decoy to help the royal heir escape being murdered by republicans. Escaping by balloon, the heir-prince lands in Wales, and he is taken in by the sympathetic aristocratic Lady Fell (Martita Hunt) and her—oddly Anglo-American—niece Virginia Traill (Belinda Lee). The orphan Louis develops an oedipal attraction for his surrogate mother, and she becomes the romantic interest of a contest between the eligible English captain Ogden (Frederick Leister) and the Gallic charms of Beauvais. This arrangement of character-ciphers and an attempt by French assassins to obliterate the royal line pits two kinds of imperfect Republicanism against the "heartfelt" and dutiful patriotism of the young king.

4.13. *Dangerous Exile*, 1957. © Rank/Carleton. Still supplied courtesy of the Ronald Grant Archive.

4.14. *Dangerous Exile*: Theatrical poster. © Rank/Carleton. Supplied courtesy of the Ronald Grant Archive.

Like *Black Tent*, the focus of such dilemmas of allegiance falls on the coming generation in the figure of the boy-king, who—despite his resolve to return to reestablish the monarchy—would like to remain in Wales where his "American" stand-in mother would marry the dashing French duke. The closing scene of the boy framed by his "adoptive" parents bears similarly inadequate resolution to final frame close-up at the *Simba* on the face of the orphaned Joshua, a Kenyan boy and mixed-race Daoud. Thus, these films mobilize melodrama as a popular genre to work through political crises. They provide an imagined line of monarchical continuity for British viewers that were witnessing their own grandee class reeling from the diplomatic, military, and domestic political crises over Abdel Nasser's rise to power that eventually brought down the British prime minister, Anthony Eden, in 1956, known as the Suez Crisis.

This clutch of films made extensive use of location shooting for their internationally set story lines, as Rank attempted to recapture the glory days of the "empire films" in the 1930s and defend its international market share.[55] Writing three years after Suez as an independent producer, Hurst publicly attacked the idea of disbanding the United Kingdom's National Film Finance Corporation, arguing that if independently produced film output were adversely affected, "their place in British and overseas cinemas would be taken by American films, insisting on the American way of life." He developed his point: "We just cannot afford to lose the opportunity which the cinema provides, to show in some way *our British way of life*, which is not without distinction, culture and integrity."[56] If a shift from "English values" to "*our* British way of life" occurred between Hurst's letters to the *Times* between 1951 and 1959, he clearly understood the importance of "soft power" exercised through cinema on international screens. His direct identification with "Britishness" remained undiminished throughout the post-1948 period, as did his professional standing within its cinema industry.

THE DIRECTOR'S CRAFT: *FILMS AND FILMING* (1957)

Within the context of that film business, Hurst was invited to contribute an essay in a "behind-the-scenes" series in the popular journal *Films and Filming*.[57] In it Hurst gives an account of the work of a film director based on his recent experiences of "making film in a hot climate," writes about the nature of filmmaking in the practical conditions of the Rank Organisation and refers in his examples to *Simba*. Hurst notes the difficulty of writing about practice: "Painting, like directing, is something one does and how one does it is not easy to describe." He also stresses the importance of having enthusiasm for the film's subject as well as noting that "the essentials for a good story or script [are] originality of theme, pace of presentation and interesting and believable characters." Hurst indicates his awareness of broader shifts in audience tastes, underlying finance models, and markets beyond just Britain: "We have to keep in mind the overseas markets which help to finance production at home. The days of the typically *British* picture for British audiences are over. Today a film has to appeal to as many nationalities as possible" (27).

The article provides its readers with a clear idea of the routine processes of planning, production, and technical requirements in filmmaking, written in an accessible, conversational tone ("You see, all the scenes in one set must be filmed before the set is 'struck'"). What is conveyed is that Hurst as a director has to understand exactly the roles of all the rest of the crew (lighting, sound recording, director of photography, editor) and that the director "be capable of understanding these skills, to feel how the members of his unit are approaching their work as the film progresses" (32).

Hurst also offers insights into how a director coaxes a performance from "the artists" (actors) and the importance, given out-of-sequence shooting, of matching the components of a scene not just technically but "dramatically" (27). Hurst isolates this part as "probably the most important single job with which the director has to cope. It is only the director who has complete command of this facet of production" (27). Hurst explains well the pressures exerted on the director as the shoot proceeds, inwardly calculating the demands of production schedule and costs against the quality of the work achieved minute by minute that will appear up on the screen: "There is a constant mental tension in my mind as I see each 'take' recorded by the camera. Shall we do another before moving on to the next set-up; or were the second and the last good enough to print?" (32).

The article itself evidences Hurst's practical knowledge, professionalism, and modesty in the role as director and his awareness of the changing conditions within the industry that was his business. As a snapshot of his own career arc, in retrospect, the year 1957 probably was the point at which his fame tilted on its fulcrum. However, at that time, he remained ambitious in actively seeking new film projects and was alert to opportunities to rekindle interests in Ireland as well as Britain.

A "NATIVE FILM INDUSTRY" AND FOUR PROVINCES PICTURES

In the previous chapter, we saw that Hurst, buoyed by the success of *Theirs Is the Glory*, felt confident enough to approach Sean Lemass with an offer to assist the Irish Free State in establishing its own viable film studio base in Ireland. As we saw, for various reasons, this offer was rejected, Fíanna Fáil lost power in 1948, and a studio was not built. However, during the mid-1950s, Hurst became involved with a small, Dublin-based, independent film production company called Four Provinces, Ltd.[58] It would be the third time that Hurst would be involved in attempting to establish an Irish-production base, but its output was modest, and an Irish state-funded studio at Ardmore was set up by rival producers in 1958 who had found the favor of Lemass. Indeed, a national film studio and also a television service were the subject of protracted debates throughout the 1950s in Ireland.[59] In fact, Lemass had returned to his old ministerial post when his party was returned to government in 1951–54 and again in 1957–59 when he also became taoiseach and was seen as a modernizing force.

In the interim, though, Labour Minister for Industry and Commerce William Norton had set up an "investigating committee to probe the possibilities of a native film industry" whose members listed (in November 1955), among others, Killanin and Michael Scott (both of Four Provinces); cinematographer George Fleischmann, a German who had adopted Ireland; members of the Irish Film Society; and Tom Sheehy of the Irish tourist board, Bord Faílte.[60] It is notable that Hurst is not mentioned, but it was probably because of his commitments with Rank working on *Simba* and *The Black Tent*. "The secret film inquiry," as it was dubbed by the *Sunday Express*, had met first on August 3 and went on to produce a report under the auspices of the National Film Institute of Ireland (NFII) a year later, titled *Report on the Means of Fostering the General Development of the Film Industry in Ireland* (dated September 1956).[61] This report, referencing European models and the National Film Board of Canada, argued for the establishment of an Irish Film Board and laid the groundwork for the setting up of a national film studio that would become Ardmore Studios in 1958.[62] It emphasized in its early drafts the establishment of film laboratories, editing facilities, and a stress on shorts and documentaries but an openness to make foreign-funded features in Ireland.[63]

While Hurst was legally one of four company directors of Four Provinces, his active role within it or work on the three short films and *The Rising of the Moon* (1957), directed by Ford, appears to have been negligible in this period. Hurst was busy, and Ford had eye problems in 1953. Hurst wrote to Killanin that he felt that the long-held plan to establish a film studio would not happen anytime soon.[64] Despite the demands of international location filming for Rank in the mid-1950s, he was, however, corresponding with Killanin from 1957 about adapting Synge's *Playboy* for the screen, to be produced by Four Provinces. That project would take five years of writing, fund-raising, and filming before it came to fruition. We explore that film and note his other unmade projects later in this chapter. But for the time being, Hurst continued to take on work that explored the changes taking place within England's professional middle class and a low-comedy farce about the "sex" wars within married life.[65]

"WHITE CORRIDOR" MELODRAMA:
BEHIND THE MASK (1958)

Behind the Mask is a hospital-set medical drama that is an unjustly overlooked film in the Hurst oeuvre and deserves comment. It was welcome to see its 2012 rerelease as a DVD from a cleaned-up print because it typifies what Hurst could do well on-screen with a half-decent script, talented artists, and crew. His treatment of the story line is informed by his knowledge of "middlebrow" British cinema, as well as the social life of professional classes in England, and is based on John Rowan Wilson's novel, originally titled *The Pack*.[66] *Behind the Mask* is emblematic of the epochal shifts quietly taking place in Britain in the 1950s, socially and culturally. Hurst had, remember, made *Irish Hearts*—a medical drama set in modernizing Ireland in the mid-1930s (see chapter 2). Here again through the prism of the medical profession, the film presents itself as a portrait of generational change, in technology, practice, and ethics among the surgeon elite of a hospital. But it also dramatizes the pressures and boundaries of behavior within the middle class more widely. Parallel to the main theme of class, there is the presence of the troubled Polish anesthetist Romek, the "foreigner"—played by Austrian actor Carl Möhner—who unsettles the narrative with a traumatic past that revisits him. We learn that he is a survivor of the Dachau death camp, marked out by his tattooed arm camp number as a victim, a displaced person, a Holocaust exile. This character is a significant alteration from the novel's

4.15. Doctor's dilemma: *Behind the Mask*, 1958. Courtesy of Studiocanal Films. Still supplied courtesy of the Ronald Grant Archive.

original scenario that featured a merely "exotic" Spanish character as a disruptive figure.

At the level of sexuality and social roles, *Behind the Mask* rehearses an interesting battle for Pamela Benson Gray's (Vanessa Redgrave) love and loyalty. This fight is between Philip Selwood (Tony Britton)—her fiancé, the newly qualified surgeon, and soon to be son-in-law—and her father, the imposing, eminent consultant Sir Arthur Benson Gray (Michael Redgrave), playing his own daughter's screen father. Romek's past experience has led to a drug dependency and an inability to form normal emotional relations with women, and he falls victim to a female blackmailer. The crux of the film is that Selwood's brilliant surgical skills with a new heart technique, filmed on the hospital's new closed-circuit teaching television, cover up Sir Arthur's faltering abilities in older age. However, Selwood is then caught up in an official inquiry into the death of the patient in recovery because he was busy saving the unfortunate Romek from an overdose. Sir Arthur tries to pull the wool over the eyes of the committee of inquiry, using his seniority to protect his own reputation and trying to save his daughter from marrying a struck-off doctor. Under questioning, Selwood has to contradict Sir Arthur, thus exposing his father-in-law's unethical practice. In the film's denouement, however, Sir Arthur retires, Selwood is offered a new job back in the hospital, and he marries Pamela. This ending is a distinct, upbeat rewriting of the novel source's text, which sees Selwood excluded from the profession and emigrating.[67] Romek is seen going off to a clinic to recover. *Behind the Mask* does maintain its dramatic tensions, and the "televised" surgery sequences are well shot. Finally, Hurst's shows great sensitivity to the male-dominated environment of the working lives of surgeons and the homosociality of the doctors' common room, but the film also captures the self-protecting behavior of the profession (see Oswold Pettiford, played by Miles Malleson) and its fierce competitiveness in the exchanges between Sir Arthur, Isherwood (played by Niall MacGinnis), Crabtree (Ian Bannen), and Selwood in some small but telling scenes.

Reviewers recognized the serious intent of the film, its "rather alarming picture of hospital politics," and noted the quality and depth of the

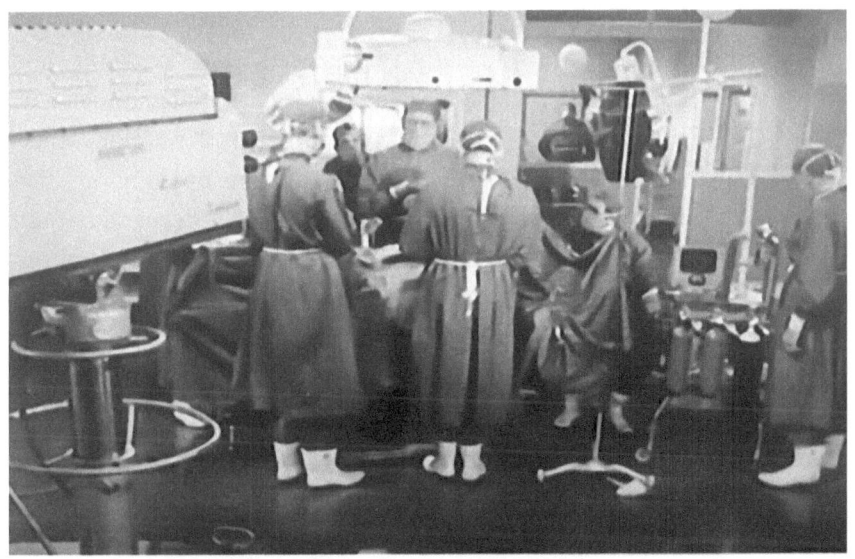

4.16.1. *Behind the Mask*: modern televised surgery. Screengrab.

4.16.2. *Behind the Mask*: male domain, the doctors' common room. Screengrab.

acting talent and that Hurst's direction had made "the dramatic rituals of the [operating] theatre unusually impressive."[68] For the *Daily Cinema*, Hurst "had never done a better job; scripting is notably literate and moral values are most praiseworthy. There are elegant interiors where required."[69] But the *Monthly Film Bulletin* felt after its opening promise, the film "failed to make its point, much less to explore the deeper questions of power corruption at which it hints."[70] *Variety* noted the film's "impressive performances," saying that it was a "sound booking" prospect, and Hurst's direction had "dignity."[71] The review went on to especially praise the heart-operation closed-circuit sequence as "uncommonly revealing," Robert Krasker's photography, and William Kellner's design as "faultless."

Following this film, Hurst allowed himself to be persuaded to take on *His and Hers* (1960), one of his rare forays into comedic film, a flimsy farce about gender relations starring Terry Thomas. Hurst knew himself that it was a poor script and a weak film, and he regretted it. It was also out of touch with political and cultural shifts of the period, but one reviewer commented that anyone "interested in the hysterical split between sex and marriage in the mind of the English middle class should not ignore the field of our more awful comedies."[72]

Film, theater, and the new medium of television meant Britain underwent a radical change between 1956 and 1963: new writers brought working-class lives, stories from beyond the metropolitan world, and new regional accents to the stage and to the screen. As the next section outlines, Hurst continued to try to develop his own projects with a view to produce some of them rather than direct. But the style of making film that he practiced was increasingly falling out of favor and looked dated, and younger talents were pushing forward around him. Not only that, but contemporaries like Roy Ward Baker had been getting projects such as *Jacqueline* (1956) that might have been ideal subject matter for him. This Catherine Cookson novel set in Belfast is about a shipyard worker suffering from vertigo and alcoholism. Maybe it was too close to home for Hurst. However, one Irish playwright's seminal play had been in development with Four Provinces since the mid-1950s. Opportunity and circumstance coincided that allowed him to complete that project.

4.17. *His and Hers*: poster, 1960. Supplied courtesy of the Ronald Grant Archive.

THE LONG GOOD FINALE?
THE PLAYBOY OF THE WESTERN WORLD (1962)

What became the last of Hurst's films to make it to the screen in the early sixties took him back to Ireland. It also took him back to an Irish playwright whose work he had first adapted at the start of his career. *The Playboy of the Western World* (1907), J. M. Synge's controversial masterpiece, "the *Hamlet* of the Irish dramatic tradition," was a play that, some argue, presaged a radical Irish liberation that failed to materialize.[73] At the time, protests in the auditorium at the Abbey Theatre greeted its staging. Some, mainly middle-class nationalists, objected to the candid, cruel tragicomedy of rural life in Mayo that Synge presented to them. Hurst's screen version, as we will see, caused a minor controversy of its own at the time of its Irish release, attracted quite severe criticism, and has not aged well, though some younger academics have tried to rehabilitate it.[74] Its relevance to the present study is as the product of the exilic imagination of its writer/director and production company. We can examine how the cultural politics of reviving a "classic" played out with audiences, critics, and a modernizing Irish establishment in the 1960s as it sought to project a new national image. Filmed on location in Kerry, the film became the chance moment of a familial reconnection for Hurst whose niece was honeymooning there at the time, but in an interview at the end of the decade in the satirical magazine *Punch*, Hurst was confirmed in his status as a "London exile."

Synge's play, set in a lonesome "country public house or shebeen," shows how a shy, vacuous young man called Christy Mahon enters a community and tells Pegeen, the pub owner's daughter, and the assembled locals that he has killed his own father with a blow from a loy (shovel). His "daring" story is retold within the community, and Christy is lionized as a hero; he displaces Pegeen's safe-choice fiancé, Shawn Keogh, and beats off advances from the local girls and the seductive older woman, Widow Quinn. But Old Mahon is *not* dead; he enters, bloody-headed, at the start of act 3. Things rapidly unravel. Pegeen has fallen badly for Christy's heroic exploits, but when Old Mahon confronts his son in front of the community and Christy kills his father off-stage outside, the locals turn on Christy, torture, and tie him up to take him to the police. In the midst of this scene, Old Mahon returns to the stage alive. Father and son team up ("We'll have great times from this out telling stories of the villainy of Mayo, and the fools is here"). But now Christy is a changed man and in charge ("Go on, you."); he looks forward ("I'll go a romancing through a romping lifetime") as father and son exit. What of Pegeen and the locals? Here the pathos kicks in: her fiancé wants things to go back as they were; she is distraught: "PEGEEN. [Hitting him a box (blow) on the ear] Quit my sight. [Putting her shawl over her head and breaking into a wild lamentation]. Oh, my grief, I've lost him surely. I've lost the only Playboy of the Western World" (167).

It is a seminal moment in Irish drama, offering perhaps *the* major female role in Irish theater, and the play has challenged actresses, directors, and audiences down the years. Marginalized by nationalists during his lifetime, Synge was canonized in his critical afterlife. Hurst well understood the weight of expectation in trying to translate what is a brilliantly inventive theater piece to the cinema screen. The film was conceived as part of a slate of films to be made by Four Provinces Films, a company that had been set up on the back of John Ford's phenomenal critical and box-office success with *The Quiet Man* (1952) and in the absence, at that point, of a state-financed film studio facility. Ford directed *The Rising of the Moon* (aka *Three Leaves of the Shamrock*), a curious three-part film released in 1957 to tempt future investors and test the market. Hurst praised Ford for the railway carriage scene in *A Minute's Wait* (one of the films), but was acutely aware that Irish audiences might well be begrudgingly critical of the film's whimsical nature.[75] Four Provinces at least offered itself as a platform for Irish production with valuable US distribution channels via Republic Pictures.

As we have seen, however, others were vying to secure backing for a studio and to monopolize film production in Ireland. In the end, this role went to Louis Ellmann and Emmet Dalton, who set up Ardmore Studios with state financing and the close support of Sean Lemass. As it worked out, Ardmore operated as much as a facility for hire by visiting foreign-backed productions as for supporting Irish-generated productions during its troubled early life in the 1960s. Four Provinces was itself a hybrid company registered in Dublin and London; its directorship was a motley

4.18. Hurst directs his last film, *Playboy*, July 1961. © Kennelly Archive, RLR002.

crew of Irish Americans, Ulster Irish in London, a Dublin architect, and an Irish earl.[76] In a sense, this situation speaks volumes for the dispersed nature of Irish cinema in this period. However, even though there was no formal film board in place, producers seeking financing for production in Ireland could apply to the Irish Film Finance Corporation (IFFC).

Hurst's *Playboy* took five years to develop, finance, script, and cast, but Hurst had to shoot it in only five weeks in the summer of 1961.[77] Early on Denis Johnston was discussed as a possible screenwriter, but perhaps because of their somewhat acrimonious past (see chapter 2), Hurst wrote the screenplay himself based on a treatment that he and Killanin had produced.[78] Their writing took place between the earl's ancestral home in Galway and Hurst's Belgravia flat.[79] Killanin and the other directors managed to raise a budget of £120,000, 85 percent of which came from the IFFC, with the rest from the UK's National Film Finance fund in London. With financing in place, the key issues for the production concerned finding a suitable location, getting the right cast, and, of course, how to adapt a one-set, three-act theater play written in Synge's idiomatic Hiberno-English stage language to a feature-length movie.

After much location scouting, it was decided it was better to shoot the film not in Mayo but on Inch Strand, in Kerry. Accounts of the production appeared in the Irish press, noting that an "authentic" Irish cottage was constructed in a matter of weeks at a photogenic spot later to be reused by David Lean in his *Ryan's Daughter* (1970). Hurst and Killanin had been corresponding on the *Playboy* project back in April 1957, discussing the title role and the key lead female of Pegeen Mike. One of the Four Provinces company directorate, actor Tyrone Power (Ty) appeared to be the favorite, but Richard Todd's name was also discussed. While finances were being finalized, Hurst was trying to schedule *Playboy* for a summer shoot (June) and was still pondering the casting of Christy, bizarrely considering Alec Guinness, Kenneth More, and upcoming "Irish" actors such as Patrick McGoohan or Sean Connery. Hurst's judgment on casting seems to be way off the mark and inaccurate (Connery is very much Scottish). But other comments from correspondence with Killanin show an alertness to the business of international distribution deals.

In the end, Hurst and Killanin did not get Tyrone Power as their leading man because he died suddenly on November 15, 1958. Killanin also wrote to John Ford (March 2, 1961) about some of his misgivings with the casting and the promotion of the film: "Brian Hearst [sic] has been over working on *The Playboy*. I think Siobhan is too old and it is very hard casting anyone opposite her. Anyhow, we are sitting down on the script. We can raise money here but the distribution will be extremely difficult and will have to be art house handled everywhere."[80]

McKenna had been cast in a Dublin theater production of the play in spring of 1961, directed by Shelah Richards, which then transferred to Belfast's Empire Theatre in May. Hurst went to Belfast to see it and, as the local press reported, had brought with him a print of *Riders to the Sea* (1935), which was screened at the Crumlin [Road] Theatre to an invited audience that included playwright Sam Thompson. McKenna was cast at this point, but the search for her "Playboy" continued, the role falling eventually to the relative unknown Gary Raymond.[81]

The film's release and distribution caused Four Provinces some difficulties. British Lion, which had a stake in its success, failed to release it in

4.19. Hurst directs Siobhan McKenna and Gary Raymond in *Playboy*. © Kennelly Archive, RLT005.

Britain, though it had been scheduled for July 1962. Although according to Hurst the film made its money back for the NFF in London, two years later it still had not had a British release.[82] At the time he wrote to Ford in the United States, complaining that British Lion had said it was "too arty" for release, with which Hurst disagreed. Hurst confessed in a letter to his mentor that although he liked some of it, most of it he did not. Citing the tight five-week shoot as a reason for its being undershot, he maintained that aesthetically it looked well.[83] In public, of course, such self-criticism evaporated.

After its world premiere in Dublin on April 25 at the Regal Cinema, it was widely reviewed. Hurst was interviewed live on Irish television's *Late Late Show*, with media reaction almost wholly negative or at best muted. Hurst recalled how he defended his casting of a young, inexperienced London-born Gary Raymond on the grounds of his Irish "gypsy" credentials and then went on the attack, decrying Dubliners as descendants of impure origins! Indeed, in press interviews during filming, Hurst had claimed his mother's Kerry origins as if they were significant in his treatment of

Synge's work.[84] The *Irish Times* critic, summing up well most of the press criticism, noted that the play's key features—"its comedy and the rhythm of its poetry—have been very much submerged," and substituted for "a sort of soft sentimentality which never appeared in Synge's original [and the rhythm of the language] has largely been sacrificed at the hands of a young actor . . . who should never have been cast in the part."[85]

Turning to the cinematographic aspects of the film, one reviewer felt "the colour is splendid and its photography, though seldom inspired (as in a shot of currachs rowing on to the beach: impressive despite the African war-drum soundtrack) is always good." The same reviewer felt in summary that the "direction is crisp and to the point, but the point is of his own screenplay . . . not the masterpiece. . . . This is not a bad film but, even in cinematic terms, has not the worth of its great original."

Hurst's memory of the film's reception was that it succeeded in quelling a typical Irish begrudgery toward successful returning exiles, and he recalled "how difficult it is to please the critical Irish about their classic authors."[86] His memory is not entirely borne out by the evidence of the newspaper reviews, but it sold tickets when it opened for the US premiere at New York's Fifty-Fifth Street "Playhouse" cinema the next spring, in March 1963, where it enjoyed a twenty-eight-week run.

It also opened the Boston Film Festival of 1963 and was screened in Edinburgh. Again, however, Hurst's assertion that it was "highly acclaimed" in US reviews does not completely stand up to scrutiny.[87] Anthony Slide notes that although the *New York Times* judged it a "ripe and rousing film," it was enjoyed by *Newsweek* and the *Herald Tribune* dubbed it "a lovely, lush offering . . . a darlin' film"; other US critics were underwhelmed by *Playboy*, again picking up on McKenna's age being mistaken casting.[88] Stanley Kauffman's blunt view, comparing play with film: "Nothing about the production compensates. Brian Desmond Hurst has directed dully. Even the outdoor scenes seem static. . . . Simple details are slovenly. . . . The cast is mediocre [and] Christy is so worried about his Irish accent, which keeps wearing thin, that he has little ebullience and vigor."[89]

Department of Foreign Affairs files show that Killanin had been very active in seeking to get very high-level support, "cooperation and coordination" from what was then called the Department of External Affairs (DEA)

4.20. *The Playboy*, 1962: the US press card. © Liam O'Leary Collection. Courtesy of the National Library of Ireland, Dublin, MS 50.000/326/23.

for the film's US premiere and release in Washington, DC, on March 28, 1963. He wrote to Hugh McCann explaining the IFFC's investment in the film, asking for support of the consul general in New York and the ambassador in Washington, stating: "The producers and distributors are more anxious if possible, for Mrs [Jackie] Kennedy (if the President [John F. Kennedy] is not able to do so himself) to attend the Washington premiere."[90]

The tart response from the Irish ambassador in Washington was to question the propriety of seeking the support of the US president for what was a commercial venture, albeit financially backed by the IFFC, and it also shows a sensitivity toward cultural marketing. A cable telegram from the ambassador back to Dublin reads: "Apart from industrial angle is film to be officially supported for cultural image. Stop. Would prefer White House first sponsorship of Our Lady Choral or other contemporary cultural manifestation of which we could be proud and which would not be primarily commercial as reference to industrial credit company suggests for this show."

Killanin's gambit failed. No promotional support was forthcoming, and two years later Four Provinces was snubbed diplomatically regarding Hurst's proposal that *Playboy* be the official Irish entry to the Moscow Film Festival, since Ireland "has no other feature film" to present. Hurst had put forward the film to the DEA via a personal letter to the Embassy of Ireland in London, just around the corner from his apartment. Meanwhile, on the other side of the Irish Sea, Siobhan McKenna had herself contacted the chairman of the Cultural Relations Committee (who also happened to be the Irish chief justice), a body responsible for disbursing public funding support, to try to persuade him to change the committee's decision not to accept Hurst's offer.

Tellingly, no one on the committee had seen the film, but the chair had contacted "a Mr Scott" for a view on the merits of the film. The secretary of the Cultural Relations Committee wrote to the DEA, advising them of their decision and a suggested course of action in replying to Hurst: "Mr Scott was of the same view as ourselves that this was not artistically a good film. He thought that the actor who played the part of Christy was poor and that Miss McKenna did not do justice to herself or the part of Pegeen. . . . Mr Scott would not favour our entering the film officially . . . and the Chair accepts this advice as final." The letter closes by instructing the ambassador to write to Hurst explaining "its view that the artistic merit of the film would not warrant entering it as an official entry for the Moscow Film Festival." A memo from the DEA tried a modicum of clumsy praise, saying "that the film was not so bad that its private entry by Hurst would 'let the country down.'"[91] This remark is a pretty damning indictment and must have upset Hurst. It is all the more telling that the Mr. Scott referred to was Hurst and Killanin's fellow company director Michael Scott! The Irish entry for Moscow was Patrick Carey's *Yeats Country*, a hauntingly beautiful sixteen-minute profile of the poet: Yeats won out over Synge in the "soft power" stakes. The episode stayed with Hurst and cannot but have fueled his sense of estrangement from the country that he had invested a considerable amount of his emotional attachment and creative effort.

Is *Playboy* such a poor film, and did it deserve the critical opprobrium? Brian McIroy has called it "a curious swansong."[92] Sanford Sternlicht gave a terse analysis of the film's many faults, critiquing the design, costume/hair, the acting of both leads, aspects of the script adaptation, and Seán Ó Riada's music track that was composed especially for the film. For Sternlicht, the age disparity between McKenna and Raymond made the supposed passionate attraction not only less credible but had, as he termed it, "the slight quality of noisome incest."[93] Some of the few positives in the production were the casting and performances of Widow Quinn, Old Mahon, and Michael (Elspeth March, Niall MacGinnis, and Liam Redmond, respectively), and although the cinematography was praised, the scenes of the sports were deemed too long and indulgent. Despite all the defects, Sternlicht still offered the kindly view that "the *Playboy* will do" and even said that it was better than *The Quiet Man*! More recent contemporary criticism has not been so forgiving of its faults: Adrian Frazier bluntly condemned it as "very bad both as a film, and as a version of *Playboy*."[94] I have to concur with this view. Press reports indicate that Hurst spent the rest of the 1960s and 1970s planning various projects, seeking to raise financing and trying to close a deal on the next film, but he never made another. If you look hard enough, traces of those attempts to make more films do survive in documents, and it is fascinating to consider briefly the evidence of those projects that never made it to the screen.

A CAREER IN CONCLUSION: UNMADE PROJECTS

Most directors' careers are littered with the debris of unrealized scripts and film projects. It is the nature of the business, and Hurst is no different in this regard. In fact, in chapter 3 we noted how, in his early years, he became adept at taking on films that had run into trouble or was hired to service mediocre scripts in order for a studio to fulfill a contractual obligation. He understood that he was pretty effective in the director-for-hire role. It's been argued earlier that, ironically, one such—*Ourselves Alone* (1936)—became his "breakthrough" film. Despite accumulating significant status and critical respect within the industry by the mid- to late 1940s, his films did not achieve the level of international critical accolades of an Academy Award. Hurst's personal "press representative," Constance "Bill" Sykes, posted a press release in 1952 announcing that *Scrooge* had received a Blue Riband Award of the American National Screen Council and Best Picture by the International Catholic Office at the Uruguayan Film Festival.[95] Although he enjoyed periods of relative contractual security first at Elstree and later with Rank, he retained an interest in developing scripts and working as an independent producer and director.

This profile accounts for at least some of the kinds of material that he started work on but failed to get through to production. Perhaps his single greatest disappointment in his career was the cancellation of his Lawrence of Arabia project, *Revolt in the Desert* in 1938, as examined in chapter 3. In the 1940s—as we have heard—Hurst was not able to complete, chose not to, or contractually was not able to receive any credit for *Freedom Radio*, *On Approval*, and *Caesar and Cleopatra*.[96] In 1946 Hurst was in correspondence with Sean O'Casey, living in Devon, about a film version of his play *Shadow of a Gunman*, and, although he met the playwright, the idea was not developed.[97] The incomplete projects of the 1950s and 1960s stalled for a variety of reasons: mostly around budget and logistics, but Hurst's quixotic taste in subjects and his approach to Ireland did not always enamor him to financiers.[98] Hurst recalled that he had developed a film based on the autobiography of the notorious Austrian Nazi commando Otto Skortzeny, who was living in exile between south County Dublin and Madrid in the 1960s, with Marlon Brando lined up at one stage for the lead role. Indeed, the background to the film is discussed fulsomely in Robbins's *Empress* but not referred to by its working title.[99] The Killanin Papers in the Irish Film Archive, Dublin, corroborate that *Jackboot in Ireland* was much discussed but remained unproduced by British Lion.

Other promising international, thriller, or historical projects all appear in correspondence and news reports but faltered, including *Kilo Forty*, *The Last Romantic* on King Ludwig II, and *Queen Nefertiti*.[100] Another newspaper story from around 1965 concerned *Napoleon of Egypt*, scripted by an apparently up-and-coming Portaferry writer called Malcolm Lee, to be produced by Hurst and directed on location by a more successful protégé, who had become a Bond director, Terence Young.[101] Other articles and sources refer to further projects that never made the screen such as *Elizabeth and Essex*, *Tess D'Urbervilles*, and *She Stoops to Conquer*.

An undated screenplay adaptation from the 1960s of James Stephens's novel *The Demi Gods* (1912), written by Hazel Murphy, is extant in the IFI archives that indicates Hurst's curiosity in trying to put Irish magic realism on-screen.[102] Hurst wanted to adapt Liam O'Flaherty's novel *Famine*—hoping to repeat the success of *The Informer*.[103] Actor Dudley Sutton cast some light on the aborted attempt to put it on-screen in the late 1960s and early 1970s. The location-hunting trip to the West of Ireland that he recalls seems to be have been Hurst's excuse for drinking with friends rather than any serious work.[104] As comically portrayed in *The Empress of Ireland*, Hurst's final film folly of the mid-1970s—working title *Darkness before Dawn*—was a biblical epic about the birth of Christ that seems to have existed as much in the, by then, octogenarian mind of Hurst as the script form, according to Christopher Robbins.[105]

Hurst was always conscious of his position of being Irish in England and the mistaken identity that could result. The risks could become greater if abroad when unsuspecting "foreigners" were unaware of intimate differences. In Moscow in 1957, adjudicating on a film-festival panel he was asked to tell the audience something that was quintessentially "British." Hurst's reply, that it was very "British" that he was there in Russia representing England but that he was Irish![106] It points up the constructed nature of "Britishness" as an identity and the ambivalence of Irish-English relations, highlighted when viewed from outside of Britain.

Hurst's quip was playing with a foreign audience, but he clearly enjoyed recalling it later in life and sometimes referred to himself as a "Britisher." It is an interesting, slightly archaic self-identification but one that in the postwar decades of the 1950s and 1960s is perhaps not surprising for a Belfast-born Irishman who had been living in England for a quarter of a century. Hurst was born in Ireland and grew up identifying as "British" until his late teens, but he was also "Irish" in a way that was common to Ulster Protestants raised in the 1886–1916 period. But he spent the bulk of his post-1920 life fashioning for himself a kind of Irish identity that took on subtly different characteristics depending on his location, the people around him, and the shifting legal/political definitions that shaped national identity in Ireland and Britain for the next sixty years. Domiciled in England, he ended up fabricating a hybrid, exilic identity that fused an Ulster Irishness with an exaggerated Britishness that alienated him from Ireland as it modernized in the 1960s.

To have *Playboy* as his last film may have colored his reputation, and that is unfortunate. But it did not stop Hurst from enjoying life as a raconteur and talking about the fun he had making the films in a not inconsiderable back catalog. Indeed, as we will see in chapter 5, Hurst attempted in the 1970s to secure a sense of himself by compiling a memoir at the suggestion and with the help of Christopher Robbins. "Travelling the Road," as the project became titled, would secure him what Liam O'Leary in a letter to Hurst assured him would be his "niche in that history" of film in Ireland.[107] The issue of receiving a considered critical appreciation as a film director and the irksome process of being written into cinema history are ones to which we turn in the final chapter of this study.

5 Forgotten
Hurst and the Wake of Fame

Up to this point, *The Last Bohemian* has focused on critically evaluating Hurst's film work, biography, and directorial reputation during his earlier life and active career. To explore what I'm calling the wake of fame, we need to examine how in later and after life he was forgotten and then see how he was critically found again. So, this final chapter offers a different focus in that it sets out to evaluate how, over the past decade or so, Hurst's profile has resurfaced, undergone a transformation, and shown signs of becoming more rounded and balanced.

Throughout this book I have tried to weave through my analyses of the films an account of Hurst's life, responding to the biographical interest kick-started by *The Empress of Ireland* and a retrospective of his films at the Cork Film Festival (2004). Biographical essays by Maume and Pettitt[1] and the considerable activities of the Hurst Estate[2] have sought to reestablish Hurst's preeminence as a film director from Ireland. The gradual rerelease of his back-catalog films under "classic" cinema DVD titles, plans to publish Hurst's memoir ("Travelling the Road"), and archive screenings have all been part of this process and are analyzed here.

What this final chapter seeks to do then is to revisit some of the themes of the introduction regarding Hurst's biography, lifestyle, and bohemian reputation. The aim is threefold. First, it examines the wake of Hurst's fame by considering the processes involved in the shaping of his cinematic legacy at three moments in the chronology of his later and posthumous life. These "moments" are elastic phases across different periods of time, but essentially the first dates from his last produced film, *The Playboy of the Western World* (1962), to the writing of "Travelling the Road" during the 1976–77 period. The genesis and problematic status of this text are discussed later in this chapter. The second phase is marked by his death in relative obscurity in London in 1986 and follows the obituary traces of his memory. The third, contemporary, phase can be dated from 2004 until the present, including his "rediscovery" via the Cork Film Festival to his "Titanic" return where *The Last Bohemian* itself began.

Indeed, the prologue and introduction noted that we are currently in a fluid moment in the reclamation of his reputation in cinematic history. In the entry on Hurst in *The A to Z of Irish Cinema*, its editors assert that "his Irish films remain important for expressing, albeit from a *British* perspective, the need for reconciliation and for appreciating Irish identity from a broader point of view."[3]

The issue of the framing of Hurst as somehow inhabiting or expressing a "British perspective" is one that recurred in reviews and criticism of his films during his lifetime. It remains a moot point as his films are re-viewed and presented in the contexts of Northern Ireland's "peace process" economy and politics, and the burgeoning screen industry in Northern Ireland in particular. The wider ambit of Irish-British relations post-1998 has added to a more open receptiveness to Hurst's films. Through TV, radio, press, and the organization of public events, people in Ireland and Britain engaged in the intensified remembrance of the centenaries of the Great War in which Hurst fought and of the Easter Rising in Dublin. The 2016 public commemoration of those conflicts and subsequent political events that unfolded in Anglo-Irish relations in the 1918–23 period all feature in resituating Hurst.

A second aim of this chapter is to pull together the different strands of the argument advanced in earlier chapters about the centrality of Hurst's Ulster exilic status and its link to his creative location. Hurst worked through all the ups and downs of the British cinema industry over a period that spanned four decades of production. But my aim has been to join up the films that he made across this extended stretch of time and to suggest an orchestration borne from the repeated demands for creative improvisation. The films were not always in themselves artistically innovative but were symptomatic of the dilemma in which many exilic directors find themselves. Such a mentality involves learning to inhabit a "foreign" though partly familiar culture, creating a new "home," and reinventing the "old country." Hurst's fugitive mobility early in his life created opportunities for class mobility, an acquired aesthetic sensibility, and a queer sexuality that played out in his bohemian social and cultural tastes.

Third, this chapter revisits the discussion that was set up in the introduction and my research published elsewhere about the relationship between a director's veridical life, (auto)biographical accounts of that life, and how reputation figures into the posthumous reception of directors in cinema history. As we have seen, Hurst's case creates difficulties, not easily fitting within the frameworks of either British or Irish cinema history. That he remained marginal, sometimes invisible, is part of the exilic and queer condition that was expressed in and through his films.

Toward the end of 1969, Hurst did an interview for the satirical magazine *Punch*.[4] The photograph illustrating it showed an impish-looking older man peeping out of the window of his Belgravia apartment, a perfect image of a mercurial, rascally persona. The interview was one in a series of three about "London exiles," the other two being about a white South African apartheid campaigner ousted from the country and a Russian count whose family had fled the post-1917 revolution. It is the first time in print that Hurst indicated his status as an exile in London, asserting his Ulster origins, the importance of returning there for what he terms "a spiritual bath." But he also spoke of the intolerance of Belfast and lack of recognition afforded artists. He spoke with veteran pride of his Gallipoli experience and of how fighting abroad in the British army dissolved sectarian differences between Catholic and Protestant Irish soldiers. Speaking highly of the English and his admiration of English culture, he voiced his support for a united Ireland, but avoided direct comment on the political conflict that had reignited in the summer of 1969 across Belfast and Derry.

The interview is salutary in a way because, despite his best efforts, the 1960s and early 1970s saw Hurst's profile decline. His country house in Buckinghamshire and its garden were photographed as the subject of a style-magazine feature with Hurst shown painting windows, laying paving stones, and tending his garden. Nothing could have conveyed the impression more that he was in retirement. He was even called upon from time to time to take part as an arts-radio pundit for the BBC, reviewing Joseph Mankiewicz's 1963 "sand and sandals" epic, *Cleopatra*, and toward the end of the decade the *Guardian* featured a short piece by him on British film,

5.1. "London Exile": Hurst in Belgravia, September 1969. Photographer unknown. *Punch* magazine.

but it was essentially a rehash of what he had written in 1950![5] When in 1974 Graham Greene's early film reviews from the *Spectator* were edited and published in book form, the acerbic critique of Hurst's 1930s output hardly encouraged a new generation to review his films, the NFT rarely screened his best work, and references to him in scholarly publications on British cinema were sparse.[6] He tried to maintain his links with the world of cinema that he had known and stayed friends with the likes of Ford and George Cukor. But they and that world soon passed away.

As we have seen, the cinephile activist Liam O'Leary in Dublin, who had known Hurst as a young man from the 1930s, had been compiling the materials for an opus magnum on Irish cinema in which Hurst would feature.[7] From O'Leary's archive, we have evidence that a sculpture of Hurst, a bust, perhaps commissioned, possibly as a gift, was made, and Hurst was photographed with it in a gallery. It was one of a very few nonphotographic likenesses of Hurst.[8] Perhaps the issue of achieving some sense of lasting permanence was pressing on the aging director. At this point, in his midseventies, obscure and critically forgotten, he was living déclassé in upmarket Belgravia. But with the help of a young English journalist called

5.2. Hurst and George Cukor, 1975. Photographer: Allan Warren. © Allan Warren, CC BY-SA 3.0, https://creativecommons.org/licenses/by-sa/3.0/deed.en, Wikimedia Commons.

Christopher Robbins, Hurst was persuaded to commit his memories to a series of audio recordings that would become the basis of a raconteur memoir. While remembering often involves a kind of forgetting, for Hurst this activity was perhaps unconsciously a way of coming to terms with his life and inadvertently writing himself into cinema history. The nature of the memoir and its significance are discussed shortly. Personally, this last decade or so of his life was a period of affectionate reconnection with his family relations in England and back in Belfast.⁹ A moment of belated recognition by the British film establishment came on the occasion of his ninetieth birthday.

BAFTA held a party in his honor to which many of the acting stars of British film in the 1950s and 1960s attended, including Sir John Mills, Richard Attenborough, Jean Simmons, and Donald Sinden. The event was reported in *Screen International* as a social piece with a one-page spread with a dozen or so photographs. Hurst is very thin, gaunt, and shrunken from his once substantial height. Two photos should attract our attention in the context of this study. While the majority of the individuals photographed are associated with British cinema, there is one photograph that features Hurst alongside a young, bearded Michael Algar (top right of figure 5.3.1). Algar was chief executive of Bord Scannan na hÉireann (the Irish Film Board), a relatively new organization inaugurated by the 1980 act to fund film production. Algar made the trip over from Dublin as a guest to present a cut-glass decanter of Irish whiskey to the elderly, white-haired Hurst and made a speech acknowledging his achievements and part in the history of Ireland's cinema. Algar's presence does show some level of recognition by Ireland's national body responsible for cinema, even if during the active part of his career the Irish state had shown little support for his filmmaking.

A second photograph to mention, featuring a strikingly good-looking younger woman, points us more to "Travelling the Road" and the process of Hurst's self-narration that has been a thread through this study. She was Astrid Frank, Hurst's close friend about whom there are few biographical details, except to say that she appeared in some erotic "Swedish" films in the 1970s. Hurst's bohemianism encompassed a wide social compass, and it is unsurprising that his birthday guests included peers and porno actresses. The key thing about Frank is that after Hurst's death a year or so later, she had the perspicacity to donate her typescript copy of the memoir to the research library of the BFI on Stephen Street in London. Evidently, she felt his account of his life and films was worth safeguarding for the future. Again, we do not know, but without her act it is highly unlikely that we would have his account to refer to. Within a year of the BAFTA party, in September 1986, Hurst passed away in a west London nursing home, visited perhaps last by Patrick Bashford.

5.3.1. Hurst's ninetieth birthday party. BAFTA, London. *Screen International* feature, 1985. BFI, National Archive. Courtesy of Screendaily.com.

5.3.2. Hurst and Astrid Frank. BAFTA, London. 1985. BFI, National Archive. Courtesy of Screendaily.com.

OBITUARY TRAILS AND AFTERLIFE REPUTATION

Hurst's death was noted by the broadsheet British national press and in the US trade journal *Variety* in the following terms:

> Brian Desmond Hurst who died aged 91 was a colourful and prolific film director and producer.

> Mr Brian Desmond Hurst, the Irish-born film director who had a long career in British cinema, died in London on September 26. He was 91. He never married.

> Brian Desmond Hurst, 86 [sic], Irish-born British film director whose career began in the 1930s, died Sept. 26 in London. Probably his most impressive (and commercially successful) pic was *Dangerous Moonlight* (*Suicide Squadron* in the USA).[10]

But it is the *Guardian* obituary column that week that catches the eye and undoubtedly would have pleased Hurst most.[11]

> OBITUARY
>
> Sir Reginald Goodwin. Labour leader of the Greater London Council from 1967 to 1980; in a Sussex nursing home, aged 78.
>
> Ruth French, former member of the Pavlova's company, distinguished ballet teacher, in London on Saturday after short illness, aged 89.
>
> Brian Desmond Hurst, the Irish film director, in a London nursing home, last Friday, aged 91.
>
> Prince Georg of Denmark, in hospital, aged 66.
>
> M. D. H. Jayewardene, a former Sri Lankan finance minister, aged 71.

Edward Vulliamy's selection of notables for the obituary neatly sums up the kind of company that Hurst liked to keep in life. It's true he preferred hereditary peers to long-serving life peers, but Pavlovian ballerinas turned teachers, European royal princes, and "exotic" Sri Lankan government ministers were the types of people with whom the former Belfast linen-mill boy turned film director mixed with socially and professionally for more than fifty years.

Brian McIlroy's retrospective-cum-biography piece in 1989 was significant, joining the work of Anthony Slide and Kevin Rockett, who had included discussion of some of Hurst's films within book-length studies of Irish cinema in the 1980s that offered an assessment of his work based on viewing in the BFI. However, as the moment of the centenary of cinema was marked, Rockett's entry on Hurst appeared in *A Companion to British and Irish Cinema*. Hurst's birth date is incorrectly entered as 1900, but more damage is done as his career is summarized thus: "Working in a number of genres, including crime, musical, war, comedy, historical romance, and horror, Hurst's career was punctuated by hits and misses, mostly the latter."[12] This pretty dismissive judgment by Ireland's foremost film historian hardly helped Hurst's critical reputation. Critics like Stephen Bourne had featured Hurst in his *Brief Encounters* history of "lesbians and gays in British cinema" and had called for him to be reevaluated, but even he categorized him as a "reliable journeyman film director," and Hurst's proper reputation would not be rescued until the new century.[13]

Part of the problem is that it is evident from his own life narrative captured by Robbins in *Empress* that Hurst gave as much thought to the pleasures of his lifestyle and friendships as to the art and business of making films. His habit of self-fashioning was not one that he had developed in later life. He had acquired the skill of embroidering the bare facts of his life and inventing much else since he had left Ireland in his teens.

His capacity to self-narrate by means of what Roy Foster terms "telling tales and making it up" was, as we have seen, part of a particular response to loss, displacement, and exile that he experienced from early on in his family, private, and more public life out in the world.[14] It was also part of defining himself professionally in a business that thrived on projected image. In particular, we have seen how Hurst changed his name, took years off his life, added details, and crafted a biography for professional reasons within the film industry. In the next section we can examine how Hurst's life was recorded as a series of anecdotal stories.

LIFE AS ANECDOTE: "TRAVELLING THE ROAD"

Hurst committed his memories to audiotape in the mid-1970s that were to become a typescript titled "Travelling the Road." The title suggests Hurst's abiding sense of a lifetime of exilic restlessness that has formed a major theme of *The Last Bohemian*. As an account, it captures life at a perpetual intersection of different personal and professional routes: of feeling out of place, of not quite being one's self, but forging a narrative of one's position and status by a career in cinema. As I have been arguing for his films, "Travelling the Road" traces the outline of an intense sense of belonging to an imagined Ireland left behind that is also transformed and projected onto the new home that he created in England.

The memoir begins conventionally enough with details of the author's birth, schooling, and family life. But as a text, its liminal provenance and problematic status make it an intriguing facet of the public forgetting of Hurst. Its opening line encapsulates his dilemma and hints at an attitude to the factual past: "I am truly in a predicament, an Irishman chained to the truth."[15] Recorded on audiotape, then transcribed, typed, and prepared for publication, his life in print is narrated in a series of anecdotes full of amusing diversions that include a recipe for Irish stew. It is structured by a series of elisions, exaggerations, and extemporizations with the truth. As a lifelong and well-practiced raconteur and self-publicist, Hurst's life story had taken its shape in interviews that appeared in newspapers, trade magazines, and PR notices from the 1930s. The memoir exists as a summative record of the stories that he repeatedly told about himself during his lifetime, were circulated by word of mouth, and got repeated in print in others' memoirs.[16]

However, while Hurst may have espoused a "live in the moment" attitude, as a man facing into his eighth decade he may well have got to thinking that he did not want the public memory of his life to be simply a series of anecdotes. To remain *anekdota*, from the Greek root word meaning "things unpublished," may have meant being not remembered. Indeed, the importance of his anecdotal recall of his life in and out of the world of cinema, his standing in the British film industry, and his Irish connections were sensed by Christopher Robbins. Nearly thirty years later, he published a "chronicle of [their] unusual friendship" as *The Empress of Ireland* (2004), a flawed but entertaining hybrid in itself. Part memoir, part biography of his old friend, it drew on Robbins's memories and diaries, the audio recordings and other interview material, and possibly a copy of the surviving spiral-bound typescript of "Travelling the Road." Robbins's book undoubtedly helped to revive interest in Hurst and his films, and while a definitive biography of Hurst may ultimately elude us, the problematic provenance of the materials is all that we are left to work with.

The audiotapes were transcribed by Valerie Martin, then a year or so later edited and reshaped by another young writer called Stephen Wyatt. This editing resulted in a 212-page typescript, left to the BFI archive by Astrid Frank. It remained there on open access until 2009 when a probate order was formalized by the Hurst Estate. The memoir's title has been used with some inconsistency by scholars who read the typescript before it was sequestered. In many ways, "Travelling the Road" reads as if it is based on

Robbins's audio recordings, and its oral provenance, implicit in its structure and verbose style, is a strength but also a weakness when read as a written text.

Fact-checking various episodes in Hurst's life does help us to point out his lapses and track down important details missed or correct others' mistakes. A number of recurring myths have been propagated about Hurst: that he was educated privately at Westminster School, or that he ran away to enlist in the army at age fourteen (it was his half brother Hugh Magill), or that he witnessed James Joyce in Paris having an epiphany at a party to complete the end of *Ulysses*—all were passed down as gospel truth.[17] The point is that Hurst reveled in the half-truths and slippages of fact that he cheerfully allowed others to circulate about him on the basis that it was the kind of thing that they wanted to hear and suited the public persona he wanted to project.

From the press release for his first production with his producer-backer on *The Tell-Tale Heart*, film bookers, managers, and journalists read that "Brian Desmond Hurst has had a varied career" (1–4) and in "Announcing Harry Clifton and Brian Desmond Hurst" (i–v), they are described in pen portraits. Clifton's interests, thus: "Landowner, West-End Clubman. Widely travelled. Scholar. Published poetry. Crack pilot, racing driver, speed-boats and cars. Horseman," whereas with Hurst it was war service ("bayonet wound, malaria, spell as a POW, Captain's commission" [the latter two were false]), then "art school training in Paris and work with John Ford"; "They sponsored Edgar Allan Poe's talkie debut. Britain has given America a lead" (ii).[18]

Hurst mischievously allowed people to think that he was born in a castle owned by his family when in fact his birthplace was on Ribble Street, in a working-class east Belfast district called Castlereagh.[19] Rather bizarrely, one critic claimed that Hurst "was the son of a distinguished surgeon," when it is clear in Hurst's written account that his father was a blacksmith at the Harland and Wolff shipyard in Belfast.[20] Critic Stephen Bourne had clearly read the typescript, since he quotes directly from it. But he has failed to pick up that Hurst writes of his youthful self, *imagining* his father being a doctor. This tendency tells us about Hurst's acute sense of social-class inferiority and a troubled relationship with his heavy-drinking father, which Robbins had usefully elicited from the candid Hurst.[21] But it also indicates that journalists, critics, and biographers can become complicit in Hurst's mythmaking and sustain a characterization of Hurst that is self-serving. Exploring Hurst's creative anecdotal inventions is germane to our understanding of Hurst as an Irish migrant film director operating in a tough environment.

It is not simply a case of supplying the facts or correcting the misreadings of scholars and journalists to reveal a "true" Hurst. Comparing "Travelling the Road" and *The Empress of Ireland* book, it is possible to detect differences that suggest the words quoted as Hurst's in Robbins's book may be closer to the original audio recordings. But this prospect does not mean that *The Empress* is itself a "cleaner" source. A close reading of the BFI typescript against passages that Robbins published shows that at times he ventriloquizes his subject via an appropriation of Hurst's words. Conscious or not, this habit masks how Robbins's own connective prose-paraphrase uses exact words and entire phrases from Hurst's "original," merely replacing "he" for Hurst's witnessing, first-person "I." This paraphrasing might be explained as a free use of material that—Robbins might argue—he elicited from Hurst in the first place or for which he acted as a kind of "ghost" author.[22]

The issue hinges on the oral provenance and formal structure of the conventional written memoir that exist in tension within Hurst's text. Although based on recorded "conversations" in late age, there is no sense of a dialogue between the teller and the listener, no inkling of opening questions or prompts along the way. Because he was a noted storyteller, we "hear" Hurst's voice narrating his life, its repetitions and oddly mannered grammar, and its tale-telling qualities. But it is difficult to figure out to whom—if anybody but himself—he is narrating. Indeed, Hurst's text demonstrates little if any reflexive "soul-searching" qualities, and it adopts instead a declarative stance. Structurally, the memoir is set up as a conventional, chronological unfolding, but the memoir fails to build up our knowledge of Hurst and does not let us feel any closer to "knowing him." The memoir in fact structurally falls apart and leads to an unsatisfactory conclusion. The reason is perhaps that Hurst could not work out how to account for the time between his last film and the time of recounting it in the mid-1970s.

At that time, Robbins ruefully recounted, Hurst still talked enthusiastically about making a film, based on a screenplay being written by Robbins for the veteran director. Based loosely on Stephen Vernon's stage play *Born to Be King*, with the working title of "Darkness before Dawn," it was to be a big-screen epic on events leading up to the birth of Christ.[23] Much of the conversation between Robbins and the elderly director in the 1970s about this never-financed movie was woven into memories of his personal life, films that he had made, and others again that he had totally forgotten that he had made! Aside from the brief ripple of obituary recognition around his passing in the mid- to late 1980s that we explored earlier, for much of the 1990s and into the early twenty-first century, Hurst's profile remained in the footnotes and entries of biographical dictionaries of film.[24] How he reemerged as a figure in Irish and British cinema is explored in the next section.

SWEENEY'S RETURN: HURST AND THE TITANIC QUARTER

How were Hurst's life and cinematic legacy reinvented? The changed political and economic circumstances of Northern Ireland at the turn of the century, including urban regeneration projects like the "Titanic Quarter" in Belfast, created favorable conditions and opportunities.[25] But not everyone was feeling the millennial love and seeing the new significance of Brian Desmond Hurst in 2000. In a review of a screening of *Hungry Hill* at the NFT, on London's South Bank, Alexander Walker, himself a native of Northern Ireland, gave an ill-informed, sour summation of Hurst: "Not everyone remembers Brian Desmond Hurst. Very few, I'd say. Michael Powell had a high opinion of this Irish-born director and praised his 'poetic realism.' He got that, I suppose, from his Hollywood mentor John Ford, but also from his native Eire [sic]—the town of Castlerea, Co. Roscommon [sic], could claim him, but I don't suppose it has bothered."[26]

This factually incorrect, dismissive presentation of Hurst to a new generation is one that would soon change. Two events—one politically momentous, the other cinematically significant—provided the catalyst for Hurst's revival. The Good Friday Agreement provided for a peace-process dividend in a number of political and economic measures that helped to transform Northern Ireland, the island of Ireland, and the nature of

Irish-British relations and carried forward into the "decade of commemorations." Coined in the Republic of Ireland, the phrase was shorthand for officially remembering the period between 1912 and 1922 from an Irish-state point of view. The second event was at the 2004 Cork Film Festival, whose director, Mick Hannigan, gave Hurst his first proper retrospective of his work in Ireland and began the process of framing him as a long-forgotten Irish talent. The event was tied in with the publication that year of Robbins's *The Empress of Ireland*.

The first London edition, generating critical acclaim and wide popular readership, put Hurst back in people's minds. The front cover of the hardback featured a photograph of a smiling elderly Hurst in a white linen suit, photoshopped in lurid pink, seated on a bench in Hyde Park a short walk from his apartment.[27] The eccentric Ulsterman portrayed became an unlikely bellwether of cultural change particularly attractive to liberal-minded unionism in Northern Ireland. While Robbins's book has been used as a source in *The Last Bohemian*, its historiographical and autobiographical methods are problematic. The book's significance was that it thrust Hurst back into the limelight of critical attention and called for a thorough reappraisal of his film work. This reassessment was partly addressed notably within Ruth Barton's authoritative *Irish National Cinema* (2004), which was cited in the introduction. Among other academic work and his inclusion on the Trinity College "Irish Film and TV Research" website, Hurst was being given a platform.[28]

The "peace process" produced a generational shift that augured well for Northern Ireland. Arms decommissioning, demilitarization and near cessation of political violence, new political structures, a period of economic upturn, and cultural openness ensued, on both sides of the Irish border. In a new era of Irish-British entente cordiale formalized in reciprocal state visits to Ireland by Queen Elizabeth II (May 2011) and to the United Kingdom by the president of Ireland, Michael D. Higgins (April 2014). A new, convivial juncture opened up, accompanied as it was by new forms of public historical inquiry and state-sponsored but also popular commemorative practices. These events provided the conditions in which Hurst as a filmmaker and public figure was rediscovered, brought home, and recuperated to represent a contemporary, inclusive kind of Northern

Ireland-ness. Not unlike the renaming of Belfast's city airport and the return of footballer George Best's body to his native Belfast in 2005, in some quarters Hurst was mobilized as a symbol of civic pride, enterprise, and a nonsectarian Northern Ireland with notions of "Hurst country" and "legacy" exhibitions in County Down. As has been evidenced, during his life Hurst was positioned within two main national frames (Irish and British), sometimes mistakenly taken for being English. But he resolutely never identified with Northern Ireland, or being "Northern Irish," and much preferred the "Ulster" affiliation. Hurst was a man of the world, cultured and cosmopolitan and unlikely to appreciate the localism and parochial Presbyterian prejudice against any nonheterosexual identity.

Hurst's image and story became tightly, professionally managed when a probate order was established by a family relative in 2009, creating the Hurst Estate and legally controlling assets associated with Hurst. A huge amount of work has taken place over the past decade, and much of the effect has been positive in raising Hurst's profile with an impressive list of research, publications, the creation of a website, lobbying, and screening events. Among others, these accolades have included Hurst being recognized in April 2011 with a blue plaque of the Directors Guild of Great Britain [sic], which was unveiled at the Queen's Film Theatre, Belfast, and the Ulster History Circle, to mark his birthplace on Ribble Street, Belfast, conferring belated legitimacy and respect. But even on these two plaques, where the Directors Guild title excludes "and Northern Ireland" and the UHC harks back to the premodern territory of "Ulster," Hurst's in-between status is conferred. In the same year, Hurst's biographer Allan Esler Smith made a radio program about his great uncle, *An Irishman Chained to the Truth*, in which he talked about his own childhood memories of Hurst and evidence of Hurst's religious conversion.

In 2011 Daniel Griffith's film *The Human Blarney Stone* was an extra on a *Scrooge* diamond-edition DVD, and the Hurst Estate-backed Quartertoten Productions produced short promo films and used YouTube to release licensed versions of *Riders to the Sea* and *Letter from Ulster*. The BFI put *The Tell-Tale Heart* out on its online viewing platform. Between 2014 and 2016, tapping into the World War I centenary, the Hurst Estate organized an eight-week exhibition (June–July 2014) at the North Down

5.4.1. Hurst's civic, local, and national recognition. Directors Guild of Great Britain plaque. 2011. Photographer: Lance Pettitt.

5.4.2. "Brian Desmond Hurst." Ulster History Circle plaque, Strand Arts Cinema 2022. Photographer: Danny Meegan.

Museum, called "Holywood Arches to Hollywood"; April 2016 saw the release of *Ourselves Alone* in a DVD version, and the BFI archive project screened the film in NFT, London, and the QFT September 2016 at QFT.

That year also saw the publication of *Theirs Is the Glory* by military historian David Truesdale and Allan Esler Smith and a screening in Arnhem with a veterans' association. There were the very welcome DVD releases from StudioCanal of *The Tenth Man*, *Sensation*, *His and Hers*, and *Behind the Mask*, for instance, and the BFI has screened *On Night of the Fire* and *Simba*, among others. Smith manages the Hurst Estate and a private collection of archive materials and ephemera on Hurst's films. As is also evident from the substantial material of the publicly accessible BFI collections and holdings at the IFI in Dublin, Hurst now very much has a presence in British and Irish cinema culture and its history. As the ceremony of naming on of the Titanic Studios film stages after him attests, Hurst's name has been made to have a currency and cultural value.

The director is justly recognized and celebrated, but this spirit should be kept in proportion: Herbert Brenon was more prolific with more than a hundred films; even Herbert Wilcox, if rumors of his birth in Cork are true, is a contender as director and producer of great significance within British cinema. Rex Ingram was surely a greater visual stylist and innovator than Hurst, had more international impact, and succeeded in establishing a film studio (albeit in France).

Questions have to be asked too of some of the focus, framing, and method in the Hurst Estate's approach to the biography and to the representation of his film work. Much new historical data has been uncovered, valuable archival work has been achieved, and Hurst's unorthodox sexuality and religious practice are liberally accepted. Despite the justifiable focus on war films, little in the analysis shows any critical discrimination between the conflicts, Hurst's positioning within them, or the limitations of his imaginative film recreations. Within that, to emphasize the undoubtedly seminal experience of Gallipoli to Hurst without fully exploring how his films helped define the men and masculinities of a generation is what has been lacking.

In this regard, the closing of public access to "Travelling the Road" and the hampering of its detailed, transparent exegesis is to be regretted. The

5.5. The Hurst and MacQuitty Sound Stages of Titanic Studios, Belfast. Photographer: Ruairi Ó Scanaill.

framing of Hurst and conflict without exploring the skill and variety of Hurst's wider, varied, and entertaining output gives a skewed picture. For its part, *The Last Bohemian* has made its own contribution to new biographical knowledge about Hurst and tried to offer an independent, critical, and theoretically informed argument about the enduring significance of his films.

In 2020 there are few people alive who knew Hurst before the 1960s and 1970s; that is, when he had ceased being an active director. Future work on Hurst and his films will of necessity be archival and probably most profitably focus on the 1920s and 1950s. It will surely require a US-based scholar with an interest in 1920s cinema and with the time to excavate film archives and social history in California. What hard evidence is there of any films that Hurst worked on as an art director, and is there a paper trail for his work with John Ford in this formative period? How did Hurst engage with the queer subculture of Los Angeles at this time? It would be fascinating but very difficult to trace Hurst's life and activities

5.6. "Hurst Stage" plaque, Titanic Studios, Belfast. Photographer: Stephen Douds.

during his time in Paris in the 1920s too. Is there any of his artwork from the 1920s extant, somewhere? In London for the 1940s and 1950s, there is probably greater chance of finding evidence of Hurst's work and social circles, and to find out, for instance, if his name ever appeared in police files connected with the cases of Angus McBean or Lord Beaulieu or other investigations. Further work too could be done exploring the papers of coworkers on his films and tracking down contemporary accounts of what contemporary cinemagoers thought of his films up and down the country.

But that is for the future and for others. For the moment, we can recall and reaffirm a summation of Hurst's current significance that was quoted earlier: "In a twenty-first century Ireland, north and south, where fluid identities were regarded more favourably than in previous decades and where increasing attention was given to audio-visual culture, Hurst has attracted increasing attention."[29] With this thought in mind, we should turn now to what conclusions can be drawn from the attention that this study has given to its subject now that he has been "found."

A quizzical subject: Hurst photo portrait, Angus McBean, ca. 1946. © Harvard Theatre Collection, MS Thr 581, Houghton Library, Harvard University.

Conclusion
Found: Critical Redemption?

> I wonder if I were to ask you if you consider yourself a British director or an Irish director, what would be your response? ... Does your Irish birth automatically make you an Irish filmmaker, or do your years in British cinema make you feel that you are a British filmmaker?
> —Anthony Slide to Brian Desmond Hurst, 1986

In the summer of 1986, US-based film historian Anthony Slide was doing research for a book that would become *The Cinema and Ireland* (1988). He had written to the aging Hurst two months before he passed away, hoping to get a definitive response to his query. Perhaps because of Hurst's worsening health or maybe because it wasn't a question that the self-styled "Empress of Ireland" felt merited an answer, Slide never got a reply. In his book Slide eventually cast Hurst as a "major British director who began his career with Irish features" but whose "work in the Irish cinema is largely forgotten."[1] I've cast Hurst as the last bohemian because he was the last of his kind, of a generation who had lived and worked through an era of cinematic modernity, producing a body of films whose worth has not until now attracted a full, critical scrutiny.

This book has examined how the Irish and British strands of his professional and personal identity were woven together. These strands are themselves related to Hurst's trajectory: manual linen worker, fine artist, art director, and then film director. This series of transformations was manifest in social-class displacement and mobility. Hurst cultivated social networks of business and creative associates as well as friendship networks and enjoyed a social life with domestic arrangements that mixed baronets, barristers and barrow boys, Russian countesses and guardsmen.

From what I can gather, he was formally engaged to be married at least once, allegedly the father of a child in Canada, and possibly the adoptive father of another. But from teenage to old age, he enjoyed a full, varied, and active bisexual queerness throughout his lifetime. It equipped him to present the codes and conventions of heterosexual "normality" on the screens of British "middlebrow" cinema, but also give glimpses and suggestions of its alternatives. As a visual artist particularly interested in the properties of light, he acquired an applied aesthetic and taste, expressed in the space of his own domestic interiors, but also crucially on-screen in even the most modestly budgeted film.

By offering the first full-scale analysis of his films and considering fresh evidence about his life and times, we are now in a better position to reassess the nature of his bohemianism and reputation as a film director. Given the emphasis that has been placed throughout on his Ulster origins and exilic status, it is logical to compare his achievements with others of Irish descent or connection from his era. Earlier we discussed the parallels and differences between Dublin-born Rex Ingram and Herbert Brenon, to London-Irish Herbert Wilcox, Alfred Hitchcock, and Montgomery Tully. Of these individuals, Ingram and Wilcox founded influential studios (respectively, the Victorine in Nice and Elstree in Hertfordshire), with the latter arguably the leading British studios of the interwar period and Wilcox a major British film producer of his era. Ingram and Hitchcock "succeeded" in Hollywood and secured international popular and critical reputations in quintessential cinema genres. Hurst's departure from Hollywood in the early 1930s was forced upon him by circumstance and before he directed any films, but the influence of John Ford, mentor and friend, on Hurst was significant and lasting.

If chapters 2, 3, and 4 explored his active years in his adopted British film industry and the core of his film output, chapter 5 went on to outline how, from the achieved cinema celebrity of the late 1940s, Hurst seemed to tail off into obscurity from the late 1960s and was forgotten. As we've seen, it would take another generation to rediscover him in the decade or so after 2004. Others of his contemporaries—Carol Reed, Anthony Asquith, Richard Attenborough, Michael Powell, Lance Comfort—received critical acclaim, peer respect, and in some case peerages, as well as academic recognition to secure a lasting status in British cinema history. But Hurst's presence failed to be widely registered until well into the twenty-first century. There is some evidence that he was discriminated against by some senior executives at Elstree because of his sexuality.[2] But Hurst was combative with anyone who attempted to slur his name, and it is a matter of record that he enjoyed extensive periods of contracted work with Rank, whose founder, J. Arthur Rank, was a practicing, devout Methodist. There was a broader tacit acceptance that the creative elements of cinema production, as in the theater and arts more generally, attracted men who were "musical" and "so."

During his working career and in fellow professionals' memoirs, Hurst was favorably compared with European art directors such as the Czech Georg Pabst (1885–1967) and French poetic realists René Clair (1898–1981) and Jean Renoir (1894–1974). Such comparisons made during his life prompt the kind of question posed earlier by Anthony Slide. Recalling Hurst's terminal biographical dates (1895–1986) and in terms of the contours of Irish cinema history, Hurst embodies a living link between North American émigré filmmaker figures—Irish born, or continental European and Scandinavian—from the silent era with those "new wave" Irish cinema directors from the 1970s and 1980s who themselves worked in Britain and the United States, such as Pat Murphy, Jim Sheridan, John T. Davis, Thaddeus O'Sullivan, and Neil Jordan. Only one of this selective list, Davis- from Holywood, County Down—is from Northern Ireland, and of Protestant, though middle-class, origins. Hurst remains distinctive then for his Ulster origins, his class background, and his queer sexuality.

The particularity of Hurst's queerness has been traced through the details of his life and in the analysis of his screen work. This screen queerness has been shown to operate at a number of levels of production, presentation, and attitude. Cinema's culture of queerdom in Hurst's life was constructed from the circles of writers, actors, technicians, designers, and directors whose sexuality was proscribed but whose creativity fed into the process of making movies. The collective fashioning of narratives of "normality" always contained other stories or just hints at the edges or were suggested by telling absences. Audiences experienced queerness as a tension on-screen between what the story offered, what the camera showed, and the emotions the viewer was invited to feel and, for some, to feel themselves validated. In certain moments, such films suggested the fragility of class norms or gender roles or ways of belonging. In his best work, Hurst showed the vulnerability of hetero masculinity and coaxed strong, spirited performances from several actresses. In his framing, lighting, and composition—especially of idealized young men, grouped or single faces—Hurst invited filmgoers to dwell on male features and physiques in ways that were unusual for popular and middlebrow cinema. Particularly when narratively a film might be striving hardest to suggest heroic masculine nationalism, Hurst gives us an image of a man in extreme physical danger, under pressure and emotional stress, that becomes sublime, almost religious.

In contrast to Slide's either-or formulation and despite Hurst's long-term residence in England, *The Last Bohemian* has located Hurst and his work between the British cinema industry and the Irish film history. It has shown that his films were mostly made in a studio context for a middlebrow popular market that typically, though not always, had quite restricted budgets. Many quickly became lost in the sheer volume of routine output, have been forgotten, or are only remembered for certain things. In an Irish context, such films form part of what has been termed a "cinema astray" by Tom Gunning, with Hurst as a twentieth-century wandering "Sweeney"-like figure.

This study has questioned the view of Hurst as "a film-maker whose contribution lay in his life rather than his films,"[3] by setting out a systematic re-view and analysis of all his screen work—including some of those films written or planned but not realized. This analysis has considered the full range of his films in the cinematic and cultural contexts within which they were made, viewed, and judged at the time. During the period taken to research this topic, Hurst's profile has undergone transformation, and *The Last Bohemian* lays claim in its own modest way to contributing to that process.

Perhaps the first outcome of the research underpinning this book to note is that we know more about the detail and shape of the life that Hurst lived, his social networks and professional connections, and his working methods as a film director. Combining various sources, including his problematic memoir, discussed in chapter 5, we also have a much better understanding of the circumstances within which his films were produced, how typical the pressures were that studio directors worked under, and a better measure of how successful he was and his status among his peers. The research confirms that Hurst was at the peak of his powers and had the greatest security of work and recognition within the industry in the five years between *Theirs Is the Glory* (1946) and *Scrooge* (1951).

Second, *The Last Bohemian* has extensively reviewed the primary sources of Hurst's films—including moving image, script, and other archival material—and the large number of critical reviews of his films. This research has included sampling US sources selectively where possible because they have been less well mined compared to Irish and British trade magazines and newspapers. I've also critically analyzed existing secondary popular and academic writing on Hurst and relevant film, historical, and theoretical literature. Perhaps most important, this research brought to fresh view three items of critical writing on filmmaking by Hurst himself written at important moments in his career—"The World's Only New Art Form" (1936), "The Lady Vanishes: Britain and the Film" (1950), and "The Director's Craft" (1957)—and it has located new photographic material documenting Hurst's film production history and social life. Each of these articles by Hurst was discussed and contextualized in chapters 2, 3, and 4, respectively. We can conclude that he did not leave behind an extensive, coherent, or developed set of reflections on his practice or film theory. However, these articles and records of other public utterances (on radio discussion, published letters, and Film Society talks) indicate that Hurst did contribute to the wider film culture of his day. Until now this facet has been insufficiently acknowledged, and it reinforces my argument that although he lived a socially unorthodox, bohemian personal life, Hurst was a shrewd, talented, and extremely effective filmmaker. His versatility and skills allowed him to reach the highest echelons of a demanding profession during a period of serial and quite disruptive transitions across the industry.

Third, unlike previous writing on Hurst that mentions his art-school training, my research—including an archival visit—has included a discussion of the context of that training as a visual artist in Toronto. It includes the influence of the "Group of Seven" school (chapter 1), but it later includes more commercial art and interior design work with Hugo Ballin in New York and Los Angeles whose influence might be fruitfully explored further. This artistic formation linked into his own intellectual development and applied practice in some theatrical production in North America, art-design work in "silent" Hollywood, and film direction in British studios. My analysis has also traced some of the lineaments of visual styles and technique that he appropriated from his autodidact studies of European and classical art and his own collection of artwork, furniture, and furnishings that he acquired to decorate his own domestic interiors in London and Buckinghamshire. Visual evidence is apparent in the National Portrait Gallery archive work of photographer Francis Goodman, interior magazines, and recollections of his contemporaries.

In relation to his film work, we have traced a recurring pictorial style, particularly in regard to the framing composition of the human form—specifically the face in arrested profile—which we can see in Hurst projects from his earliest independent films such as *Riders to the Sea* to his later studio output, as in *Malta Story*. We have also noted his favored use of a tracking-shot "tableaux vivants" setup and a facility for combining popular music in set-piece scenes across his films, such as *Dangerous Moonlight*, *A Letter from Ulster*, *Hungry Hill*, and *Trottie True*. They feature a capacity to adapt an acquired visual sense to the rigorous demands of the film medium and the cinema system within which he worked. An idea of Hurst's creative outlook that underpinned his visual sense is suggested in a statement that he made in 1938: "A film director like a novelist must be a man of wide sympathies, of great experience. He must see humanity as individuals, not as a collective mass; he must understand their problems and have an imagination vivid enough to share their point of view. That is an ideal to aim at but one which few of us attain."[4] Hurst's "wide sympathies" were coupled with that quality of adaptability that *The Last Bohemian* has highlighted by its reference to the optic of exile.

Fourth, the introductory section of the book, "Fugitive," explained the ways in which Hurst's particular origins were the basis for an "Ulster exilic" identity that then went through a series of transformations over the course of his life. As "Formation" (chapter 1) outlined, with the cumulative result of travel, encounter, and circumstance in particular locations and under pressure of certain historical moments, Hurst evolved a self-fashioned exilic Irishness that took its final domicile form in London. Hurst's pre-1921 birth, class roots, British military service, desertion, lack of contact with most of his family back in Belfast until the 1960s, sexual nonconformity, and conversion to the Roman Catholic faith all kept him on the move and always slightly at a remove from home and never feeling a sense of being in a "steady state."

Moreover, it gave a particular definition to an *Ulster* Irishness that was distinct even from writers like MacNeice, Hewitt, and Greacen, with whom he shared an Ulster Protestant upbringing. Hurst's "Irishness" was anomalous: through his own invented lineage ("Desmond" suggesting Anglo-Norman antecedents; "Brian" was a high king of Ireland) and his avid cultivation of Irish aristocratic friends (notably Michael Killanin), Hurst affected a connection to premodern Ireland and an Ulster nobility. This assumed identity hardly enamored him to the Irish Free State or Éire that complied with the "annexation" of Ulster while its constitution claimed it as part of the "national territory." Nor did his assumed status align him in class terms to the majority of Irish emigrants in Britain, many of whom were Catholic rural workers, or indeed Ulster's Protestant middle class that sought work and social advancement through business and the professions in the metropolis. In another important sense, Hurst's exilic status was strongly influenced by his social and creative interaction with a generation of European, Russian, and other international artistic émigrés whom he encountered in North America and Paris in the 1920s and particularly in the British cinema business whose epicenter was London during the 1930s and 1940s.

Fifth, Hurst's film versions of Ireland and his self-styled Irish identity were not eccentrically "individual": they were determined by the contexts of the shifting power relations of Anglo-Irish affairs from the mid-1930s to the late 1960s. But sharing the diasporic space of England with other exile groups, accented by his social position (close to, but *not quite* Anglo), Hurst was part of a generation of creative migrants who helped define Britishness, its developing middlebrow culture, and the cinema associated with it over a thirty-year period. Thus, in the specific and extended senses outlined above, the exilic—inflected through the vectors of nationality, class, and sexuality—helps to illuminate the films that he directed. It suggests that over three decades, his body of work offers a set of connections, despite its generic range, and it reflects on these themes. These recur because the wider politics, society, and cinema themselves anxiously dwelt on them. The films as cultural artifacts sanctioned sources of pleasure and stories of (be)longing, public aspiration, and personal fulfillment to offset emotional pain and loss.

Sixth, one of the main aims of this study was to evaluate the films and the critical reputation of Hurst. By giving a series of close visual and contextual analyses of his films, *The Last Bohemian* argues for a more rounded, balanced evaluation of Hurst's significance as a filmmaker in British and Irish cinema history. I've shown that there was more to Hurst's method and career than the colorful, "crazy Irishman" of popular biography and much academic comment. In terms of the critical interpretation of moving image, I've offered new interpretations of Hurst's well-known films and have drawn greater attention to perhaps neglected ones with fresh analyses. In chapter 2, for example, an analysis of *Ourselves Alone* was counterpointed with that of an unmade *Lawrence of Arabia*, drawing out the exilic and more subversive potential in the latter in terms of its politics and queerness. In chapter 3, queer readings of *Dangerous Moonlight* and *Alibi* were given, connecting back to earlier, adjacent, and later postimperial film narratives. My analysis has critiqued the much-touted documentary patriotism of *Theirs Is the Glory* and the sensitivity to Irish history unpinning his treatment of *Hungry Hill*, giving contrary interpretations, based on script, visual text, and contextual materials. In chapter 4, analyses of English literary "classics"—*Tom Brown's School Days* and *Scrooge*—World War II, and empire films were reinterpreted using postcolonial, queer, and gothic critical lenses. Viewed with these optics, *Simba* and *The Black Tent*, and even *Dangerous Exile*, show the limits and representational contradictions of British monarchical imperialism, as films produced from Hurst's intermediary position within an attenuated studio system. These latter films also yield readings that show the precariousness of heterosexual social institutions, the economic and colonial relations that rely on them, and the fragility of masculinity when queered or hybridized.

On the "positioning" of Hurst in relation to his national identity and affiliations, and his creative and professional attainment, we can conclude the following points. First, we can show that his Ulster Protestant birth and upbringing stayed with him in exile, but they adapted and reshaped at different geographical locations and career stages. Once domiciled in England, his Irish British status was modified in ways that were specific to the changing nature of Anglo-Irish relations in the interwar, World War II, and postwar periods. In this he was not unlike Bernard Shaw, who considered that being Irish and a British subject gave him the status of being a "citizen of Nowhere" after 1948. Hurst's response to the legal fact that Ulster had been "replaced" with "Northern Ireland" was to fashion himself an Ulster "Irishness" in Britain and continue to believe in an "Ireland" unified in his imagination.

Practically, working on Irish topics and shooting on location in Ireland for British studios, Hurst also made concerted attempts with others to establish a national film studio in Ireland in the 1930s and 1940s, which failed or were rejected. As an entrepreneurial figure, he falls short of an Ingram or a Wilcox, though the latter did go spectacularly bankrupt in the 1950s. In Ireland, Hurst and his codirectors lost out to the producer-businessman Emmet Dalton, who set up Ardmore Studios in 1958. In the 1950s he was a partner in the "Four Provinces Films" production company registered in Dublin but with London letterheads in "County Knightsbridge." His last film, *Playboy* (1962), a tribute to Ireland's foremost playwright, received 85 percent of its budget from the Irish state, but on completion Ireland's cultural diplomats distanced themselves from its screenings abroad and refused to submit it officially as an "Irish" entry at an international festival in 1965. British Lion, the film's minor stakeholder, failed to secure it a release in UK cinemas. Attempts to be Irish in Ireland were scorned; British institutions could be coolly indifferent to his difference. As we have noted, even he joked about being mistaken for being a "Britisher" when abroad.

In detailing his career arc, *The Last Bohemian* has drawn on and contributed to a growing literature on Irish diaspora studies, applying existing theoretical concepts, and in effect added a case study in the underresearched area of Irish Protestant migration to England in the twentieth century. This conclusion began by noting how the research underpinning this study has generated a greater biographical knowledge of Brian Desmond Hurst and that chapter 5 discussed the period that saw Hurst's belated recognition in the appearance of entries in the standard biographical volumes of *ODNB*, *DIB*, and *DUB*. Sections of the chapters titled "Fugitive" and "Found" addressed the perplexing issue of (auto)biographical writings by Irish migrants, particularly in relation to analyzing creative expression such as novels, plays, and film.

I have explored the process of self-narration insofar as it sheds light on migrant adaptation, survival, and the professional image creation required to succeed in the cinema business. But I've argued that Hurst's social mobility, his facility in crisscrossing class boundaries, and his bisexuality have been shown to inflect his exilic sensibilities in his treatment of film material. He may have embodied an artistic, bohemian life and social attitudes in the 1920s. But as he matured, Hurst, although sexually maverick, became culturally and politically conservative, extolling the virtues of outmoded versions of "Englishness" and dated expressions of "Irishness." And as Ford commented drily to Killanin in the mid-1950s: "I suspect he's bucking for a Knighthood. . . . Nothing third rate about Brian: he's really a first class snob."[5]

Understanding the films and the contexts of their production, including his own partial narrative of them, provides valuable insights into the class tensions and hidden sexualities in play in midcentury Britain. Indeed, his autobiography offers a counternarrative to a metropolitan "gay liberation" leading up to Wolfenden (1957) and beyond to decriminalization and equality (1993 in Ireland, 1997 in most of the United Kingdom; Northern Ireland remained excluded until January 2020). He stands in contrast to figures like Quentin Crisp and Kenneth Williams—arch, camp, queer, sexually ascetic—but like them he seemed to hide in the light of public performance. Nearer to home for Hurst was the Belfast comedian Jimmie Young, who in the local vernacular was a "Protestant fruit" who stayed in Belfast/Northern Ireland and became a hugely popular comic actor and much-loved performer from the 1940s to the 1970s. In contrast, Hurst was successful in London. Profligate and priapic, well into his later years, he retained a socially bohemian disruptiveness even as he cleaved toward a cultural and political conservatism. Allan Warren's photograph of Hurst from 1973 on the cover of this book beautifully captures these lived contradictions. As a figure, we can't recuperate Hurst into a liberal story, just as his films in all their messy, generic variety and unevenness defy categorization within strictly national boundaries.

This study has been researched as Hurst in his critical afterlife has been recast since 2004 as—in his own self-styled fashion—the "Empress of Ireland." More lately, as we have seen in chapter 5, he has been brought back to his "mother city" of Belfast by the Hurst Estate's "legacy" initiatives since 2010. It's ironic, surely, to observe Hurst's rediscovery by a Northern Irish civic unionism, performing a middle-class "peace-process" recuperation of a figure who said disdainfully of his home city: "It's not just the lack of money, it's the lack of appreciation that gets you in the end."[6] Hopefully, as part of a journey to critical redemption, *The Last Bohemian* goes some way to ensuring that Hurst's films will be more widely seen and better appreciated in the future.

Appendixes

Notes

Bibliography

Films Referenced

Index

Appendix A
Irish and Irish-Related Films Released in IFS and UK during the 1930s

Note: Hurst's films are **in bold**.

1929
The Informer d. Robison

1930
Juno and the Paycock d. Hitchcock, A.
By Accident d. s/p Davidson, J. N. G.
Film produced in TCD by the Irish Amateur Films

1931
None

1932
Lucky Ladies d. Rawlings, John
A Lucky Sweep d. Bramble, A. V.
A Night Like This d. Walls. T
The Voice of Ireland p./d./sp. Haddick, Col. Victor. First indigenous sound feature.

1933
The Blarney Stone d. Walls, Tom p. Herbert Wilcox
Colonel Blood d. Lipscombe, W. P.
General John Regan d. Edwards, Henry
Hundred to One d. West, Walter
Lily of Killarney d. Elvey, Maurice

1934
Danny Boy d. Mitchell, O. and Sanderson, Challis
Evensong d. Saville, Victor
Irish Hearts d. Hurst, B. D.
Man of Aran d. Flaherty, Robert J.
Some Say Chance p.d./sp Michael Farrell. Film unreleased. Silent.
Sweet Inniscarra d. Moore, Emmet

1935
The Informer d. Ford, J.
Father Flynn d. Noy, W. T.
Jimmy Boy d. Baxter, J.
Mr Cohen Takes a Walk d. Beudine, W.
Peg of Old Drury d. Wilcox, H.
Old Mother Riley (1935–)
Riders to the Sea d. Hurst, B. D.
Guests of the Nation d. Johnston, D. s/p Mary Manning.
Luck of the Irish d. Pedelty, D.
Oidhche Sheanchais (Storyteller's Night) d. Flaherty, R. Irish language short, filmed in London. First sound film in Irish.

1936
Café Mascot d. Huntingdon, L.
Irish For Luck d. Woods, A.
Ourselves Alone d. Hurst, B. D. Released in the United States as *River of Unrest*.
The Dawn d. Cooper Released in the United States as *Dawn over Ireland*.
The Early Bird d. Pedelty, D.
Irish and Proud of It d. Pedelty, D.

1937
Kathleen Mavoureen d. Lee, Norman
The Last Rose of Summer d. Williamson, W. K.
Macushla d. Bryce, Alex
The Minstrel Boy d. Morgan, Sydney
Oh, Mr Porter! D. Varnel, Marcel
Old Mother Riley d. Mitchell, Oswald
Rose of Tralee d. Mitchell, Oswald

Said O'Reilly to McNab d. Beudine, William
Storm in a Teacup d. Saville, Ian D.
The Vicar of Bray d. Edwards, H.
Wings of the Morning d. Schuster, Harold, D., and Tyron, G.
Le Puritain (*The Puritan*) d. Siossian, Armand. s/c Liam O'Flaherty. French language.

1938
The Londonderry Air d. Bryce, A.
Mountains O'Mourne d. Hughes, Harry
My Irish Molly d. Bryce, A.
Old Mother Riley in Paris d. Mitchell, O.
Penny Parade d. Reed, Carol
Blarney d. O'Donovan, H.
Devil's Rock d. Hayward, R. Burger, G. G.
The Islandman d. Heale, Patrick K. National Film Corporation. English with some Irish dialogue. Released in the United States as *Men of Ireland*.
Uncle Nick d. Cooper, T.

1939
Cheer Boys Cheer d. Ford, Walter
Let's Be Famous d. Forde, Walter
Old Mother Riley Joins Up d. Rogers, Maclean
Old Mother Riley MP d. Mitchell, Oswald

Source: Kevin Rockett, *The Irish Filmography: Fiction Films, 1896–1996*

Appendix B
Hurst's Filmography

Prepared from the BID Online database of the British Film Institute (2004), Reuben BFI Research Library (accessed Dec. 19, 2008) and cross-checked with Irish Film and TV Research Online. The BFI Collection now integrates its holdings, which are fully searchable at http://collections-search.bfi.org.uk/web.

KEY	
Title (+release date)	**(in the United States or alternative title)**
P. (Producer)	D. (Director)
Ad. (Adaption)	Sc. (Screenplay)
Production Company	
Studio	

The Tell-Tale Heart (1934)
P. Harry Clifton
Ad. David Plunkett Greene
Clifton-Hurst Productions
Blattner Studios

(*A Bucket of Blood*)
D. Brian Desmond Hurst
Sc. Desmond Hurst

Irish Hearts (1934)
P. Harry Clifton
Clifton-Hurst Productions
Cricklewood Studios

(*Nora O'Neale*)
D. Brian Desmond Hurst
Sc. Brian Desmond Hurst

***Riders to the Sea* (1935)**
P. John Patrick Flanagan
Ad. Francis Stuart, Patrick Kirwan
Flanagan Hurst Productions
Marylebone Studios

P/D. Brian Desmond Hurst
Sc. Wolfgang Wilhelm,
    Brian Desmond Hurst

***The Tenth Man* (1936)**
P. Walter C. Mycroft
British International Pictures
Elstree Studios

D. Brian Desmond Hurst
Sc. Dudley Leslie, Marjorie Deans,
    William Freshman

***Ourselves Alone* (1936)**
P. Walter C. Mycroft
British International Pictures
Elstree Studios

(*River of Unrest*)
D. Brian Desmond Hurst
Sc. Dudley Leslie, Marjorie Deans,
    Denis Johnston

***Sensation* (1936)**
P. Walter C. Mycroft
British International Pictures
Elstree Studios

D. Brian Desmond Hurst
Sc. Dudley Leslie, Marjorie Deans,
    William Freshman

***Glamorous Night* (1937)**
P. Walter C. Mycroft
Ad. L. Tavelli
Ad. Ivor Novello (from his stage
    play) with Dudley Leslie
Associated British Pictures
    Corporation

D. Brian Desmond Hurst

***Prison without Bars* (1938)**
AP. Irving Asher
Ad. Egon Eis, O. Eis, Gina Klaus,
    Hans Wilhem (from a film by
    Egon Eis)
London Film Productions
Denham Studios

D. Brian Desmond Hurst
Sc. Arthur Wimperis

The Lion Has Wings (1939)
P. Alexander Korda
AP. Ian Dalrymple
London Film Productions/Alexander Korda Film Productions
Denham Studios

D. Michael Powell, Adrian Brunel, Brian Desmond Hurst

On the Night of the Fire (1939)
P. Josef Somlo
G and S Films
Denham Studios

(*The Fugitive*)
D. Brian Desmond Hurst
Sc. Brian Desmond Hurst, Patrick Kirwan, Terence Young

Miss Grant Goes to the Door (1940)
Ministry of Information
Denham and Pinewood Studios

D. Brian Desmond Hurst
Sc. Brian Desmond Hurst (with Thorold Dickinson, Rodney Ackland)

A Call for Arms! (1940)
Ministry of Information
Denham and Pinewood Studios

D. Brian Desmond Hurst
Story. Rodney Ackland, Terence Young
Sc. Brian Desmond Hurst

Dangerous Moonlight (1941)
P. William Sistrom
RKO Radio Pictures
Denham Studios

(*Suicide Squadron*)
D. Brian Desmond Hurst
Sc. and Original Story. Terence Young

Alibi (1942)
P. Josef Somlo
Corona Films/British Lion Film Corporation
Denham Studios

D. Brian Desmond Hurst
Sc. Jacques Companeez, Herbert Juttke, R. Carter
Ad. Dialogue. Rodney Ackland
Shoot Sc. Brian Desmond Hurst

The Hundred Pound Window (1943)

Warner Brothers/First National Productions
Teddington Studios

D. Brian Desmond Hurst
Sc. Abem Finkel
Adp. Brock Williams
Ad. Dialogue: Rodney Ackland

Letter from Ulster (1943)

P. William MacQuitty
Ass. P. Shaun Terence Young
Crown Film Unit

D. Brian Desmond Hurst
Sc. Shaun Terence Young

Theirs Is the Glory (1946)

P. Castleton Knight
Rank Organisation Film Production
Denham Studios

D. Brian Desmond Hurst
Sc. Louis Golding

Hungry Hill (1947)

P. William Sistrom
Two Cities Films
Denham Studios

D. Brian Desmond Hurst
Sc. Daphne de Maurier, Terence Young
Ad. Dialogue. Francis Crowdy

The Mark of Cain (1948)

P. W. P. Lipscomb
Two Cities Films/General Film Distributors
Denham Studios

D. Brian Desmond Hurst
Sc. Francis Crowdy
Adp. W. P. Lipscomb

Trottie True (1948)

P. Hugh Stewart
Two Cities Films
Denham Studios

D. Brian Desmond Hurst
Sc. C. Denis Freeman

Tom Brown's School Days (1951)
P/D. Brian Desmond Hurst
P. George Minter
George Minter Productions/Talisman Productions
Nettlefold Studios

D. Gordon Parry
Sc. Noel Langley

Scrooge (1951)
P/D. Brian Desmond Hurst
Renown Pictures
Nettlefold Studios

(*A Christmas Carol*)
Adp/Sc. Noel Langley

Malta Story (1953)
P. Peter de Sarigny
Theta Film Production/Rank Organisation
Denham and Pinewood Studios

D. Brian Desmond Hurst
Sc. William Fairchild, Nigel Balchin

Simba (1955)
P. Peter de Sarigny
Group Film Productions
Pinewood Studios

D. Brian Desmond Hurst
Sc. John Baines (with Robin Estridge)

The Black Tent (1956)
P. William MacQuitty
Rank Organisation Film Productions
Pinewood Studios

D. Brian Desmond Hurst
Sc. Robin Maugham, Brian Forbes

Dangerous Exile (1957)
P. George H. Brown
Rank Organisation Film Productions
Pinewood Studios

D. Brian Desmond Hurst
Sc. Robin Estridge
Ad. Dialogue. Patrick Kirwan

***Behind the Mask* (1958)**
P. Josef Somlo, Sergei Nolbandov
G. W. Films

D. Brian Desmond Hurst
Sc. John Hunter

***His and Hers* (1960)**
P. Hal E. Chester
Eros Films/Sabre Films Production

D. Brian Desmond Hurst
Sc. Stanley Mann, Jan Lowell, Mark Lowell

***Playboy of the Western World* (1962)**
P. Michael Killanin
Four Provinces Films
Shot on location in Kerry

D. Brian Desmond Hurst
Sc. Brian Desmond Hurst

Notes

INTRODUCTION

1. Tom Gunning, "Waking and Faking: Ireland and Cinema Astray," 19–20. By "cinema astray," Gunning means "the full field of cinema, including the margins of that field which I find often to be as rich and revealing as its more familiar centre [that] maintains a particular relation to the marginal figures of tricksters and travellers, roamers and illusionists," which seems to me to capture Hurst, how his work is located, and of course neatly alludes to the exiled king Suibhne Geilt (tr. "Sweeney astray" or "mad") from Irish myth, cursed and cast into the wilderness by Saint Ronan for transgression.

2. Patrick O'Sullivan discusses the term in his "Introduction: The Creative Migrant," in *The Irish World Wide*, ed. O'Sullivan, 2.

3. Kevin Rockett, *The Irish Filmography*, i–ii; Ruth Barton, ed., *Screening Irish-America: Representing Irish-America on Film and Television*; Ruth Barton, "Introduction: Screening the Irish in Britain"; Gary D. Rhodes, *Emerald Illusions: The Irish in Early American Cinema*, 8, 20, offers an argument against what he views as "a problematic expansion of Irish Cinema" and the "illusion of an Irish-American cinema."

4. Louis MacNeice, *The Strings Are False*, 78.

5. David Truesdale and Allan Esler Smith, *"Theirs Is the Glory": Arnhem, Hurst and Conflict on Film*, 211–12, 218–19.

6. Virginia Nicholson, *Among the Bohemians: Experiments in Living, 1900–1939*, xvii.

7. Jerrold Seigel, *Bohemian Paris: Culture, Politics and the Boundaries of Bourgeois Life, 1830–1930*, 9, 11.

8. Hurst's family are most likely of Anglo-Saxon origin. Moore is a topographical family name in England and personal name introduced by the Normans. In some instances in Ireland/Scotland, Moore is the anglicized version of "Ó Mordha," or "mor" (great, large); "Hawthorne" is an Ulster variation of an English surname from the seventeenth century associated with Puritan settlement of North America and the Plantation of Ulster; "Hurst" is also of English origin, mainly from Yorkshire but also with examples from lower Saxony (for example, Horst) via southern England. Patrick Hanks and Flavia Hodges, eds., *A Dictionary of Surnames*, 374, 245, 289.

9. Louis MacNeice, "Carrickfergus," 345. The 1911 Census of Ireland record can be viewed online by typing in "Hurst" and "Tamor St.," http://www.census.nationalarchives

.ie/pages/1911/Down/Victoria__part_of_/Tamor_Street/226868/. Margaret Hurst is listed as "Head of Family" probably because her husband may have been away working in Glasgow on the census date. Her eldest daughter, "Martha Sheer," and granddaughter "Meta Beer" [sic] are part of the household and her son-in-law is not resident.

10. His desertion was officially recorded on his Medal Card record. National Archives, Kew, London.

11. "Arts and Artists," *Toronto Globe*, Apr. 30, 1923, reported a luncheon at the Heliconian Club to mark the departure of four OCA students bound for Belgium, "to see, to observe and to learn," as Hurst is quoted. Hurst's traveling companions were Norman Deans, T. A. Stone, and Donald Philip.

12. Kevin Kenny, "Irish Emigration in a Comparative Perspective," 414.

13. Avtar Brah, *Cartographies of Diaspora: Contested Identities*, 209.

14. Seamus Heaney, "Correspondences: Emigrants and Inner Exiles," 20.

15. Stuart Hall, "Minimal Selves," 44.

16. Adrian Frazier, *Hollywood Irish: John Ford, Abbey Actors and the Irish Revival in Hollywood*, 32.

17. Sean Campbell and Roger Swift, "The Irish in Britain: Since 1914," 523.

18. Bernard Shaw, "Fragment of Autobiography (1902)," 10.

19. MacNeice, *The Strings Are False*, 17.

20. Seamus Heaney, "Frontiers of Writing," 198–99.

21. The letter from 1948 is cited in Liam Harte, ed., *The Literature of the Irish in Britain: Autobiography and Memoir, 1725–2001*, 180.

22. C. W. Reid, "Citizens of Nowhere: Longing, Belonging and Exile among Irish Protestant Writers in Britain, c. 1830–1970."

23. John Wilson Foster, "Culture and Colonisation: View from the North," 23.

24. Hamid Naficy, "Situating Accented Cinema," 113.

25. Hamid Naficy, "Between Rocks and Hard Places: The Interstitial Mode of Exilic Cinema," 134 (emphasis added).

26. Ruth Barton has analyzed the performance of Irishness by emigrant actors in the United States from the studio period to the present day, adapting Naficy in *Acting Irish in Hollywood*. See in particular "Introduction: Acting Exile," 1–20.

27. The academic literature on film, authorship, and the idea of the auteur is vast, but C. Paul Sellor, *Film Authorship: Auteurs and Other Myths*, 6–32, offers a succinct summary of key issues. Colin McCabe, "The Revenge of the Author," and Dudley Andrew, "The Unauthorised Auteur Today," offer examples of the "auteur" being mobilized by two critics in writing about film.

28. "Index of British Feature Directors," 297.

29. Graham Greene, "*The Spectator*, 1 December 1939," In *The Pleasure-Dome: The Collected Film Criticism, 1935–1940*, 256.

30. C. S. [Constance Sykes], "Brian Desmond Hurst," *Screen* (June 1942): 3.

31. All three men worked with Hurst in the 1950s. Respectively, Gavin Lambert, *Mainly about Lindsay Anderson: A Memoir*, 50; actor and scriptwriter Brian Forbes, *A Divided Life: Memoirs*, 307, 254, 308; Alan Strachan summarizing Michael Redgrave's impressions, *Sweet Dreams: A Biography of Michael Redgrave*, 327.

32. The late Philip French, *Observer* film critic of long-standing, has argued that because of the publication of Greene's *The Pleasure-Dome* collection in the early 1970s Hurst's reputation took a hit that would last a generation. Email to the author, May 15, 2009.

33. Anthony Slide, *The Cinema and Ireland*, 22.

34. Jeffrey Richards, *Films and British National Identity*, 244.

35. Ruth Barton, *Irish National Cinema*, 56, uses these terms in her synopsis of Hurst, particularly the problematic one: "Northern-Irish."

36. Ruth Barton's *Rex Ingram: Visionary Director of the Silent Screen*, is the second monograph on the director, the other is by Liam O'Leary; Sean Boyle, *Emmet Dalton: Somme Soldier, Irish General, Film Pioneer*; and finally, Ian Graham, *Herbert Brenon: An American Odyssey*.

37. See Slide, *The Cinema and Ireland*; and Joseph Curran, *Hibernian Green on the Silver Screen: The Irish and American Movies*.

38. Sources for this paragraph include Herbert Wilcox, *Twenty-Five Thousand Sunsets: The Autobiography of Herbert Wilcox*; and Charles Barr's public lecture on Hitchcock at St. Mary's University, May 2014. My thanks to Professor Barr for providing me with his PowerPoint slides and Peter Power-Hynes for his 1901 Census work on Tully. See also Wheeler Winston Dixon, introduction to *Re-viewing British Cinema, 1900–1992*, 3–4; W. W. Dixon, "The Marginalised Vision of Montgomery Tully." Two more Irish figures about which very little is known or written who appear to have been involved in film in Britain preceding Hurst, namely, Creighton Hale from Cork (b. Patrick Fitzpatrick, May 24, 1892 [d. unknown]), who was educated in England but emigrated to make films in the United States in 1909; and Roy William Neill (1886–1946) allegedly born on a boat on the Irish Sea who worked in England from 1915 until late 1930s in British cinema. Slide, *The Cinema and Ireland*, 85–89.

39. John Hill, "Revisiting British Film Studies," 308.

40. These have included 35mm film on Steenbeck at the BFI; public digital screenings at NFT in Dublin and London; VHS and DVD at IFI, the IWM, and private collections; and online streamed modes such as the BFI Player and YouTube.

41. Virginia Woolf, "Middlebrow," in *The Death of the Moth, and Other Essays*, 115. See, notably, Lawrence Napper, *British Cinema and Middlebrow Culture in the Interwar Years*.

42. Michael Powell, *A Life in Movies: An Autobiography*, 329.

43. Brian McIlroy, "British Filmmaking in the 1930s and 1940s: The Example of Brian Desmond Hurst," 38–39 (emphasis added).

44. Nicholson, *Among the Bohemians*, 28; Juliet Gardiner, *The Thirties: An Intimate History*, 652.

45. Both quotations are from Andy Medhurst, "That Special Thrill: *Brief Encounter*, Homosexuality and Authorship," 47.

46. *Dictionary of Irish Biography*, s.v. "Brian Desmond Hurst," by Patrick Maume, accessed Nov. 23, 2013, http://www.dib.cambridge.org.

1. FORMATION

1. "Ulster Day" and the "Ulster Covenant," Belfast, PRONI n.d., https://www.nidirect.gov.uk/articles/about-ulster-covenant. Hurst's signature—a simple cursive "Hans Hurst" of "Welland Street"—on the Covenant is available at https://apps.proni.gov.uk.

2. For two essays on notions of Irishness in the context of Englishness and Irishness within the context of the British Empire, see, respectively, David George Boyce, "The Marginal Britons: The Irish"; and Keith Jeffrey, "An 'Irish Empire'? Aspects of Ireland and the British Empire."

3. Roy Foster, *Paddy and Mr Punch: Connections in Irish and English History*, 282–83.

4. Brah, *Cartographies of Diaspora*, 181. See also Wendy Webster's *Englishness and Empire, 1939–1965*.

5. Hall, "Minimal Selves," 44.

6. Raymond Williams, *Culture*, 71–74.

7. A visual sense of the character of the city in this period can be gathered from the archival film of Belfast in the *Mitchell and Kenyon in Ireland* DVD.

8. National Census of Ireland, 1911, National Library, Dublin, http://www.census.nationalarchives.ie/pages/1911/Down/Victoria__part_of_/Tamor_Street/226868/.

9. Francis Stewart Leland Lyons, *Ireland since the Famine*, 60–67.

10. Boyce, "Marginal Britons," 242.

11. Jeffrey, "'Irish Empire'?," 2–3.

12. Boyce, "Marginal Britons," 232–34.

13. Sarah Burton, *Imposters: Six Kinds of Liar—True Tales of Deception*, 3–4. Burton distinguishes between "opportunist" and "pragmatic imposters": "The first group pretend they *have* achieved (or inherited); the second group pretend *in order* to achieve." At different stages, Hurst seems to have been a bit of both. Official papers indicate his rank in the army as a rifleman; that is, a private, whereas in his memoir he assumed the rank of sergeant and by the 1930s his PR material elevated him to captain.

14. John Wilson Foster, "Making Representation: The Literary Imagery of Ulster Protestants—Some Historical Notes," 12.

15. Lynd, from his memoir *Home Life in Ireland* (1909), is quoted in Barry Sloan, "Journeys into the Protestant Mind," 97.

16. Roy F. Foster, "Protestant Magic: W. B. Yeats and the Spell of Irish History," 221–22.

17. Selina Guinness, "Protestant Magic Reappraised: Evangelicalism, Dissent and Theosophy."

18. F. Archer, "Psychic Film Director Recalls: Spirit Led Him Away from Enemy Lines."

19. Christopher Robbins, *The Empress of Ireland: Chronicle of an Unusual Friendship*, 271. Joanna Bourke has written on this area in a couple of essays with some searching insights into the difficulties of veterans putting memories of their experience into public discourse. See her essays "'Remembering' War" and on the mythology surrounding the "purity" of bayonet killing and hand-to-hand combat, "'Irish Tommies': The Construction of Irish Manhood, 1914–18."

20. See Joanna Bourke, *Rape: A History from 1860 to the Present Day*.

21. See Eve K. Sedgwick, *Between Men: English Literature and Male Homosocial Desire*.

22. Frazier, *Hollywood Irish*, 26–33.

23. Montagu, Lord Pitt-Rivers, and Peter Wildeblood were convicted in 1954 for having sex with young servicemen at a party on Montagu's estate when consensual sex between males was illegal.

24. Robbins, *Empress of Ireland*, 213–16.

25. Key texts here are Sheila Rowbotham's excellent biography *Edward Carpenter: A Life of Liberty and Love* (London: Verso, 2008); and Peter Wildeblood, *Against the Law*, written out of his personal experience of prosecution and imprisonment in the 1950s in the "Montagu sex scandal."

26. See Jonathan Dollimore's deft essay "Bisexuality," 253–55.

27. See Christina Grandy, *Heroes and Happy Endings: Class, Gender and Nation in Film and Fiction in Interwar Britain*.

28. Audio of Hurst's voice and accent is virtually nonexistent, but people who knew him have reported this to me and a rare snippet of his voice can be heard on Allan Esler Smith's radio program *An Irishman Chained to the Truth*.

29. J. C. Beckett, *The Making of Modern Ireland, 1603–1923*, 449.

30. Records show that Hurst did not revert to calling himself "Hans" after his war service and actually added "Desmond" to the "Brian," which appeared in the credits of his early films.

31. Ontario College of Art, *OCA Prospectus, 1921–22*.

32. The others who constituted the seven were Franklin Carmichael, Lawren Harris, A. Y. Jackson, and Franz Johnston, but other artists were in this loose constellation.

33. Lismer, *Canadian Theosophist*, Feb. 15, 1925, quoted in Fred B. Housser, *A Canadian Art Movement: The Story of the Group of Seven*, 13.

34. Angela N. Grigor, *Arthur Lismer: Visionary Arts Educator*, 65.

35. Quoted in Housser, *Canadian Art Movement*, 143.

36. MacDonald quoted in Housser, *Canadian Art Movement*, 16.

37. See, for example, Lynda Jessup, "The Group of Seven and the Tourist Landscape of Western Canada . . . or the More Things Change."

38. *Toronto Globe*, Dec. 18, 1922. This newspaper was on microfiche at the British Library, Colinsdale. The *Telegram* articles were located at the OCAD Archive of newspaper cuttings with no page numbers shown.

39. Charles C. Hill, *The Group of Seven: Art for a Nation*, 126.

40. R. F. Foster, *W. B. Yeats*, 462–69. The work of Forest Reid (1875–1947) from Belfast would be one novelist writing out of a curious Ulster Protestant blend of classicism, the esoteric, and Twilight theosophy laced with bachelor homoeroticism.

41. C. Hill, *Group of Seven*, 126.

42. *Hart House Theatre: A Description of the Theatre and a Record of Its First Nine Seasons, 1919–28*, 6–8.

43. *Toronto Telegram*, ca. 1924.

44. *Toronto Sunday World*, Apr. 27, 1924.

45. Ian Christie, "Histories of the Future: Mapping the Avant-Garde," 7.

46. Vincent Bouvet and Gerard Durozoi, *Paris between the Wars: Art, Style and Glamour in the Crazy Years*.

47. Ernest Hemingway, *Ernest Hemingway on Paris*, 21. Essays in this collection were first published in the *Toronto Star*, 1922–23.

48. Email correspondence with author from Emmanuel Schwartz at the archive of Ecole, Feb. 29, 2009.

49. Bouvet and Durozoi, *Paris between the Wars*, 218.

50. Bouvet and Durozoi, *Paris between the Wars*, 217–24.

51. Lance Pettitt, "Life by Anecdote: Memoir, Irish Cinema and Cultural History."

52. Denise Hooker, *Nina Hamnet: Queen of Bohemia*, 74.

53. Her birth name was Mary Duff, but she also went by her mother's maiden name of Smurthwaite. Her husband was in fact Lieutenant Commander Sir Roger Thomas Twysden Bart (1894–1934). Married in 1917, she found her aristocratic marriage utterly stifling and took Patrick Guthrie as her lover, divorced her husband in 1926, and in Paris befriended the literary crowd around Hemingway and Faulkner. Vol. 3 of *Who Was Who, 1929–1940*, 2nd ed. (London: Andrew and Charles Black, 1967). Liam O'Flaherty (1896–1984) was an Aran Islander who had trained as a priest, but then fought in the British army during World War I. He developed sympathies with communism, married, and then lived between Paris and Dublin as a writer. By the end of the 1920s, he had separated and moved to London where he lived as a recluse in a room in Ebury Street but remained remarkably productive, and his fiction remained of interest to Hurst and John Ford as source material for films like *The Informer* (1928). Nina Hamnet (1890–1956) was a renowned English painter, bohemian, and memoirist, remembered in London and Paris for

her slow transformation from early-twentieth-century promise to the rather tatty, alcoholic ending in fifties Fitzrovia. *The Laughing Torso* (1932) is her most notorious book and caused several litigations, but see also *Is She a Lady? A Problem in Autobiography* (1955).

54. Once again, Hurst *knew* people who *knew* Ford Maddox Ford—connected to Joyce, the Hemingway/Faulkner set through Twysden and so on, but records or correspondence showing direct connections to Hurst are not apparent from extant papers.

55. Leger (1881–1955) was a French artist who had initially trained as a draftsman and couldn't get into the Ecole. He became very active in the 1920s under the influence of the cubists and futurists. Juan Gris (1887–1927) was a Spanish cubist painter who moved from his native Madrid to Paris in 1906. An associate of Picasso, he also designed sets for the Russian Ballet in Paris in 1924–25 and lectured on art theory at the Sorbonne; Georges Braque (1882–1963) was a Parisian and cofounder of cubism. Having served an apprenticeship as a painter-decorator, he met Picasso in 1907, and they each developed a "fractured" style. He fought in World War I but returned injured to painting in 1917. A salon exhibition in 1922 cemented his mature reputation for still life and interiors; Ossip Zadkine (1890–1967) was a Russian-born painter and sculptor who had trained in London and moved to Paris in 1910. He had served in the French medical corps during the war; Constantin Brancusi (1876–1957) was a Romanian abstract sculptor who moved to Paris in 1904 and established himself in a range of materials and studied for a time under Auguste Rodin.

56. Robert Phelps, *Professional Secrets: An Autobiography of Jean Cocteau*, 69.

57. Robbins, *Empress of Ireland*, 59.

58. Joseph McBride, *Searching for John Ford: A Life*, 160–61.

59. The synagogue is at 3663 Wilshire Boulevard in Los Angeles, and its website does indeed confirm that it was refurbished in 1928–29 under the direction of artist Hugo Ballin, commissioned by film studio owner Jack Warner. Its main interior ceiling was lavishly decorated with Old Testament murals. My inquiries with the synagogue, however, suggest that the rabbi's library ceiling was not decorated with murals as claimed by Hurst. Rebecca Sills Nudel, email to the author, Jan. 15, 2009.

60. Kate Summerscale, *The Queen of Whale Quay: The Extraordinary Life of "Joe" Carstairs, the Fastest Woman on Water*.

61. Henry Talbot de Vere Clifton (1907–79) was the heir to Lytham Hall, Lancashire; Kildalton Castle on the Isle of Islay; and various other properties in London and Dublin. Robbins, *Empress of Ireland*, 115.

62. Ito (1892–1961) was trained classically in dance in Tokyo but immigrated to Paris in 1911 and thence to London during World War I where he met W. B. Yeats, for whom he choreographed a staging of *At the Hawk's Well* (1915). In 1916 he moved to the United States, where he divided his time between Broadway revue and avant-garde theater and in Los Angeles with both stage and film work during the 1930s. Ito was deported in 1941 after Pearl Harbor. M. Fleischer, "W. B. Yeats and Ito."

63. Bruce Posner, *Unseen Cinema: Early American Avant-Garde Film, 1893–1941*, 40.

64. The career of English set designer and theater and film director James Whale provides an interesting parallel to Hurst at this moment, though his movement was from east to west, from England to the United States. Whale transferred his theatrical success of *Journey's End* (1928) in London to New York and then took up a film contract in Los Angeles for the screen version (1930) and then achieved phenomenal success with *Frankenstein* (1931). Whale was also openly homosexual and shared a working-class/skilled labor background with military service in World War I, became socioeconomically successful through his creative talents, and remained a long-term exile.

65. Constance Sykes, "Director with Ideals and How He Acquired Them."

66. *Dictionary of Irish Biography Online*, s.v. "Brian Desmond Hurst," by Patrick Maume, accessed November 23, 2013, http://www.dib.cambridge.org.

67. Kevin Kenny, *The American Irish*, 182.

2. FILMMAKER

1. Sarah Street, *British National Cinema*, 30.

2. Naficy, "Situating Accented Cinema," 113.

3. Virginia Woolf, "Middlebrow," in *Death of the Moth*, 115.

4. Lawrence Napper, *British Cinema and Middlebrow Culture in the Interwar Years*, 8–9, 12.

5. Jamie Sexton, *Alternative Film Culture in Interwar Britain*; Mo Moulton, *Ireland and the Irish in Interwar England*.

6. Sanford Sternlicht, "Synge on Film: Two Playboys," 161–62.

7. Tom Ryall, "A British Studio System: The Associated British Picture Corporation and the Gaumont-British Picture Corporation in the 1930s," 34.

8. For *Ourselves*, see Brian McIlroy, "Appreciation—Brian Desmond Hurst, 1895–1986: Irish Filmmaker"; and John Hill, "'Purely Sinn Fein Propaganda': The Banning of *Ourselves Alone*." See also Allan Esler Smith, "*Ourselves Alone*: Conflict in 1920s Ireland," sleeve notes for rereleased DVD of *Ourselves Alone* in the British Film/StudioCanal series. For the Lawrence of Arabia film, see Andrew Kelly, Jeffrey Richards, and James Pepper, eds., *Filming T. E. Lawrence: Korda's Lost Epics*.

9. "Brian Desmond Hurst, who directed *Ourselves Alone*, is forming an Irish film company in association with young Lord Killanin. Headquarters will be the giant hangars at Gormanstown, 25 miles from Dublin, which have stood empty since the War [World War I]." "Brian Desmond Hurst," press release, BFI Microfiche.

10. Moulton, *Ireland and the Irish*, 6–7.

11. Conor Cruise O'Brien quoted in Declan Kiberd, *Inventing Ireland: The Literature of the Modern Nation*, 251.

12. Moulton, *Ireland and the Irish*, 3.

13. See Appendix A, listing Irish-made and Irish-themed films of the 1930s.

14. Juliet Gardiner notes that with more than three and half million unemployed in Britain in 1932, it was "the deepest trough of the Depression." Gardiner, *Thirties*, 27.

15. "Honolulu, Hawaii, Passenger and Crew Lists, 1900–1959," Canadian National Archives, roll 188, no. 236–37, microfilm. But ship-passage documentation and other evidence corroborates the fact that he had taken up residence in London by 1932. Adrian Frazier is incorrect in asserting that Hurst "began his directing career in 1934 working with DuWorld Pictures in Hollywood on a version of Poe's *The Tell-Tale Heart*," before returning to Ireland to make *Riders to the Sea* (1935). Frazier, *Hollywood Irish*, 27. Hurst made *Tell-Tale Heart* in north London at the Blattner Studios in 1934.

16. Allan Esler Smith showed the audience and talked about glowing letters of reference kept by Hurst in his private collection when introducing a public screening of *On the Night of the Fire* at NFT3, London.

17. Hurst ensured that his "apprenticeship" in Hollywood under Ford made its way into press-pack material and mentioned it in interviews, which is evidenced in many reviews of his films or director profiles.

18. Paula Gilligan, "'A Monotonous Hell': Space, Violence and the City in the 1930s Films of Liam O'Flaherty."

19. Francis Stuart recalls "ringing up those people who make London so dear to me: Brian at his office making films," or being at the Café Royal "watching to see if Brian is down below with some cinema mogul selling films." Stuart, *Things to Live For: Notes for an Autobiography*, 74–75.

20. Patrick Maume has unearthed from Johnston's personal papers in Trinity College, Dublin, the fact that Hurst had at one point lodged temporarily on Johnston's boat moored in London. Their early friendly relations soured later as Hurst began to achieve some status and power as an Elstree director. He appears to have treated Johnston badly over payment for script work and allowed him to lose out on an acting role in *Ourselves Alone*.

21. Jack Finegan, "Irish Films: What of the Future?," *Picture Daily*, Oct. 25, 1934. Writing on the appearance of *Irish Hearts*, Finegan claimed that "Dublin is one of the most film-conscious capitals in Europe," with over thirty cinemas, and "looks forward to the day when we shall have a regular supply of Irish films in our cinemas." J. A. P., "Film Projects for the Free State," *Irish Times*, Mar. 9, 1935, also picked up on the positive idea "that in Ireland there are abundant resources for the enterprising film producer," as coming productions were introduced.

22. Street, *British National Cinema*, 10–11.

23. Sexton, *Alternative Film Culture*, 4–10, for his definition of alternative film-culture networks and preference for "alternative" rather than "avant-garde" in a British context.

24. Kevin Gough-Yates, "Exiles and British Cinema," 170, 173. As Tom Ryall points out, not everyone in the industry at the time thought it was necessarily a good thing, some

complaining it was detrimental to the "projection of our national life" on-screen and others saying that the technical skills and development of young English workers were hampered. He cites from an issue of *World Film News* (Sept. 1937) in *Alfred Hitchcock and the British Cinema*, 66.

25. See Robert James, "*Kinematograph Weekly* in the 1930s: Trade Attitudes towards Audience Taste."

26. See Jeffrey Richards's edited collection of essays, *The Unknown 1930s: Alternative history of the British Cinema, 1929–1939*, viii–ix, where he makes the case for the reevaluation of "quota quickies," "melodrama as a legitimate and powerful mode of cinematic expression," and the project of contextualizing films in "the wider cultural scene" of the period.

27. See *Kinematograph Weekly*, Dec. 17, 1936. Compare it to Denis Johnston's essay "The Last Refuge of Nationality" on his own film *Guests of the Nation* (1935) and the possibilities for film in the same period.

28. George Warrington, "At the Theatre: Arts and Reality."

29. *Tell-Tale* may be viewed in person at the BFI but was uploaded on the BFI Player (viewed Sept. 26, 2016); the IFI has a *Riders to the Sea* VHS viewing copy, but the Hurst Estate released the film on YouTube on its eightieth anniversary (Feb. 12, 2015). *Irish Hearts* was viewed at the BFI and the IFI.

30. BFI, *The Tell-Tale Heart*, publicity material, microfiche (London: BFI, 1934), 1. Hurst is referring to a Charles Klein's adaptation of 1928, a twenty-four-minute silent version that Klein adapted and directed himself with Otto Matieson as the young insane man. BBFC papers "*Tell-Tale Heart* 1-1-91 (February 22, 1932)," held at the BFI, indicate that a scenario was submitted to the BBFC by a R. H. Kinsman, esq.; whether it was a rival project or someone acting on Hurst's behalf is unclear. A report was delivered on a proposed film with the title of *Tell-Tale Heart* that commented: "The subject is morbid, details may be gruesome and it does not sound very attractive entertainment, but it is doubtful if we can call it prohibitive. It might give dramatic scope to a strong actor. Unless very well done it would almost certainly prove objectionable." There is no record of a film being submitted.

31. On-screen credits and BFI's BIDs Online, accessed Dec. 19, 2008, indicate that it was adapted and designed by David Plunkett Greene, from a scenario by Hurst. It was photographed by two British journeymen cinematographers, Walter Blakely, who had worked for the German E. A. Dupont on *Menschen Im Kafig* (1931), and the more experienced D. P. Cooper, as well as a much younger photographer credited only as "Van der Horst." The latter might be the Dutchman Herman Van der Horst (1910–76) who went on to direct films back in his native Netherlands in the postwar period, per IMDb.

32. Edgar Allan Poe, "The Tell-Tale Heart," in *Selected Tales*, 186.

33. This painting adds a layer of self-reference to the film, with Hurst inserting himself into a film scene. The Saint Thérèse is his own work from the 1920s period, and the

other nudes are probably his work too, though their provenance cannot be verified. And, as outlined in chapter 1, the young man is played by the Canadian Norman Dean, though credited as Norman Dryden, Hurst's art-college lover and long-term companion. Comparing a photograph of Dean from the 1920s to a publicity still from the film can visually corroborate this idea. The Dean photograph is reproduced in Robbins, *Empress of Ireland*, 128, but I have been able to trace only one other likeness. From the evidence of the film, Dean's accent in performance is, unsurprisingly, "mid-Atlantic," tending toward educated middlebrow for the period.

34. Ian Conrich, "Horrific Films and the 1930s British Cinema," 64–65.

35. Poe, "The Tell-Tale Heart," 188.

36. "The Beauties of Unscreened England," unidentified press cutting (London: BFI microfiche, 1934).

37. Andrew Moor, *Powell and Pressburger: A Cinema of Magic Spaces*, 5.

38. BFI, *Tell-Tale Heart*, press release, microfiche (London: BFI, 1934), 1. It is highly probable that Hurst wrote or contributed directly to the press-release materials of his early independent productions.

39. "Beauties of Unscreened England" (emphasis added).

40. J. W. Foster, "Culture and Colonisation," 23.

41. See Liam O'Dowd's discussion of Albert Memmi's *The Colonizer and the Colonized* (London: Earthscan, 1990), 131. In particular, adopting Memmi's analysis, Hurst would exemplify a "refusal" of his Ulster Protestant origins. Hurst's skilled Protestant working-class status within the historical power bloc of unionism, its relative privilege as a colonial settler caste within Ireland, and its structured dominance that took state form when "Northern Ireland" was created in 1920 results in an "exultation-resentment" relationship with the "mother country" (England) and the actual place of his birth in Ireland.

42. *Picturegoer*, Aug. 4, 1934, 24; *Kinematograph Weekly*, Mar. 22, 1934, 26; *The Cinema: Film Booking and Ready Reference Guide* (2nd quarter, 1934), 18.

43. The narrator in the story relates that "first of all I dismembered the corpse. I cut off the head and the arms and legs." Poe, "The Tell-Tale Heart," 189. Such graphic details are not reproduced in Hurst's version, but a silhouette of a bucket of bloodied water being poured is highly suggestive and provided the US version with its gripping title.

44. Kauf, *Tell-Tale Heart*, *Variety*, June 19, 1934, in *Bowker "Variety" Film Reviews, 1934–37*, vol. 5.

45. Harry T. Smith, "An Edgar Allen Poe Thriller: 'The Tell-Tale Heart,'" June 15, 1934, in *The "New York Times Film" Reviews, 1932–1938* (New York: New York Times, 1970), 1070.

46. James Johnston Abraham, *The Night Nurse*, now kept as a rare book held at the British Library.

47. *By Accident* (1930) survives as an example of pre–Irish Film Society work. Incomplete, without sound and badly damaged, it features a young man's disturbed, subjective

view of Dublin's streets, monuments, and parks intercut with a dreamlike childhood scene of trauma at one of Dublin's coastline Martello towers. His vertigo, the nonlinear action, and certain surreal effects convey his obsession with his inability to express himself to a young woman, an incapacity shared by Dermot in *Irish Hearts*. *By Accident* gets its title from the crisis point when, riding as a passenger in a car in Phoenix Park, the young man witnesses the car knock down a pedestrian, who—when he gets out to look—is himself! Kevin Rockett, Luke Gibbons, and John Hill, *Cinema and Ireland*, 45–46. Viewed on IFI Player.

48. Kevin Rockett, ed., *The Irish Filmography: Fiction Films, 1896–1996*, lists *Irish Hearts* as being seventy minutes' running time, but the mini DVD viewing copy in the IFA Dublin is only twenty-two minutes long. The print viewed is titled "Nora O'Neale," not "Irish Hearts," suggesting it may be a copy of the US release print. The title credits of the director's name are given in Irish as "Brian Deasmumnac Ó hOrsasg," further Hibernizing the product.

49. The BBFC report on the film scenario noted: "Several scenes objected to, all of which were noted in our letter of 16 August 1934. Script writer: BD Hurst. Producer: Harry Clifton." *BBFC Reports* Films Submitted 10-9/1934, 1-3-330, BFISC.

50. Cited in Rockett, *Irish Filmography*, 137. The photography for the film is credited to two cinematographers, the British-born Walter Blakeley (1894]1941), who had worked on Hurst's first movie, and the German in exile Eugen Schüfftan, whose impressive list of credits in the decade leading up to working on this film included cinematography/special effects for no less than Fritz Lang's *Metropolis* (1927), a further film by Max Ophuls, and four films for G. W. Pabst in the early 1930s.

51. Unfortunately, Hurst seems to have faithfully transposed Abraham's somewhat florid prose style when describing the interior thoughts of Nora and his efforts at capturing the dialogue of young male Trinity medicals. Here is a post-boat-race exchange of young medical rowers, Pip and his opponent: "Thanks awfully, old man." "It's all right, old chap," he said swaying slightly. "We will be right as ninepence when we've had a tub. Sides," he called automatically (44). And Nora, on seeing the finished painting *The Stooping Princess*, by an artist friend La Touche, for whom she has modeled, is overcome by the fact that the likeness of the "Knight" figure in it startlingly resembles that of Pip, Dermot's handsome younger nephew: "It was this [the head of the knight] that now absorbed her growing consciousness, intensifying the effect to a degree disturbingly intimate, reverberating on the shores of her soul in lapping waves of unexpected amplitude" (51).

52. A recently restored, "partially reconstructed" version of the film by Dean Kavanagh at the Irish Film Archive combined new elements and recovered "rushes" to produce a longer, new version of the film. It remains incomplete and is an amateur production, but is a fascinating celluloid document of Irish social life and the state of Irish film culture from the mid-1930s. It was screened at the Barbican Cinema in London in November 2016

with a presentation by Sunniva O'Flynn and with live musical accompaniment as part of the IFFL/IFI "Century of Cinema" strand cocurated by Lance Pettitt and Kelly O'Connor.

53. John Millington Synge, "Riders to the Sea," in *Plays, Poems and Prose*, 29–30.

54. Hurst was impressed by Carl Dreyer's *The Passion of Joan of Arc* (1928), taking John Ford to see it at an "art" cinema on Vine Street, Los Angeles. Wilhelm had worked in the German film industry but fled in 1933; Stuart, born in Australia to Antrim-born parents, was schooled in Rugby, England, fought as a Republican in 1916–21, and married Iseult Gonne. Living and writing between Ireland, France, and London until in 1939, Stuart moved to Berlin to teach at university and broadcast to Ireland on cultural matters under the Nazi regime. The uncredited "art director" of the film may be John Rattersbury Skeaping (1901–80) who went to Goldsmith's College, London, and the Royal Academy. He had a traveling scholarship to Paris and Rome in the mid-1920s where he and Hurst may have become acquainted.

55. Robbins, *Empress of Ireland*, 169.

56. Robbins, *Empress of Ireland*, 170. The frame still is reproduced in *A Seat among the Stars: The Cinema and Ireland*, ed. George Fleeton, 8. This publication accompanied the six-part television series broadcast in 1984.

57. Synge, "Riders to the Sea," 23.

58. Synge, "Riders to the Sea," 26.

59. Barry Monahan, "John Milligan Synge and Ireland by Brian Desmond Hurst," 74.

60. "Synge Play to Be Filmed: Producer Working in Connemara," *Irish Times*, May 28, 1935. See also next quotation.

61. Rockett, Gibbons, and Hill, *Cinema and Ireland*, 96–97.

62. Our Special Representative, "Filming Synge in the West: Producers at the Whim of the Weather," *Irish Times*, July 24, 1935.

63. The amount the Fields put into the film varies from £3,000 to £6,000 in different reports. "Private Pre-view Screening in London 'Film Backed by Gracie Fields'" was reported in the *Yorkshire Post*, Sept. 19, 1935; "A Synge Film," *Birmingham Post*, Oct. 8, 1935; "'Riders to the Sea' Film," *Irish Independent*, Nov. 9, 1935, which noted that it "makes an impressive film" and the script was by "Messrs Francis Stuart and Patrick Kirwan."

64. *Sunday Express*, n.d., 15.

65. A. P. Luscombe Whyte, "Gracie Fields: Helps to Make Screen History," *Evening Standard*, n.d. (ca. 1935).

66. There is one record of how a Dublin audience reacted to the film screening. It comes from a reviewer of a Radio Eireann adaptation of *Riders* produced to commemorate fifty years of the play's stage debut. He recalls how he first encountered the play: "I first met Synge's little play not in the Abbey but in the [Theatre] Royal where in 1936 a film version . . . offered an inauspicious contrast to a robust vaudeville bill headed by Gracie Fields. It was a very poorly wrought little picture, in spite of Sarah Allgood's presence, and it took drastic liberties, as I learned later, with Synge's text." He concludes: "The instinct of the

Theatre Royal audience to laugh at it was a healthy instinct; be that as it may, we laughed." R. A. Olden, "R.E. [Radio Eireann] Treated Synge with Respect," *Irish Times*, Jan. 28, 1954.

67. *Sunday Times*, Dec. 15, 1935.

68. "Limerick Cinemas: Savoy," *Limerick Leader*, Nov. 7, 1935.

69. "Synge Play on the Screen: *Riders to the Sea*," *Kinematograph*, Dec. 19, 1935; "Epic of Irish Tragedy," no source (Dec. 18, 1935). From BFI Microfiche of press cuttings.

70. "R. P.," *Monthly Film Bulletin* 4, no. 39 (1937): 55.

71. National Film Archive 35mm print (London, BFI). It does not appear on the IFI, Dublin print. Both prints do have opening and closing frames of a Celtic cross image. Of course, many local to this area spoke Irish as a first language or were bilingual, using English when dealing with city folk, tourists, and visiting film crews.

72. G. A. Atkinson, "Epic of Irish Tragedy: *Riders to the Sea*," *Era*, n.d.

73. *Spectator*, Dec. 20, 1935, cited in Greene, *Pleasure-Dome*, 40.

74. *Spectator*, Dec. 20, 1935, cited in Greene, *Pleasure-Dome*, 40.

75. Robert Herring, *Life and Letters Today* 14, no. 3 (1936): 79.

76. Robbins, *Empress of Ireland*, 193.

77. Robbins, *Empress of Ireland*, 170. On 1935 average wage, see Gardiner, *Thirties*, xv.

78. On the business of making use of unproduced film material, see Dan North, "Finishing the Unfinished," 3–8.

79. See James Barr, *A Line in the Sand: Britain, France and the Struggle That Shaped the Middle East*. Covering the period from 1919 to 1948, the chapters most relevant to the mid- to late 1930s are 12–15, from the "Arab Revolt" of April 1936 until the outbreak of World War II.

80. Deirdre McMahon, *Republicans and Imperialists: Anglo-Irish Relations in the 1930s*, provides a highly detailed account and analysis.

81. General Sir Henry Wilson, quoted in Barr, *Line in Sand*, 101, and Frank Kitson likening policing in Palestine to that of the Black and Tans in Ireland, also in Barr, *Line in Sand*, 185–86.

82. The key films are *The Informer* (United States, Ford, 1935), *Guests of the Nation* (Ireland, Johnston, 1935), *The Dawn* (Ireland, Cooper, 1936), *The Plough and the Stars* (United States, Ford, 1936), and *Beloved Enemy* (United States, Potter, 1936). Korda produced a trilogy of celebratory "Empire" films in *Sanders of the River* (1935), *The Drum* (1935), and *The Four Feathers* (1939); other titles in this mode would include *Rhodes of Africa* (1936) and *Elephant Boy* (1937).

83. See also Donal Lowry, "The Captive Dominion: Imperial Realities behind Irish Diplomacy, 1922–49."

84. Sturrock was a former captain in the British army who served in World War I in the RASC, the same regiment that Hurst was redeployed to or reenlisted under a false name after returning from illness and desertion following the Gallipoli campaign. Both men served in the same regiment, both men also served in the Middle East, and it is

highly likely that they knew each other from this period. I have not been able to locate the play in the Lord Chamberlain's Register at the British Library, suggesting it did not have a public production in Britain, nor have I been able to locate the short story. More sinisterly perhaps, Sturrock's main qualification for serving as military adviser for *Ourselves* was for his post–World War I counterinsurgency work as an intelligence officer and his alleged membership of the so-called Cairo Gang that was responsible for the killing of several IRA men in the dirty war of 1919–20 in Ireland. Sturrock's and Hurst's combined military experience and Hurst's ambivalent Irishness clearly fed into the script revision, editing and filming of the location work, and ambush scenes. "The Cairo Gang," accessed Feb. 4, 2017, http://www.cairogang.com.

85. John Hill, "'Ulster Will Fight Again': Cinema and Censorship in the 1930s," in *Cinema and Northern Ireland: Film, Culture and Politics*, 47–77.

86. Robbins, *Empress of Ireland*, 170.

87. J. Hill, "'Purely Sinn Fein Propaganda,'" 328. See also *Ourselves Alone*, press book PBM-40399 (BFI, London).

88. J. Hill, "'Purely Sinn Fein Propaganda,'" 329.

89. The headlines are from, respectively, *Sunday Mercury* (Birmingham), May 10, 1936; and *Daily Mail*, July 20, 1936.

90. *Evening Standard*, July 18, 1936.

91. "Jolo," "*Ourselves Alone*," *Variety*, May 13, 1936.

92. "Jolo," "*Ourselves Alone*."

93. Frank S. Nugent, "*Ourselves Alone*," *New York Times*, July 31, 1936.

94. "Kauf," "*Ourselves Alone*," *Variety*, Aug. 11, 1937.

95. "Film Making in Ireland," *Sligo Champion*, Sept. 26, 1936. The same article mentions "an aeroplane hangar possibly at Gormanstown, to be converted into a studio," as a facility site in Meath, north of Dublin.

96. Robbins, *Empress of Ireland*, 309.

97. See Phillip Orr, "The Road to Belgrade: The experiences of the 10th (Irish) Division in the Balkans, 1915–17," for a lucid account of this theater of engagement. It is perhaps significant that one of the few possessions recovered from Hurst's Belgravia flat after his death was a copy of T. E. Lawrence's *Seven Pillars of Wisdom*. An abridged version, *Revolt in the Desert*, was optioned by Korda.

98. Hurst's account of this appears to tally in some respects with what is known of Lawrence's movements. Robbins, *Empress of Ireland*, 279. Kevin Brownlow makes the claim that Hurst, "an Irishman who had fought the Turks himself, and *who had known Lawrence in the Middle East*," though he gives no indication of his source. Brownlow, *David Lean: A Biography*, 406 (emphasis added). In appendix 1 of his *Seven Pillars of Wisdom* titled "Nominal Roll: Hejaz Armoured Car Company" under the RASC, Lawrence lists the names of men in his unit, which includes no less than two Hursts: an "R. W. Hurst" and a "W. Hurst," 685. However, these initials do not tally with the "Brian

Henry Hurst" that Truesdale and Smith claim became his alias when he reenlisted to avoid being charged for desertion.

99. Kelly, Richards, and Pepper, *Filming T. E. Lawrence*, 4. Much of this introduction is based on Jeffrey Richards and Jeffrey Hulbert's earlier "Censorship in Action: The Case of *Lawrence of Arabia*," 158.

100. James Chapman and Nicholas J. Cull, "The Watershed: *Lawrence of Arabia* (1962)," 90–92, offer a fascinating account of the film's genesis in an imperial context and in particular the tensions in the different script versions as the film was developed between 1935 and 1938.

101. The BFI Special Collection holds a "Treatment" (S.9756), two "Scenarios" (S.10359, a 121-page document with only Hurst's name on it), another (S.8735) and "Screenplay" (S.8755) of "Revolt in the Desert"/"Lawrence of Arabia," the last dated Oct. 4, 1938. Malleson (1888–1969) was an actor and busy screenwriter, whose credits in the 1930s included *Nell Gwyn* (1934) and the hugely successful *Victoria the Great* (1937). By contrast, Guthrie (1911–94) had worked on the script of *Riders to the Sea*.

102. Jeremy Wilson, *Lawrence of Arabia: The Authorized Biography of T. E. Lawrence*, 941.

103. Yeats had written to Lawrence in 1932, asking him if he would accept a nomination as an associate of the Irish Academy of Letters, to which Lawrence replied, writing in acceptance: "I am Irish, and it has been a chance to admit it publicly. . . . It is not my fault, wholly, if I am not more Irish: family, political, even money obstacles will hold me in England always. I wish it were not so" (Oct. 12, 1932), cited in J. Wilson, *Lawrence of Arabia*, 896.

104. Cited in Brownlow, *David Lean: A Biography*, 405.

105. Kevin Jackson, *Lawrence of Arabia*, 117, citing Malcolm Brown's study of T. E. Lawrence's correspondence.

106. Chapman and Cull, "Watershed," 108.

107. Kelly, Richards, and Pepper, *Filming T. E. Lawrence*, 47.

108. For a concise account of political, diplomatic, and constitutional frictions from the External Relations Act (1936) and the Constitution (1937), through negotiations on treaty ports, land annuities, partition, and trade tariffs (1938), see John A. Murphy, *Ireland in the Twentieth Century*, 86–96.

109. Kelly, Richards, and Pepper, *Filming T. E. Lawrence*, 33. The BFI's *Lawrence of Arabia* "Scenario" has nude Arabs bathing at an oasis (53) and a strong sequence depicting the cruelty of battle against the Turks (59–63). Another note added in handwriting warns that such a scene might be too graphic (66); another extremely graphic scene involves flogging (86–87). We can also get a sense of how an encampment in the desert at night was envisioned, describing the Arab men as having faces like sculptures and the dramatic mood of scene lit by a campfire (102).

110. Robbins, *Empress of Ireland*, 170–71.

111. *The Tenth Man* was subtitled "A Play by W. Somerset Maugham" that was "retold and edited by C. M. Martin," but inside carried the cast list and credits for the film production! It was published in London by Heinemann in its "Pocket Edition" series.

112. For once, Graham Greene had a good word to say about a Hurst film in his *Spectator* review that focused on these very sequences and its ending: "Mr B. D. Hurst has upset prophecies this week with a well-directed film. . . . There was nothing in Mr Hurst's two previous films . . . to show him capable of these humorous and satirical political sequences, and the very fine melodramatic close. The credit is all Mr Hurst's, for the dialogue is stagy, and the principal actor, Mr John Lodge, continues to suffer from a kind of lockjaw." *Spectator*, Dec. 11, 1936, in *The Graham Greene Film Reader: Mornings in the Dark*, 165.

113. C. A. Lejeune, *Observer*, Dec. 6, 1936.

114. The quotation from the *Times* review of the original Embassy Theatre production and the comments on its staging from the *Era* in November 1935 are cited from an Internet facsimile source, accessed Feb. 6, 2017, http://charlesmortimer.weebly.com/murder-gang-1935.html.

115. See Ryan Linkof, "'Gross Intrusions': *Sensation*, Early Queer Film, and the Trouble with Crime Reporting in 1930s Britain," which discusses the film's fascination with sensationalist journalism of the mid-1930s linking Hurst's sexuality to the fear of revelation and shame.

116. C. A. Lejeune, "The Six Deadly Sins," *Observer*, Jan. 31, 1937, 14.

117. G. S. Street, "Reader's Report of *Glamorous Night*," Lord Chamberlain's Papers, LCP/Corr1935/13863, Mar. 8, 1935, British Library, London.

118. Ivor Novello, *Glamorous Night*, script, Lord Chamberlain's Papers, LCP/1935/13. References to the script are shown in parenthesis. © British Library Board.

119. The screenplay of *Glamorous Night* is extant (1–64) and carries a "Producer's Note" referencing the play's success at Drury Lane theater in 1935. It was adapted by Dudley Leslie, Hugh Brooke, and William Freshman. BFI Special Collection, S10644. Graham Greene gave his view in *Spectator*, May 7, 1937, that "it is about as bogus as a film could be" but—exemplifying damnation by faint praise—was "quite well-directed by Mr Brian Desmond Hurst," reproduced in Greene, *Pleasure-Dome*, 150.

120. *Prison sans barreaux*, directed by Leonide Moguy, was released in France in February 1938. The director of photography was Claude Renoir with Christian Matras, based on a screenplay by Hans Wilhelm, Egon Els, and Gina Kaus. One can see some vindication in comparisons made by some critics between Hurst and "newer continental" directors. http://www.UniFrance.org.

121. Robbins, *Empress of Ireland*, 315.

122. E. P., *Monthly Film Bulletin*, 5, no. 57 (1938): 218.

123. *Motion Picture Herald*, 138, no. 1 (1940): 44. Source: Lantern: Media History Digital Archive, University of Wisconsin–Madison, Film Magazine and Periodical Collection, accessed May 14, 2018, http://lantern.mediahist.org.

124. C. R., "*On the Night of the Fire*: A Fine British Film," *Manchester Guardian*, Nov. 25, 1939, wrote: "One of the most promising British films since *Blackmail* and *Murder*. Not that Brian Desmond Hurst experiments as the young Hitchcock did, but if his manifest virtues are derivative it is from the Ford of *The Informer* and from the newer French directors that he has copied his deliberate pans and his emphasis on the rich sprawling life of the slum."

125. In Green's original, Will or Walter Kobling is given a more sinister, troubled interior than we see in the film: "Affable, like most barbers, handsome, vain and proud in his soul, crafty and envious by nature." Frederick Lawrence Greene, *On the Night of the Fire*, 10. Green was described by his publicity on the book's flyleaf biography as "a writer with a realistic outlook. Besides reflecting the influence of the French writers of the nineteenth century, his work is in the tradition of Defoe . . . the conglomerate life of a large city."

126. In the novel, Walt anticipates this outcome: "It was the end. He knew this was the end. . . . He was frightened, angry, disappointed. An immense desire was rising in his heart, and he knew he would never be able to satisfy it. He knew he had reached the end of his freedom. Despair became intolerable then, and he mourned what he had lost, feeling grief and despair stun him. Darkness closed in on his senses: a peculiar darkness coming from within him" (219–20).

127. See Laurence Miller, "Evidence for a British Film Noir Cycle." But interestingly, Miller does not name Hurst's film in his survey.

128. *Monthly Film Bulletin* 6, no. 71 (1939): 202.

129. Greene, *Spectator*, Dec. 1, 1939, reproduced in *Pleasure-Dome*, 256.

130. *Motion Picture Herald* 138, no. 1 (1940): 44.

131. In his essay "British Film Noir," Andrew Spicer writes that *On the Night of the Fire* was "directed with typical sensitivity by Hurst" and that "with its sustained, doom-laden atmosphere, Gunther Krampf's expressive cinematography, its adroit mixture of location shooting and Gothic compositions . . . clearly shows that an achieved mastery of film noir existed in British cinema before the war" (183). It was screened as part of the "Projecting the Archive" program at the NFT3 in 2014. BFI program notes.

132. Hurst's sexuality was an "open secret" within the industry, and he recalls reported instances where an executive in a meeting referred to him as a "bugger" and as a reason not to be offered *Prison without Bars*. Robbins, *Empress of Ireland*, 315.

133. Robbins, *Empress of Ireland*, 57.

134. Clair Wills, *That Neutral Island: A History of Ireland during the Second World War*, 37–39.

135. Hurst, born in 1895, would have been forty-three. He joined the army at age nineteen and remained a private throughout his military service; he deserted in July 1917. He never studied medicine and never formally studied painting in Paris.

3. FAME

1. Cited in Sykes, "Director with Ideals."

2. Hurst had written to Ford on June 4, 1940. Ford Papers, Lilly Library. Again, my thanks to Charles Barr for generously allowing me access to his research notes.

3. Diana Dors, *Behind Closed Dors*, 97–98. Dors was clearly duped by Hurst's blarney about his "aristocratic relations" wealth, but her observations of the "carved wooden saints and religious statues" indicate his "Catholic" aesthetic taste in fine-art interior decor.

4. Edward Montagu [Lord Montagu of Beaulieu], *Wheels within Wheels: An Unconventional Life*, 80; and in telephone interview with the author, 2008.

5. Quentin Crisp, *The Naked Civil Servant*, 157.

6. Robbins, *Empress of Ireland*, 338.

7. Rodney Ackland, with Elspeth Grant, *The Celluloid Mistress; or, The Custard Pie of Dr. Caligari*, 189. Hurst co-owned the house, according to the title deed papers, with a Mr. Warner and Mr. Young (Terence). My thanks to Angela Waters for allowing me to see legal papers and view the house.

8. Ackland, *Celluloid Mistress*, 189.

9. Ackland, *Celluloid Mistress*, 104–5.

10. See James Chapman, *The British at War: Cinema, State and Propaganda, 1939–1945*.

11. In "'Is It His War as Well as Hers?': The View from Ealing," Charles Barr explores the tensions in Michael Balcon's Ealing Studios films that featured Irish settings and narratives and how they were handled by Éire's wartime censor.

12. Chapman, *British at War*, chaps. 3–4, covering material specific to Hurst's involvement, include a focus on the MOI, its shorts and documentaries, and feature-film propaganda.

13. Harrison's article on documentary filmmaking is reproduced in Jeffrey Richards and Dorothy Sheridan, eds., *Mass-Observation at the Movies*, 210–11.

14. Nov. 3, 1939. Quoted in Robert Murphy, *Britain Cinema and Second World War*, 18. Rodean School is a private, fee-paying school for upper-class young women associated with a particular accent.

15. For a comprehensive military account and reconstructive analysis of the film, see Truesdale and Smith, *"Theirs Is the Glory."* It is possible that Hurst and the production team based their scenario and planning on Louis Hagen's account based on his firsthand experience, published immediately after the event in 1945, reprinted as a new edition, *Arnhem Lift: A German Jew in the Glider Pilot Regiment*.

16. Ian Dalrymple, in "On the Lion Having Wings," talks of the "imaginative direction" (12) of Hurst and explains that in making the film "our duty was to reassure and 'hearten' the audience" (10). Overall it is a bit defensive in tone.

17. Richards and Sheridan, *Mass-Observation*, 209–16, collates material from reports from individual observers, survey data, a letter from Adrian Brunel's (one of the film's co-directors) son on his knowledge of the making of the film, newspaper reviews, and so on.

18. *Observer* critic C. A. Lejeune, "London Comes Up for Air," *New York Times*, Nov. 19, 1939.

19. Quoted in Richards and Sheridan, *Mass-Observation*, 324 (emphasis in the original).

20. Robbins, *Empress in Ireland*, 317.

21. "'Themes, Trends and Preferences,' Report: Mass-Observation Report (FR24, 1940)," quoted in Richards and Sheridan, *Mass-Observation*, 153.

22. R. Murphy, *British Cinema*, 16–17.

23. Anthony Asquith, "Realler than the Real Thing," 25.

24. Ackland, *Celluloid Mistress*, 89.

25. Dialogue transcribed from screen, 6:40–6:58. See note 27.

26. Richards and Sheridan, *Mass-Observation*, 210 (emphasis added).

27. Notes to *Miss Grant Goes to the Door* on the BFI Player, accessed June 10, 2017, http://www.bfi.org.uk/films-tv-people/4ce2b69db43c1.

28. *A Call to Arms!* (1940) can be viewed on the BFI. Accessed June 10, 2017, http://player.bfi.org.uk/film/watch-call-for-arms-1940/.

29. Ackland, *Celluloid Mistress*, 85, 87.

30. Robbins, *Empress of Ireland*, 317.

31. Ackland, *Celluloid Mistress*, 88.

32. Harrison in *Documentary News Letter* (Nov. 1940) quoted in Richards and Sheridan, *Mass-Observation*, 210 (emphasis in the original).

33. For a discussion of class in postwar film, see Philip Gillett, *The British Working Class in Postwar Film*, especially his "five-dimensional model" for analyzing working-class images in film (16–21).

34. Hollie Price, "The MOI Film Division and Their Finest."

35. Robbins, *Empress of Ireland*, 320.

36. John Gielgud narrates the "airman's letter" from Michael Powell's *An Airman's Letter to His Mother* (1941). YouTube, accessed June 10, 2017. At time of writing, only voice-over is available, https://www.youtube.com/watch?v=STxjFPVf_Rs.

37. Robbins, *Empress of Ireland*, 321.

38. Allan Esler Smith's booklet *Revisiting a Letter from Ulster* (2012) performs a commemorative recapitulation of this process marking as it did the seventieth anniversary of troop arrival in Northern Ireland.

39. J. Hill, *Cinema and Northern Ireland*, 93.

40. It is also interesting to note that the extant script of the film does not have indication of the action, shots, or setup for this sequence. Is this a rare instance of unscripted cinematography in Hurst? *Letter from Ulster* (London: BFISC, S.15108).

41. William MacQuitty, *A Life to Remember*, 276–77.

42. "Letter from Ulster," accessed July 11, 2018, http://www.briandesmondhurst.org/letterfromulster.html.

43. William MacQuitty (1905–2004) was born and educated in Belfast, but joined the Charted Bank and worked in India, Australia, and the Far East. He saw military service in India and returned to Ireland in 1939. He began to study medicine in London, but served an informal apprenticeship in film with Sydney Box and made a short film about Ulster agriculture that got the interest of the Ministry of Information. He moved into film production during World War II but is best known as the producer of *A Night to Remember* (1958). Over a busy, industrious life, he was also a professional writer and photographer specializing on the history of the Middle East, notably *Abu Simblel* (1965) and *Tutankhamun: The Last Journey* (1972). His autobiography, *A Life to Remember* (1991), is a fascinating account of a polymath film producer who was a good friend of Hurst.

44. "'Themes, Trends and Preferences,' Report: Mass-Observation Report (FR24, 1940)," quoted in Richards and Sheridan, *Mass-Observation*, 144.

45. Robbins, *Empress of Ireland*, 317.

46. Len England's report (dated Sept. 15, 1941) is cited from Richards and Sheridan, *Mass-Observation*, 219.

47. *Documentary News Letter* (Nov. 1940) cited in Richards and Sheridan, *Mass-Observation*, 210.

48. Compare, for example, the scenario of Anthony Asquith's *The Way to the Stars* (1943), cowritten by Terence Rattigan and produced by the Russian-born Anatole de Grunwald.

49. The film was released in the United States with the title *Suicide Squadron*. See *Harrison's Reports and Film Reviews, 1941–43*, 66. The *Variety* review, based on a screening in London (June 27, 1941), thought that Young's screenplay "glosses a lot, dialog is okay, but plot is short on action" and thought Hurst's direction was "prosaic" but praised the cinematography: "pianissimo mood of soft-lighted interiors; air stuff also tops from his department."

50. All quotations in this paragraph, Richards and Sheridan, *Mass-Observation*, with page numbers in parentheses, but emphases are mine.

51. Reported in the round-up of 1946 by Peter Noble, *The British Film Yearbook, 1947–48*, 130–31.

52. Chapman, *British at War*, 197–98.

53. Barton, *Irish National Cinema*, 54.

54. Stephen Bourne, *Brief Encounters: Lesbians and Gays in British Cinema*, 54–55; Barton, *Irish National Cinema*, 51–56.

55. Richard Dyer, "Believing in Fairies: The Author and the Homosexual," 35. Page numbers of subsequent quotations shown in parentheses.

56. Robbins, *Empress of Ireland*, 320. See also Birkbeck's "Queer Fifties" conference, May 2009, especially Elizabeth Wilson's notion of "war damage."

57. The quotation about the poor-quality script is from an unnamed reviewer for the *Sunday Times*, and the second is taken from the prerelease publicity booklet for the film, both on microfiche for *Dangerous Moonlight*. BFI microfiche collection, London.

58. Terence Young, *Dangerous Moonlight*, 60. Script. "Shot No. 331: CU Insert. On portion of letter [FROM CAROL]: 'At least send me his address. I don't know how to reach him you see.'"

59. Bombardier, humorist, and jazz musician Spike Milligan begged to differ. He recalls seeing the film in Neasden, remembering the "bloody awful Warsaw Concerto," in *Adolf Hitler: My Part in His Downfall*, 57.

60. Offscreen, the piano was played by the Hungarian-born classical pianist Lajos, known as Louis Kentner (1905–87), who became a British national.

61. Ruth Barton, "'The Potency of Cheap Music': Exile, Ballads and Performance in Irish Cinema," 205–6.

62. Robbins, *Empress of Ireland*, 319.

63. Chapman, *British at War*, 98.

64. *Harrison's Reports and Film Reviews, 1941–43*, Apr. 3, 1943, 55.

65. Quoted from "Red Devils Revisit Arnhem," *Pathé News Reel*, Dec. 10, 1945, and also (mute, unreleased) "Pilgrimage to Arnhem 1946," accessed July 27, 2017, https://www.britishpathe.com/video/red-devils-revisit-arnhem/query/Arnhem. See also "Stanley Maxted in Return to Arnhem," BBC Home Service, Sept. 16, 1949, 22:15. The British Library's National Sound Archive also holds recordings of actual broadcast pieces made by Stanley Maxted that are the basis for the film's "commentary."

66. Robbins, *Empress of Ireland*, 323.

67. Truesdale and Smith, *"Theirs Is the Glory,"* 173. The "making and marketing of *Theirs Is the Glory*" is detailed extensively in chap. 6.

68. Film critic Philip French recalled his time as a former paratrooper in this period to me. Correspondence with the author, Dec. 22, 2013.

69. Truesdale and Smith, *"Theirs Is the Glory."* The book's approach is critiqued by Eunan O'Halpin in *Estudios Irlandeses*; and in Lance Pettitt, "Belfast-Born WWI Deserter," *Irish Times*, review of *Theirs Is the Glory* (2016), Jan. 22, 2018, https://www.irishtimes.com/culture/books/the-belfast-born-wwi-deserter-who-became-one-of-the-greatest-war-film-directors-1.3361502?utm_source=dlvr.it&utm_medium=twitter.

70. Halpin, *"Theirs Is the Glory."*

71. Robbins, *Empress of Ireland*, 322.

72. K. F. B., *Monthly Film Bulletin* 13, no. 152 (1946): 135.

73. Robbins, *Empress of Ireland*, 323.

74. Peter Noble, ed., *British Film Year Book, 1949–50*, 580.

75. Elizabeth Bowen, "The Mysterious Kor," 728.

76. Peter Noble, ed., *British Film Year Book, 1947–48*, 143.

77. Lemass (1899–1971) was a Republican who fought in the 1916 Rising and was later interned for IRA activities. He joined the Fianna Faíl party, served effectively in its governments in the 1930s and 1940s, and replaced de Valera as party leader in 1959.

78. Roddy Flynn, "Raiders of the Lost Archives: The Report of the Inter-Departmental Committee on the Film Industry, 1942." A concise account of his research appears in *The A to Z of Irish Cinema*, ed. Roddy Flynn and Pat Brereton, 170–74.

79. See also slightly later in this period T. J. M. Sheehy, "Towards an Irish Film Industry." He argues for a Europe-wide realistic perspective on the viability of film production in Ireland before "our orators build Irish studios in the clouds" and dismisses calls for a government-financed studio that "might lead to a tottery documentary movement. It might also lead to a Civil Service dominated home for people in search of easy jobs, or for sincere enthusiasm experiment at public expense. . . . Departing radically from all suggestions on Irish Production offered by various interests, may I suggest that unprotected Irish private enterprise unblushingly cash in on the Irish-American ties, and on Hollywood's European headache, and hire a studio to those who can pay partially in dollars" (420).

80. See Liam O'Leary, "Developments in Éire"; Rex Mac Gall, "Towards an Irish Film Industry"; Kathleen O'Dwyer, "The Child and the Cinema in Éire"; and Patricia Hutchins, "News from Ireland."

81. Sheila Greann, [no title], *Irish Press*, Jan. 9, 1947 (National Library, Dublin, LOLNLI, MS 50.000/326/25). Bingham is quoted from this report.

82. "Rank Director's Plan for Irish Film Industry," Jan. 1, 1947, newspaper clipping (National Library, Dublin, LOLNLI, MS 50.000/326/25).

83. Robbins, *Empress of Ireland*, 194.

84. De'ath, "Exiles in London," 576.

85. Hurst did became briefly involved in film production in Ireland in the 1950s through his partnership in an independent company with Ford, Killanin, and Tyrone Powers, prior to the establishment of Ardmore Studios by Lemass in 1958. This context is discussed in chapter 4.

86. Richard Traubner's gem of an essay "Angus McBean," xi.

87. Adrian Woodhouse, *Angus McBean: Face-Maker*, 224.

88. McBean's photographs of Hurst are held in the Theatre Archive, Houghton Library, Harvard University, Cambridge, MA.

89. "Court Circular," *Times*, Mar. 1, 1949.

90. Gavin Lambert talks of this period in his memoir, *Mainly about Lindsay Anderson*, 50–53. He recalls that "with a mandate to establish *Sight and Sound* in the marketplace, I boldly fished for famous names, that included Renoir, Dreyer, von Sternberg, Redgrave, Powell, Tynan, Beaton and so on." Hurst was in good company. Lambert also notes that "he had become friendly with Brian Desmond Hurst," whom he refers to as the

"Anglo-Irish [sic] film director" and a "raging pansy in Beddington's words." This is in the context of a discussion of the supposed homosexuality of John Ford. Jack Beddington worked at the Ministry of Information and clearly knew Hurst professionally through this work. Lambert also recalls that Hurst paid him a small fee to adapt *She Stoops to Conquer* for the screen, working at Wardrobe's Lodge, but that it never went into production.

91. Brian D. Hurst, "The Lady Vanishes" (page references in parentheses). This article, with very little amendment or updating, was regurgitated by Hurst for the *Guardian* in a piece retitled "The Films," *Guardian*, Sept. 5, 1970.

92. Robert Murphy, "Rank's Attempt on the American Market," in *British Cinema History*, ed. James Curran and Vincent Porter, 172–78.

93. "Two Directors and an Editor Will Lecture to Film Society" reported that Hurst shared a platform with Jill Craigie, "Britain's only woman film director [sic] with *Blue Scar* to her credit," and Paul Sheridan, "'Editor of Impact on film' who would survey European cinema." Hurst, it said "will tackle the thorny question of the nationalization of the film industry." *West London Observer*, Sept. 2, 1949, 4.

94. John Oliver, "*Hungry Hill*: Projecting the Archive."

95. Postproduction script, S.916. Quotations that follow are from this version. The BFI Special Collections holds three scripts for *Hungry Hill*. See the bibliography for details.

96. On this defiant line, the camera has pulled Arthur Sinclair (Donovan)'s head into a close-up, an "unnatural" profile facing left to right as Broderick leaves in his carriage; the shot on the side of Donovan's face is held, filling the screen, into a dissolve to Broderick's "castle" house.

97. McIlroy, "British Filmmaking," 81.

98. Noël Coward, "10 November 1946," In *The Noël Coward Diaries*, ed. Graham Payn and Sheridan Morley, 68.

99. Oliver, "*Hungry Hill*." All newspaper reviews cited are from this source.

100. Geoffrey Bell, *Troublesome Business: The Labour Party and the Irish Question*. See esp. chap. 4, "Making Partition Concrete."

101. Barton, *Irish National Cinema*, 56.

102. Monahan, "Synge and Ireland," 85–86.

103. *Hungry Hill*, "Final Shooting Script," S.114 (London: BFISC, Scene 58), 55.

104. *Hungry Hill*, "Second Draft Script," S.10872 (London: BFISC, Scene 60), 68 (emphasis added).

105. See Andrew Spicer, "British Film Noir," 185–86, where he offers definitions of subcategories as follows: (1) gothic melodramas that continued the exploration of Victorian hypocrisy, (2) psychological thrillers that probed mental traumas produced by war, (3) crime thrillers that investigated the social upheavals and discontents, and (4) a small group of semidocumentaries that were an unstable mix of social realism and noir melodrama.

106. C. A. W., review of *Mark of Cain*, *Today's Cinema*, Jan. 4, 1948, 10.

107. C. A. W., review of *Mark of Cain*. More recent evaluations have not been any less forgiving to the film. M. F. Keaney, *British Film Noir Guide*: "*Mark of Cain* is a disappointing period noir that promises much but delivers little" (123), but the film was rescreened by the NFT in an archive season retrospective of Portman's screen work.

108. McIlroy, "British Filmmaking," 82 (emphasis in the original).

109. *Trottie True*, "Final Shooting Script," 114.

110. Harold Wilson, "Seven Directors," 67.

111. Wilson, "Seven Directors," 83, 84.

112. "Brian Desmond Hurst Will Lecture to Film Society," *West London Observer*, Aug. 19, 1949.

4. FINALE

1. Brian Desmond Hurst, "The Future of Telecinema," *Times*, Aug. 2, 1951, 7.

2. Webster, *Englishness and Empire*, 7–11, explains the difficult transition in terminology from "empire" to "commonwealth" in the 1939–65 period, and notes that the Dominions Office of the Empire had its name changed to Commonwealth Relations Office in 1947 as symptomatic of wider shifts.

3. Nicholas Mansergh, *Nationalism and Independence: Selected Irish Papers*. See, especially, chapter 11, "The Implications of Éire's Relationship with the British Commonwealth of Nations," 148–68.

4. See Clair Wills, *The Best Are Leaving: Post-war Irish Culture*; and Liam Ryan, "Irish Emigration to Britain since WWII," 47.

5. Mica Nava calls this process "visceral cosmopolitanism," which she sees at work in mainly urban centers, cities like Liverpool, London, Birmingham, and Glasgow. Her emphasis is on the unconscious, nonintellectual, and emotional features of cosmopolitanism, arguing that "music, dance and voice facilitate these processes more so than the scopic regimes of modernity." Mica Nava, *Visceral Cosmopolitanism: Gender, Culture and the Normalisation of Difference*, 8–9.

6. Catherine Dunne, *An Unconsidered People: The Irish in London*, explores the generation of the 1940s and 1950s who left Ireland to settle in London through analysis based on a series of extended interviews.

7. "Ireland Eternal and External," originally published Oct. 30, 1948, in the *New Statesmen*, in *The Matter with Ireland*, ed. David H. Green and Dan H. Laurence, 340.

8. Perilli's survey of cinema admissions for 1950 shows 13.96 million, down from a peak of 15.85 in 1945. In 1950 but 343,882 thousand TV licenses had been purchased. By mid-decade (1955) cinema admissions had dropped to 11.82 million, whereas TV license sales had risen to 4.53 million. By 1960 these trends had continued: cinema numbers had more than halved to 5.01 million, whereas TV ownership had reached 10.46 million. Curran and Porter, *British Cinema History*, table 1, 372.

9. Sue Harper and Vincent Porter, "Independent Producers," chap. 8 in *British Cinema of the 1950s: The Decline of Deference*, 153–84, offers succinct analysis with case studies of nine figures, including Herbert Wilcox, George Minter, and Michael Balcon.

10. Harper and Porter, *British Cinema*, 267–68, 272.

11. The original Dickens text was published in 1843 and Thomas Hughes's novel in 1857.

12. My summary here is indebted to Joseph Bristow's chapter "Schoolboys," in *Empire Boys: Adventures in a Man's World*, 53–92. References to the novel here are to *Tom Brown's School Days*. Page numbers in parentheses.

13. Press book located at BFI. The theatrical trailer voice-over stresses that "the stars from *Oliver Twist*"—Newton and Davies—were appearing in *Tom Brown*, that its characters were "fiction's great names that have written themselves on our memory" [*sic*], and that Tom Brown "brings back all the nostalgic excitement of *our youth*, the courage, the sentiment," suturing the viewer into an assumed memory of reading and a projected sense that "we" share the "thrill of a great public school."

14. Myro, "*Tom Brown's School Days*," *Variety*, May 2, 1951.

15. K. R., *Monthly Film Bulletin*, 18, no. 208 (1951): 260.

16. K. R., *Monthly Film Bulletin*, 260.

17. Robbins, *Empress of Ireland*, 306.

18. Robbins, *Empress of Ireland*, 309. In fact, a Ewen Fergusson was a pupil at Rugby between 1945 and 1951 and, it turns out, went on to Oxford University, played international rugby for Scotland, became a UK diplomat, and was knighted for his services. He served as chair on the Rugby School Governing Body (1995–2002) and died in 2017. Information supplied by Dr. Jonathan Smith, archivist at Rugby School. Letter to the author, Sept. 28, 2017.

19. See Hughes, *Tom Brown's School Days*, 271–73, for instance, on the "inner life" and "intimacy" shared between Tom, East, and Arthur.

20. Two essays provide useful case studies: Andrew Spicer, "Male Stars, Masculinity and British Cinema"; and Andy Medhurst's analysis, "*Victim*: Text as Context," 17–31.

21. Hughes, *Tom Brown's School Days*, 170 (emphasis added).

22. The European tradition of boys and young men in art is explored by Germaine Greer, *The Boy*, and for a more direct queer angle on photography and gay life, see James Gardiner's *Who's a Pretty Boy Then?*

23. Jeffrey Richards, "Dickens—Our Contemporary," in *Films and British National Identity*, 342.

24. Charles Dickens, *A Christmas Carol, and Other Christmas Writings*, xxvii and the illustration itself on 93.

25. *Daily Graphic*, Dec. 10, 1951, 6 (British Library, British Newspaper Archive, microfilm). The "picture serialisation" ran for a week, Dec. 10–17, 1951, in the run-up to Christmas.

26. *Scrooge*, press book (London, BFI Microfiche, Renown Pictures, 1951).

27. Quotations from *Saturday Review*, Dec. 1, 1951; and John McArdle, Dec. 8, 1951, respectively.

28. Quotations from *Variety*, Nov. 14, 1951; and *New York Film Review*, Nov. 29, 1951. This point is also made in an interview by Richard Gordon in "*Scrooge* by Another Name: Distributing *A Christmas Carol*" on *A Christmas Carol*, "Diamond Edition, Extras" (Renown Pictures/VCI Entertainment, 2001), DVD.

29. *Monthly Film Bulletin*, 18, no. 214 (1951): 359.

30. *Independent* (review section), Dec. 3, 1999, 10.

31. Robbins, *Empress of Ireland*, 303.

32. Sir Christopher Frayling, "The Darker Side of a Classic." The cricketing reference to "second-eleven" refers to a "reserve"; that is, second-best, team.

33. This point was made by Anna Laura Zambrano, *Dickens and Film*, who noted specifically its juxtapositions of fantasy and reality that resulted in a film presenting a "dark view of the human soul, leaving the viewer with an uneasy sense of the permanence of social injustice and misery" (318).

34. It comes at the end of Stave One, where "the air filled with phantoms, wandering hither and thither in restless haste, and moaning as they went. . . . The misery with them all was, clearly, that they sought to interfere, for good, in human matters, and had lost the power for ever." Dickens, *Christmas Carol*, 52.

35. *The Empress of Ireland* features some of Hurst's recollections of the origins, development, and location shooting of *Malta Story*, including his casting and direction of Alec Guinness. See Robbins, *Empress of Ireland*, 295–96, and other anecdotes about a cocktail party hosted by Admiral of the Fleet (later Lord) Louis Mountbatten, 99–100.

36. Josh Billings, *Kinematographic Weekly*, June 18, 1953, 9. According to John Ramsden, citing Josh Billings's annual listing in *Kinematographic Weekly*, *Malta Story* was the fourth-highest-earning war film of the 1950s, "The People's War: British War Films of the 1950s," 62.

37. See Terry Teachout, on Guinness's embodiment of middle-class male uncertainties and the cultural confusions of national decline, in "Alec Guinness: The Great Little Briton," 85. Ironically, Guinness actually served as a Royal Naval Reserve officer, leading landing craft offensive on Sicily in 1942, the action that the film reports in its denouement.

38. Andrew Spicer, *Typical Male: The Representation of Masculinity in British Popular Culture*, 33–39.

39. "Clem," *Variety*, July 8, 1953.

40. "Hift," *Variety*, July 14, 1953.

41. Wendy Webster, "Domesticating the Frontier: Gender, Empire and Adventure Landscapes in British Cinema, 1945–59," 88, 92–94.

42. Christine Geraghty, "The Commonwealth Film and the Liberal Dilemma," 125.

43. Robbins, *Empress of Ireland*, 301.

44. Robbins, *Empress of Ireland*, 302.

45. Truesdale and Smith, "Theirs Is the Glory," 324.

46. Transcribed from DVD viewing copy of *Simba* (Granada International/Classic Movie Collection, 390099, 2005). Hughes's speech is at 23:50–25:15 (emphasis added). The film script is at the BFISC. See the bibliography.

47. Review comments featured include C. Dixon, *Daily Telegraph*, Jan. 21, 1955; P. Brough, *News of the World*, Jan. 23, 1955; H. Conway, *Daily Sketch*, Jan. 21, 1955; John H [?], *Evening News*, Jan. 20, 1955; and W. D. Hare, *Evening Standard*, Jan. 20, 1955 (London, BFI Microfiche). One review, *Monthly Film Bulletin* 22, no. 254 (1955): 35–36, stood out as a largely negative review. Of contemporary academic analyses, Geraghty's treatment in "Commonwealth Film and the Liberal Dilemma" usefully discusses *Simba* alongside *Windom's Way* (1957).

48. For a brief accounts of the film's production, see Bryan Forbes, *Notes for a Life*, 253–54; and MacQuitty, *A Life to Remember*, 318–21. The Tudor manor house featured is Compton Wynyates in Warwickshire.

49. Albert Hourani, *A History of the Arab Peoples*, 353–69.

50. The resolution is scene 280, *The Black Tent*, "Shooting Script," July 21, 1955 (London, BFISC, S.2773), 96.

51. Forbes, *A Divided Life: Memoirs*, 310. Forbes recalls that he also shot the scene as an Italian soldier "for the Italian market," but neither version survived. This point is corroborated in "Shooting Script," 38–39.

52. Robin Maugham, "The Black Tent," in *The Black Tent, and Other Stories*, 50.

53. See notes to the production, *The Black Tent*, "General Information," July 28, 1955, 1–5.

54. See the "Shooting Script" for swift montage marriage ceremony celebrations (scenes 220–29), 70–73. For much more progressive explorations of interracial relationships and racism in British film, see, for example, Basil Dearden's *Pool of London* (1951) and *Sapphire* (1959).

55. *The Black Tent*, "General Information," July 28, 1955, 1–5. Libya had gained independence in 1951, and as well as providing logistical information about the production, these notes intended for cast and crew provide historical, political, and cultural advice about behavior and attitudes as well as how not to cause offense.

56. Brian Desmond Hurst, "British Films" [letter], *Times*, July 23, 1959 (London, British Newspaper Archive) (emphasis added).

57. "Come into the Studio . . . the Director," *Films and Filming* (Feb. 1957): 27, 32. Page references shown in text.

58. Michael Killanin formed Four Provinces Films, Ltd., in 1954. Its other directors were John Ford, Irish American actor Tyrone Power, former actor turned architect Michael Scott (1905–88), and Brian Desmond Hurst. It was set up to be the vehicle for film production in Ireland and to build a film studio designed in the modernist style of Scott,

who had produced the Irish trade pavilion in 1939, Busarus (Dublin's central bus station), the new Abbey Theatre and the Eblana Theatre, hospitals, and a host of other notable public buildings. Largely through Ford's influence and the success of *The Quiet Man* in 1952, Four Provinces had apparently swayed Republic Pictures in the United States to agree to a distribution deal in Ireland and the United Kingdom. Flynn and Brereton, *The A to Z of Irish Cinema*, 126; Irish Architects Association, https://iarc.ie/collections/drawings/. Michael Scott 89/44, accessed Aug. 31, 2017; Killanin Collection, Irish Film Archive, Dublin.

59. For the debates about the television service, see Robert Savage, *Irish Television: The Political and Social Origins*.

60. Reported by Brian MacWilliams in *Films and Filming* 2, no. 2 (1955): 24. Materials in the Killanin Papers, KAIFA, 07/1343, Dublin.

61. *Report on the Means of Fostering the General Development of the Film Industry in Ireland*, Sept. 11, 1955.

62. See Rockett, Gibbons, and Hill, *Cinema and Ireland*, 95–100, for an account of the postwar governmental debates and competition to capture the business that it was thought would follow the establishment of a purpose-built studio.

63. *Report on the Means of Fostering the General Development of the Film Industry in Ireland* (KAIFA, 07/1343, Dublin).

64. References to these letters are in Killanin's memoir notes that explicitly make these links: "Recall Brian Hearst [sic] and our first efforts at the film industry in the early thirties and the purchase of Gormanston and his last picture THE PLAYBOY OF THE WESTERN WORLD." See "Brian Hearst [sic] to K.[illanin]," Apr. 21, 1953 (KAIFA, Dublin).

65. *Behind the Mask* (OPTD 2347) and *His and Hers* (7954139) were released on DVD in 2012 and 2014, respectively, the latter under "The British Film" series in the United Kingdom by StudioCanal.

66. Published originally with this title by Heinemann in 1955, it was republished to coincide with the release of the film under the new title of *Behind the Mask*. It can be found now in the rare-books collection of the British Library.

67. Wilson's novel writes of Selwood's exclusion from the circle, "a person of no significance, he had no further place in this world at all," whereas John Hunter's film script presents him as part of what Wilson calls the "conspiratorial realignment of the profession." John Rowan Wilson, *The Pack*, 272.

68. W. L. W., "Hospital Life with the Starch Left In," *Observer*, Nov. 24, 1958; C. A. Lejeune, "Horse-Play in the Wild West," *Observer*, Nov. 9 1958.

69. F. J., "Behind the Mask," *Daily Cinema*, Oct. 27, 1958.

70. P. J. D., *Monthly Film Bulletin* 25, no. 299 (1958): 150.

71. "Rich," *Variety*, Nov. 12, 1958.

72. Penelope Gilliat, "Censorship in the Torture Chamber," *Observer*, Jan. 22, 1961.

73. Christopher Murray, *Twentieth-Century Irish Drama*, 80. See also Kiberd, *Inventing Ireland*, 166–88.

74. Monahan, "John Milligan Synge and Ireland," 76–87.

75. Ford Papers, Lilly Library, Indiana University, Bloomington. The letter from Hurst to Ford is dated June 4, 1956. My thanks to Charles Barr for generously sharing his notes from an archive trip.

76. In a letter to Killanin, John Ford welcomed the news that Hurst had agreed to come onto the Board of Four Provinces and, it seems, had designed the new company's stationery. Mar. 13, 1955, KAIFA, 07/4116, Dublin.

77. Robbins, *Empress of Ireland*, 191–92. For an account of the shoot from the uncredited assistant director I interviewed Gerald O'Hara, Oct. 9, 2008, audiotape.

78. *Playboy of the Western World*, "Script," typed 126 pages, 07/1319; and "Final Shooting Script," 07/1321, KAIFA, Dublin.

79. Ford Papers. Thanks to Charles Barr for this reference.

80. Letter to John Ford, Mar. 24, 1961. Quoted from Killanin's memoir notes. KAIFA, 07/1416, Dublin.

81. "Ulsterman to Film 'Playboy,'" unidentified newspaper clipping (possibly *Belfast Telegraph*), n.d, Cuttings Collection, Central Library, Belfast. The difficulties were commented on by Hurst's associates and friends in correspondence, Liam O'Flaherty noting to a correspondent that "Brian Hurst is filming 'The Playboy' in Kerry, using Siobhan McKenna as the female lure and God knows how many pansies as the male ones." Andrew A. Kelly, ed., *The Letters of Liam O'Flaherty*, 363.

82. It received a private fund-raising screening at the Institut Français, London, to help raise money for a leper-colony charity whose patron was Lady Diana Cooper. I can find no record of a UK release date. Robbins, *Empress of Ireland*, 193.

83. Hurst had written to Ford, Nov. 4, 1964, Ford Papers, based on Charles Barr's notes.

84. Robbins, *Empress of Ireland*, 192–93. Sadly, this interview was not recorded. "Seamus Kelly Visits Kerry to See an Irish Classic Being Filmed," *Irish Times*, July 26, 1961.

85. David Nowlan, "*The Playboy* as a Film," *Irish Times*, Apr. 26, 1962.

86. Robbins, *Empress of Ireland*, 193.

87. Robbins, *Empress of Ireland*, 192.

88. Quoted in Slide, *The Cinema and Ireland*, 23. See also the US promotional flier for the film's release, which is in the Liam O'Leary Archive, National Library, MS 50.000/326/24, Dublin.

89. *The Playboy of the Western World*, in *A World on Film* (New York: Harper & Row, 1966), 219.

90. Killanin's letter went to McCann, Mar. 9, 1963. Department of Foreign Affairs, DFA 323/268, National Archives, Dublin. My thanks to Roddy Flynn for generously sharing his research notes documenting this and another diplomatic incident about *Playboy* in Russia in 1965. Quotations below are from same DFA file in the National Archives, Dublin. With permission.

91. A letter from Mr. Ronan to Ambassador of Ireland, London, July 8, 1965, from the Cultural Relations Committee and an earlier DEA memorandum to a Mr. Coffey, dated May, 14 1965. With permission.

92. McIlroy, "Appreciation," 113.

93. Sternlicht, "Synge on Film," 164.

94. Frazier, *Hollywood Irish*, 32. See also his earlier essay "'Quaint Pastoral Numbsculls': Siobhan McKenna's Playboy Film."

95. Constance Sykes, "Brian Desmond Hurst: Career of an Irish Film Director," press release, Feb. 6, 1952 (London: BFI Microfiche). This document also gives news of Hurst's appointment by the Dutch government to be artistic adviser on a "tough seafaring story of the ocean-going tugs and dry docks" with a screenplay written by Jan de Hartog. The PR closes by mentioning Hurst's "own production of *The Last Romantic*, a film of Ludwig II the so-called 'mad' King of Bavaria, will be uninterrupted; negotiations are in the final stages for shooting to commence early summer, probably in two languages."

96. Discussing *On Approval* (1944), Googie Withers (in an interview with Brian McFarlane) recalls: "We started off with Brian Desmond Hurst as director, but Clive Brook didn't see eye to eye with him at all. They had some awful rows. The film was finished and put on the shelf, then a few months later my agent told me that Clive was putting up his own money because he believed it would be a money spinner." Brian McFarlane, ed., *Sixty Voices: Celebrities Recall the Golden Age of British Cinema*, 233.

97. Letter from Hurst to Sean O'Casey, in *Sean O'Casey: Collected Letters*, vol. 2, *1942–54*, ed. David Krause, 394.

98. There is significant correspondence during the years 1958–60 between Hurst and Killanin about making *Jackboot in Ireland*, even involving a letter (Apr. 22, 1960) from Marlon Brando to Killanin on the lack of a market for the project in the United States. KAIFA, LK/B3/8, Dublin.

99. Robbins, *Empress of Ireland*, 324–29.

100. M. Walsh, "Nasser Film Deal with Britain," *Daily Express*, June 8, 1964, reports that "British independent film producer Brian Desmond Hurst has clinched a £15 million deal with the Nasser Government to make 12 feature pictures in the next six years." The ambitious "Anglo-Egyptian venture" would combine productions made in English at British studios with location work in Egypt, including one titled *Queen Nefertiti*. The first film, *Kilo 40*, would star Trevor Howard, with whom Hurst had spent a week in Cairo in discussions with the Egyptian minister of culture, Dr. Abdul Hatim. Hurst's own film company, Glade Films, based in Piccadilly, would be involved. There is no archival record of this company to the author's knowledge.

101. The inaccurately titled newspaper clipping, "The Diary: Twelve Projects of Two Ulster Film Makers," is undated, but ca. 1965 owing to internal date reference to *Thunderball* (1965). Cuttings Collection, Central Library, Belfast. Writer "Malcolm Lee" appears in no search of online databases or film reference books.

102. Hazel Murphy, Killanin Papers, box 33, Irish Film Institute, Dublin.

103. According to O'Flaherty's correspondence, Hurst initially bought the film rights for a year in 1946 and in 1962 was still trying to cut a deal with O'Flaherty that consisted of £500 for a six-month option on *The Famine*, a further £1,500 if the option was taken up, and a final £4,000 sum when the film cleared its costs, plus a 5 percent cut of the profits. Kelly, *Letters of Liam O'Flaherty*, 299, 363.

104. Dudley Sutton, interview with the author, Oct. 9, 2008, Chelsea Arts Club, London, audiotape.

105. Robbins, *Empress of Ireland*, 346.

106. This exchange was recalled by Dudley Sutton impersonating Hurst for me! Oct. 9, 2008, Chelsea Arts Club, London, audiotape.

107. Liam O'Leary to Brian Desmond Hurst, Feb. 9, 1985, LOLNL, MS 50.000/326/1, National Library.

5. FORGOTTEN

1. Patrick Maume's essay is in the *Dictionary of Irish Biography* (Cambridge: Cambridge Univ. Press, with the Royal Irish Academy, 2009), but only in the online edition, dated as 2012.

2. Launched in 2010, the "official legacy website" www.briandesmondhurst.com is authored and published by Hurst biographer Allan Esler Smith, who also represents the Hurst Estate. As of September 2020, this URL is inactive.

3. Roddy Flynn and Pat Brereton, eds., *The A to Z of Irish Cinema*, 157–58 (emphasis added).

4. De'ath, "Exiles in London."

5. "New Comment: The Blockbuster Discussion," BBC Third Programme, Aug. 8, 1963, BBC Written Archives; "The Films," *Guardian*, Sept. 5, 1970.

6. In Durgnat's seminal *Mirror for England* (1970), Hurst is in fact mentioned six times, but referring to just four titles: *On Night of the Fire, Theirs Is the Glory, Hungry Hill*, and *Dangerous Exile* (three times!). Durgnat combines praiseworthy mentions (*Hungry Hill* is noted as "the boldest" of a group of post-1945 films addressing class [23]) and damning critique, such as "After a colourful start, [*Dangerous Exile*] dwindles into Orczy tosh" (219). Roy Armes, *A Critical History of British Cinema*, gets Hurst's birth date wrong (1892), mentions just *Glamorous Night* and *The Lion Has Wings*, and attributes Hurst with the codirection of *Caesar and Cleopatra* (1945). George Perry, *The Great British Picture Show*, does not feature Hurst in the "Biographical Guide to British Cinema" section, but does mention *Dangerous Moonlight* with its "immensely popular but sugary story," whose Addinsell music "became an incessant theme on the radio" (90).

7. O'Leary had discussed Hurst and cited his professional views on the viability of filmmaking as an industry in Ireland in his book *Invitation to the Film* (1947). As

an archivist/curator, O'Leary wrote key text in the catalog/pamphlet accompanying Ireland's first major exhibition in Dublin held as part of the Dublin Arts Festival, Mar. 5–20, 1976. Hurst got only the briefest of mentions to the effect that he "was to make many films," citing only three Irish films from the 1930s (see chapter 2 above), *Cinema Ireland, 1895–1976* (Dublin: Dublin Arts Festival, 1976), 23. In London in 1980 an extensive festival of Irish arts called "A Sense of Ireland" was held in multiple locations across music, art, literature, and cinema and included various seminars and talks, with Kevin Rockett as the film programmer. Although one still image from *Ourselves Alone* featured in the booklet that accompanied the festival (162), none of Hurst's films was actually screened. *A Sense of Ireland* (Dublin and London: A Sense of Ireland, 1980).

8. The undated black-and-white photograph of Hurst next to the sculpture in an unnamed gallery (or is it a church?) is located in the Liam O'Leary Archive, NLI, LOL MS 50.000/276, Dublin.

9. Smith, *Irishman Chained*.

10. These articles appeared, respectively, in "Brian Desmond Hurst," *Daily Telegraph*, Oct. 4, 1986; "Mr B. D. Hurst," *Times*, Oct. 2, 1986; and *Variety*, Oct. 1, 1986, 129.

11. Ed Vulliamy, *Guardian*, Sept. 30, 1986.

12. Kevin Rockett, with John Caughie, *The Companion to British and Irish Cinema*, 87.

13. Bourne, *Brief Encounters*, 31.

14. The phrase comes from Foster's subtitle to his *The Irish Story* (2001).

15. Quoted in Smith, *Irishman Chained*.

16. See, for example, the memoirs of Diana Dors, Brian Forbes, and William Roach. For full details, see the bibliography.

17. Bourne, *Brief Encounters*, 11; Robbins, *Empress of Ireland*, 28. Interestingly, Hurst can actually be heard recounting the anecdote of hosting a party in Paris, James Joyce being present, and announcing the inspired last words of Molly Bloom in *Ulysses*. In what is believed to be the only extant recording of Hurst's voice, he was being interviewed by sociolinguist Tom Boyd circa the 1970s. See Smith, *Irishman Chained*.

18. The two documents under "Brian Desmond Hurst" are in the BFI, Microfiche Collection, 1935, 1–4, i–v.

19. Sykes, "Brian Desmond Hurst," 3–4; Dors, *Behind Closed Doors*, 79; Slide, *The Cinema and Ireland*, 22.

20. Stephen Bourne, "Behind the Masks: Anthony Asquith and Brian Desmond Hurst," 41.

21. Robbins, *Empress of Ireland*, 164.

22. Although the author was in email contact with Robbins in 2008–9, sadly he died in 2012 and the whereabouts of the audiotapes remain unknown. Marcus Hearn produced a short film featuring Robbins's memories of Hurst captured on-screen, called "The Legendary Brian Desmond Hurst," that was a DVD extra on a two-disk collectors edition of *Scrooge* (UK, DD Entertainment, 2005).

23. Ronan Farren, "Memoir of the Making of a Non-existent Film," *Sunday Independent*, Oct. 10, 2004.

24. In contrast to the dismissive tone of Rockett, Stephen Bourne was notable in the mid-1990s by suggesting that "perhaps the time has come for a reassessment of his career. In some ways he is difficult to pigeon-hole, because he worked in different genres. But he did excel at making melodramas, in which he often cast gay actors, or included gay characters." Bourne, *Brief Encounters*, 27.

25. See "Belfast's Titanic Quarter," *Economist* 8690 (2010): 30–31; and the essays in *Relaunching the Titanic*, ed. W. J. V. Neil, M. Murray, and B. Grost.

26. Alexander Walker, reviewing *Hungry Hill* screening at NFT for "Hot Ticket" section, *Evening Standard*, Mar. 16, 2000.

27. A paperback edition, published in 2005, appeared with a redesigned cover with the Hurst Estate's photograph removed.

28. The Irish Film and Television Research, Trinity College, was developed from Rockett's book *The Irish Filmography* (1996) into an online database with Eugene Finn. https://www.tcd.ie/irishfilm/index.php. Hurst was notably absent from the BFI's Screenonline website listing biographical essays on British directors. Hurst began to appear in print reference works such as Brian McFarlane, ed., *The Encyclopaedia of British Film*; and Robert Murphy, ed., *Directors in British and Irish Cinema: A Reference Companion*, with a well-written entry by J. C. Robertson.

29. *Dictionary of Irish Biography*, s.v. "Brian Desmond Hurst," by Patrick Maume, accessed Nov. 23, 2013, http://www.dib.cambridge.org.

CONCLUSION

1. Slide, *The Cinema and Ireland*, 22.

2. Robbins, *Empress of Ireland*, 315.

3. Tom Dewe Matthews's review in *Independent on Sunday* is cited in Robbins, *Empress of Ireland*, front matter.

4. Hurst was expatiating on the release of *Prison without Bars*, quoted in *Film Weekly* 20, no. 519 (1938), 23.

5. John Ford to Michael Killanin, July 30, 1953, John Ford Archive, Lilly Library, Indiana University, Bloomington.

6. Hurst is quoted in De'ath, "Exiles in London." Perhaps it is a version of the Irish: "Ní hé an bochtanas is measach an tarcaisne a leanann" (It's not poverty that is the worst thing, but the insult that follows it). Quoted in Declan Kiberd, *After Ireland: Writing the Nation from Beckett to the Present Day*, 13–14.

Bibliography

ARCHIVES

BBC Written Archives, Reading
BFI Special Collection, London
British Newspaper Archive (formally at Colindale)
Hart House Theatre Archive, Ontario, Canada
Hurst Estate Archive (Private)
Irish Film Institute, Dublin
Liam O'Leary Collection, National Library of Ireland
Lord Chamberlain's Register, British Library, London
National Film and TV Archive, London
Ontario College of Art and Design Archive, Canada

PRIMARY SOURCES

All sourced at the Reuben BFI Library/Special Collections (BFISC) unless otherwise indicated.

Screenplays

In order of production date with BFISC reference unless otherwise indicated.

Glamorous Night (1937). S.10644.
Revolt in the Desert (n.d.). "Scenario" by Brian Desmond Hurst. SCR-15131. Script number S.10359. "Unrealised project."
Revolt in the Desert (n.d.). BFI SC "Unrealised project." SCR-15128. Script number S.8735. "Outline script" by John Monk Saunders. GB London Film Productions. Dir. Brian Desmond Hurst.
Lawrence of Arabia (1935). "Screenplay" by James Lansdale Hodson. SCR-15130. Script number S.8755. "Unrealised project."

Revolt in the Desert (1938). "Scenario" by Brian Desmond Hurst and Duncan Guthrie. SCR-15132. Script number S.8738 (3-1938 [Mar.]).

Lawrence of Arabia from *Revolt in the Desert* (1938). "Scenario" by Brian Desmond Hurst, Duncan Guthrie, and Miles Malleson. SCR-15133, Oct. 4, 1938.

The Lion Has Wings (1939). S.1838. SCR-11335. Release Script.

Miss Grant Goes to the Door (1940). Shot sheet and script. Imperial War Museum, London, MI-43. Typescript. Viewing copy: https:film.iwmcollections.org.uk/record/18045.

Dangerous Moonlight (1942). S.442. Continuity/Cutting Script.

Hungry Hill (1945). S.114. Final Shooting Script.

Hungry Hill (1945). S.10872. Second Draft Script.

Hungry Hill (1946). S.916. Postproduction script.

Letter from Ulster (1943). S.15108. Continuity/Dialogue Sheets from treatment.

Letter from Ulster (1943). Northern Ireland Screen. Digital Film Archive, https://digitalfilmarchive.net/media/a-letter-from-ulster-81.

Theirs Is the Glory (1946). Screenplay by Louis Golding and Terence Young.

The Mark of Cain (1948), aka *Closed Carriage*. S.14827. Play by J. Shearing.

Trottie True (1948), aka *The Gay Lady*. S.10858. Novel by S. J. Simon/Caryl Brahms. Final Shooting Script.

Scrooge (1951). S.6429. Postproduction script.

The Malta Story (1953). Draft "Bright Flame." Thorold Dickenson Collection. Item 8.

Simba (1955). S.1262.

The Demi-Gods (ca. 1955). "Treatment," Hazel Murphy. KAIFI, Dublin. Box 33. B.7.2/S1, 61 pages. Typescript.

The Black Tent (1956). S.2773. Dated 21/7/55 Bryan Forbes. Shooting Script.

Dangerous Exile (1957). S.14034. Postproduction script. From novel by Vaughan Wilkins.

His and Hers (1958). S.13539. Release script.

The Playboy of the Western World (1962). S.14903.

Playboy of the Western World (1962). Typescript. Dublin: Film Institute of Ireland, Killanin Collection. 07/1319, 126 pages. See also 07/1320 and "Final Shooting Script," 07/1321.

Press Books (BFISC Reference).

Ourselves Alone. PBM40399.

On the Night of the Fire. PBS40175 and PBM40175.

The Tenth Man. PBM47647.

Glamorous Night. SCR-8748; PBM-30960.
Prison without Bars. PBM-41918.

Hurst Interviews/Contributor, BBC Written Archives

"Film Time: Pastimes of the Picture Makers." BBC Home Service radio, Dec. 13, 1951.
"Kaleidoscope." BBC Television, Nov. 29, 1948.
"New Comment: The Blockbuster Discussion." Aug. 8, 1963.
"Northern Film News Goes to Pinewood Studios." Interviewed by John Stratton. North Region, July 1, 1957.

IRISH FILM INSTITUTE, DUBLIN

Killanin Archive. Dublin, IFI. Hurst Papers: KAIFA includes 07/1416; 07/1319, 07/1320, 07/1321.

LIAM O'LEARY ARCHIVE, NATIONAL LIBRARY OF IRELAND, DUBLIN

Ford, John. Papers. MS 50.000/327.
Hurst, Brian Desmond. Papers. MS 50.000/326.

SECONDARY SOURCES

Place of publication is London unless otherwise specified.

Abraham, James Johnston. *The Night Nurse*. George Newness, 1932.
Ackerley, Joe Randolph. *My Father and Myself*. 2nd ed. New York: Coward-McCann, 1969.
Ackland, Rodney, with Elspeth Grant. *The Celluloid Mistress; Or, The Custard Pie of Dr. Caligari*. Alan Wingate, 1954.
Andrew, Dudley. "The Unauthorised Auteur Today." In *Film Theory Goes to the Movies*, edited by R. Stam and T. Miller, 20–29. Oxford: Blackwell, 2000.
Archer, Fred. "Psychic Film Director Recalls: Spirit Led Him Away from Enemy Lines." *Psychic News*, Nov. 14, 1959, 1–2.
Armes, Roy. *A Critical History of British Cinema*. Secker & Warburg, 1978.

Ashby, Justine, and Andrew Higson, eds. *British Cinema: Past and Present*. Routledge, 2000.
Asquith, Anthony. "Realler than the Real Thing." *Cine-Technician* 11 (Mar.–Apr. 1945): 25–27.
Austin, Aubery. "The Picture They Never Made." *Picture Post*, Dec. 15, 1945, 2.
Bairner, Alan. "Simply the (George) Best: Ulster Protestantism, Conflicted Identity and the Belfast Boys." *Canadian Journal of Irish Studies* 32, no. 2 (2006): 34–41.
Barr, Charles. "Is It His War as Well as Hers? The View from Ealing." *Irish Studies Review* 19, no. 1 (2011): 31–40.
Barr, James. *A Line in the Sand: Britain, France and the Struggle That Shaped the Middle East*. Simon & Schuster, 2012.
Bartlett, Neil. *Who Was That Man? A Present for Mr Oscar Wilde*. Serpent's Tail, 1988.
Barton, Ruth. *Acting Irish in Hollywood*. Dublin: Irish Academic Press, 2006.
———. "Introduction: Screening the Irish in Britain." *Irish Studies Review* (Feb. 2011): 1–4.
———. *Irish National Cinema*. Routledge, 2004.
———. "The Potency of Cheap Music: Exile, Ballads and Performance in Irish Cinema." In *Ireland: Space, Text and Time*, edited by Liam Harte, Yvonne Whelan, and Patrick Crotty, 199–207. Dublin: Liffey Press, 2005.
———. *Rex Ingram: Visionary Director of the Silent Screen*. Lexington: Univ. Press of Kentucky, 2014.
———, ed. *Screening Irish-America: Representing Irish-America on Film and Television*. Dublin: Irish Academic Press, 2009.
BBFC. *Alibi*. Report. BBFC-1-9-989, Feb. 10, 1941.
———. *Irish Hearts* (a.k.a. Nora O'Neale). Report. BBFC-1-3-330, Aug. 3, 1934).
———. *Tell-Tale Heart*. Report. BBFC-1-1-91, Feb. 22, 1932.
Beckett, James Camlin. *The Making of Modern Ireland, 1603–1923*. 2nd ed. Faber, 1981.
Bell, Desmond, ed. *Dissenting Voices/Imagined Communities: Ulster Protestant Identity and Cinema in Ireland*. Belfast: Belfast Film Festival, 2001.
Bell, Geoffrey. *Troublesome Business: The Labour Party and the Irish Question*. Pluto Press, 1982.
Bergfelder, Tim. "Surface and Distraction: Style and Genre at Gainsborough in the Late 1920s and 1930s." In *Gainsborough Pictures: Rethinking British Cinema*, edited by Pam Cook, 31–46. Cassell, 1997.

Bielenberg, Andy, ed. *The Irish Diaspora*. Pearson Education, 2000.

The Black Tent. "General Information on Production." BFISC S.277328, July 1955, 1–5.

Bourke, Joanna. "'Irish Tommies': The Construction of Irish Manhood, 1914–18." *Bullan* 3, no. 2 (1997–98): 20–23.

———. *Rape: A History from 1860 to the Present Day*. Virago, 2007.

———. "'Remembering' War." Special issue, *Journal of Contemporary History* 39, no. 4 (2004): 473–85.

Bourne, Stephen. "Behind the Masks: Anthony Asquith and Brian Desmond Hurst." In *British Queer Cinema*, edited by R. Griffiths, 35–46. Routledge, 2006.

———. *Brief Encounters: Lesbians and Gays in British Cinema*. Cassell, 1996.

Bouvet, Vincent, and Gerard Durozoi. *Paris between the Wars: Art, Style and Glamour in the Crazy Years*. Thames & Hudson, 2010.

Bowen, Elizabeth. "The Mysterious Kor." In *Collected Stories*. Vintage, 1999.

Bowker "Variety" Film Reviews, 1934–37. New York: R. R. Bowker, 1983.

Bowman, Timothy. *Irish Regiments in the Great War: Discipline and Morale*. Manchester: Manchester Univ. Press, 2003.

Boyce, David George. "The Marginal Britons: The Irish." In *Englishness*, edited by R. Colls and P. Dodd, 230–53. Croom Helm, 1986.

Boyle, Sean. *Emmet Dalton: Somme Soldier, Irish General, Film Pioneer*. Sallins, Co. Kildare: Merrion Press, 2015.

Brah, Avtar. *Cartographies of Diaspora: Contested Identities*. Routledge, 1996.

"Brian Desmond Hurst." Press release, BFI Microfiche, Oct. 3, 1936.

"Brian Desmond Hurst." Press release, Denham Studios, June 30, 1938.

Bristow, Joseph. *Empire Boys: Adventures in a Man's World*. HarperCollins, 1991.

"British Feature Directors: An Index to Their Work." *Sight and Sound* 27, no. 6 (1958): 289–304.

Brownlow, Kevin. *David Lean: A Biography*. Richard Cohen, 1996.

Burton, Sarah. *Imposters: Six Kinds of Liar—True Tales of Deception*. Penguin, 2001.

Campbell, Sean, and Roger Swift. "The Irish in Britain: Since 1914." In *The Cambridge Social History of Modern Ireland*, edited by Eugenio F. Biagini and Mary E. Daly, 523–33. Cambridge: Cambridge Univ. Press, 2017.

Chapman, James. *The British at War: Cinema, State and Propaganda, 1939–1945*. I. B. Tauris, 1998.

Chapman, James, and Nicholas J. Cull. "The Watershed: *Lawrence of Arabia* (1962)." In *Projecting Empire: Imperialism and Popular Cinema*, 87–111. I. B. Tauris, 2009.

Chapman, James, Mark Glancy, and Sue Harper, eds. *The New Film History*. Houndmills, Hampshire: Palgrave, 2007.

Christie, Ian. "Histories of the Future: Mapping the Avant-Garde." *Film History* 20, no. 1 (2008): 6–13.

Condon, Dennis. *Early Irish Cinema: 1895–1921*. Dublin: Irish Academic Press, 2008.

Conrich, Ian. "Horrific Films and the 1930s British Cinema." In *British Horror Cinema*, edited by S. Chibnall and J. Petley, 58–70. Routledge, 2000.

Cook, Pam, ed. *Gainsborough Pictures*. Cassell, 1997.

Cousins, Mark. *The Story of Film*. Pavillion, 2011.

Crisp, Quentin. *The Naked Civil Servant*. Flamingo, 1985.

Curran, James, and Vincent Porter, eds. *British Cinema History*. Weidenfeld & Nicolson, 1983.

Curran, Joseph. *Hibernian Green on the Silver Screen: The Irish and American Movies*. New York: Greenwood Press, 1989.

Dalrymple, Ian. "On the Lion Having Wings." *Cine-Technician* 6, no. 24 (1940): 10–13.

De'ath, Wilfred. "Exiles in London." *Punch*, Oct. 8, 1969, 575–76.

Delaney, Enda. *The Irish in Post-war Britain*. Oxford: Oxford Univ. Press, 2013.

"Desmond Hurst in Ulster." *Kinematograph Weekly*, July 30, 1942, 38.

Dickens, Charles. *A Christmas Carol, and Other Christmas Writings*. Edited by M. Slater. Penguin, 2003.

Dixon, Wheeler Winston. "The Marginalised Vision of Montgomery Tully." *Classic Images* 224–25 (1994): 8, 10, 12, 56–57, 303.

———, ed. *Re-viewing British Cinema, 1900–1992*. Albany: State Univ. of New York Press, 1994.

Dollimore, Jonathan. "Bisexuality." In *Lesbian and Gay Studies: A Critical Introduction*, edited by A. Medhurst and S. Munt, 250–60. Cassell, 1997.

Dors, Diana. *Behind Closed Dors*. W. H. Allen, 1979.

Dunne, Catherine. *An Unconsidered People: The Irish in London*. Dublin: New Island Books, 2003.

Dusinberre, Deke. "The Avant-Garde Attitude in the Thirties." In *British Cinema: Traditions of Independence*, edited by D. MacPherson, 34–49. BFI, 1980.

Dyer, Richard. "Believing in Fairies: The Author and the Homosexual." In *The Culture of Queers*, 31–45. Routledge, 2002.

Edwards, Steve. *Art and Its Histories: A Reader*. New Haven, CT: Yale/Open Univ. Press, 1999.

Elder, Bruce R. *Harmony and Dissent: Film and Avant-Garde Art Movements in the Early Twentieth Century.* Toronto: Wilfrid Laurier Univ. Press, 2008.

Evans, Mary. *Missing Persons: The Impossibility of Auto/Biography.* Routledge, 1999.

Fer, Briony, David Batchelor, and Paul Wood. *Realism, Revolution and Surrealism: Art between the Wars.* Oxford: Oxford Univ. Press, 1993.

"Five Minutes in a Film Studio" [on set of *Alibi*]. *Picture Post*, Mar. 6, 1942, 21.

Fleeton, George, ed. *A Seat among the Stars: The Cinema and Ireland.* Belfast: UTV/Channel Four TV, ca. 1984.

Fleischer, Mary. "W. B. Yeats and Ito." In *Embodied Texts: Symbolist Playwright-Dancer Collaboration*, 149–213. Amsterdam: Rodolfi Press, 2007.

Fleming, Marie, and John R. Taylor. *100 Years: The Evolution of the Ontario College of Arts.* Ontario: Art Gallery of Ontario/Ontario College of Art, 1976.

Flynn, Roddy. "Raiders of the Lost Archives: The Report of the Inter-Departmental Committee on the Film Industry, 1942." *Irish Communications Review* 10 (2007): 30–40.

Flynn, Roddy, and Patrick Brereton, eds. *The A to Z of Irish Cinema.* Lanham, MD: Scarecrow Press, 2007.

Forbes, Bryan. *A Divided Life: Memoirs.* 2nd ed. Heinemann, 1992.

———. *Notes for a Life.* Heinemann, 1974.

Foster, John Wilson. "Culture and Colonisation: A View from the North." *Irish Review* 5 (Autumn 1988): 17–26.

———. "Making Representation: The Literary Imagery of Ulster Protestants—Some Historical Notes." In *Dissenting Voices/Imagined Communities: Ulster Protestant Identity and Cinema in Ireland*, edited by D. Bell, 12–14. Belfast: Belfast Film Festival, 2001.

Foster, R. F. "Marginal Men and Micks on the Make: The Uses of Irish Exile." In *Paddy and Mr Punch: Connections in Irish and English History*, 281–305. Penguin, 1993.

———. *Paddy and Mr Punch: Connections in Irish and English History.* Penguin, 1993.

———. "Protestant Magic: W. B. Yeats and the Spell of Irish History." In *Paddy and Mr Punch: Connections in Irish and English History*, 212–32. Penguin, 1993.

———. *W. B. Yeats: A Life.* Vol. 1, *The Apprentice Mage.* Oxford: Oxford Univ. Press, 1998.

Frayling, Sir Christopher. "The Darker Side of a Classic." In *A Christmas Carol.* Ballyhoo Pictures/VCI Entertainment, 2011. DVD.

Frazier, Adrian. *Hollywood Irish: John Ford, Abbey Actors and the Irish Revival in Hollywood.* Dublin: Lilliput Press, 2011.

———. "'Quaint Pastoral Numbsculls': Siobhan McKenna's Playboy Film." In *Playboys of the Western World: Production Histories*, edited by A. Frazier, 59–74. Dublin: Carysford Press, 2004.

Gardiner, James. *Who's a Pretty Boy Then?* Serpent's Tail, 1996.

Gardiner, Juliet. *The Thirties: An Intimate History.* HarperPress, 2010.

Geltzer, George. "Herbert Brenon." *Films in Review* 6 (Mar. 3, 1955): 116–25.

Geraghty, Christine. "The Commonwealth Film and the Liberal Dilemma." In *British Cinema in the Fifties: Gender, Genre and the "New Look,"* 112–32. Routledge, 2000.

Gillespie, Michael Patrick. *The Myth of an Irish Cinema: Approaching Irish-Themed Films.* Syracuse, NY: Syracuse Univ. Press, 2008.

Gillett, Phillip. *The British Working Class in Postwar Film.* Manchester: Manchester Univ. Press, 2003.

Gilligan, Paula. "'A Monotonous Hell': Space, Violence and the City in the 1930s Films of Liam O'Flaherty." *Early Popular Visual Culture* 5, no. 3 (2007): 301–16.

Gingold, Hermione. *How to Grow Old Disgracefully.* Gollancz, 1989.

Gledhill, Christine. "Play as Experiment in 1920s British Cinema." In "Experiment in Film before World War II." Special issue, *Film History* 20, no. 1 (2008): 14–34.

Gough-Yates, Kevin. "Exiles and British Cinema." In *The British Cinema Book*, edited by R. Murphy, 170–76. BFI, 2001.

Graham, Ian. *Herbert Brenon: An American Cinema Odyssey.* Privately published, 2017.

Grandy, Christine. *Heroes and Happy Endings: Class, Gender and Nation in Popular Film and Fiction in Interwar Britain.* Manchester: Manchester Univ. Press, 2014.

Gray, Michael. *Stills, Reels and Rushes: Ireland and the Irish in 20th Century Cinema.* Dublin: Blackhall, 1999.

Greacen, Robert. *Rooted in Ulster: Nine Northern Writers.* Belfast: Lagan Press, 2000.

Green, David H., and Dan H. Laurence, eds. *The Matter with Ireland.* Rupert Hart Davies, 1962.

Green, Frederick Lawrence. *On the Night of the Fire.* 2nd ed. Penguin, 1942.

Greene, Graham. *The Graham Greene Film Reader: Mornings in the Dark.* Edited by D. Parkinson. Manchester: Carcanet, 1993.

———. *The Pleasure-Dome: The Collected Film Criticism, 1935–1940*. Edited by J. R. Taylor. 2nd ed. Oxford: Oxford Univ. Press, 1980.

———. *Reflections*. Edited by J. Adamson. Reinhardt Books, 1990.

Greer, Germaine. *The Boy*. Thames & Hudson, 2003.

Griffith, Daniel. *The Darker Side of a Classic*. Ballyhoo Motion Pictures/VCI Entertainment, 2011. DVD.

———. *The Human Blarney Stone: The Life and Films of Brian Desmond Hurst*. Ballyhoo Motion Pictures/VCI Entertainment, 2011. DVD.

Griffiths, Robin, ed. *British Queer Cinema*. Routledge, 2006.

Grigor, Angela N. *Arthur Lismer: Visionary Arts Educator*. Montreal: McGill–Queens Univ. Press, 2002.

Guinness, Selina. "Protestant Magic Reappraised: Evangelicalism, Dissent and Theosophy." *Irish University Review* 33, no. 1 (2003): 14–27.

Gunning, Tom. "Waking and Faking: Ireland and Cinema Astray." In *National Cinema and Beyond*, edited by K. Rockett and J. Hill, 19–31. Dublin: Four Courts Press, 2004.

Hagen, Louis. *Arnhem Lift: A German Jew in the Glider Pilot Regiment*. 2nd ed. Stroud: History Press/Spellmount, 2012.

Hall, Stuart. "Minimal Selves." In *The Real Me: Postmodernism and the Question of Identity*, edited by L. Appignanesi, 44–46. Institute of the Contemporary Arts, 1987.

Hamnet, Nina. *Is She a Lady? A Problem in Autobiography*. Allan Wingate, 1955.

———. *The Laughing Torso*. Constable, 1932.

Hanks, Patrick, and Flavia Hodges, eds. *A Dictionary of Surnames*. Oxford: Oxford Univ. Press, 1998.

Hannigan, Mick. "Tribute to Brian Desmond Hurst." In *49th Cork Film Festival Programme*, 84–85. Cork: Cork Film Festival, 2004.

Harper, Sue, and Vincent Porter. *British Cinema of the 1950s: The Decline of Deference*. Oxford: Oxford Univ. Press, 2003.

Harrison's Reports and Film Reviews, 1941–43. Edited by D. Richard Baer. Hollywood: Hollywood Film Archive, 1992.

Harte, Liam, ed. *The Literature of the Irish in Britain: Autobiography and Memoir, 1725–2001*. Houndmills: Palgrave, 2009.

———. "Migrancy, Performativity and Autobiographical Identity." *Irish Studies Review* 14, no. 2 (2006): 225–27.

———, ed. *Modern Irish Autobiography*. Houndmills: Palgrave, 2007.

Harte, Liam, Yvonne Whelan, and Patrick Crotty, eds. *Ireland: Space, Text, Time*. Dublin: Liffey Press, 2005.

Hart House Theatre: A Description of the Theatre and a Record of Its First Nine Seasons, 1919–28. Toronto: Thomas Fisher Library, Hart House Theatre Archives, 1928.

Head, Jill. "Cecil Beaton Dresses a Girl for a Film" [Dangerous Moonlight]. *Picture Post*, Apr. 12, 1941, 25–27.

Heaney, Seamus. "Correspondences: Emigrants and Inner Exiles." In *Migrations: The Irish at Home and Abroad*, edited by R. Kearney, 21–31. Dublin: Wolfhound Press, 1990.

———. "Frontiers of Writing." In *The Redress of Poetry: Oxford Lectures*, 186–203. Oxford: Oxford Univ. Press, 1995.

Hearn, Marcus. "Viewing Notes: Scrooge." In *Scrooge: The 50th Anniversary*. Feature Film/Dandelion Distribution, 2001. DVD.

Hemingway, Ernest. *Ernest Hemingway on Paris*. Hesperus Press, 2010.

Higson, Andrew. "The Limiting Imagination of National Cinema." In *Transnational Cinema*, edited by E. Ezra and T. Rowden, 15–25. Routledge, 2006.

Hill, Charles C. *The Group of Seven: Art for a Nation*. Toronto: National Gallery of Canada, 1995.

Hill, John. *Cinema and Northern Ireland: Film, Culture and Politics*. BFI, 2006.

———. "'Purely Sinn Fein Propaganda': The Banning of *Ourselves Alone*." *HJFRTV* 20, no. 3 (2000): 317–33.

———. "Revisiting British Film Studies." *Journal of British Cinema and Television* 7, no. 2 (2010): 299–310.

Hobsbawm, Eric. *Fractured Times: Culture and Society in the Twentieth Century*. Little, Brown, 2013.

Hooker, Denise. *Nina Hamnet: Queen of Bohemia*. Constable, 1986.

Houlbrook, Matt. *Queer London: Perils and Pleasures in the Sexual Metropolis*. Chicago: Univ. of Chicago Press, 2005.

Hourani, Albert. *A History of the Arab Peoples*. Faber and Faber, 1991.

Housser, Fred B. *A Canadian Art Movement: The Story of the Group of Seven*. 2nd ed. Toronto: Macmillan, 1974.

Huddleston, Sisley. *Bohemian Literary and Social Life in Paris*. Harrap, 1928.

Hughes, Thomas. *Tom Brown's School Days*. 6th ed. Penguin "Popular Classics," 1994.

Hurst, Brian D. "Hurst and Dilys Powell." *New Comment* [BBC radio transcript], July 31, 1963, 1–12.

———. "Into the Studio." *Films and Filming*, Feb. 1957, 27, 32.
———. "The Lady Vanishes." *Sight and Sound*, Aug. 1950, 253–55.
———. "The World's Only New Art Form." *Kinematograph Weekly*, Dec. 17, 1936, 4.
Hurst, Brian D., with Stephen Wyatt. "Travelling the Road." Unpublished MS. BFI, ca. 1976.
Hutchins, Patricia. "News from Ireland." *Sight and Sound* (Summer 1947): 50–51.
"Index of British Feature Directors." *Sight and Sound* (Autumn 1958): 289–304.
Jackson, Kevin. *Lawrence of Arabia*. BFI, 2007.
James, Lawrence. *The Golden Warrior: The Life and Legend of Lawrence of Arabia*. Weidenfeld & Nicholson, 1990.
James, Robert. "*Kinematograph Weekly* in the 1930s: Trade Attitudes towards Audience Taste." *Journal of British Cinema and Television* 3, no. 2 (2006): 229–43.
Jeffrey, Keith, ed. *Ireland and Empire*. Manchester: Manchester Univ. Press, 1996.
———. "An 'Irish Empire'? Aspects of Ireland and the British Empire." In *Ireland and Empire*. Manchester: Manchester Univ. Press, 1996.
Jessup, Lynda. "The Group of Seven and the Tourist Landscape of Western Canada . . . or the More Things Change." *Journal of Canadian Studies/Revue d'Études Canadiennes* 37, no. 1 (2002): 144–79.
Johnston, Denis. "The Last Refuge of Nationality." *Film Art*, 2, no. 6 (1935): 63–64.
"Joy Absolute" [review of *Playboy*]. *Newsweek*, Dec. 13, 1962, 57.
Keaney, M. F. *British Film Noir Guide*. Jefferson, NC: McFarland, 2008.
Kelly, Andrew A., ed. *The Letters of Liam O'Flaherty*. Dublin: Wolfhound Press, 1996.
Kelly, Andrew, Jeffrey Richards, and James Pepper, eds. *Filming T. E. Lawrence: Korda's Lost Epics*. I. B. Tauris, 1997.
Kennedy, Denis. "Brian Desmond Hurst." In *Dictionary of Ulster Biography*. http://www.newulsterbiography.co.uk/index.php.
Kenny, Kevin. *The American Irish*. Pearson Education, 2000.
———. "Irish Emigration in a Comparative Perspective." In *The Cambridge Social History of Modern Ireland*, edited by Eugenio F. Biagini and Mary E. Daly, 405–22. Cambridge: Cambridge Univ. Press, 2017.
Kiberd, Declan. *After Ireland: Writing the Nation from Beckett to the Present Day*. Head of Zeus, 2017.
———. *Inventing Ireland: The Literature of the Modern Nation*. Jonathan Cape, 1995.

Krause, David, ed. *Sean O'Casey: Collected Letters*. Vol. 2, *1942–54*. New York: Macmillan, 1980.

Lambert, Gavin. *Mainly about Lindsay Anderson: A Memoir*. Faber & Faber, 2000.

Lawrence, Thomas Edward. *Seven Pillars of Wisdom*. Penguin, 2000.

Leslie, Shane. "France and the Latin Quarter." In *The Film of Memory*, 208–33. Michael Joseph, 1938.

Linkof, Ryan. "'Gross Intrusions': *Sensation*, Early Queer Film, and the Trouble with Crime Reporting in 1930s Britain." *Media History* 20, no. 2 (2014): 107–25.

Low, Rachael. *The History of the British Film, 1929–1939: Film Making in the 1930s*. George Allen & Unwin, 1985.

Lowry, Donal. "The Captive Dominion: Imperial Realities behind Irish Diplomacy, 1922–49." *Irish Historical Review* 36, no. 142 (2008): 202–26.

Lyons, Francis Stewart Leland. *Ireland since the Famine*. Collins/Fontana, 1973.

Mac Gall, Rex. "Towards an Irish Film Industry." *Bell* (June 1946): 234–42.

MacKillop, James. "Herbert Brenon." In *Dictionary of Irish Biography*, edited by J. McGuire and J. Quinn. Cambridge: Cambridge Univ. Press/Royal Irish Academy, 2009.

MacNeice, Louis. "Carrickfergus." In *The New Oxford Book of Irish Verse*, edited and translated by T. Kinsella, 345–46. Oxford: Oxford Univ. Press, 1989.

———. *The Strings Are False*. Faber & Faber, 1982.

MacQuitty, William. *A Life to Remember*. Quartet Books, 1991.

MacRaild, Donald. *The Irish Diaspora in Britain, 1750–1939*. Houndmills, Basingstoke: Palgrave Macmillan, 2011. Ebook.

Mansergh, Nicholas. *Nationalism and Independence: Selected Irish Papers*. Edited by Diana Mansergh. Cork: Cork Univ. Press, 1997.

Maugham, Robin. *The Black Tent, and Other Stories*. W. H. Allen, 1973.

Maugham, William Somerset. *The Tenth Man: A Tragic Comedy in Three Acts*. 1910. Reprint, Chicago: Dramatic, 1913. https://archive.org/details/tenthmantragiccooomaugrich.

McBride, Joseph. *Searching for John Ford: A Life*. Faber, 2003.

McCabe, Colin. "The Revenge of the Author." In *The Eloquence of the Vulgar*, 33–41. BFI, 1999.

McFarlane, Brian, ed. *An Autobiography of British Cinema*. Methuen, 1997.

———, ed. *The Cinema of Britain and Ireland*. Wallflower, 2005.

———, ed. *The Encyclopaedia of British Film*. 3rd ed. Methuen, 2008.

———, ed. *Sixty Voices: Celebrities Recall the Golden Age of British Cinema*. BFI, 1992.
McGerr, Celia. *René Clair*. Boston: Twayne, 1980.
McGuire, James, and James Quinn, eds. *Irish Dictionary of Biography from Earliest Times to the Year 2002*. Cambridge: Cambridge Univ. Press/Royal Irish Academy, 2009.
McIlroy, Brian. "Appreciation—Brian Desmond Hurst, 1895–1986: Irish Filmmaker." *Éire-Ireland* 24, no. 4 (1989): 106–13.
———. "British Filmmaking in the 1930s and 1940s: The Example of Brian Desmond Hurst." In *Re-viewing British Cinema, 1900–1992*, edited by W. Winston Dixon, 25–39. Albany: State Univ. of New York Press, 1994.
McMahon, Dierdre. *Republicans and Imperialists: Anglo-Irish Relations in the 1930s*. New Haven, CT: Yale Univ. Press, 1984.
Medhurst, Andy. "That Special Thrill: *Brief Encounter*, Homosexuality and Authorship." *Screen* 32, no. 2 (1991): 197–208.
———. "*Victim*: Text as Context." In *Dissolving Views: Key Writings on British Cinema*, edited by A. Higson, 17–31. Cassell, 1996.
Mellen, Peter, ed. *The Group of Seven*. Montreal: McClelland and Steward, 1970.
Miller, Laurence. "Evidence for a British Film Noir Cycle." In *Re-viewing British Cinema, 1900–1992*, edited by W. W. Dixon, 155–64. Albany: State Univ. of New York Press, 1994.
Milligan, Spike. *Adolf Hitler: My Part in His Downfall*. Penguin, 1972.
Mitchell and Kenyon in Ireland. Directed by Sagar Mitchell and James Kenyon. BFI, 2007. DVD and notes.
Monahan, Barry. "John Milligan Synge and Ireland by Brian Desmond Hurst." In *Ireland's Theatre on Film*, 66–87. Dublin: Irish Academic Press, 2010.
Monks, Bob (Robert). *The Liam O'Leary Archive*. Dublin: National Library, n.d.
Montagu, Edward [Lord Montagu of Beaulieu]. *Wheels within Wheels: An Unconventional Life*. Weidenfeld & Nicolson, 2000.
Moor, Andrew. *Powell and Pressburger: A Cinema of Magic Spaces*. I. B. Tauris, 2005.
Mort, Frank. *Capital Affairs: London and the Making of the Permissive Society*. New Haven, CT: Yale Univ. Press, 2010.
———. "Crisis Points: Masculinities in History and Social Theory." *Gender and History* 6, no. 1 (1994): 124–30.
Moulton, Mo. *Ireland and the Irish in Interwar England*. Cambridge: Cambridge Univ. Press, 2014.

Murphy, John A. *Ireland in the Twentieth Century*. Dublin: Gill & Macmillan, 1975.
Murphy, Robert, ed. *Britain Cinema and Second World War*. Continuum, 2000.
———. *British Cinema: Critical Concepts in Media and Cultural Studies*. 4 vols. Routledge, 2014.
———, ed. *The British Cinema Book*. BFI, 1997.
———, ed. *Directors in British and Irish Cinema: A Reference Companion*. BFI, 2006.
Murray, Christopher. *Twentieth-Century Irish Drama*. Manchester: Manchester Univ. Press, 1997.
Naficy, Hamid. "Between Rocks and Hard Places: The Interstitial Mode of Exilic Cinema." In *Home, Exile and Homeland*, edited by H. Naficy, 125–47. Routledge/AFI, 1999.
———. "Situating Accented Cinema." In *Transnational Cinema: The BFI Film Reader*, edited by E. Ezra and T. Rowden, 111–29. Routledge, 2006.
Napper, Lawrence. *British Cinema and Middlebrow Culture in the Interwar Years*. Exeter: Exeter Univ. Press, 2009.
———. "A Despicable Tradition? Quota Quickies in the 1930s." In *The British Cinema Book*, edited by R. Murphy, 45–52. BFI, 2001.
National Library of Ireland. National Census, 1911. http://www.census.national archives.ie.
Nava, Mica. *Visceral Cosmopolitanism: Gender, Culture and the Normalisation of Difference*. Oxford: Berg, 2007.
Neil, W. J. V., M. Murray, and B. Grost, eds. *Relaunching the Titanic*. Routledge, 2013.
Newman, Kate. *Dictionary of Ulster Biography*. Belfast: Institute of Irish Studies, 1993.
Nicholson, Virginia. *Among the Bohemians: Experiments in Living, 1900–1939*. Penguin, 2003.
Noble, Peter, ed. *British Film Yearbook, 1947–48*. Skelton Robinson, 1948.
———, ed. *British Film Yearbook, 1949–50*. Skelton Robinson, 1950.
North, Dan. "Finishing the Unfinished." In *Sights Unseen: Unfinished British Films*, 1–13. Newcastle: Cambridge Scholars Press, 2008.
O Cleire, Eamonn. "Belfast Queens and Republican Film Makers." Online review of *Empress of Ireland*, n.d.
O'Dwyer, Kathleen. "The Child and the Cinema in Éire." *Sight and Sound* (Summer 1946): 46.
O'Flaherty, Liam. *Two Years*. Jonathan Cape, 1930.

O'Halpin, Eunan. "*Theirs Is the Glory*." *Estudios Irlandeses* 12 (2016): 249–51. https://www.estudiosirlandeses.org/reviews/theirs-is-the-glory-arnhem-hurst-and-conflict-on-film/.

O Laoghaire, Liam. *Invitation to the Film*. Tralee: Kerryman, 1945.

O'Leary, Liam. "Developments in Éire." *Sight and Sound* (Summer 1943): 12.

———. *The Silent Cinema*. Dutton Vista, 1965.

Oliver, John. "*Hungry Hill*: Projecting the Archive." Program notes. BFI, n.d.

Ontario College of Art. *OCA List of Awards Session, 1921–22*. Toronto: OCA, 1922.

———. *OCA List of Awards Session, 1922–23*. Toronto: OCA, 1923.

———. *OCA Prospectus, 1921–22*. Toronto: Ontario College of Art Design Archive.

Orr, Phillip. *Field of Bones: An Irish Division at Gallipoli*. Dublin: Lilliput Press, 2006.

———. "The Road to Belgrade: The Experiences of the 10th (Irish) Division in the Balkans, 1915–17." In *Ireland and the Great War*, edited by A. Gregory and S. Pašeta, 171–89. Manchester: Manchester Univ. Press, 2002.

O'Sullivan, Patrick, ed. *The Creative Migrant: The Irish World Wide*. Vol. 3. Leicester Univ. Press/Cassell, 1997.

Payn, Graham, and Sheridan Morley, eds. *The Noel Coward Diaries*. Weidenfeld & Nicolson, 1982

Perry, George. *The Great British Picture Show*. 1974. Reprint, Boston: Little, Brown, 1985.

Pettitt, Lance. "Belfast's Cinenigmatic Émigré." Screening introduction to Hurst's *Playboy of the Western World* (1962), Studio Cinema, 7. Belfast: Belfast Film Festival, 2009.

———. "Brian Desmond Hurst." In *Oxford Dictionary of National Biography*. Oxford: Oxford Univ. Press, 2014.

———. "Irish Exilic Cinema in England." *Irish Studies Review* 19, no. 1 (2011): 41–54.

———. "Life by Anecdote: Memoir, Irish Cinema and Cultural History." In *A Garland of Words: A Festschrift for Maureen Murphy*, edited by M. Mutran, B. Kopschitz Bastos, and L. Izarra, 483–95. São Paulo: Humanitas, 2010.

Phelps, Robert. *Professional Secrets: An Autobiography of Jean Cocteau*. New York: Farrar, Straus & Giroux, 1970.

Poe, Edgar Allan. *Selected Tales*. Edited by J. Symons. Oxford: Oxford Univ. Press, 1980.

Posner, Bruce. *Unseen Cinema: Early American Avant-Garde Film, 1893–1941*. New York: Anthology of Film Archives, 2001.

Powell, Michael. *A Life in Movies: An Autobiography*. Faber and Faber, 2000.

Price, Hollie. "The MOI Film Division and Their Finest." *MOI Digital* (blog), May 10, 2017. http://www.moidigital.ac.uk/blog/moi-films-division-and-their-finest-ii/#_ftn3.

Ramsden, John. "The People's War: British War Films of the 1950s." *Journal of Contemporary History* 33, no. 1 (1998): 35–63.

Raymond, Ernest, ed. *Tell England: A Study in a Generation*. New York: George H. Doran, 2002.

Reid, Colin W. "Citizens of Nowhere: Longing, Belonging and Exile among Irish Protestant Writers in Britain, c. 1830–1970." *Irish Studies Review* 24, no. 3 (2016): 255–74.

Rentschler, Eric. "The Problematic Pabst: An Auteur Directed by History." In *The Films of G. W. Pabst: An Extraterritorial Cinema*, 1–23. New Brunswick, NJ: Rutgers Univ. Press.

Rhodes, Gary D. *Emerald Illusions: The Irish in Early American Cinema*. Dublin: Irish Academic Press, 2012.

Richards, Jeffrey. *The Age of the Dream Palace: Cinema and Society, 1930–1939*. Routledge & Kegan Paul, 1984.

———. *Films and British National Identity*. Manchester: Manchester Univ. Press, 1997.

———, ed. *The Unknown 1930s: An Alternative History of the British Cinema, 1929–1939*. I. B. Tauris, 2000.

Richards, Jeffrey, and Jeffrey Hulbert. "Censorship in Action: The Case of *Lawrence of Arabia*." *Journal of Contemporary History* 19, no. 1 (1984): 153–70.

Richards, Jeffrey, and Dorothy Sheridan, eds. *Mass-Observation at the Movies*. Routledge & Kegan Paul, 1987.

Robbins, Christopher. *The Empress of Ireland: Chronicle of an Unusual Friendship*. Scribner, 2004.

Robertson, James C. *The BBFC: Film Censorship in Britain, 1896–1950*. Croom Helm, 1985.

———. "Brian Desmond Hurst." In *Directors in British and Irish Cinema: A Reference Companion*, edited by R. Murphy, 314. BFI, 2006.

Rockett, Kevin. *Irish Film Censorship: A Cultural Journey from Silent Cinema to Internet Pornography*. Dublin: Four Courts Press, 2004.

———, ed. *The Irish Filmography: Fiction Films, 1896–1996*. Dublin: Red Mountain Media, 1996.

———. "The Irish Migrant and Film." In *The Creative Migrant*, vol. 3, *The Irish World Wide*, edited by P. O'Sullivan, 170–91. Leicester Univ. Press, 1994.

Rockett, Kevin, with John Caughie. *The Companion to British and Irish Cinema*. Cassell, 1996.

Rockett, Kevin, Luke Gibbons, and John Hill. *Cinema and Ireland*. Routledge, 1988.

Roper, Michael. "Between Manliness and Masculinity: 'The War Generation' and the Psychology of Fear in Britain, 1915–1950." *Journal of British Studies* 44, no. 2 (2005): 342–62.

Rowbotham, Sheila. *Edward Carpenter: A Life of Liberty and Love*. Verso, 2008.

Ryall, Tom. *Alfred Hitchcock and the British Cinema*. Beckenham, Kent: Croom Helm, 1986.

———. "A British Studio System: The Associated British Picture Corporation and the Gaumont-British Picture Corporation in the 1930s." In *The British Cinema Book*, edited by Robert Murphy, 27–36. BFI, 1997.

Ryan, Liam. "Irish Emigration to Britain since WWII." In *Migrations: The Irish at Home and Abroad*, edited by Richard Kearney. Dublin: Wolfhound Press, 1990.

Saler, Michael T. *The Avant-Garde in Interwar England: Medieval Modernism and the London Underground*. Oxford: Oxford Univ. Press, 1999.

Savage, Robert. *Irish Television: The Political and Social Origins*. Cork: Cork Univ. Press, 1996.

Sedgwick, Eve K. *Between Men: English Literature and Male Homosocial Desire*. 1985. Reprint, New York: Columbia Univ. Press, 2016.

Seigel, Jerrold. *Bohemian Paris: Culture, Politics and the Boundaries of Bourgeois Life, 1830–1930*. Penguin, 198.

Sellor, C. Paul. *Film Authorship: Auteurs and Other Myths*. Wallflower, 2010.

Sexton, Jamie. *Alternative Film Culture in Interwar Britain*. Exeter: Exeter Univ. Press, 2008.

Shaw, George Bernard. "Fragment of Autobiography (1902)." In *The Matter of Ireland*, edited by David H. Greene and Dan H. Laurence. Rupert Hart-Davies, 1962.

———. *The Matter of Ireland*. Edited by D. H. Greene and D. H. Laurence. Rupert Hart-Davies, 1962.

Sheehy, T. J. M. "Towards an Irish Film Industry." *Irish Monthly*, Sept. 1948, 417–20.

Sinfield, Alan. *Literature, Politics and Culture in Postwar Britain.* Dublin: Athlone Press, 1997.

———. *A Wilde Century.* Serpent's Tail, 1994.

Slide, Anthony. *The Cinema and Ireland.* Jefferson, NC: McFarland, 1988.

Sloan, Barry. "Journeys into the Protestant Mind." In *Writers and Protestantism in the North of Ireland,* 92–122. Dublin: Irish Academic Press, 2000.

Smith, Allan Esler. *An Irishman Chained to the Truth.* RTE Radio 1, Aug. 6, 2011. http://www.rte.ie/radio1/doconone/2011/0718/646821-radio-documentary-irishman-chained-to-the-truth-brian-desmond-hurst/.

———. "*Ourselves Alone*: Conflict in 1920s Ireland." DVD notes to *Ourselves Alone.* British Film/Studio Canal, 2016.

———. *Revisiting a Letter from Ulster.* Northern Ireland War Memorial Home Front Exhibition pamphlet. Belfast: Northern Ireland War Memorial, 2012.

———. "*Theirs Is the Glory*: The Epic Film of the Airborne Forces at Arnhem." *Pegasus* (Winter 2012).

Smith, Murray. "Modernism and the Avant-Gardes." In *The Oxford Guide to Film Studies,* edited by J. Hill and P. Church-Gibson, 395–412. Oxford: Oxford Univ. Press, 1988.

Spicer, Andrew. "British Film Noir." In *British Cinema: Critical Concepts,* vol. 4, edited by Robert Murphy. Routledge, 2014.

———. "Male Stars, Masculinity and British Cinema." In *The British Cinema Book,* edited by R. Murphy, 144–53. BFI, 1997.

———. *Typical Male: The Representation of Masculinity in British Popular Culture.* I. B. Tauris, 2001.

Steel, Nigel, and Peter Hart. *Defeat at Gallipoli.* Macmillan, 1994.

Sternlicht, Sanford. "Synge on Film: Two Playboys." In *Contemporary Irish Cinema,* edited by J. MacKillop, 161–68. Syracuse, NY: Syracuse Univ. Press, 1999.

Strachan, Alan. *Sweet Dreams: A Biography of Michael Redgrave.* Orion Books, 2004.

Street, Sarah. *British Cinema in Documents.* Routledge, 2000.

———. "British Film and the National Interest, 1927–39." In *The British Cinema Book,* edited by R. Murphy, 28–34. BFI, 2001.

———. *British National Cinema.* 2nd ed. Routledge, 2009.

Stuart, Francis. *Things to Live For: Notes for an Autobiography.* Jonathan Cape, 1934.

Summerscale, Kate. *The Queen of Whale Quay: The Extraordinary Life of "Joe" Carstairs, the Fastest Woman on Water.* Harper Perennial, 2008.

Sykes, Constance. "Brian Desmond Hurst: Career of an Irish Film Director." *Screen* (June 1942): 3–4, 8.

———. "Director with Ideals and How He Acquired Them." *Picturegoer*, May 30, 1942, 7.

Synge, John Milligan. *Plays, Poems and Prose*. Dent/Everyman's Library, 1980.

Teachout, Terry. "Alec Guinness: The Great Little Briton." *Commentary* (May 2009). https://www.commentary.org/articles/terry-teachout/alec-guinness-the-great-little-briton/.

Traubner, Richard. "Angus McBean." In *The Theatrical World of Angus McBean: Photographs from the Harvard Theatre Collection*, edited by F. W. Wilson. Boston: David R. Godine, 2009.

Truesdale, David, and Allan Esler Smith. *"Theirs Is the Glory": Arnhem, Hurst and Conflict on Film*. Solihull, West Midlands: Helion Press, 2016.

"Ulster Covenant." Northern Ireland Public Record Office. https://www.nidirect.gov.uk/services/search-ulster-covenant.

Unseen Cinemas: Early American Avant Garde Film, 1894–1941. Curated by Bruce Posner. DVD (NTSC), 2005.

Warrington, George. "At the Theatre: Arts and Reality." *Country Life*, Feb. 6, 1937, 152.

Webster, Wendy. "Domesticating the Frontier: Gender, Empire and Adventure Landscapes in British Cinema, 194555." *Gender and History* 15, no. 1 (2003): 85–107.

———. *Englishness and Empire, 1939–1965*. Oxford: Oxford Univ. Press, 2007.

Welch, Robert Anthony, ed. *The Oxford Companion to Irish Literature*. Oxford: Oxford Univ. Press, 1996.

Wilcox, Herbert. *Twenty-Five Thousand Sunsets: The Autobiography of Herbert Wilcox*. Bodley Head, 1976.

Wildeblood, Peter. *Against the Law*. Wiendenfeld & Nicolson, 1955.

Williams, Raymond. *Culture*. Glasgow: Fontana, 1981.

Wills, Clair. *The Best Are Leaving: Post-war Irish Culture*. Cambridge: Cambridge Univ. Press, 2015.

———. *That Neutral Island: A History of Ireland during the Second World War*. Faber and Faber, 2008.

Wilson, Harold. "Seven Directors." In *British Film Yearbook, 1949–50*, edited by P. Noble, 67–84. Skelton Robinson, 1950.

Wilson, Jeremy. *Lawrence of Arabia: The Authorized Biography of T. E. Lawrence*. Minerva, 1990.

Wilson, John Rowan. *The Pack*. Heinemann, 1955.
Woodhouse, Adrian. *Angus McBean: Face-Maker*. Alma, 2006.
Woolf, Virginia. *The Death of the Moth, and Other Essays*. Hogarth, 1942.
Zambrano, Anna Laura. *Dickens and Film*. New York: Bowling Green Station, 1977.

Films Referenced

n.d. = no date; typically indicated film was not completed.

An Airman's Letter to His Mother (1941)
Alibi (1942)
L'Alibi—French original (1937)
Another Shore (1949)
Arrowsmith (1931)
Behind the Mask (1958)
The Black Tent (1956)
A Bright Flame—alternate title of *Malta Story*.
A Bucket of Blood (1934)—alternate title of *Tell-Tale Heart*.
By Accident (1930)
Caesar and Cleopatra (1945)
A Call for Arms! (1940)
Cavalcade (1933)
A Christmas Carol (1951)—see also *Scrooge*
Cleopatra (1963)
The Cruel Sea (1953)
Dangerous Exile (1957)
Dangerous Moonlight (1941)—see also *Suicide Squadron*
Darkness before Dawn (n.d.)—see also *Millions Like Us*
Daughter of Darkness (1948)
The Demi Gods (n.d.)
Elizabeth and Essex (n.d.)
Famine (n.d.)
Freedom Radio (1941)
The Gentle Gunman (1952)

A Gift for a King (n.d.)
Glamorous Night (1937)
Half Way House (1944)
Hangman's House (1928)
Henry V (1945)
His and Hers (1960)
The Hundred Pound Window (1943)
Hungry Hill (1947)
In Which We Serve (1942)
Irish Hearts (1934)
I See a Dark Stranger (1946)
Jackboot in Ireland (n.d.)
Jacqueline (1956)
Jamaica Inn (1936)
Kilo Forty (n.d.)
The Last Romantic (n.d.)
Lawrence of Arabia (1938)—see also *Revolt in the Desert*
Lawrence of Arabia (1962, Lean)
A Letter from Ulster (1943)
The Life and Death of Colonel Blimp (1943)
The Lion Has Wings (1939)
M (Fritz Lang, 1931)
Malta Story (1953)
Man of Aran (1935)
The Mark of Cain (1948)
Millions Like Us (1943)
A Minute's Wait (1957)
Miss Grant Goes to the Door (1940)

Napoleon of Egypt (n.d.)
Night Boat to Dublin (1946)
Nora O'Neale—see *Irish Hearts*
Odd Man Out (1947)
Old Mother Riley's New Venture (1949)
On Approval (1944)
On the Night of the Fire (1939)
Ourselves Alone (1936)
The Passion of Joan of Arc (1928)
Playboy of the Western World (1962)
Prison sans barreaux
Prison without Bars (1938)
Revolt in the Desert (n.d.)
Queen Nefertiti (n.d.)
The Quiet Man (1952)
Rebecca (1938)
Riders to the Sea (1935)
The Rising of the Moon (1957)—see also *Three Leaves*
Rivers of Unrest (US title for *Ourselves Alone*)
Ryan's Daughter (1970)

Sabotage (1936)
Scrooge (1951)—see also *A Christmas Carol*
Shadow of a Gunman (n.d.)
Shanghai Express (1932)
She Stoops to Conquer (n.d.)
Simba (1955)
Some Say Chance (1934)
Suicide Squadron—see also *Dangerous Moonlight*
The Tell-Tale Heart (1934)
The Tenth Man (1936)
Tess of the D'Urbervilles (n.d.)
Theirs Is the Glory (1946)
This German Freedom (n.d.)
This Happy Breed (1944)
Three Leaves of a Shamrock (1957)—see also *Rising of the Moon*
Trottie True (1948)
The Way to the Stars (1945)
Went the Day Well? (1944)
The Wizard of Oz (1939)
Yeats Country (1965)

Index

Italic page numbers denotes illustrations/captions.

Abbey Theatre, Dublin, 68, 71, 72, 206
Abraham, J. Johnston: *The Night Nurse*, 63–64, *65*
Achard, Marcel: *L'Alibi*, 130
Ackland, Rodney, 107, 111, 113, 121, 133
Act of Union (1801), 24, 25
Agate, James, 145
Algar, Michael, 223, *224*
Alibi (1942), 129, 130–33, 157, 175, 246; budget, 133; poster, *132*; still from, *131*
Allgood, Sara, 67, 68, 71, 98
Alpert, Hollis, 179–80
Andrews, John M., 120
Anglo-Irish Treaty (1921), 76, 118, 152
Antheil, George, 41
Antwerp: study tour to, 5, 38
Archers film company, 158
Ardmore Studios, Bray, 13, 166, 199, 200, 207, 247
Arts and Letters Club, Toronto, 33
Art Students League of New York, 5, 43
Asquith, Anthony, 1, 13, 56, 110, 142, 146, 164, 240; *Freedom Radio* (1941), 120; *Way to the Stars* (1945), 124
Asquith, Herbert, 20
Associated British Picture Corporation (ABPC), 146, 169; British International Pictures (BIP), 75, 77, 79, 96
Attenborough, Richard, 223, 240
Attlee, Clement, 171, 181

auteur criticism, 11

Baddley, Hermione, 176
BAFTA dinner in Hurst's honor, 223; *Screen International* report, 223, *224, 225*
Baines, John, 188
Baker, Roy Ward, 142; *Jacqueline* (1956), 204
Balchin, Nigel, 185
Baldwin, Ruth, 45
Ballet mécanique (1924), 41
Ballin, Hugo, 43–44, 244
Bannen, Ian, 202
Barr, Charles, 13
Barton, Ruth, 12, 80, 124, 125, 126, 153, 232
Bashford, Patrick, 223
BBC, 54; Hurst featured as arts pundit, 220
Beardsley, Aubrey, 47
Behind the Mask (1958), 200–204; released on DVD, 235; stills from, *201, 203*; "televised surgery," 202, *203, 204*
Belfast: Harland and Wolff shipyard, 229; renaming of airport, 233; sectarian conflict, 3–4, 5, 31, 220; socioeconomic conditions, 22–23; Titanic Quarter, 19, 219, 231

Best, George, 233
Betts, Ernest, 72
Beveridge, William, 171
Bingham, Richard, 140–41
BIP. *See* Associated British Picture Corporation
bisexuality of Hurst, 12, 29–30, 40, 124, 240, 248
Black Tent, The (1956), 170, 172, 191–94, 197, 199, 246; still from, *193*
Bogarde, Dirk, 183, 185, 188
Bon Echo Inn, 37–38
Boru, Brian, 25
Boston Film Festival, 1963, 211
Boulting, Roy, 142
Bourne, Stephen, 124, 125, 229
Bowen, Elizabeth, 145
Box, John and Betty, 167
Boyce, George, 23
Brah, Avtar, 6, 21
Brahms, Caryl, 148, 160
Brancusi, Constantin, 41
Brando, Marlon, 215
Brandt, Ivan, 100, 112
Braque, Georges, 41
Brenon, Herbert, 13, 235, 240
Brent, Romney, 98
Brinton, Ralph, 176
British Broadcasting Company. *See* BBC
British Commonwealth, 167–68, 188, 194
British film industry, 55, 102, 108, 146–47, 166, 169, 245; Crown Film Unit, 108; European influences on, 56; postwar, 139; US dominance of, 146, 169, 197
British Film Institute (BFI), 64, 73, 113, 226, 233, 235; archive project, 228, 235; Hurst's memoir donated to library, 223, 228. *See also Sight and Sound*

British Legion, 5
British Lion/Gainsborough Studios, 130, 209–10, 215, 247
British Nationality Act (1948), 168
Britton, Tony, 202
Brooke, Basil, 152
Browne, Beral, 96
Browne, Dominick, Fourth Baron Oranmore, 129
Brunel, Adrian, 56, 111; codirection of *The Lion Has Wings*, 107–8
Bull, Donald, 111
Bushell, Anthony, 194
Butler Act (1944), 171

Caesar and Cleopatra (unmade), 215
Callas, Maria, 145
Call for Arms, A (1940), 113–15; "Thumbs Up Patriotism," *114*
Canada: Hurst in, 4, 5, 7, 8, 13, 31–32; landscape painting style, 47
Carey, Patrick: *Yeats Country*, 213–14
Carpenter, Edward, 30
Carstairs, Betty "Joe," 45
Casement, Roger, 85
Castles in the Air (children's play), 38
Castleton-Knight, Leonard, 136
Catholicism: Hurst's conversion to, 23, 26, 37, 181, 233, 244
Cavalcanti, Alberto, 176, 181; *The Life and Adventures of Nicholas Nickleby* (1947), 170; *Went the Day Well?*, 113
Cellier, Antoinette, 77
Charlesworth, John, 173
Churchill, Diana, 92, 145
Churchill, Winston, 121, 171
Cinematograph Films Acts (1927, 1938), 55
Clair, René, 1, 241

Clare, Mary, 111
class culture: in Belfast, 3, 5, 10, 23, 26; in Britain, 8–9, 17, 21, 30, 31, 151, 156–57, 162
Clifton, Harry, 45, 53, 55, 59, 229
Cocteau, Jean: *Sang d'un poète*, 41
color use for films, 160
Comfort, Lance, 1, 167, 240; *Daughter of Darkness* (1948), 168
Connery, Sean, 209
Cookson, Catherine: *Jacqueline*, 204
Cork Film Festival (2004), 218, 219, 232
Coward, Noël, 45, 126, 151
Craigie, Jill, 147
Crawford, Andrew, 160
Crisp, Quentin, 248
Crowdy, Francis, 148, 158
Crowe, Eileen, 154
Crowley, Dave, 100
Crowther, Bosley, 180–81
Cukor, George, 105, 221, 222

Daily Graphic serialization of Scrooge, 178–79, *180*
Daily Mail National Film Award, 123–24
Dalton, Emmet, 1, 13, 166, 207, 247
Dangerous Exile (1957), 170, 172, 194–97, 246; poster from, *196*; still from, *195*
Dangerous Moonlight (1942), 2, 59, 103, 116, 120–29, 175, 176, 226, 244, 246; exilic signification, 124, 126, 129; music for, 121, 122, 123, 126; queer reading of, 124–26, 128, 129, 133, 246; stills from, *122*, *123*, *125*, *127*
Darkness before Dawn, 216
Davies, John Howard, 173
Davis, John T., 241

Dawson, Beatrice, 174
Dean, Norman, 8, 29, *36*, 38; in London, 48, 54; in Paris, 40
Deans, Marjorie, 77, 87
Dearman, Glyn, 173
decadent movement, 47
de Grunwald, Anatole, 142
Del Giudice, Filippo, 142
Denham Studios, 103, 106
Dennison, Flora MacDonald, 37
Dennison, Merrill, 36–37
Depression of interwar period, 6, 53
de Valera, Eamon, 51, 76, 107, 152; "external association," 168
Dickens, Charles: *A Christmas Carol*, 170, 171, 172, 176, 181, 182; illustration from, *178*
Dickinson, Thorold, 111, 146, 184, 185
Dietrich, Marlene, 44
"Director's Craft, The." See *Films and Filming*
Directors Guild of Great Britain plaque, *233*, 234
documentary filmmaking, 56, 110, 140, 163, 164, 200; funded by Ministry of Information, 108, 110, 121
Donald, James, 160
Dreyer, Carl, 47, 68; *The Passion of Joan of Arc* (1928), 44
Drury Lane (Theatre Royal), Covent Garden, 92, 95
Dudley, Lesley, 77
du Marney, Derrick, 124
Du Maurier, Daphne, 148; *Hungry Hill*, 148, 149, 151
Dyer, Richard, 124–25

Eady Levy, 169
Eakins, Thomas, 175

École des Beaux Arts, Paris, 39, 179; annual ball, 40
Eden, Anthony, 197
Edward VIII, King of England, 87; affair with Mrs. Simpson, 90
Eisenstein, Sergei, 74
Elizabeth and Essex (unmade), 216
Elizabeth II, Queen of England, 165, 167; state visit to Ireland, 232; televised coronation, 170
Ellis, Mary, 93
Ellmann, Louis, 207
Elstree Studios, 49, 79, 80, 87, 215, 240, 241; Hurst becomes contract director in 1936, 6, 51, 75
Empire Theatre, Belfast, 209
Empress of Ireland, The. *See* Robbins, Christopher
England, Len, 120
European Economic Community (EEC), 167
exilic identity, 124, 125, 171; of Hurst, 1–2, 6–8, 46, 47–48, 49–50, 51, 62, 103, 170, 183–84, 206, 216–17, 219–20, 240, 244–46, 248; of T. E. Lawrence, 85, 246
External Relations Act (1936), 152

Fairchild, William, 185
Farrell, Michael: *Some Say Chance*, 67
fascism: rise of, 87, 94
Festival of Britain (1951), 165
Fields, Gracie, 54, 55; funds *Riders to the Sea*, 59, 72
Films and Filming: "The Director's Craft" (1957 essay), 166, 197–99, 243
film societies, 56, 57, 64, 95, 147, 164, 199, 243
Film Society of Ireland, 64, 199

Flaherty, Robert, 13; *Man of Aran*, 64, 66, 67, 82
Flanagan, Aubrey, 100
Flanagan, John, 54, 55, 67, 68; Flanagan-Hurst Productions, 67
Fleischmann, George, 199
Forbes, Bryan, 194
Ford, John, 1, 5–6, 13, 21, 28, 44, 45, 47, 49, 50, 71, 89, 119, 138, 166, 179, 184, 209, 210, 221, 229, 236, 240, 248; *Arrowsmith* (1931), 44; *Hangman's House* (1928), 41–43, 44; Hurst holidays in Honolulu with, 45, 53; *The Informer* (1935), 54, 82, 216; *The Quiet Man* (1952), 207, 214; *The Rising of the Moon* (1957), 200, 207; works for US army, 105
Forsyth, Bertram, 38
Foster, John Wilson, 10, 25, 62
Foster, Roy, 10, 21, 27, 227
Four Provinces Films, 13, 199, 200, 204, 207, 209, 213, 247; hybrid nature of, 207–8; problems with releasing *Playboy* in Britain, 209–10
Fowle, Chick, 119
Fox Corporation, 5–6, 21, 41, 44, 45; distributes *Tell-Tale Heart*, 63
Frank, Astrid, 223, 225, 228
Frayling, Christopher, 181–83
Frazier, Adrian, 8
Freedom Radio (unmade), 215
Freeman, C. Denis, 160

Gallipoli, 4, 5, 20, 23, 27, 103, 220, 235
G and S Films, 107
Gate Theatre, Dublin, 54
George V, King of England, 3, 84
George VI, King of England, 135
Gielgud, John, 29, 115

Gingold, Hermione, 105, 106
Glamorous Night (1937), 45, 51, 87, 92–95; still from, *94*
Glover, Charles, 128
Golden, Michael, 150
Goldwyn, Samuel, 43
Goodman, Francis, 244
Gormanston Castle, County Meath, 140
gothic genre, 46, 153, 157; in *Scrooge* 176, 181, 246
Govan shipyards, Glasgow, 8
Government of Ireland Act (1920), 25
Grafton cinema, Dublin, 79
Gray, Sally, 121, 129, 158; photographed with Hurst, *128*
Greacen, Robert, 9, 245
Green, F. L., 87, 98; *Odd Man Out*, 98; *On the Night of the Fire*, 98
Greene, Graham, 11, 74, 108; harsh criticism of Hurst, 100–101, 221
Griffith, Daniel: *The Human Blarney Stone*, 233
Gris, Juan, 41
Grosvenor House Hotel dinner, 142, *143*
Group of Seven, 32, 33, 34, 36, 46, 244; exhibition catalog, *35*
Guardian: Hurst on British film, 220–21
Guinness, Alec, 183, 185, *187*, 188, 209
Gunning, Tom, 1, 242
Guthrie, Duncan, 84
Guthrie, Kevin, 68, 71
Guthrie, Patrick, 40

Hagen, Julius, 64
Hall, Stuart, 8
Hammersmith Film Society, 147
Hamnet, Nina, 40, 54
Hannigan, Mick, 232

Harrison, Kathleen, 114
Harrison, Tom, 108, 113, 114, 115, 121
Hart House Theatre, 36, 38
Harvey, Walter J., 77
Hawkins, Jack, 185
Hay, Will, 118
Heaney, Seamus, 7
Hedde, Muriel, 38
Heliconian Club: lunch hosted by college, 38
Hemingway, Ernest: on Paris, 38–39
Hepburn, Audrey, 143
Herlie, Eileen, 149
Hewitt, John, 9, 245
Higgins, Michael D., 232
Hill, John, 12, 14, 79, 80, 115, 118
Hillier, Erwin, 158
Hinton, Mary, 160
His and Hers (1950), 204; poster, *205*; released on DVD, 235
Hitchcock, Alfred, 1, 13, 240; *Sabotage*, 89
Hodson, James Lansdale, 83
Hollywood, 7, 16, 44, 46, 47, 49, 51, 81, 179, 240, 244; Hurst studies mural painting in, 5
Holt, Patrick, 158
Home Rule, 20, 23, 25
Horden, Michael, 176
Hughes, Thomas, 172; *Tom Brown's School Days*, 166, 173, 175
Hundred Pound Window, The (1944), 129; still from, *130*
Hungry Hill (1947), 2, 105, 141, 148–57, 174, 231, 244, 246; ballroom dance scene, 153, 154–56, 160; stills from, *149, 154, 155, 156, 157*
Hunt, Martita, 111, 195
Hurst, Margaret (Hurst's stepmother), 5, 22

Hurst, Patricia, (Hurst's sister) 5, 22, 53
Hurst, Robert (Hurst's father), 5, 8, 22, 229–30
Hurst Estate, 218, 228, 233, 235, 249; North Down Museum exhibition, 233–35

impressionism, 34, 41, 47
Inch Strand, County Kerry, 209
India and Pakistan partition, 167
Ingram, Rex, 1, 13, 83, 84, 235, 240, 247
Inter-Departmental Commission on the Film Industry (1938), 140
Ireland: Anglo-Irish war, 3, 52, 76, 85, 151; Black and Tans, 77, 151, 189; Civil War, 52, 85; Constitution (1937), 51, 67, 118, 152, 245; cultural revival, 65, 165; "decade of commemorations," 232; Easter Rising (1916), 52, 85, 219; immigration to Britain, 168, 245, 247; External Relations Act (1936), 51; Great Famine, 150; Hurst plans to set up national film studio, 51, 55, 72, 82, 139, 141, 165, 166, 199–200, 207, 247; leaves British Commonwealth, 168; National Film Institute, 140, 141; neutrality in the "Emergency," 105, 107, 118; partition (1920), 3, 5, 52, 76, 118, 151; War of Independence (1916–21), 3, 76, 77, 189. *See also* Belfast
Irish Film Board, 200, 223
Irish Film Finance Corporation (IFFC), 208, 212
Irish Film Institute (IFI), 216, 235
Irish Free State, 3, 8, 32, 52, 67, 76, 118, 245; policy on cinema, 139, 152
Irish Hearts (1934; released as *Nora O'Neale* in US), 2, 50, 58–59, 63–67,

201; Abbey Players appear in, 67; Dublin filming location, 64, 66, 67
Irish Republican Army (IRA), 151, 153, 191; bombing campaign in Britain, 107
Ito, Michio, 45

Jackboot in Ireland (unmade), 215
James, C. L. R., 74
Jenkins, "Mabs," 45
Johns, Mervyn, 176
Johnston, Denis, 54, 68, 77, 208
Jordan, Neil, 241
Jory, Victor, 93
Jourdan, Louis, 194
Joyce, James, 229

Kauffman, Stanley, 211
Kellner, William, 204
Kennedy, John F., 212
Kent, Jean, 160
Kenyan independence campaign, 167, 188
Keynes, Maynard, 171
Killanin, Lord. *See* Morris, Michael
Kilo Forty (unmade), 215
Kirwan, Patrick, 54, 68, 87, 98
Korda, Alexander, 49, 82, 83, 96, 103; *The Lion Has Wings*, 107–8
Korda, Vincent, 96
Korda, Zoltan, 84
Krampf, Günter, 98
Krasker, Robert, 185, 188, 204
Kruger, Otto, 93

Labour Party, Britain, 152, 157, 171, 181, 182
Lachman, Harry, 63

"Lady Vanishes, The." See *Sight and Sound*
Laffan, Bridie, 68, *70*, 71
Lambert, Gavin, 146
Lang, Fritz, 158; *M.*, 98
Langley, Noel, 173, 175, 176
Last Romantic, The (unmade), 215
Late Late Show, RTE: Hurst interview, 210
Lawrence, T. E., 84, 185; *Revolt in the Desert*, 75, 83, 215; *The Seven Pillars of Wisdom*, 83, 86
Lawrence of Arabia (unmade), 51, 75, 76, 82–83, 86, 120, 246
Lean, David, 142, 146, 167, 176; codirection of *The Lion Has Wings* (1939), 107–8; *Great Expectations* (1948), 170; *Lawrence of Arabia* (1962), 75, 83, 85; *Oliver Twist* (1946), 170; *Ryan's Daughter* (1970), 209
Leaver, Philip, 131
Le Corbusier, 41
Lee, Belinda, 195
Lee, Malcolm, 216
Leech, John, 178
Léger, Fernand, 41
Leigh, Vivien, 145
Leister, Frederick, 195
Lejeune, C. A., 89, 90
Lemass, Sean, 139–40, 141, 199, 207
Letter from Ulster, A (1942), 108, 115–20, 138, 139, 174, 244; stills from, *116*, *117*, *119*; on YouTube, 233
Lexy, Edward, 158
Life and Letters Today, 74
Lillie, Beatrice, 145
Lion Has Wings, The, 105, 107–8, 120; still from, *109*
Lipscomb, W. P., 158
Lismer, Arthur, 33, 34
Locke, Shamus, 149

Lockwood, Margaret, 133, 149, 151, 152
Loder, John, 77
Lodge, John, 77, 80, 87, 91
l'Oeil de Paris, 41, *42*
London: Belgravia apartment, 30, 54, 55, 105–6, 107, 179, 208, 220, *221*; the Blitz, 27, 28, 99, 105; Hurst moves to (1931), 5, 7–8, 9, 21, 26, 45, 48, 53; Hurst retires to Knightsbridge, 6, 145; Hurst works at Elstree, 51, 53
Los Angeles, 4, 7, 17, 20, 39, 44, 45, 46, 244; Laurel Canyon (Hurst's residence) 44
Lovell, Raymond, 131
Lye, Len, 56

MacDonald, J. E. H., 33
MacDonald, Philip, 77
MacGinnis, Niall, 77, 202, 214
MacNeice, Louis, 3, 9, 245
MacQuitty, William (Bill), 18, 30, 119–20, 192
Magill, Hugh, 229
Malleson, Miles, 84, 86, 202
Malta Story, The (1953), 170, 184–88, 244; film poster, *184*; locals participate in, 185; stills from, *186*, *187*
Mamoulian, Rouben, 63
Mankiewicz, Joseph: *Cleopatra*, 220
March, Elspeth, 214
Marion, Joan, 91, 92
Mark of Cain, The (1947), 148, 157, 158–60, 162; still from, *159*
Martin, C. M., 87
Martin, Denis, 116
Martin, Valerie, 228
Marylebone Spiritualist Association, 27
Mason, James, 98, 133
"Masquerade par Excellence," 37

Massine, Léonide, 41
Mass-Observation, 108, 113, 120, 122
Mathieson, Dock, 155
Maugham, Robin, 191, 192
Maugham, W. Somerset, 87, 88
Maume, Patrick, 18, 47, 181, 218
McBean, Angus, 29, 237, 142–45; photo-portraits of Hurst, *xvii*, *142*, *144*, *238*
McCann, Hugh, 212
McCormack, John, 126
McCormick, F. J., 154
McGoohan, Patrick, 209
McGuinness, Martin, 18
McIlroy, Brian, 12, 16, 80, 162, 214, 226
McKay, Barry, 93
McKenna, Siobhan, 209, *210*, 211, 213, 214
McKenna, Virginia, 183, 188
Medhurst, Andy, 17
Mercury Films (Ireland) Ltd., 140
MGM, 44, 176
"middlebrow" British cinema, 49–50, 58, 95, 167, 200, 240, 242, 245
Milestone, Lewis, 84
Mills, John, 223
Minter, George, 176, 179
Miss Grant Goes to the Door (1940), 111–13; title credit, *111*
Mitchell-Cotts, Campbell, 145
Modigliani, Amedeo, 47
Möhner, Carl, 201
Montagu-Scott, Edward, Lord Montagu of Beaulieu, 15, 29, 237
Mooney, Ria, 68
More, Kenneth, 209
Morell, Andre, 192
Morris, Michael, Third Baron Killanin, 9, 55, 72, 82, 139, 141, 166, 199, 200, 215, 245, 248; collaboration on *Playboy*, 208, 209; promotion of *Playboy*, 211–13

Morrison, Herbert, 152
Moulton, Mo, 50, 52
Mountbatten, Louis, 105
Munro, George, and Basil Dean: *Murder Gang* (1935), 90
Murphy, Dudley, 41
Murphy, Hazel: *The Demi Gods*, 216
Murphy, Pat, 241
Musgrove, Gertrude, 99
music used in Hurst's films, 90, 104, 116, 121, 122, 164, 214, 244; exilic resonances of, 124, 126, 128; in *Hungry Hill* dance scene, 155; "Rose of Tralee," 116, 117, 126–28; in *Tom Brown's School Days*, 174; Warsaw Concerto, 122, 123, 124
Mycroft, Walter, 75, 77

Naficy, Hamid, 10, 49
Napoleon of Egypt, 215–16
Napper, Lawrence, 49, 50
Nasser, Abdel, 197
National Film Finance Corporation (NFFC), 147, 197, 208, 210
National Film Institute of Ireland (NFII): *Report on . . . Film Industry in Ireland*, 199–200
National Film School, Beaconsfield, 147
National Film Theatre (NFT), London, 74, 75, 221, 231; screen *Ourselves Alone*, 235. *See also* British Film Institute
National Health Service (NHS), Britain, 171
National Theatre, London, 165
neorealism, 110, 164
Nettlefold Studios, 176
Newfield, Wally, 115, 118
Newton, Robert, 173

New York, 4, 7, 13, 43, 46, 244
Niven, David, 183
Nolan, Coleen, 114
Northern Ireland, 3, 32, 52, 108, 141, 151, 152, 153, 191, 232, 241, 247; decriminalization of homosexuality (2020), 248; Good Friday Agreement, 231, 232; location for *A Letter from Ulster*, 115, 118, 120; screen industry, 219; Stormont, 76; urban regeneration, 231
Norton, William, 199
Novello, Ivor, 29, 143; *Glamorous Night*, 45, 87, 92, 93, 96

Oberon, Merle, 110
obituaries for Hurst, 219, 225–27, 231
O'Casey, Seán: *Shadow of a Gunman* (correspondence with Hurst) 140, 215
O'Dea, Denis, 158
O'Dea, Jimmy, 118
Odeon, Marble Arch, 176, 179
O'Flaherty, Liam, 40, 54; *Famine*, 216; *The Informer*, 54; *Shame the Devil*, 54
O'Hara, Gerald, 15 (uncredited, assistant director *Playboy*)
Olcott, Sidney 13
O'Leary, Liam, 64, 140, 217, 221
Olivier, Laurence, 142, 145; *Henry V* (1945), 170
On Approval (unmade), 215
O'Neill, Maire, 67
Ontario College of Art (OCA), 5, 20, 32, 33, 34, 35, 243; Arts Ball, 35; "Merrie Pageant" Ball, 38
On the Night of the Fire (1939), 11, 51, 87, 96–101, 107, 130; screened by BFI, 235; still of, 99

Ó Riada, Seán, 214
Oscar, Henry, 97
O'Sullivan, Richard, 194
O'Sullivan, Thaddeus, 241
Ourselves Alone (1936), 6, 50, 51, 57, 75, 76–82, 83, 86, 120, 139, 215, 246; released on DVD, 235; three-way profile, 78; US reviews of, 80–81

Pabst, Georg, 1, 241
Paris, 20, 38, 46, 102, 237; avant-garde scene, 38–40; Exposition Internationale (1925), 41
Parker, Cecil, 150
Parry, Gordon, 173
Pascal, Gabriel, 72, 145; *Caesar and Cleopatra* (1945), 145
Pathé News, 136
Pavlow, Muriel, 183, 185
Pennington-Richards, C., 176
Perinal, Georges, 96
Picasso, Pablo, 41
Picot Treaty (1919), 85
Pinewood Studios, 184, 191
Pitt-Rivers, Michael, 29
Playboy of the Western World, The (1962), 2, 166, 200, 206–14, 217, 218, 247; photos of Hurst directing, 208, 210; refused as entry to Moscow Film Festival, 213, 247; US press card, 212; US reviews, 211
Playhouse, Fifty-Fifth Street, New York, 211
Pleasance, Donald, 193
Poe, Edgar Allan, 58, 59, 63, 229
Portman, Eric, 158, 159
Powell, Michael, 1, 13, 16, 61, 103, 111, 138, 142, 158, 167, 231, 240; *An Airman's Letter to His Mother* (1941), 115

Index

Power, Hartley, 133
Power, Tyrone, 209
Pressburger, Emeric, 61, 142, 158, 167
Price, Dennis, 149
Price, Hollie, 114–15
Prill, Don, 115
Prison without Bars (1938), 51, 87, 95–96, 103, 107, 130; still from, *97*
Punch interview, 1969, 220; photograph of Hurst, 220, *221*

Quartertoten Productions, 233
Queen Nefertiti (unmade), 215
Queen's Film Theatre (QFT), Belfast: blue plaque for Hurst, 233; screen *Ourselves Alone*, 235
queerness/homosexuality, 28–29, 30, 220, 236, 240, 241–42, 244, 246; boy nudes in art, 175; decriminalization, 248
Quinn, Anthony, 181
"quota quickies," 18, 56, 64

Rank, J. Arthur, 241; photographed with Hurst, *163*
Rank Organisation, 141, 142, 146, 147, 157, 169, 173, 183, 184, 188, 194, 197, 198, 199, 200, 215, 241
Raymond, Gary, 209, *210*, 214
Redgrave, Michael, 202
Redgrave, Vanessa, 202
Redmond, Liam, 214
Reed, Carol, 89, 142, 146, 240; *Odd Man Out* (1947), 98
Regal Cinema, Dublin, 210
Renoir, Jean, 1, 241
Renown Pictures Corporation, 170, 176
Renvyle House Hotel, Galway, 71

Republic Pictures, 207
Richards, Jeffery, 12, 176
Richards, Shelah, 209
Richards, Sheila, 68
Richardson, Ralph, 96, 110
Riders to the Sea (1935), 50, 58–59, 68–75, 116, 138, 139, 209, 244; crew shot, *72*; sketch drawing of Bridie, 68, *69*; on YouTube, 233
Robb, Nesca, 9
Robbins, Christopher: *The Empress of Ireland*, 15, 27, 28–29, 30, 138, 171, 181, 189, 215, 216, 217, 222, 227–31, 232
Robinson, Peter, 18
Robson, Flora, 183, 186
Rockett, Kevin, 226–27
Rodin, Auguste, 41
Roosevelt, Teddy, 120
Royal Army Service Corps, 23
Royal Festival Hall, London, 165
Royal Irish Rifles, 3, 23, 25

Saint Thérèse, 26
Sandri, Anna Marie, 192
Sarigny, Peter de, 184
Satie, Erik, 41
Saunders, John Monk, 83
School of Paris, 40
Scott, Michael, 199, 213
Scott, Noel: "River of Unrest," 76
Screen profile, 12
Scrooge (1951), 2, 157, 166, 170, 171, 176–83, 233, 243, 246; awards, 215; stills from, *177*, *179*, *182*
Seigel, Jerrold, 4
Sensation (1936), 51, 90–92, 98, 130; released on DVD, 235; theme music, 90
Sexton, Jamie, 49, 56
Sharkey, Terence, 193

Shaw, George Bernard, 9, 10, 72, 84; "citizen of nowhere," 168, 247
Shearing, Joseph: *Airing in a Closed Carriage*, 148
Sheehy, Tom, 199
Sheridan, Jim, 241
She Stoops to Conquer (unmade), 216
Sight and Sound: "The Lady Vanishes" (1950 essay), 104, 146–47, 243
"silent" movies, 1, 46, 50, 59, 68, 241, 244
Sim, Alistair, 176, *177*, 180
Simba (1955), 82, 170, 172, 188–91, 197, 198, 199, 246; screened by BFI, 235; stills from, *189*, *190*, *192*
Simmons, Jean, 223
Simon, S. J., 148
Sinclair, Arthur, 150
Sinclair, Hugh, 133
Sinden, Donald, 190, 192, 223
Sistrom, Walter: photographed with Hurst, *163*
Sitwell, Edith, 74
Skortzeny, Otto, 215
Slide, Anthony, 12, 211, 226, 239, 241, 242
Smith, Allan Esler: *An Irishman Chained to the Truth*, 233; manages Hurst Estate, 235; *Theirs Is the Glory*, 235
Somlo, Josef, 107, 142
Steel, Anthony, 192
Stephens, James, 40
Sternlicht, Sanford, 50, 214
Stock, Nigel, 186
Street, Sarah, 55
Stuart, Francis, 54, 68
Sturrock, Dudley: *The Trouble*, 76
Suez Crisis (1956), 166, 167, 197
Summers, Walter, 76, 77
Sutton, Dudley, 15, 216
Sykes, Constance "Bill," 215
synchronous film sound, 44

Synge, John Millington, 1; *The Playboy of the Western World*, 166, 200, 206–7, 208, 211; *Riders to the Sea*, 38, 47, 67–68, 71, 73, 74

Talisman Films, 170
Taylor, Elizabeth, 145
"telecinema" plans, 165
Tell-Tale Heart, The (1934), 51, 57–63, 74, 75, 89, 229; banned by some local authorities in Britain, 63; on BFI online platform, 233; exilic context, 61; Hurst in cameo role, *89*
Tenth Man, The (1936), 51, 87, *88*, 89, 91; released on DVD, 235
Tess d'Urbervilles (unmade), 216
Thalberg, Irving, 54
Theirs Is the Glory (1946), 2, 108, 110, 133–38, *139*, 145, 164, 185, 199, 243, 246; screened in Arnhem, 235; stills from, *134*, *135*, *137–38*; use of surviving soldiers, 134–35, 136, 138
theosophy, 37
Thomas, Terry, 204
Thompson, Sam, 209
Titanic Film Studios, Belfast, 18–19, 235; Hurst and MacQuitty sound stages, *236*; Hurst stage plaque, *237*
Todd, Richard, 209
Tom Brown's School Days (1951), 166, 170–76, 246; stills from, *174*, *175*
Tomelty, Joseph, 190–91
Toronto. *See* Ontario College of Art
"Travelling the Road," 14, 15, 40, 217, 218, 223, 227–31; closing of public access to, 235
Trottie True (1949), 148, 160–62, 174, 244; still from, *161*
Tuke, Henry Scott, 175

Tully, Montgomery, 13–14, 240
Twickenham Studios, 64
Two Cities Films, 142, 148, 157, 158; dinner, *143*
Twysden, Lady Duff, 40

Ulster Covenant, 5, 20, 23
Ulster History Circle plaque, 233, *234*
Ulster Presbyterianism, 3, 7, 26, 37, 233, 247
Ulster Volunteer Force (UVF), 23
United Nations Charter (1948), 167
unmade film projects of Hurst, 214–17. *See also Lawrence of Arabia*
Unsworth, Geoffrey, 192
Ustinov, Peter, 142

Varley, F. Horsman, 33
Verno, Jerry, 77, 91
Vernon, Stephen: *Born to Be King*, 231
Vetchinsky, Alex, 133, 158
Victorine studio, Nice, 240
Von Sternberg, Josef, 47; *Shanghai Express* (1932), 44
Vulliamy, Edward, 226
Vyner, Margaret, 91

Walbrook, Anton, 30, 121, 122, 123, 124, 126, 128
Walker, Alexander, 231
Walker, Frederick, 175
Wall Street crash, 6, 44, 53
Walsh, Raoul, 1, 13
Wardrobes Lodge, Buckinghamshire (Hurst residence) *106*, 107
Warner, Jack, 54, 176

Watt, Harry, 110
Wayne, John, 43
Welch, Elizabeth, 105, 131
West, Mae, 145
Whiley, Manning, 111
Wilcox, Herbert, 13, 83, 235, 240, 247
Wilde, Oscar, 47
Wildeblood, Peter, 29, 30
Wilhelm, Wolfgang, 68
Williams, Kenneth, 248
Williams, Raymond, 21
Wilson, Harold, 147, 181
Wilson, John Rowan: *The Pack*, 200
Woolf, Virginia, 49–50
"World's Only New Art Form, The," 57, 243
World War I, 3, 4, 7, 20, 23, 27, 40, 52, 56, 84, 219; centenary, 233; Hurst deserts from British army, 5, 7, 19, 25
World War II, 6, 18, 54, 55, 56, 96, 98, 103, 140, 246, 247; Battle of Britain, 121; the Blitz, 27, 28, 99, 105; government-sponsored films, 107, 110–15; invasion of Arnhem, 108, 133–34, 135; and Malta, 185–86; US service personnel based in Britain and Northern Ireland, 108, 115, 116, 118, 119, 121
Wyatt, Stephen, 228
Wynyard, Diane, 96

Yeats, Jack B., 47, 68
Yeats, William Butler, 27, 84, 173
Young, Jimmie, 248
Young, Terence, 55, 87, 98, 115, 216; co-owns house with Hurst, 106; *Hungry Hill*, 148, 151; script for *Dangerous Moonlight*, 120, 121, 148

LANCE PETTITT is an independent film scholar and emeritus professor of screen media based in London. He was an associate research fellow at Birkbeck, University of London (2019–22) and an Irish government–funded traveling professor of Irish studies at Bergische Universität, Wuppertal, Germany (2021–22).

His publications include *Screening Ireland: Film and Television Representation* (2000), *December Bride* (2001), a DVD, *Thaddeus O'Sullivan: Early Films, 1973–1986* (2014), articles in the *Oxford Dictionary of National Biography* (2013) and *Eire-Ireland* (2015, 2017), and recent critical essays on Pat Murphy and George Best in volumes published in 2020.

He is founding coeditor (with Beatriz Kopschitz Bastos) of Ireland on Film, whose four volumes to date include *The Uncle Jack* (2011), *The Woman Who Married Clark Gable* (2013), *The Road to God Knows Where* (2014), and *Maeve* (2022). His latest research, funded by a British Academy small grant award—on Eugene McCabe's screen writing of the Irish border—is published in *HJEAS* 28, no. 2 (2022).

www.ingramcontent.com/pod-product-compliance
Lightning Source LLC
Chambersburg PA
CBHW051206300426
44116CB00006B/452